Download Your [...] Ebook Tod[...]

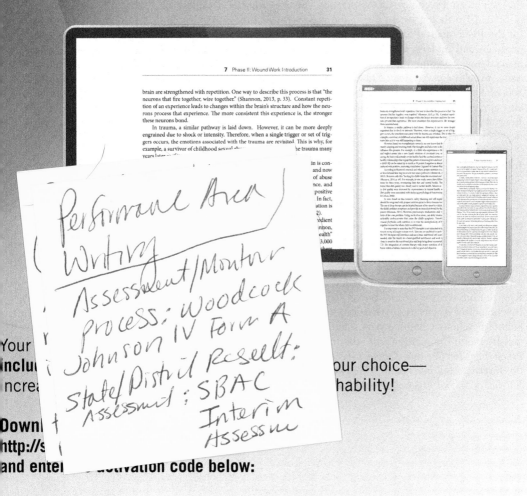

Handwritten note:

Performance Area

Writing

Assessment/Monitor

Process: Woodcock

Johnson IV Form A

State/District Result:

Assessmt: SBAC

Interim

Assessme

SPRINGER PUBLISHING COMPANY

Sally L. Grapin, PhD, NCSP, is an assistant professor of psychology in the College of Humanities and Social Sciences at Montclair State University. She received her PhD in school psychology from the University of Florida (UF). Her scholarly interests include the implementation of multi-tiered systems of support (MTSS), academic screening for at-risk students, and social justice advocacy in school psychology. She has received awards from national organizations such as the American Psychological Association, Society for the Teaching of Psychology, and Trainers of School Psychologists. In 2017, she received the Innovative Teaching Award from the Society for the Psychological Study of Social Issues. Dr. Grapin has taught both lecture- and field-based graduate and undergraduate courses in school psychology. In particular, she has taught courses in academic assessment, psychotherapeutic interventions, diversity in education, and professional issues in school psychology. Dr. Grapin serves on the editorial boards of several journals, including *School Psychology International, Psychology in the Schools,* and *School Psychology Forum.* She also currently serves as Co-Chair of the National Association of School Psychologists' Graduate Recruitment and Awareness Development (GRAD) subcommittee, which seeks to promote awareness of school psychology among prospective practitioners.

John H. Kranzler, PhD, is a professor and director of the School Psychology Program in the School of Special Education, School Psychology, and Early Childhood Studies at the University of Florida (UF). He joined the faculty at UF in 1990 after receiving his PhD in school psychology from the University of California, Berkeley. Dr. Kranzler served as Associate Dean for Research and Graduate Studies in the College of Education from 2001 to 2005 and from 2007 to 2010. and as Acting Associate Dean for Research and Faculty Development from 2008 to 2011. He has taught classes in school psychology, learning and cognition, the theory of intelligence, psychoeducational assessment, statistics, ethics and law, and individual differences. His major areas of scholarly interest concern the nature, development, and assessment of human cognitive abilities. Dr. Kranzler has written several books and numerous journal articles. He is a Fellow of the American Psychological Association (Division 16) and an elected member of the Society for the Study of School Psychology. He has won a number of awards for his research from the Mensa Education and Research Foundation and other organizations, as well as Article of the Year awards in *School Psychology Review* and *School Psychology Quarterly.* He currently serves as Associate Editor of the *International Journal of School and Educational Psychology* and on the editorial boards of the *Journal of School Psychology* and *Psychological Assessment.*

School Psychology
Professional Issues and Practices

SALLY L. GRAPIN, PhD, NCSP

JOHN H. KRANZLER, PhD

Editors

SPRINGER PUBLISHING COMPANY

Springer Publishing Company, LLC
11 West 42nd Street
New York, NY 10036
www.springerpub.com

Acquisitions Editor: Kate Dimock
Compositor: Exeter Premedia Services Private Ltd.

ISBN: 978-0-8261-9473-2
ebook ISBN: 978-0-8261-9474-9

Instructor's Materials: Qualified instructors may request supplements by emailing textbook@springerpub.com:
Instructor's Manual: 978-0-8261-9475-6
Instructor's PowerPoints: 978-0-8261-9477-0
Instructor's Test Bank: 978-0-8261-9476-3

The author and the publisher of this Work have made every effort to use sources believed to be reliable to provide information that is accurate and compatible with the standards generally accepted at the time of publication. The author and publisher shall not be liable for any special, consequential, or exemplary damages resulting, in whole or in part, from the readers' use of, or reliance on, the information contained in this book. The publisher has no responsibility for the persistence or accuracy of URLs for external or third-party Internet websites referred to in this publication and does not guarantee that any content on such websites is, or will remain, accurate or appropriate.

Library of Congress Cataloging-in-Publication Data

Names: Grapin, Sally L. | Kranzler, John H.
Title: School psychology : professional issues and practices / Sally L.
   Grapin, PhD, NCSP, John H. Kranzler, PhD Editors.
Description: New York, NY : Springer Publishing Company, [2018]
Identifiers: LCCN 2017053218 | ISBN 9780826194732
Subjects: LCSH: School psychology—Study and teaching. | School
   psychologists—Training of. | School psychologists—In-service training. |
   School psychology.
Classification: LCC LB3013.6 .S29 2018 | DDC 370.15—dc23
LC record available at https://lccn.loc.gov/2017053218

Printed in the United States of America.

To my wonderful parents, Julie and Larry Grapin, who were my first and most influential examples of what it means to be a compassionate advocate for children.

To my brother, Scott Grapin, whose zest for the field of education inspires me every day.

To my husband and the love of my life, Peter Nurnberg, whose insight, empathy, and kindness to everyone around him will always amaze me.
—Sally L. Grapin

To the next generation of school psychologists—it has been my privilege to help in some small way with your training – you will make a difference.
—John H. Kranzler

Contents

SECTION III: LOOKING AHEAD

Contributors

Scott P. Ardoin, PhD, BCBA, is a professor of school psychology, department head of the Department of Educational Psychology, and codirector of the Center for Autism and Behavioral Education Research at the University of Georgia. His research focuses on applying the principles of applied behavioral analysis to improving classroom management practices as well as academic assessment and intervention practices implemented in the schools.

Nicholas F. Benson, PhD, NCSP, is an associate professor of school psychology within the Department of Educational Psychology at Baylor University. His research interests focus broadly on psychological and educational assessment, with an emphasis on examining the validity of interpretations and uses of test scores. Dr. Benson also serves on editorial boards for several journals and is an associate editor for the *Journal of School Psychology.*

Amy M. Briesch, PhD, NCSP, is an associate professor in the Department of Applied Psychology at Northeastern University and codirector of the Center for Research in School-Based Prevention. Her research interests include the role of student involvement in intervention design and implementation as well as the development of feasible and psychometrically sound measures for the assessment of student behavior in MTSS. Dr. Briesch has authored three books and more than 50 peer-reviewed journal articles to date, and she was the 2014 recipient of the Lightner Witmer award from the American Psychological Association for early career scholarship.

Alexa Dixon, BA, is a current school psychology doctoral student at the University of Florida. She received her BA from Elon University. Upon receiving her doctoral degree, she plans to pursue a career in pediatric school psychology, working with children and adolescents with health issues.

Ashley Donohue, BA, is pursuing an educational specialist degree through the School Psychology Program at Baylor University. She is currently a school psychology intern at Belton Independent School District in Texas. She earned her baccalaureate degree in psychology from Southern Illinois University, Carbondale.

William P. Erchul, PhD, ABPP, is a professor and the director of the School Psychology Program at the University of California, Riverside. His interests include processes and outcomes associated with school consultation as well as social influence and interpersonal communication. He has served as president of the American Academy of School Psychology and president of the Society for the Study of School Psychology.

Aaron J. Fischer, PhD, BCBA-D, is an assistant professor of school psychology and adjunct assistant professor of psychiatry at the University of Utah. His interests include using technology to provide individuals in remote and underserved areas with access to school consultation services as well as the assessment and treatment of behavior problems in individuals with disabilities.

Dan Florell, PhD, NCSP, is an associate professor at Eastern Kentucky University. He is a trainer in the School Psychology Specialist Program and has a private practice. He has presented and written on the topics of the history of school psychology and the use of technology in the field.

Randy G. Floyd, PhD, is a professor of psychology, training director for the School Psychology doctoral program, and associate chair in the Department of Psychology at the University of Memphis. His research focuses on understanding the measurement properties of psychological assessment techniques and reducing error in measurement. He is the former editor of the *Journal of School Psychology* (2010–2014).

Susan G. Forman, PhD, is a university professor at Rutgers, the State University of New Jersey, where she has served as Director of Clinical Training for the School Psychology Program, Chair of the Department of Applied Psychology, and Vice President for Undergraduate Education. Her research and scholarship focus on factors that influence intervention implementation, implementation of interprofessional collaborative approaches to pediatric behavioral health care, and the effectiveness of behavioral and cognitive behavioral interventions in educational settings. She is a Fellow of the American Psychological Association and has been elected to membership in the Society for the Study of School Psychology.

Sally L. Grapin, PhD, NCSP, is an assistant professor in the School Psychology Program at Montclair State University. Her scholarly and professional interests include social justice advocacy in schools and the implementation of multi-tiered systems of support (MTSS) to promote positive academic outcomes for youth. She currently serves as Co-Chair of the National Association of School Psychologists' Graduate Recruitment and Awareness Development (GRAD) subcommittee and as Publications and Communications Chair for the American Psychological Association's Early Career Workgroup.

Erin A. Harper, PhD, is an assistant professor in the School Psychology Program at Miami University. She was a school psychologist in urban public schools for 8 years prior to joining the faculty at Miami. Her interests include culturally responsive school mental health supports and positive youth development. She has presented her work at professional conferences and published research in numerous peer-reviewed journals.

Stacy-Ann A. January, PhD, NCSP, is an assistant professor in the Department of Psychology at the University of South Carolina and a nationally certified school psychologist. Her research interests include academic assessment and interventions in schools.

Diana Joyce-Beaulieu, PhD, NCSP, is a faculty member at the University of Florida, where she has taught numerous graduate courses. As a licensed psychologist and nationally certified school psychologist, she also administers the practica program. Her publications include three books, 25 chapters, and numerous peer-reviewed articles. She has served as coprincipal investigator for two professional development grants to research training models for MTSS.

John H. Kranzler, PhD, is Professor of School Psychology at the University of Florida, where he serves as Director of the School Psychology Program. Dr. Kranzler's major area of scholarly interest concerns the nature, development, and assessment of human cognitive abilities.

Kathleen M. Minke, PhD, NCSP, is a professor in the School Psychology Program at the University of Delaware. Her interests include counseling, family–school collaboration, and MTSS. She is a former president of the National Association of School Psychologists (2010–2011) and serves as a consultant to Delaware's Positive Behavior Supports project.

Laura W. Monahon, PsyD, NCSP, is a licensed psychologist in New Jersey as well as a school psychologist. She currently works primarily in private practice, specializing in cognitive behavioral therapy. Dr. Monahon also works as a consulting school psychologist in addition to teaching graduate-level courses in ethics and cognitive behavioral therapy.

Amity L. Noltemeyer, **PhD, NCSP,** is a professor in the School Psychology Program at Miami University. Her interests include MTSS, disproportionality and bias in school discipline, resilience, and school climate. She is editor-in-chief of the *School Psychology International* journal and comanages several externally funded grants.

Philip Oliveira, MA, is a doctoral student in the Graduate School of Applied and Professional Psychology, School Psychology PsyD program. His work in the Newark, New Jersey, public school system as a teacher has influenced his interests in the application of psychological interventions in urban districts with diverse and lower-socioeconomic populations.

Natalie N. Politikos, PhD, NCSP, is presently an associate professor of psychology and director of the School Psychology Program at the University of Hartford. A licensed psychologist and the chair of the Program Accreditation Board for the National Association for School Psychologists, which oversees program accreditation for school psychology programs throughout the United States, her interests include accreditation and licensing, ethics, and gifted education.

Sherrie L. Proctor, PhD, is an associate professor in the School Psychology Program at Queens College, City University of New York. Her primary research interests are in the recruitment, retention, and attrition of students of color from school psychology programs. She is also interested in the use of qualitative methodology to examine issues relevant to diverse student populations. She is the coeditor of the *Handbook of Multicultural School Psychology: An Interdisciplinary Perspective,* Second Edition.

Joseph S. Prus, PhD, NCSP, is a professor of psychology, chair of the Department of Psychology, and director of the School Psychology Program at Winthrop University in Rock Hill, South Carolina. He has published and presented extensively in school psychology and has chaired, cochaired, and served on many national committees related to school psychology. He was the recipient of the 2015 National Association of School Psychologists' Lifetime Achievement Award.

Eric Rossen, PhD, NCSP, is a nationally certified school psychologist and licensed psychologist in Maryland. He has experience working in public schools as well as in independent practice and is currently Director of Professional Development and Standards for the National Association of School Psychologists.

Robert J. Volpe, PhD, is professor and chair of Applied Psychology at Northeastern University and codirector of the Center for Research in School-Based Prevention. His research focuses on behavioral assessment in school-based problem-solving models and evaluating classroom interventions for students with behavior problems. He is past-president of the Society for the Study of School Psychology and serves on the editorial boards of *Journal of School Psychology, School Psychology Review, School Mental Health,* and *Journal of Attention Disorders.*

Barbara Bole Williams, PhD, NCSP, is professor and coordinator of the School Psychology Program at Rowan University, Glassboro, New Jersey. She has served on the National Association of School Psychologists' (NASP) Ethics Committee as representative from the Northeast region of the United States and currently chairs the Ethics Committee for the New Jersey Association of School Psychologists. She is the lead author of the NASP publication *Professional Ethics for School Psychologists: A Problem-Solving Model Casebook* (2008) and its second edition (2011), coauthored by Leigh Armistead and Susan Jacob. She is the recipient of the 2011 Lifetime Achievement Award from NASP.

Foreword

OPPORTUNITIES ABOUND FOR SCHOOL PSYCHOLOGISTS

This book, *School Psychology: Professional Issues and Practices*, offers valuable information and insights regarding the profession of school psychology, with particular emphasis on social justice in preparing school psychologists who are effective advocates for children and families. It is important to highlight that there are tremendous opportunities for school psychologists in the United States and around the world. For instance, considering multiple factors, including salary, job market, future growth, and work life balance, the profession of School Psychologist was recently ranked #1 among the *Best Social Service Jobs in the United States* (U.S. News & World Report, 2017). While there are over 30,000 school psychologists in the United States (Jimerson, Stewart, Skokut, Cardenas, & Malone, 2009), there are documented shortages, highlighting the need for more school psychologists across the United States (National Association of School Psychologists, 2017). Thus, individuals interested in pursuing a career that contributes to supporting: (a) the education and development of children, (b) teachers and school staff, (c) families and communities, and (d) social justice, will find this book and the job of school psychologist to be both informative and rewarding. The following paragraphs highlight important emphases and contributions featured within *School Psychology: Professional Issues and Practices*.

SOCIAL JUSTICE AND SCHOOL PSYCHOLOGY

As the roles and functions of school psychologists continue to evolve, a social justice perspective provides a framework to guide their efforts (Shriberg, Song, Miranda, & Radliff, 2013). Considering the diversity of children, families, and communities throughout the United States, this book emphasizes the importance of the practice and profession of school psychology through a social justice lens. The editors, Grapin and Kranzler, describe and emphasize a broad view of social justice that incorporates concepts of equity, advocacy, and fairness, noting; "*When applied to the field of school psychology specifically, social justice work involves building safe, supportive, and welcoming environments that promote the healthy development and educational success of all students*" (Chapter 1). Furthermore, as Grapin and Kranzler highlight; "*In the context of school psychology, promoting social justice involves advocating for the well-being of all children and families and fostering school communities that reflect diverse values*" (Preface). Each of the chapters featured in this book emphasizes that social justice considerations should be prominent and intentional in all areas of school psychology service delivery.

THE PROFESSION OF SCHOOL PSYCHOLOGY

The editors have compiled an excellent collection of informative chapters that provide a foundation for fully considering a career as a school psychologist, including chapters addressing the breadth of professional activities that many school psychologists are commonly engaged in. As described in the chapters of this book, the specialty of school psychology has been characterized as one that collectively provides individual assessment of children who may display cognitive, emotional, social, or behavioral difficulties; develops and implements primary and secondary intervention programs; consults with teachers, parents and other relevant professionals; engages in program development and evaluation; conducts research; and helps prepare and supervise others (Jimerson, Oakland, & Farrell, 2007, p. 1). Professional associations such as the National Association of School Psychologists (NASP) in the United States and the International School Psychology Association (ISPA) provide comprehensive descriptions and standards of preparation for school psychologists. Around the world, professionals who provide these services use a variety of titles, including counselor, educational psychologist, professional of educational psychology, psychopedagog, psychologist, psychologist in education, psychologist in the schools, or school psychologist. In most countries throughout Europe, the term educational psychologist is most commonly used to describe these professionals. The term *school psychologist* is used throughout this book to refer to these professionals.

FOUNDATIONS OF SCHOOL PSYCHOLOGY

The first five chapters included in the foundations of school psychology section provide valuable information regarding the profession of school psychology, including important information pertaining to the historical foundations of the field and the essential aspects of the training and credentialing of school psychologists. The chapters include important information highlighting the professional preparation standards delineated by national and international school psychology associations. In addition, important topics such as multicultural, legal, and ethical foundations are also reviewed in this section. Each of the chapters in this section provide thoughtful summaries of key considerations relevant to the profession and practice of school psychology. Given the increasingly diverse populations of students and families in communities across the United States and around the world, it is imperative that school psychologists are knowledgeable of these important considerations. For those considering or preparing for a career as a school psychologist, this foundational knowledge will be very valuable to informing your understanding of the profession.

SERVICE DELIVERY IN SCHOOL PSYCHOLOGY

As previously described, the roles and responsibilities of school psychologists vary across contexts. One role that is often included among the roles of most school psychologists is using assessments to inform interventions to support students and teachers at school. The importance of assessment and intervention are reflected in the contemporary emphasis on implementing multi-tiered systems of support (MTSS) for students (see for instance, Jimerson, Burns, & VanDerheyden, 2016). This section of the book highlights the importance of assessment and intervention and offers important information to understand the breadth of knowledge that is needed for school psychologists to fulfill these responsibilities. For instance, assessment includes applications for planning (before intervention), monitoring (during intervention), and evaluating (after intervention) services, and there is a breadth of domain-specific assessments and interventions (e.g., academic, behavioral, social, and emotional). Furthermore, consistent with an MTSS emphasis, there are interventions that aim to support all students in a classroom setting, some students in smaller groups, and also individual students. The importance of consultation for supporting teachers and families, as well as program evaluation and systems reform, are also topics featured in this section. The chapters in this section of the book discuss each of these topics and also highlight the importance of school psychologists advocating for the use of evidence-based interventions (i.e., those strategies that have empirical evidence to support their effectiveness for supporting specific needs).

THE FUTURE AND PREPARING FOR A CAREER IN SCHOOL PSYCHOLOGY

The chapters in this final section of the book provide valuable information and insights regarding what may be on the horizon in the field of school psychology (e.g. personnel shortages, virtual psychological service delivery, and the evolution of professional organizations and standards) and also delineate a range of career options in school psychology. As discussed in each of these chapters, there is a tremendous need for school psychologists, including: those who will work as practitioners in the schools; those who will become faculty in programs that prepare the next generation of practitioners and scholars; those who will engage in scholarship to advance knowledge, science, and practice relevant to school psychology; and those who will work in other settings to help support children and families (e.g., hospital systems, juvenile justice systems, community agencies, military schools, international schools). The chapters in this section offer readers knowledge and insights that will inform their understanding of how they may pursue a career as a school psychologist.

Overall, *School Psychology: Professional Issues and Practices* provides a contemporary resource to introduce the field of school psychology. For those currently considering or pursuing a degree in school psychology, this book offers extensive information to enhance your understanding of the history, roles, responsibilities, preparation, and opportunities for school psychologists. This book also highlights a range of social justice considerations relevant to the field of school psychology. Grapin and Kranzler have carefully selected important topics to facilitate further understanding, and the chapters are authored by many leading experts in the field of school psychology. As highlighted throughout this book, the breadth of knowledge, roles, and responsibilities among school psychologists provides an incredible opportunity to contribute to the well-being of children, families, schools, and communities. For those who share a commitment to understanding, advocating, and helping others, school psychology presents a wonderful career opportunity.

Shane R. Jimerson, PhD, NCSP
Professor and Department Chair,
Counseling, Clinical, and School Psychology
University of California, Santa Barbara

REFERENCES

Jimerson, S. R., Burns, M. K, & VanDerHeyden, A. M. (Eds.) (2016). *The handbook of response to intervention: Science and practice of multi-tiered systems of support* (2nd. ed.). New York, NY: Springer US.

Jimerson, S. R., Oakland, T. D., & Farrell, P. T. (Eds.). (2007). *The handbook of international school psychology*. Thousand Oaks, CA: Sage.

Jimerson, S. R., Stewart, K., Skokut, M., Cardenas, S., & Malone, H. (2009). How many school psychologists are there in each country of the world? International estimates of school psychologists and school psychologist-to-student ratios. *School Psychology International, 30,* 555–567. doi:10.1177/0143034309107077

National Association of School Psychologists. (2017). *Shortages in school psychology: Challenges to meeting the growing needs of U.S. students and schools*. Bethesda, MD: Author.

Shriberg, D., Song, S. Y., Miranda, A. H., & Radliff, K. M. (2013). *School psychology and social justice: Conceptual foundations and tools for practice*. New York, NY: Routledge.

U.S. News & World Report. (2017). Best social service jobs. Retrieved from https://money.usnews.com/careers/best-jobs/rankings/best-social-services-jobs

Preface

This book provides a comprehensive introduction to the practice and profession of school psychology through a social justice lens. The term *social justice* has been defined in many ways by different scholars. In the context of school psychology, promoting social justice involves advocating for the well-being of all children and families and fostering school communities that reflect diverse values. We join many others in affirming that the goals of social justice and school psychology are inextricably linked. School psychologists strive to promote the welfare of all children and families, and in the absence of socially just learning environments, this goal cannot be fully achieved. Therefore, social justice issues must be studied in tandem with all areas of school psychological service delivery.

We believe that both *infusion* and *intentional* approaches are essential to the study of social justice. *Infusion* refers to the teaching of multicultural and social justice principles throughout the curriculum rather than as separate modules (Newell et al., 2010). In infusion approaches, social justice principles are integrated as core concepts across all areas of psychoeducational service delivery. We believe that an infusion approach is essential for encouraging students to draw clear connections between practice and advocacy across the curriculum.

Intentionality refers to the deliberate and visible emphasis of social justice issues in school psychology curricula. All too often, these issues are discussed as an afterthought, which reinforces a passive approach to addressing injustice. As we state in Chapter 1, continuing with routine practices is always easier and more comfortable than challenging the status quo. Thus, school psychologists must deliberately identify practices and policies that marginalize diverse students and take steps to challenge these practices and policies in an intentional manner.

We believe that employing a combination of infusion and intentional approaches is the best way to prepare effective advocates for children and families. The structure of this book reflects these two approaches. Specifically, social justice principles are *infused* throughout the chapters as well as addressed clearly and explicitly (i.e., with *intentionality*).

ORGANIZATION AND CONTENT

This book is organized into three main sections: *Foundations of School Psychology* (Section I), *Service Delivery in School Psychology* (Section II), and *Looking Ahead* (Section III). The goals and rationale for each of these sections are described below.

Section I: Foundations of School Psychology

This section describes the foundations of school psychology, including the field's historical, multicultural, legal, and ethical foundations. These areas are described first because they permeate all areas of practice and therefore are integral to understanding the roles and functions of school psychologists. By covering multicultural issues within the first few chapters, we frame them as a primer for subsequent reading. Similarly, studying legal and ethical issues early on allows the reader to consider the many ways in which school psychologists protect the rights and dignity of all children and families.

In Chapter 1, we present a general overview of the field of school psychology by introducing readers to the National Association of School Psychologists' Model for Comprehensive and Integrated School Psychological Services (NASP Practice Model). We also describe the meaning of the term *social justice* and the value of studying school psychology through a social justice lens. Chapter 2 describes the history and development of the field. Only a little more than a century old, school psychology continues to be heavily influenced by its historical foundations. Knowledge of these foundations is critical for understanding contemporary practice and anticipating future directions. Recognizing that school psychology has undergone significant paradigm shifts in recent years, this book not only covers the field's early history but also advances and trends of the last 20 years (i.e., the early 2000s onward). To provide a comprehensive overview, this section of the book also includes chapters on graduate preparation and credentialing (Chapter 3), multicultural foundations (Chapter 4), and legal and ethical foundations (Chapter 5).

Section II: Service Delivery in School Psychology

Whereas Section I describes the broad foundations of school psychology, Section II centers on the specific roles and functions of school psychologists. This section begins with an overview of two types of services that permeate all major areas of practice: *assessment* and *intervention*. Chapter 6 assumes a broad approach to conceptualizing assessment by considering its applications for planning (before intervention), monitoring (during intervention), and evaluating (after intervention) services. Chapter 7 describes foundational concepts in intervention, which we believe are important prerequisites for understanding domain-specific interventions (e.g., academic, behavioral, social, and emotional interventions). Thus, Chapter 7 describes a number of essential terms, including *evidence-based interventions*, *randomized controlled trials*, and *random assignment*.

Chapter 8 describes academic assessment and intervention, and Chapter 9 describes social, emotional, and behavioral (SEB) interventions. These two chapters are written in similar formats (describing universal, targeted, and indicated interventions) to assist the reader in understanding how multi-tiered systems of support (MTSS) are applied in both academic and SEB domains. Chapter 10 describes intellectual assessment in school settings. The latter chapters of this section describe services for empowering school personnel and systems to better serve children. These services include consultation (Chapter 11), program evaluation and systems-level reform (Chapter 12).

Section III: Looking Ahead

This section discusses the future of school psychology as well as considerations for preparing for a career in the field. Unlike similar books, the chapters in this section consider not only future directions for the field but also future professional pathways for the reader. Chapter 13 describes emerging issues and anticipates future directions for the field. Topics include personnel shortages, virtual psychological service delivery, and the evolution of professional organizations and standards. Chapter 14 describes considerations for pursuing a career in school psychology. It covers topics such as choosing specialization coursework, selecting mentors, and identifying potential career paths. It also includes resources such as a curriculum vitae (CV) development checklist and graduate planning worksheet.

UNIQUE FEATURES

Social Justice Orientation

The social justice orientation of this book is one of its most essential features. In Chapter 1, we provide a rationale for studying social justice and school psychology in tandem. By explicitly communicating this rationale at the beginning of the book, we reinforce the idea that social justice considerations should have a prominent and intentional presence in all areas of service delivery.

This book addresses a range of social justice issues related to school psychology practice, including discriminatory assessment and disciplinary practices and the implementation of MTSS to promote equity in educational access. Such topics are featured in "Social Justice Connections" boxes, which appear in all of the book's chapters (with the exception of Chapter 1, which introduces key concepts in social justice). Each box poses a question related to the chapter's content and offers a thoughtful response. These responses are designed to provide concrete, actionable recommendations for aspiring advocates.

In line with its social justice focus, this book emphasizes the research and practice contributions of racial, ethnic, and linguistic (REL) minority scholars. All too often, the history of psychology is told from a predominantly White, Eurocentric perspective that obscures the contributions of diverse scholars. One of our goals in developing this book was to illustrate the rich intellectual legacy of REL minority scholars who shaped the field of school psychology. This legacy is most clearly illustrated in Chapter 2, which describes the revolutionary contributions of scholars such as Albert Sidney Beckham, Kenneth and Mamie Clark, Beverly Inez Prosser, Ena Vazquez-Nuttall, and Deborah Crockett. By featuring these individuals, we paint a more comprehensive picture of school psychology's past, present, and future.

Voices of Experts

Most introductory school psychology books are authored rather than edited books, meaning that they are written by, at most, several authors. This book, however, is an edited one and comprises chapters from nearly 30 different contributing authors. There are two primary advantages to the edited book format. First, producing an edited book allowed us to leverage the wide range of backgrounds and orientations represented in school psychology. Our field is a complex one that thrives on this diversity of perspectives. School psychologists may approach service delivery in many different ways, and it is important for readers to understand how different perspectives shape both research and practice.

Second, an edited format allows readers to learn about theory, research and practice in school psychology directly from experts in those areas. As illustrated in the brief biographies of contributors (presented in the frontmatter), we have recruited a group of highly regarded, accomplished, and prolific scholars to develop the various chapters of this book. The authors represented in this group include journal editors and editorial board members, principal investigators of major research grants, and leaders in school psychology's primary professional associations. Rather than summarizing their work, we connect readers directly to the experts.

Clear Connections to the NASP Practice Model

At this time, the most prominent and widely regarded model of school psychological service delivery is the NASP Practice Model. As described in Chapter 1, this model comprises 10 domains that illustrate the diverse roles and services that school psychologists perform.

The content of this book is designed to align with the Practice Model. In some cases, entire chapters are dedicated to single domains, including *Consultation and Collaboration* (Domain 2; Chapter 11), *Interventions and Instructional Supports to Develop Academic Skills* (Domain 3; Chapter 8), and *Interventions and Mental Health Services to Develop Social and Life Skills* (Domain 4; Chapter 9). Other domains, such as *Preventive and Responsive Services* (Domain 6), *Family-School Collaboration Services* (Domain 7), and *Data-Based Decision Making and Accountability* (Domain 1), are integrated across several chapters. For example, *Preventive and Responsive Services* are addressed extensively in Chapter 7 as well as in Chapters 8 and 9. By drawing clear connections to the NASP Practice Model, we provide a comprehensive overview of the roles and functions of school psychologists as well as introduce readers to a widely accepted framework of service delivery.

LEARNING TOOLS AND RESOURCES

One goal of this book is to make school psychology accessible to a wide range of audiences. Its intended audiences are undergraduate and graduate students, related school personnel, caregivers, and others who wish to explore the field. Thus, we have included a number of features that are designed to facilitate the accessibility of content. Each chapter includes four to five chapter objectives as well as a brief introduction section to orient readers to its main ideas. The chapters also incorporate bold and italicized key terms, which are accompanied by clear and concise definitions in text. Similar to the chapter objectives, these key terms are designed to orient readers to the book's main ideas.

One important feature of the book is that it takes care to review prerequisite concepts in psychological research and practice that are essential for understanding service delivery in school psychology. For example, terms such as *reliability* and *validity* (introduced in Chapter 6) are important for understanding concepts in assessment and intervention. To bridge concepts from previous coursework (e.g., introductory psychology and research methodology courses), we clearly define these terms and describe their relevance for school psychology practice and research. These bridges allow learners to better contextualize and integrate new concepts with previous learning.

For instructors who wish to use this book as the core text for an introductory school psychology course, a number of resources are available. At the end of each chapter, discussion questions are included, which can be used to facilitate both face-to-face and online discussion. These questions involve summarizing key concepts from the text and then applying those concepts to extend learning. Other resources include materials for fostering students' professional development, such as the CV development checklist and the graduate planning worksheet included in Chapter 14. Instructors can encourage students to use these resources in class or during independent assignments. Finally, sample syllabi are available to potential and current course instructors. **For more information regarding instructor resources, qualified adopters should contact textbook@springerpub.com.**

It has been a tremendous privilege to work with all of the book's contributing authors to portray the landscape of school psychology practice in the United States. We hope that this book will serve as a resource for undergraduate and graduate students, school personnel, caregivers, and other stakeholders who are invested in protecting the welfare of youth.

Sally L. Grapin, PhD, NCSP
John H. Kranzler, PhD

REFERENCE

Newell, M. L., Nastasi, B. K., Hatzichristou, C., Jones, J. M., Schanding, G. T., & Yetter, G. (2010). Evidence on multicultural training in school psychology: Recommendations for future directions. *School Psychology Quarterly, 25,* 249-278. doi:10.1037/a0021542

Acknowledgments

We would like to acknowledge the tremendous support we received from colleagues, family, and Springer Publishing Company. In particular, we are grateful to all of the authors who contributed chapters to this book. It has been a privilege to work with each of them, and we immensely appreciate their expertise, incisive perspectives, eloquent writing, and willingness to share their work with us.

We are grateful to Shane Jimerson for sharing his insights with us and for developing the foreword of this book. We also are grateful for the input of Randy Floyd and Thomas Fagan as well as for the meticulous editorial support of Meaghan Pereiras. Finally, we are grateful to Springer Publishing Company for their guidance and support throughout the publication process.

—*Sally L. Grapin and John H. Kranzler*

I would like to thank the many people who supported me during the development of this book. First, I am grateful to my co-editor, John Kranzler, for partnering with me on my first edited book and for providing ongoing support for this project and many others. I also appreciate the support of my wonderful colleagues at Montclair State University.

I would like to thank my parents, Larry and Julie Grapin, who provided unwavering encouragement throughout this process. I am especially appreciative of the support I received from my brother, Scott Grapin, to whom I frequently turned to discuss ideas for this book. He is a true asset to the field of education, and I am constantly learning from him.

I am grateful to my husband, Peter Nurnberg, for his endless love and encouragement. Thank you for supporting me through all of the late nights, for all of your humor when I needed it most, and for being the loving companion I still cannot believe I was lucky enough to find.

—*Sally L. Grapin*

SECTION I

Foundations of School Psychology

CHAPTER 1

Introduction to School Psychology

SALLY L. GRAPIN ■ JOHN H. KRANZLER

CHAPTER OBJECTIVES

- Define *school psychology*
- Describe the primary roles and employment contexts of school psychologists
- Define *social justice* and *multiculturalism*
- Describe the rationale for studying school psychology through a social justice lens

As compared with other areas of applied psychology, the profession of school psychology is relatively lesser known. For example, school psychology is less widely represented in introductory psychology books than areas such as clinical, counseling, and industrial/organizational psychology (Haselhuhn & Clopton, 2008; Lucas, Raley, Washington, & Blazek, 2005). In some cases, even school staff, such as general and special education teachers, lack knowledge about the precise roles and job responsibilities of their school psychologist colleagues. As a result, they may infrequently call upon these colleagues to deliver essential services such as individual counseling, group counseling, and crisis intervention (Gilman & Medway, 2007). Overall, there is a considerable need to educate school personnel, parents, legislators, and the general public about the value of school psychological services.

We begin this book on school psychology by providing a general orientation to the field. Although school psychology is widely represented internationally, this book specifically addresses the practice of school psychology in the United States. First, we examine contemporary definitions of *school psychology*. Next, we provide a brief description of school psychologists' primary roles and employment contexts as well as the ways in which their roles differ from those of other related professionals (e.g., school counselors). Finally, we discuss the meaning of social justice and its relevance to the study of school psychology.

DEFINING SCHOOL PSYCHOLOGY

Although the field of *school psychology* has been defined in different ways over the years, definitions provided by the two most prominent national organizations representing school psychologists—the American Psychological Association and the National Association of School Psychologists—are particularly important. The *National Association of School Psychologists* (*NASP*) is a U.S. professional organization that represents school psychologists. As of the writing of this chapter, NASP comprises more than 25,000 members, including practitioners, graduate educators, graduate students, and others. Presently, it is the largest association of school psychologists in the United States and the world (NASP, n.d.-a). In response to the question "Who are school psychologists?" NASP (2017b) provides the following answer on its website:

> School psychologists are uniquely qualified members of school teams that support students' ability to learn and teachers' ability to teach. They apply expertise in mental health, learning, and behavior, to help children and youth succeed academically, socially, behaviorally, and emotionally. School psychologists partner with families, teachers, school administrators, and other professionals to create safe, healthy, and supportive learning environments that strengthen connections between home, school, and the community.

Unlike NASP, the *American Psychological Association* (*APA*) is a professional organization that represents many different types of psychologists, including social, clinical, health, counseling, cognitive, and forensic psychologists. In 2015, APA (2016) reported 117,575 members (most of whom were not school psychologists), including faculty, practitioners, and student members. At this time, APA comprises more than 50 divisions, each of which represents a different area of psychology. Division 16 represents the profession of school psychology.

The APA recognizes school psychology as one of 15 approved specialty areas in professional psychology. A *specialty* is a defined area of psychological practice that requires advanced knowledge and skills acquired through an organized sequence of education and training (APA, 2011). On its website, the APA (n.d.) defines the specialty area of school psychology as follows:

> School Psychology is a general practice and health service provider specialty of professional psychology that is concerned with the science and practice of psychology with children, youth, families; learners of all ages; and the schooling process. The basic education and training of school psychologists prepares them to provide a range of psychological diagnosis, assessment, intervention, prevention, health promotion, and program development and evaluation services with a special focus on the developmental processes of children and youth within the context of schools, families and other systems.
>
> School psychologists are prepared to intervene at the individual and system level, and develop, implement, and evaluate preventive programs. In these efforts, they conduct ecologically valid assessments and intervene to promote positive learning environments within which children and youth from diverse backgrounds . . . have equal access to effective educational and psychological services that promote healthy development. (APA, n.d., paragraphs 1 and 2)

What do the definitions provided by NASP and APA have in common? First, both definitions focus on the essential characteristics of school psychology rather than on specifying what school psychologists actually do or ideally should do. They state that school psychology is a profession whose activities facilitate the development of healthy environments to promote the psychological and educational well-being of children and youth. In addition, they state that school psychologists collaborate with professionals in schools and other settings to provide a range of direct and indirect psychological services.

One of the main differences between these two definitions concerns the context within which school psychologists work. Although both emphasize the delivery of psychological services within educational systems, the NASP definition mentions only that school psychologists work as members of school-based teams. In contrast, the APA definition indicates that these services are delivered in settings beyond schools as well (e.g., clinics and hospitals). Despite their differences, however, both definitions describe school psychology as involving the delivery of psychological services that promote positive academic and mental health outcomes for youth.

SCHOOL PSYCHOLOGICAL PROFESSIONAL PRACTICES

As already stated, school psychologists work in schools and a variety of other settings. Within each of these settings, their professional practices are likely to vary as a function of the context in which they work. One widely accepted framework for describing the delivery of school psychological services is NASP's *Model for Comprehensive and Integrated School Psychological Services*, also known as the **NASP Practice Model** (NASP, 2010). The Practice Model is NASP's official policy statement on comprehensive service delivery in school psychology. It is meant to serve as a guide for the organization and delivery of services, with an emphasis on the delivery of school psychological services in the context of educational programs and settings.

The NASP Practice Model comprises two major parts: (1) Professional Practices and (2) Organizational Principles. The Professional Practices delineate the domains of knowledge and skills in which all school psychologists are expected to have competency. The Organizational Principles describe the structures and support systems that need to be in place in school systems to facilitate effective service delivery. Because the purpose of this chapter is to describe the professional roles and functions of school psychologists, it focuses specifically on the Professional Practices part of the Practice Model.

Figure 1.1 displays a graphic representation of the Professional Practices of the NASP Practice Model. The model includes 10 practice domains that are organized into three major areas: (1) *Foundations of School Psychologists' Service Delivery*, (2) *Practices That Permeate All Aspects of Service Delivery*, and (3) *Direct and Indirect Services for Children, Families, and Schools*. In the following section, we briefly describe each of the domains within these three areas of practice.

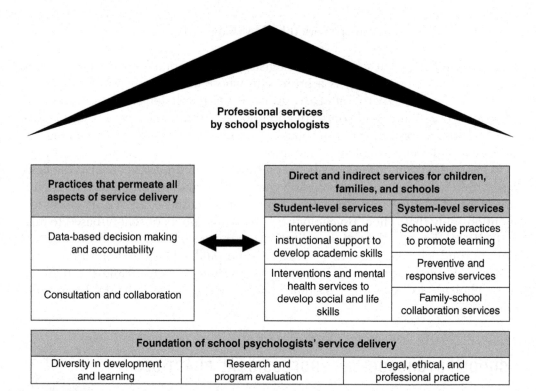

FIGURE 1.1 NASP MODEL FOR COMPREHENSIVE AND INTEGRATED SCHOOL PSYCHOLOGICAL SERVICES.

Source: National Association of School Psychologists. (2010). *Model for comprehensive and integrated school psychological services.* Bethesda, MD: National Association of School Psychologists. Reprinted/Adapted with permission of the publisher. www.nasponline.org

Practices That Permeate All Aspects of Service Delivery

The first two domains of the Practice Model are categorized as *Practices That Permeate All Aspects of Service Delivery.* Specifically, the two domains that constitute this area are *Data-Based Decision Making and Accountability* (Domain 1) and *Consultation and Collaboration* (Domain 2). These domains fall under this category because they are critical for providing a wide variety of direct and indirect services to students, families, and school systems.

Data-Based Decision Making and Accountability (Domain 1)

Data-based decision making involves the use of individual, group, or school-wide data to make informed decisions regarding educational and psychological service delivery. According to the Practice Model, "School psychologists have knowledge of varied models and methods of assessment and data collection for identifying strengths and needs, developing effective services and programs, and measuring progress and outcomes" (NASP, 2010, p. 4). Examples of practices in this area include (a) using "valid and reliable assessment techniques to assess progress toward academic and behavioral goals" and (b) systematically collecting "data from multiple sources as a foundation for decision-making" (NASP, 2010, p. 4).

Consultation and Collaboration (Domain 2)

Domain 2 refers to school psychologists' knowledge and skills in collaborating and communicating effectively with teachers, caregivers, administrators, community members, and others to facilitate positive outcomes for youth. The Practice Model states that "school psychologists have knowledge of varied models and strategies for consultation, collaboration, and communication applicable to individuals, families, groups, and systems and methods to promote effective implementation of services" (NASP, 2010, p. 4). Examples of practices in this area include (a) using "a consultative problem-solving process as a vehicle for planning, implementing, and evaluating academic and mental health services" and (b) consulting and collaborating "at the individual, family, group, and systems levels" (NASP, 2010, pp. 4–5).

Direct and Indirect Services for Children, Families, and Schools: Student-Level Services

School psychologists may provide a variety of student-level services. **Student-level services** are those that involve working with individuals or groups of students. Student-level services may be either direct or indirect. **Direct services** are those in which the provider has firsthand client contact (typically face-to-face contact, although some services may be provided through other media). Common examples of direct services include individual and group counseling, in which the school psychologist interacts *directly* with the client. **Indirect services** are those in which the provider does not have firsthand contact with the client, but rather supports the client's functioning through contact with a third party. Common examples of indirect services include consultation with teachers and administrators, in which school psychologists provide support to staff who subsequently deliver services to students. The following subsections describe the domains in this area of the Practice Model.

Interventions and Instructional Support to Develop Academic Skills (Domain 3)

Domain 3 includes knowledge and skills related to supporting the academic success of students (e.g., success in areas such as reading, writing, math, and science). According to the Practice Model, "School psychologists have knowledge of biological, cultural, and social influences on academic skills; human learning, cognitive, and developmental processes; and evidence-based curricula and instructional strategies . . . to implement and evaluate services that support cognitive and academic skills" (NASP, 2010, p. 5). Examples of practices in this area include (a) using "assessment data to develop and implement evidence-based instructional strategies that are intended to improve student performance" and (b) working with "other school personnel to develop, implement, and evaluate effective academic interventions for increasing the amount of time students are engaged in learning" (NASP, 2010, p. 5).

Interventions and Mental Health Services to Develop Social and Life Skills (Domain 4)

Domain 4 describes school psychologists' role in supporting the social, emotional, and behavioral well-being of students. The Practice Model states that

> School psychologists have knowledge of biological, cultural, developmental, and social influences on behavior and mental health, behavioral and emotional impacts on learning and life skills, and evidence-based strategies . . . to promote social–emotional functioning, and mental and behavioral health to implement and evaluate services that support socialization, learning, and mental and behavioral health. (NASP, 2010, p. 5)

Examples of practices in this area include (a) facilitating the "design and delivery of curricula to help students develop effective behaviors, such as self-regulation and self-monitoring, planning/organization, empathy, and healthy decision-making," and (b) providing "a continuum of developmentally appropriate mental health services, including individual and group counseling, behavioral coaching, classroom and school-wide social-emotional learning programs, positive behavioral support, and parent education and support" (NASP, 2010, pp. 5–6).

Direct and Indirect Services for Children, Families, and Schools: Systems-Level Services

School psychologists also provide a variety of systems-level services. Unlike student-level services, **systems-level services** involve working with organizations (or specific organizational levels, such as a grade level) to impact client outcomes on a larger scale. Systems-level services may also be either direct or indirect. The following describes each of the domains included in this section of the Practice Model.

School-wide Practices to Promote Learning (Domain 5)

Domain 5 describes school psychologists' knowledge and skills in fostering respectful, supportive, and high-quality learning environments for all students. According to the Practice Model,

> School psychologists have knowledge of school and systems structure, organization, and theory; general and special education; technology resources; and evidence-based school practices that promote learning and mental and behavioral health . . . to develop and implement practices and strategies to create and maintain effective and supportive learning environments for children and others. (NASP, 2010, p. 6)

Examples of practices in this area include (a) promoting "high rates of academic engaged time" and (b) working collaboratively "with other school personnel to create and maintain a multi-tiered continuum of services to support all students' attainment of academic, social, emotional, and behavioral goals" (NASP, 2010, p. 6).

Preventive and Responsive Services (Domain 6)

Domain 6 refers to competencies in identifying and promoting protective and adaptive factors that influence student functioning. The Practice Model states that

> School psychologists have knowledge of principles and research related to resilience and risk factors in learning and mental health, services in schools and communities to support multi-tiered prevention, and evidence-based strategies for effective crisis response . . . to promote services that enhance learning, mental and behavioral health, safety, and physical well-being through protective and adaptive factors and to implement effective crisis preparation, response, and recovery. (NASP, 2010, p. 6)

Examples of practices in this area include (a) promoting "recognition of risk and protective factors that are vital to understanding and addressing systemic programs such as school failure, truancy, dropout, bullying youth suicide, or school violence," and (b) participating "in the implementation and evaluation of programs that promote safe and violence-free schools and communities" (NASP, 2010, p. 7).

Family—School Collaboration Services (Domain 7)

Domain 7 refers to school psychologists' knowledge and skills in understanding, supporting, and communicating with diverse families. According to the Practice Model, "School psychologists have knowledge of principles and research related to family systems, strengths, needs, and culture; evidence-based strategies to support family influences on children's learning and mental health; and strategies to develop collaboration between families and schools" (NASP, 2010, p. 7). Examples of practices in this area include (a) using "effective evidence-based strategies to design, implement, and evaluate effective policies and practices that promote family, school, and community partnerships to enhance learning and mental health outcomes for students" and (b) promoting "strategies for safe, nurturing, and dependable parenting and home interventions to facilitate children's healthy development" (NASP, 2010, p. 7).

Foundations of School Psychological Service Delivery

At the base of the NASP Practice Model are the *Foundations of School Psychological Service Delivery* (see Figure 1.1). The domains within this section represent core areas of knowledge and skill that are essential for high-quality, ethical, and effective practice. The three domains in this section are *Diversity and Development in Learning* (Domain 8), *Research and Program Evaluation* (Domain 9), and *Legal, Ethical, and Professional Practice* (Domain 10).

Diversity in Development and Learning (Domain 8)

Domain 8 of the Practice Model refers to school psychologists' knowledge and skills in serving multicultural student and family populations. Specifically, the model states that

School psychologists have knowledge of individual differences, abilities, disabilities, and other diverse characteristics; principles and research related to diversity factors for children, families, and schools, including factors related to culture, context, and individual and role differences; and evidence-based strategies to enhance services and address potential influences related to diversity. (NASP, 2010, p. 7)

Examples of practices in this area include (a) providing "culturally competent and responsive services in all areas of service delivery and in the contexts of diverse individual, family, school, and community characteristics" and (b) promoting "fairness and social justice in educational programs and services" (NASP, 2010, p. 8). Because school psychologists work with a diverse range of students, families, and school personnel, knowledge and skills in this area are critical for effective service delivery.

Research and Program Evaluation (Domain 9)

Domain 9 refers to knowledge and skills in conducting research and assessing program outcomes through the use of sound analytic tools. According to the model,

School psychologists have knowledge of research design, statistics, measurement, varied data collection and analysis techniques, and program evaluation sufficient for understanding research and interpreting data in applied settings. School psychologists demonstrate skills to evaluate and apply research as a foundation for service delivery and, in collaboration with others, use various techniques and technology resources for data collection, measurement, and analysis. (NASP, 2010, p. 8)

Examples of practices in this area include (a) using "techniques for data collection, analysis, and accountability in evaluation of services at the individual, group, and system levels" and (b) providing "support for classroom teachers in collecting and analyzing progress monitoring data" (NASP, 2010, p. 8).

Legal, Ethical, and Professional Practice (Domain 10)

Finally, Domain 10 encompasses professional behaviors, knowledge of the field of school psychology itself, and skills in applying legal and ethical principles to practice. Specifically, the Practice Model states that "school psychologists have knowledge of the history and foundations of school psychology; multiple service models and methods; ethical, legal, and professional standards; and other factors related to professional identity and effective practice as school psychologists" (NASP, 2010, p. 8). Examples of practices in this area include (a) practicing "in ways that are consistent with ethical, professional, and legal standards and regulations" and (b) using "supervision and mentoring for effective practice" (NASP, 2010, p. 8).

Summary of the NASP Practice Model

The NASP Practice Model provides a comprehensive framework for conceptualizing service delivery in school psychology. Collectively, the domains in this model describe the range of knowledge and skills that school psychologists use to support the well-being of children and families, especially in educational settings. Although this model illustrates the many services that school psychologists can provide, roles and responsibilities may vary considerably across employment contexts throughout the United States, as discussed in the next section.

PROFESSIONAL ACTIVITIES AND EMPLOYMENT OF SCHOOL PSYCHOLOGISTS

It has been estimated that more than 32,000 school psychologists are practicing in the United States (Jimerson, Stewart, Skokut, Cardenas, & Malone, 2009). These individuals work in a variety of school and nonschool settings, including K–12 public and private schools, colleges and universities, independent practice, and hospital and medical settings. Some data have been published on the demographics, qualifications, and professional activities of school psychologists. Typically, these data are collected by individual research teams (e.g., scholars collaborating across higher education institutions) or professional organizations (e.g., NASP). For example, every 5 years, NASP surveys a random sample of its members across the United States regarding their training and professional activities. The most recent of these membership surveys was conducted in 2015 (Walcott, Charvat, McNamara, & Hyson, 2016). Notably, NASP's survey includes only data from organizational members (and. therefore. is not necessarily representative of school psychologists who are not NASP members). Nevertheless, it provides some of the most comprehensive data on the practice of school psychologists nationwide.

Employment Contexts

The 2015 NASP membership survey indicated that school psychologists serve in a variety of roles, including practitioners (approximately 83%), university faculty (approximately 7%), administrators (approximately 5%), and other roles (approximately 5%) (Walcott et al., 2016). They also work in a variety of settings, including public schools, private schools, higher education institutions, and independent (private) practice. Table 1.1 displays the percentage of school psychologists who worked in various primary full-time employment settings (according to the results of the NASP membership survey). As seen in the table, the majority of school psychologists were employed full-time in some type of pre-K–12 school setting, with more than 80% working in the public schools. Among those school psychologists employed in pre-K–12 settings, many worked in suburban school systems (43.4%), whereas others were employed in urban (26.5%) and rural (24.0%) settings.

Professional Activities of School Psychologists

Professional activities vary significantly among school psychologists depending on the individual's job title (e.g., practitioner and faculty member) and employment context. Figure 1.2 displays the professional activities of school psychologists, as indicated by the 2015 NASP membership survey results. Respondents were asked

TABLE 1.1 Employment Settings of NASP Members

Employment *Setting*	Percentage of NASP Members
Public school	86%
College/university	10%
Private school	8%
Independent (private) practice	7%
Faith-based school	7%
State department of education	2%
Hospital/medical setting	2%

Source: Adapted from Walcott, C. M., Charvat, J., McNamara, K. M., & Hyson, D. (2016). *School psychology at a glance 2015, member survey results.* Paper presented at the Annual Convention of the National Association of School Psychologists, New Orleans, LA. Copyright (as applicable) by the National Association of School Psychologists, Bethesda, MD. Reprinted/Adapted with permission of the publisher. www.nasponline.org

to rate the frequency with which they participated in a variety of psychological and educational practices. Frequency ratings were based on a scale of values ranging from 0 to 4, with a value of 0 indicating no involvement in the activity and a value of 4 indicating a great deal of involvement. Mean ratings for each activity are displayed in Figure 1.2.

On average, NASP members reported spending a considerable amount of time conducting assessments to determine students' eligibility for special education services. They also devoted considerable time to developing Individualized Education Programs (IEPs), which are formal, individualized plans that specify the range of services to which a student with a disability is entitled. (IEPs are described in Chapter 5.) Collectively, these data suggest that many school psychologists spend a significant amount of time in activities related to special education eligibility and services, meaning that they work frequently with students with disabilities.

Conversely, NASP members reported spending less time in activities such as promoting family–school collaboration and developing school-wide strategies and programs to support learning. Notably, these roles are integral functions of the school psychologist, according to the NASP Practice Model. For many years, professional organizations and leaders in the field have advocated for the expansion of the school psychologist's role to include not only special education assessment activities but also a wide range of systems-level prevention and intervention activities (Dawson et al., 2004). Despite the findings of this survey, the roles of school psychologists vary considerably across settings, and many do engage in a variety of systems-level activities to promote positive academic, behavioral, social, and emotional outcomes for students.

SCHOOL PSYCHOLOGY AND RELATED PROFESSIONS

How does school psychology differ from other related fields in psychology? What makes the profession of school psychology unique? To some extent, the roles of school psychologists and other mental health providers overlap. For example,

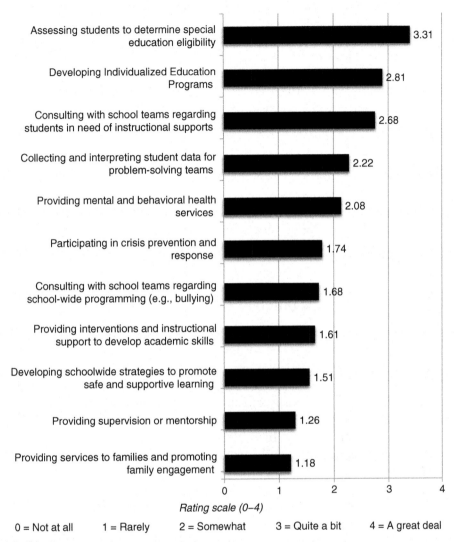

Rating scale (0–4)

0 = Not at all   1 = Rarely   2 = Somewhat   3 = Quite a bit   4 = A great deal

FIGURE 1.2 PROFESSIONAL PRACTICES OF SCHOOL PSYCHOLOGISTS.

Source: Adapted from Walcott, C. M., Charvat, J., McNamara, K. M., & Hyson, D. (2016). *School psychology at a glance 2015, member survey results.* Paper presented at the Annual Convention of the National Association of School Psychologists, New Orleans, LA,. Copyright (as applicable) by the National Association of School Psychologists, Bethesda, MD. Reprinted/Adapted with permission of the publisher. www.nasponline.org

school psychologists, school counselors, and clinical psychologists are similar in that all three groups of professionals can provide counseling services to children and adolescents. Nevertheless, the training, credentialing, expertise, and roles of these professionals also differ in important ways. This section describes these differences.

How Is School Psychology Different From School Counseling?

School psychology and ***school counseling*** differ in several ways. First, school counselors typically require only 2 years of graduate education (including a 600-hour supervised internship), whereas school psychologists typically require 3 years of training (including a 1,200-hour supervised internship). Moreover, school counselors typically do not practice outside of school settings, while school psychologists may practice in a variety of settings (depending on their degree and training), including private practice, mental health clinics, and hospitals (NASP, n.d.-b).

In K–12 public schools, the roles of school counselors and school psychologists overlap to some extent but also differ in significant ways. Both school psychologists and school counselors are trained in mental health counseling, crisis prevention, and other intervention activities. In addition to these activities, school counselors typically work with all students in a school to assist with course scheduling, career planning, and family and academic problems. Although school psychologists also provide supports to all students in a school building, they spend a considerable amount of time providing assessment and intervention services to students with disabilities. Generally, school psychologists are more likely to have training in the areas of behavioral analysis, mental health diagnosis, and research methods (NASP, n.d.-b).

How Is School Psychology Different From Child Clinical Psychology?

One of the primary distinctions between **child clinical psychology** and school psychology concerns the degrees required to practice in these fields. Whereas school psychologists may practice at either the doctoral or the non-doctoral level, the entry-level degree for independent practice as a child clinical psychologist is the doctoral degree. The majority of school psychologists are employed in K–12 school settings, although some are employed in hospitals, mental health centers, and other clinical settings. In contrast, clinical psychologists are less likely to be employed in elementary and secondary school settings and more likely to be found in hospitals, mental health clinics, private practice, and other settings (NASP, n.d.-b).

While both clinical and school psychologists have training in child development, psychopathology, and other areas of psychology, school psychologists have expertise in issues that concern the intersection of education and psychology. Thus, as compared with clinical psychologists, school psychologists are much more likely to have skills in facilitating school change and organizational development, consulting with educators, and promoting students' academic success. School psychologists also are more likely to be knowledgeable about instruction, curriculum, and classroom behavior management (NASP, n.d.-b).

SOCIAL JUSTICE AND SCHOOL PSYCHOLOGY

As mentioned earlier, this book describes the practice and profession of school psychology through a social justice lens. We believe that all school psychologists must be well versed in the pervasive social, cultural, and political issues that impact children, families, teachers, special services staff, and the settings in which these individuals interact. These issues should be discussed in relation to all areas of practice, including each of the 10 domains of the NASP Practice Model. Why is it important to study school psychology through a social justice lens? To answer this question, we must first define the term *social justice*.

Defining Social Justice

Broadly, Bell (2013) defined **social justice** as the "full and equal participation of all groups in a society that is mutually shaped to meet their needs" (p. 21). This term has been defined in many ways by a number of different scholars, but there are commonalities among these definitions. For example, Shriberg et al. (2008) investigated the meaning of social justice by surveying a panel of cultural diversity experts. In two rounds of feedback, the panelists were asked to define the term *social justice*, identify topics salient to this term, and describe the ways in which school psychologists can promote social justice. Experts most frequently generated definitions aligned with two primary categories: (a) ensuring the protection of rights and responsibilities for all and (b) assuming an ecological/systemic view (i.e., moving beyond the immediate school context to consider the larger impact of educational decision making). Moreover, when asked to rank the salience of various topics to social justice work, participants generally assigned the highest rankings to topics such as institutional power (e.g., dynamics of privilege and oppression in government) and advocacy. Generally, Shriberg's experts believed that social justice work is best characterized by a focus on issues of power, privilege (which is described in Chapter 4), equity, and advocacy. **Advocacy** refers to the practice of proactively representing and supporting a cause or group of individuals. More specifically, social justice advocacy involves empowering and promoting the well-being of traditionally marginalized individuals and groups.

In this book, we embrace a broad view of social justice that incorporates concepts of equity, advocacy, and fairness. When applied to the field of school psychology specifically, social justice work involves building safe, supportive, and welcoming environments that promote the healthy development and educational success of all students. From this perspective, we acknowledge that pervasive injustices permeate the larger contexts in which schools are situated, including their cultural, social, economic, and political environments. Social justice advocacy involves recognizing and proactively addressing these injustices, rather than simply accepting the status quo. Presently, a number of social injustices impact children and families in schools, including the over- and under-representation of racial and ethnic minority students in certain categories of special education and related services (e.g., intellectual disability and giftedness), discrimination against gender and sexual minority youth, and disparities in disciplinary practices between racial and ethnic minority and non-minority students. This book describes many of these social justice issues in the context of school psychology practice.

Social Justice and Multiculturalism

To understand social justice, it is important to understand how this concept differs from **multiculturalism**. Multiculturalism is described extensively in Chapter 4. For now, however, we provide a basic definition of the term: a worldview that acknowledges and values diverse individuals and cultural backgrounds (Carroll, 2009). Multicultural knowledge, awareness, and skills are undoubtedly critical to effective psychological service delivery. Although inextricably linked, the terms *social justice* and *multiculturalism* have somewhat different meanings. More specifically, social justice is often described as the latest development in multicultural psychology (Ratts, 2011). Whereas multicultural competence generally refers to the awareness, knowledge, and skills needed to work effectively with diverse populations, social justice competencies center on skills in recognizing and challenging systemic inequities, which often transcend the school context (Shriberg et al., 2008). Promoting social justice involves taking proactive measures to rectify pervasive societal inequalities and to promote equal access to educational opportunity for diverse groups (Shriberg et al., 2008).

To illustrate the differences between the terms *social justice* and *multiculturalism*, recall Shriberg and colleagues' (2008) findings regarding the meaning of *social justice*. Now, consider a similar study by Rogers and Lopez (2002), who also surveyed a panel of experts in providing culturally competent services to racial, ethnic, and linguistic minority populations. After conducting a comprehensive literature review of cross-cultural competence research and soliciting feedback from panelists, they identified 102 critical competency items across 14 major categories (e.g., *Assessment, Consultation, Counseling, and Organizational Skills*). Panelists were asked to rate competencies based on perceived importance, and average ratings for items were calculated for each category. Of the 14 categories, panelists assigned the highest mean ratings to competencies in the *Assessment* and *Report Writing* categories. Examples of highly rated items in these categories included the following: (a) "using instruments sensitive to cultural and linguistic differences"; (b) possessing "knowledge about non-biased assessment"; and (c) "incorporating information about family origins . . . into report." Conversely, *Working with Organizations* (i.e., competency related to organizational change) was ranked the second least important of the 14 categories. Overall, the multicultural experts in this study generally rated skills in culturally responsive service delivery (e.g., providing assessment and counseling services to diverse populations) as more central to cultural competence than skills in advocacy and facilitating organizational change.

Undoubtedly, Rogers and Lopez's (2002) and Shriberg and colleagues' (2008) studies suggest that there is considerable overlap in the meaning of the terms *multiculturalism* and *social justice*. For example, Rogers and Lopez's participants endorsed competencies in facilitating organizational change. Likewise, many of the experts in Shriberg and colleagues' (2008) study acknowledged the central role of cultural competence in social justice advocacy. Nevertheless, these studies also suggest that there are fundamental nuances that differentiate the two terms.

Despite their differences, multiculturalism and social justice clearly are inextricably linked. Concepts such as oppression and discrimination cannot be properly understood without first understanding multicultural principles. In fact, Ratts (2011) cautioned that engaging in social justice advocacy in the absence of multicultural competence may result in the selection of advocacy strategies that disregard important cultural variables. Developing multicultural competence is an essential prerequisite for promoting social justice; however, the latter term generally places greater emphasis on advocacy within and beyond school walls, as compared with the former.

Why Study School Psychology and Social Justice in Tandem?

Returning to our earlier question, why is it important to study school psychology through a social justice lens? Issues in school psychology and social justice should be studied in tandem for many reasons. In the following list, we enumerate several of these reasons, which provide an underlying rationale for the orientation and content of this book.

1. ***Social justice advocacy is being increasingly prioritized in school psychology.*** As described in Chapter 13, professional organizations that represent school psychology are increasingly emphasizing the importance of social justice work. For example, in Domain 8 (*Diversity in Development and Learning*) of its Practice Model, NASP states that "an understanding and respect for diversity in development and learning and advocacy for social justice are foundations for all aspects of service delivery." As is discussed in Chapter 13, NASP (2017a) will explicitly recognize *social justice* as one of its strategic goals through at least 2022. Generally, social justice principles are embedded in the core training and practice standards of school psychology's major professional organizations. By embracing a social justice orientation, school psychologists will be better prepared to align themselves with future directions for the field.

2. ***Social justice issues must be studied with intentionality.*** Social justice advocacy involves challenging both the overt and covert injustices that impact students and their families. Some injustices are seemingly less conspicuous, because they are part of the status quo, or the existing state of school affairs. For example, we noted earlier that, on average, assessment activities (typically special education assessments) consume more than half of school psychologists' daily routines. When school psychologists spend a great deal of time in assessment activities, they have less time to engage in prevention and intervention activities, which may be vital for supporting our nation's most vulnerable youth. Without these services, such youth are likely to fall even further behind their peers. The assessment-laden routine of the school psychologist can easily be overlooked, because it is simply part of the typical practitioner's day (and ultimately, part of the status quo). As for all social justice issues, changing the status quo requires careful and intentional scrutiny of one's own practices and their impact on others. Thus, social justice issues must be studied with intentionality.

3. ***We have a long way to go before the aspirational goals of social justice are realized.*** This means that taking immediate steps to educate oneself about social justice issues is an imperative for all practitioners. As described in Chapter 12, systems-level change in schools is a slow and painstaking process. As an example, the landmark court case that led to the racial integration in public schools (i.e., *Brown v. Board of Education*) was decided more than half a century ago (in 1954). However, well into the 21st century, the public school system continues to proliferate many forms of racial injustice. For example, African American students are more likely to be subject to harsher disciplinary action in schools than their White peers (Skiba et al., 2011). Promoting social justice is a slow and laborious undertaking that will require the commitment and collaboration of a variety of stakeholders. School psychologists are among these stakeholders.

4. *School psychologists must possess knowledge and skill in the area of social justice advocacy to be effective in their work.* One of the authors of this chapter (SLG) often asks her students, "Is it necessary for school psychologists to become social justice advocates to be effective in their roles?" Most often, this question is met with a long, thoughtful pause followed by slow, tentative head nodding that gradually becomes more vigorous and self-assured. We believe these students are correct in answering this question affirmatively. As Shriberg (2012) contended, the goals of social justice are integrally linked with the goals of school psychology. School psychologists are ethically responsible for acting in the best interest of all students. At this time, many school-age youth face a range of injustices that compromise their overall well-being and opportunities for success. If school psychologists do not advocate vigorously for these students, they cannot fulfill their ethical and professional obligation to act in the best interest of all children.

For all of these reasons and others, this book describes the practice of school psychology through a social justice lens. To highlight social justice applications in each area of practice, every chapter includes a section on "Social Justice Connections." The purpose of these sections is to encourage readers to consider the pervasive social justice issues that permeate school systems and to provide concrete strategies for addressing these issues.

SUMMARY AND CONCLUSIONS

This chapter provided an overview of the field of school psychology. In particular, it defined the profession, described the ways in which school psychology differs from other related professions, presented the 10 domains of the NASP Practice Model, and described the typical roles and functions of school psychologists in the schools. The NASP Practice Model is referenced frequently throughout the remainder of the book; thus, the figure provided in this chapter may assist readers in understanding how various components of practice are interrelated. Finally, this chapter defined the term *social justice* and presented a rationale for the orientation of this book. It is our sincere hope that readers will reflect on the social justice concepts presented throughout the remaining chapters and consider them in their future professional development and practice.

DISCUSSION QUESTIONS

1. What is school psychology? What makes the profession of school psychology unique?
2. What is the significance of the NASP Practice Model for the field of school psychology?
3. What are direct and indirect psychological services? Why are both types necessary for comprehensive school psychological service delivery?

4. Shriberg (2012) contended that the goals of school psychology and social justice are integrally linked. Do you agree or disagree? Why?
5. Identify three domains of the NASP Practice Model. How might each of these domains intersect with social justice principles?

REFERENCES

American Psychological Association. (n.d.). School psychology. Retrieved from http://www.apa.org/ed/graduate/specialize/school.aspx

American Psychological Association. (2011). *Principles for the recognition of specialties in professional psychology.* Washington, DC: Author.

American Psychological Association. (2016). Annual report of the American Psychological Association. *American Psychologist, 71,* S1–S50.

Bell, L. A. (2013). Theoretical foundations. In M. Adams, W. J. Blumenfeld, C. Castañeda, H. W. Hackman, M. L. Peters, & X. Zúñiga (Eds.), *Readings for diversity and social justice* (3rd ed., pp. 21–26). New York, NY: Routledge.

Carroll, D. W. (2009). Toward multicultural competence: A practical model for implementation in the schools. In J. M. Jones (Ed.), *The psychology of multiculturalism in schools* (pp. 1–16). Bethesda, MD: National Association of School Psychologists.

Dawson, M., Cummings, J. A., Harrison, P. L., Short, R. J., Gorin, S., & Palomares, R. (2004). The 2002 multisite conference on the future of school psychology: Next steps. *School Psychology Review, 33,* 115–125.

Gilman, R., & Medway, F. (2007). Teachers' perceptions of school psychology: A comparison of regular and special education teacher ratings. *School Psychology Quarterly, 22,* 145–161.

Haselhuhn, C. W., & Clopton, K. L. (2008). The representation of applied psychology areas in introductory psychology textbooks. *Teaching of Psychology, 35,* 205–209. doi:10.1080/00986280802189130

Jimerson, S. R., Stewart, K., Skokut, M., Cardenas, S., & Malone, H. (2009). How many school psychologists are there in each country of the world? International estimates of school psychologists and school psychologist-to-student ratios. *School Psychology International, 30,* 555–567.

Lucas, J. L., Raley, A. B., Washington, C., & Blazek, M. A. (2005). Where are the non-traditional applied areas of psychology in introductory psychology textbooks? *North American Journal of Psychology, 7,* 379–388.

National Association of School Psychologists. (n.d.-a). About NASP. Retrieved from https://www.nasponline.org/utility/about-nasp

National Association of School Psychologists. (n.d.-b). A career in school psychology: Frequently asked questions. Retrieved from https://www.nasponline.org/about-school-psychology/becoming-a-school-psychologist/a-career-in-school-psychology-frequently-asked-questions

National Association of School Psychologists. (2010). *Model for comprehensive and integrated school psychological services.* Bethesda, MD: National Association of School Psychologists. Copyright (as applicable) by the National Association of School Psychologists, Bethesda, MD. Reprinted/Adapted with permission of the publisher. www.nasponline.org

National Association of School Psychologists. (2017a). Strategic plan: 2017–2022. Retrieved from https://www.nasponline.org/utility/about-nasp/vision-core-purpose-core-values-and-strategic-goals

National Association of School Psychologists. (2017b, April). Who are school psychologists? [Webpage]. Retrieved from https://www.nasponline.org/about-school-psychology/who-are-school-psychologists

Ratts, M. (2011). Multiculturalism and social justice: Two sides of the same coin. *Journal of Multicultural Counseling and Development, 39,* 24–37.

Rogers, M., & Lopez, E. (2002). Identifying critical cross-cultural school psychology competencies. *Journal of School Psychology, 40,* 115–141.

Shriberg, D. (2012). Graduate education and professional development. In D. Shriberg, S. Song, A. Miranda, & K. Radliff. (Eds.), *School psychology and social justice: Conceptual foundations and tools for practice* (pp. 311–326). New York, NY: Routledge.

Shriberg, D., Bonner, M., Sarr, B., Walker, A., Hyland, M., & Chester, C. (2008). Social justice through a school psychology lens: Definitions and applications. *School Psychology Review*, *37*, 453–468.

Skiba, R. J., Horner, R. H., Chung, C., Rausch, M. K., May, S. L., & Tobin, T. (2011). Race is not neutral: A national investigation of African American and Latino disproportionality in school discipline. *School Psychology Review*, *40*, 85–107.

Walcott, C. M., Charvat, J., McNamara, K. M., & Hyson, D. (2016). *School psychology at a glance 2015, member survey results*. Paper presented at the Annual Convention of the National Association of School Psychologists, New Orleans, LA.

Historical Foundations

DAN FLORELL

- Define and describe the major epochs of school psychology's history (i.e., Hybrid and Thoroughbred Years)
- Describe foundations in psychology and education that prompted the inception of the field
- Describe the development and contributions of school psychology's major professional associations
- Describe influential legislation and court cases that shaped the development of school psychology
- Describe the contributions of diverse individuals to the development of the field

Although relatively brief, the history of school psychology is brimming with innovation, missteps, successes, and challenges. Over the past 120 years, the profession of school psychology has been shaped by a number of influences, including developments in the fields of psychology and education, the changing sociopolitical environment of the United States, and, ultimately, the evolving contexts and needs of public schools. Many of these influences continue to be evident in contemporary practice.

Studying the history of school psychology is essential for understanding the current status of the field. In particular, knowledge of school psychology's history allows current scholars, practitioners, and graduate educators to avoid repeating past mistakes and to capitalize on opportunities for rectifying past injustices. This chapter describes important events and trends that contributed to the development of the field.

OVERVIEW OF SCHOOL PSYCHOLOGY'S HISTORY

According to Fagan (1986a), school psychology's roots can be traced back to the 1890s. The history of school psychology has been described as two periods: the **Hybrid Years** (1896–1969) and the **Thoroughbred Years** (1970–present). The term *hybrid* is used to describe a time in school psychology's history when the profession comprised a diverse range of practitioners in psychology and education who were loosely organized around the mission of providing psychoeducational services to school-aged youth (Fagan & Wise, 2007). For the most part, these services centered on assessing children for the purpose of educational "sorting" or placement. The term *thoroughbred*, however, refers to the period of time in which school psychology's professional identity became more cohesive and established. In particular, this time period saw a growing number of graduate preparation programs, school positions, and publication outlets specifically devoted to the practice and profession of school psychology. The turning point marking the transition from the Hybrid Years to the Thoroughbred Years was the formation of the National Association of School Psychologists (NASP), the profession's first national organization devoted specifically to the practice of school psychology. This chapter describes both time periods and the events and trends that shaped them.

THE HYBRID YEARS

The Emergence of Psychology in Europe and the United States

The foundations of school psychology began to take root only a fewdecades after the larger field of psychology was established. The field of psychology itself was a mixture of medicine and philosophy that emerged in Germany in the late 1800s. German pioneers of psychology, such as Herman von Helmholtz and Wilhelm Wundt, focused their work on understanding the human mind through *introspection* (i.e., the observation of one's own mental state and conscious thoughts) and the measurement of physiological reactions. In England, individuals such as Francis Galton also experimented with methods of mental measurement as a means for understanding individual differences (Fancher, 1990).

Not long after the roots of psychology took hold in Europe, the United States began to contribute to the field as well. For example, William James, who studied under von Helmholtz in the late 1860s and later came to be regarded as "the Father of American Psychology," wrote one of the profession's most influential books, *The Principles of Psychology* (Angell, 1911; Evans, 1990). This work sparked great interest in the field of psychology among U.S. scholars. Inspired by James and his contemporaries, students in the United States and abroad began to specialize in the field of psychology.

The Changing Landscape of the Labor Force and Education

As the larger field of psychology began to take shape, the U.S. education system experienced significant changes as well. In the mid- to late 1890s, relatively few individuals enjoyed full access to formal education. The country was only a few decades removed from the Civil War, and racial and ethnic discrimination was rampant. For example, mandated racial segregation in public spaces resulted in Black students attending under-resourced, inferior schools or their exclusion from public education altogether. Native Americans also were marginalized by the U.S. education system during this time. When Native American youth were included in schooling, it was often for the purpose of forced assimilation (Noltemeyer, Mujic, & McLoughlin, 2012). Regardless of cultural background, financial circumstances prevented many children who worked in factories, mines, and other labor-intensive jobs from attending school (Rury, 2016).

As poor work conditions continued and concerns for children's rights mounted, social movements advocating for the formal education of youth gained momentum. According to Field (1976), these social movements were motivated by the desire for an educated workforce and the preservation of society's character and moral structure. State legislators became increasingly aware that child labor negatively impacted the workforce and therefore needed to be regulated. Organized labor unions and other social organizations were instrumental in many states to ban child labor. Early on, however, these laws often were not enforced (Siegel & White, 1982).

As various industries began to require a more highly skilled and educated workforce, states began to pass compulsory schooling legislation, which was more successful in removing children from the labor force. **Compulsory schooling** refers to the legal requirement that children of particular ages attend school for a designated period of time. The surge in compulsory schooling legislation between 1870 and 1890 was a major driving force in the development of school psychology, as it resulted in an influx of youth with diverse characteristics and needs into the U.S. public school system (Braden, DiMarino-Linnen, & Good, 2001; Kaplan & Kaplan, 1985). With the welfare and needs of children rising to the forefront of the American conscience, a child study movement began.

Child Study Movement

Among the many social movements of the late 1800s, the **child study movement** was the one that most directly facilitated the birth of school psychology (Fagan, 2000). During this time, scholars became increasingly aware that children were not simply "miniature adults," but rather were distinctly different in their mental and behavioral functioning. As a result, greater numbers of people and organizations committed to working with children. This increased interest was motivated by four primary goals: (1) the need to teach children about a community's shared beliefs and values; (2) the desire for partial regulation of the labor market; (3) the need to prepare children for adult economic roles; and (4) the desire to provide services and support for at-risk children (Siegel & White, 1982). These goals significantly influenced the development of social institutions that continue to serve and impact children.

The increasing diversity of the student population in public schools initially presented a number of new challenges for school personnel (Fagan, 1992; Hildreth, 1930). Many children who came to school were coping with a range of issues, including malnutrition, economic hardship, learning problems, and chronic disease. Whereas such problems previously had deterred these students from enrolling in public schools, compulsory schooling laws paved the way for their attendance. In response, schools developed special programs to address the needs of students who were experiencing learning problems (Siegel & White, 1982).

A number of psychologists contributed to the study of children's abilities, needs, and development. For example, Granville Stanley Hall was instrumental in drawing attention to the need for school-based services for children and adolescents. In 1880, Hall presented a series of lectures at Harvard University on the applications of psychology to education. Moreover, he studied the use of questionnaire methodology as a means for assessing the "common problems of school children" (Fagan, 1992, p. 238). Although Hall's questionnaire methodology was later discredited, he inspired other psychologists, such as Edward Thorndike, to pursue more scientifically rigorous studies of children (Ross, 1972). Ultimately, Hall's goal was to understand the basic nature of children and to apply this knowledge to the development of school programs (White, 1992).

Inspired by the child study movement, Lightner Witmer also made significant contributions to the study of children and schooling. In 1892, Witmer began teaching at the University of Pennsylvania, where he established the world's first applied psychological clinic in 1896 (Tulchin, 1956). Witmer focused on the assessment of schoolchildren who were referred by teachers, parents, and local community agencies (Fagan, 1992). Witmer's assessment techniques included interviews, naturalistic observations, record reviews, physical exams, and mental testing, all of which he used to ascertain the client's functioning while noting relevant environmental and social influences (Baker, 1988). He promoted a multidisciplinary approach centered on high-quality communication with parents and teachers to develop effective interventions (McReynolds, 1996; Routh, 1996). At the fifth annual meeting of the American Psychological Association (APA), Witmer (1897) emphasized the need for psychological experts "who [were] capable of treating the many difficult cases that resist the ordinary methods of the school room" (p. 117). Lightner Witmer is regarded as the founder of both school psychology and clinical psychology (Fagan, 1996; McReynolds, 1996).

Intelligence-Testing Movement

Interest in the measurement of individual differences in physiological and mental functioning significantly shaped the development of school psychology. Although many scholars contributed to the early development of intelligence testing, Alfred Binet, Victor Henri, and Theodore Simon are credited with the breakthrough in this area that most directly influenced school psychology. Commissioned by the French government to develop a measure that would identify students with intellectual disabilities, Binet, Henri, and Simon constructed the first modern intelligence test, the *Binet-Simon Intelligence Scale*, which was published in 1905 (Kaufman, 2000). As part of the development of this intelligence scale, Binet and colleagues identified age-related differences in children's cognitive development (Sattler, 2001).

Soon after the *Binet-Simon Intelligence Scale* was published in France, it was translated into English and distributed in the United States. Henry Goddard was the first to translate the test in 1908, and Lewis Terman followed with his own version in 1916. In his 1916 version, Terman introduced the concept of the intelligence quotient (which is described in Chapter 10; Braden et al., 2001; Kehle, Clark, & Jenson, 1993). Between 1910 and 1920, other psychologists began to develop aptitude and achievement tests (Fagan, 2000; Kehle et al., 1993). Even though some school districts and child study bureaus embraced these tests, they were not well known by the general public.

Recognition of intelligence testing increased when the United States entered World War I. At the time, the U.S. military was relatively small and searching for a way to screen the intellectual and emotional functioning of soldiers. In response to this need, Robert Yerkes, who was the president of the APA at the time the United States declared war, recruited several prominent psychologists, including Henry Goddard, to develop a group-administered intelligence test (Boake, 2002; Kaufman, 2000). These psychologists developed the Army Alpha intelligence test. They quickly realized, however, that not all recruits would be able to complete the test, due to cultural barriers, limited English proficiency, or illiteracy. Subsequently, the committee developed the Army Beta test, which emphasized nonverbal items to increase accessibility (Kaufman, 2000). The widespread use of the Army Alpha and Beta tests contributed to the legitimization of psychological testing in the public eye (Fagan, 1985). As these tests began to enter schools, they gradually ushered school psychologists into an assessment-focused role (Fagan & Wise, 2007).

The advent of intelligence testing legitimized the need for school staff with psychological training; however, it also introduced a number of controversial social issues. Results from the Alpha tests indicated that, on average, Whites performed better than members of other racial groups (e.g., African Americans) did. Some scholars used these findings as a vehicle for suggesting that Whites were intellectually superior to African Americans. In response, several African American psychologists, including Horace Mann Bond, Herman Canady, Martin Jenkins, and Albert Beckham, set out to debunk these claims (Graves & Mitchell, 2011; Urban, 1989). For example, Albert Sidney Beckham, the first African American school psychologist, examined the impact of environmental variables (e.g., socioeconomic status) on intelligence test scores (Graves, 2009). Debate regarding the use of intelligence tests with diverse populations intensified in subsequent decades and would eventually become a source of heated controversy in state and federal courts.

An Emerging Profession

The confluence of sociopolitical forces and advances in child studies, intelligence testing, and other areas made it increasingly clear that school psychological services were necessary for supporting a diverse student body. As student populations continued to grow, public schools began conducting health screenings and providing preventive care to students. Many schools focused on assisting children with disabilities, including students with visual, auditory, physical, and intellectual impairments. These services required the expertise of specialists with multidisciplinary skill sets, and, consequently, laid the foundations of school psychology.

Organizations devoted to the welfare of children, such as the Illinois Society for Child Study (ISCS; established in 1894), contributed to the development of school-based services. For example, W. S. Christopher, who was a member of the Chicago Board of Education and the ISCS, assisted the Chicago Board of Education in establishing the nation's first **child study bureau** in 1899 (Slater, 1980). These child study bureaus conducted research on students to establish typical development and then identify students who were atypically developing so as to provide more appropriate educational services. Over the next few decades, the developments in Chicago began to spread to other urban school districts, which formed their own child study bureaus. Subsequently, child study bureaus were founded in major cities such as St. Louis, Baltimore, Cleveland, Los Angeles, New Haven, Louisville, and Detroit (Fagan, 1985; Hildreth, 1930; Wallin, 1920). Many of the psychologists in these bureaus devoted their time to measuring the physiological characteristics and mental aptitude of children (Gesell, 1921; Mullen, 1981; Slater, 1980). Employees in these bureaus also embraced the topic of teaching pedagogy, as teachers were becoming increasingly interested in learning effective techniques for educating students with a wide range of abilities.

Although pedagogical innovations were emerging, many students continued to struggle in the classroom. As a result, some school districts developed classification systems that would allow children to be targeted for specialized services. Parents and teachers referred students with a range of difficulties, including behavior problems and intellectual disabilities, for consideration for these services. Some districts even developed the earliest forms of special education services (Fagan, 2000).

The expansion of the child study bureaus and various student services led to an increase in the number of psychologists working with children in school settings. This trend eventually prompted the Connecticut State Board of Education to hire Arnold Gesell as the first school employee to hold the title of *school psychologist*. Gesell's role was to assist in mental examination case studies and to conduct survey research with students attending public schools. He also provided consultative services and in-service trainings to school staff (Fagan, 1987).

Growth of Training

Although increasing numbers of school psychologists were being hired by school districts, there was little consensus regarding the professional preparation necessary to serve in this role. Advances in training gained momentum in the 1920s, when New York University became the first higher education institution to offer a school psychology program (Trachtman, 1987). Other institutions began to offer specialized courses for students who were training to be school psychologists, and in the late 1930s, Pennsylvania State University established the first doctoral program in school psychology (Reynolds & Clark, 1984).

As more universities began offering courses related to school psychology, the need for literature and textbooks in this area arose. In 1930, Gertrude Hildreth wrote the first book on school psychology, *Psychological Service for School Problems*. This book presented a model of school psychological services and described the roles and functions of school psychologists. Additionally, Hildreth described the typical daily schedule of school psychologists, which included conferencing with staff and parents, conducting in-service trainings, and testing individual students. In many respects, the various activities described by Hildreth are similar to those performed by contemporary practitioners. Hildreth's textbook would stand alone for 25 years before the next book written specifically for school psychologists appeared, which was a summary of the Thayer Conference of 1954

(French, 1986). Ultimately, the availability of training programs and textbooks paved the way for the first state credentialing systems for school psychologists in New York and Pennsylvania. These systems were in place by the mid-1930s (Fagan & Wise, 2007).

Professional Organizations

As training programs and state credentialing systems populated the nation, professional organizations were slowly developing as well. Even though APA was established in 1893, it primarily emphasized academic psychology (i.e., research and scholarship) and placed relatively less emphasis on applied psychology (i.e., practice). As the number of applied psychologists grew, other psychological associations began to form. One of the most notable of these organizations was the American Association of Applied Psychologists (AAAP), which emerged in 1937 as APA's most significant competitor. The AAAP represented four broadly defined specialties (i.e., clinical, educational, consulting, and business and industrial psychology), with school practitioners belonging predominantly to the clinical or educational sections. Despite the existence of these two national psychological associations, most school practitioners did not belong to either (Fagan & Wise, 2007).

APA and AAAP merged into one organization in 1945, and APA's subsequent reorganization led to the formation of its current division system. One of the original divisions established in 1945 was the Division for School Psychologists (Division 16). This was the first national organization devoted specifically to school psychologists. The division struggled to maintain a consistent membership for several years thereafter, but its establishment marked an important milestone in the formation of school psychology's professional identity (Fagan & Wise, 2007).

On the Brink of a Professional Identity

Impact of World War II

Similar to World War I, World War II had a significant impact on the development of the broader field of psychology. Whereas World War I introduced psychological assessment to the public, World War II increased public awareness of the ability of psychologists to provide counseling services. The atrocities of World II and the Holocaust (in which millions of Jews, racial and ethnic minorities, people with disabilities, sexual minorities, and many others were executed in concentration camps) left many witnesses and victims deeply traumatized. It was at this point that applied psychologists began to focus on counseling as one of their primary functions.

Following World War II, the United States experienced a spike in its population as a result of the "baby boom." Between 1945 and 1961, more than 60 million children were born in the United States (Colby & Ortman, 2014) and flooded into the public school system. Consequently, even more psychologists were needed in schools to meet this demand. In response to the baby boom, the profession of school psychology experienced reciprocal growth, with the number of practitioners increasing from 500 to 5,000 between 1940 and 1970. There also was a corresponding increase in training programs from merely a handful to more than 100 programs that collectively enrolled over 3,000 graduate students (Batsche, Knoff, & Peterson, 1989; Reynolds & Clark, 1984). During this time, more states began to recognize the need for professional certification systems for school psychologists. The number of states implementing credentialing systems increased from 13 in 1946 to 23 in 1960. By 1970, the majority of states (approximately 40) had established credentialing systems for school psychologists.

Impact of the Civil Rights Movement

Beginning in the early 1950s, simmering tensions regarding the education of racial and ethnic minority students came to a boil. During the first half of the 20th century, U.S. public schools operated in accordance with the doctrine "separate but equal," which emerged in 1896 from the infamous court case known as ***Plessy v. Ferguson***. This landmark ruling upheld state laws requiring the racial segregation of public facilities (including schools) under the premise that "separate but equal" facilities would be provided to individuals from White and non-White backgrounds. As a result of this ruling, African American and other non-White students frequently were educated in schools with fewer resources and less qualified teachers than White students (Benjamin, Henry, & McMahon, 2005). When such schools were not accessible, many non-White students were excluded from the public school system all together.

The *Plessy v. Ferguson* ruling sparked considerable debate among educators and psychologists regarding the best way to educate students from racial and ethnic minority backgrounds. In the 1930s, psychological research made a notable shift from focusing on racial differences (as a means of asserting superiority) to exploring the impact of racial prejudice (Samelson, 1978). For example, Inez Beverly Prosser, one of the first African American women to earn a doctorate in psychology, examined the relationship between school environment (i.e., racially segregated or mixed) and nonacademic variables (e.g., family relationships, personality characteristics, and social participation) in African American students. She found that African American students in racially mixed schools experienced higher levels of social maladjustment as well as less security and satisfaction in their social relations. Based on these findings, Prosser argued that segregated environments were preferable for supporting the healthy development of African American children, although she believed some students (depending on personality type) would fare well in mixed schools (Benjamin et al., 2005).

Others argued that school segregation would justify segregation in other aspects of society and would perpetuate misguided beliefs about African American inferiority (Benjamin et al., 2005). Advocates of this viewpoint included Kenneth Clark and Mamie Phipps Clark, a married couple who were among the first African American scholars to receive doctoral degrees in psychology. The Clarks studied African American children who attended either segregated or integrated schools and found that the students who attended segregated schools were more likely to internalize negative racial stereotypes (Gibbons & Van Nort, 2009).

In 1954, the U.S. Supreme Court rendered a decision in the landmark ***Brown et al. v. Board of Education of Topeka*** case that overturned the "separate but equal" doctrine that had emerged from *Plessy v. Ferguson* more than 50 years earlier. The 1954 ruling declared that state laws establishing separate schools for

White and African American students were unconstitutional. This case was not only a significant victory for the public education system, but also a major milestone for the field of psychology. The research of Kenneth and Mamie Clark played a key role in the decision rendered in *Brown v. Board of Education* (1954) and was one of the first pieces of psychological research to be incorporated in a Supreme Court decision that effected monumental social change (Benjamin & Crouse, 2002; Jackson, 1998). The importance of this case cannot be overstated, as it not only desegregated schools but also incited a variety of subsequent lawsuits advocating for the rights of other marginalized populations (e.g., children with disabilities). The *Brown v. Board of Education* case and others would lead to immense change in the practice of school psychology, as described later in this chapter.

Thayer Conference

Following World War II and with the emerging need for diagnostic and therapeutic services, leaders in clinical psychology training and practice convened to discuss the roles, functions, and training standards for clinical psychologists. This meeting became known as the Boulder Conference of 1949 (held at the University of Colorado Boulder). At this conference, participants discussed specific directions for the proper training of clinical psychologists. These discussions led to the development of the **scientist-practitioner model** of training, which called for an emphasis on training in both research and clinical practice (Baker & Benjamin, 2000).

Unfortunately, the Boulder Conference was primarily focused on serving the adult population and provided little guidance on training standards for psychologists who specialized in serving children and schools. This omission prompted the organization of the **Thayer Conference**, which took place in West Point, New York, in 1954 (French, 1992). The Thayer Conference was one of the first professional gatherings exclusively focused on the professional practice of school psychologists. The main goals of the conference were to define the roles and functions of school psychologists and to specify training standards for the field. The proceedings of this conference were recorded in the second school psychology book to be published (25 years after Hildreth's book), *School Psychologists at Mid-Century: A Report of the Thayer Conference on the Functions, Qualifications, and Training of School Psychologists* (Cutts, 1955). Shortly following the publication of this book, several other school psychology books were published, including Stanley Marzolf's (1956) *Psychological Diagnosis and Counseling in the Schools* and W. D. Wall's (1956) *Psychological Services for the Schools* (French, 1986).

Formation of NASP and State Associations

Throughout the 1940s and 1950s, professional organizations representing school psychology continued to develop. Membership in APA Division 16 rose to 601 members in 1956. Moreover, a number of state school psychological associations were formed throughout the 1950s and into the 1960s. In 1943, Ohio became the first state to develop an association for school psychologists (*School Psychologists of Ohio,* which was renamed the *Ohio School Psychology Association* in the early 1960s). California, Illinois, Massachusetts, New York, and New Jersey all followed suit in the 1950s. By the end of the 1960s, there were 17 state associations and a strong interest in forming a national association exclusively for school psychologists (Fagan, Hensley, & Delugach, 1986).

Ohio's state association initiated efforts to increase communication among the various state associations. In 1968, leaders in school psychology convened the National Invitational Conference of School Psychologists in Ohio, which led to the resolution to form a national association devoted specifically to school psychologists. During the following year, the St. Louis planning convention was held, and the NASP was officially established. At this time, it comprised more than 900 members. Pauline Alexander was elected the first president of NASP (Farling & Agner, 1979). The formation of NASP was particularly significant because it recentered school psychology's national representation. As noted by Fagan and Wise (2007), "Whereas Division 16 carried the national banner for school psychology from 1945 to 1970, NASP has carried it since" (p. 60).

As practicing school psychologists began to organize, a professional literature began to take hold. The journals *Psychology in the Schools*, *Journal of School Psychology*, and *Professional Psychology* were established in the 1960s, marking some of the first times that school psychologists had outlets devoted specifically to research in their field (Fagan & Jack, 2012). Around the same time, there was a corresponding increase in the number of school psychology books available, with approximately 13 being written between 1960 and 1969 (French, 1986). This growth in school psychology's literature would pave the way for tremendous growth in the number of graduate preparation programs.

THOROUGHBRED YEARS

As noted previously, the formation of NASP marked the transition from the Hybrid Years to the Thoroughbred Years. With the establishment of this national association, school psychology took a momentous step in its development and professionalization. As school psychology entered the Thoroughbred Years, many of the social changes and advances that took root in the Hybrid Years continued to gain momentum. These changes had a significant impact on the continued evolution of school psychology.

The Emergence of Federally Mandated Special Education Services

The ramifications of the *Brown v. Board of Education* ruling continued to reverberate throughout the 1960s and the civil rights movement. One of the widespread sentiments that emerged was the notion that all children and adolescents should have a right to public education and, in particular, a free and appropriate public education (FAPE). The emphasis on educational rights for all students spurred a series of court cases regarding the fair treatment of individuals with disabilities in school settings. The rationale for many of these cases was that children with disabilities were not being afforded equal protection under the law (as required in the 14th Amendment to the U.S. Constitution). For example, in 1972, the Pennsylvania Association for Retarded Children (PARC) challenged the state of Pennsylvania regarding its failure to provide equal access to public education for students with intellectual disabilities. Similarly, in the case of *Mills v. District of Columbia Board of Education* (1972), a class action suit was brought on behalf of a group of children with a variety of disabilities (e.g., behavioral and intellectual disabilities) who had been denied access to educational services due to their disability status. In both cases, students represented in these cases were granted numerous rights, including access to a free public education, documentation of an individualized education program to support the students' success, and due process rights. Ultimately, these court decisions and others diversified the student population and expanded the range of services provided by public schools (Kuriloff, 1975).

Increasing advocacy for the educational rights of students with disabilities led to several important pieces of legislation. In 1973, Congress passed the Rehabilitation Act, which prohibited institutions receiving federal funds (including schools) from discriminating against individuals with disabilities. In addition, Congress passed the Education for All Handicapped Children Act (EAHCA; PL 94-142) in 1975. This legislation required school districts to provide a FAPE to all students with disabilities ages 5 through 21 years. It also required schools to develop an Individualized Education Program (IEP) for each student with a disability who qualified for special education services. This IEP described the specific range of services to which a student was entitled and specific goals for educational progress. Ultimately, PL 94-142 marked the advent of widespread, federally mandated special education services for students with disabilities. In 1986, PL 94-142 was reauthorized as PL 99-457. This reauthorization mandated states to provide services for children ages 3 through 21 years, thereby requiring schools to expand their services to include preschool and home-based services for infants and toddlers. This legislation and its subsequent iterations are discussed in greater detail in Chapter 5.

Both the EAHCA (reauthorized as the Individuals with Disabilities Education Act [IDEA] in 1990) and the Rehabilitation Act of 1973 had a significant impact on the roles and functions of school psychologists. For example, the 1986 reauthorization of the EAHCA (PL 99-457) prompted school psychologists to expand their range of competencies to include working with preschool-age children (McLinden & Prasse, 1991; Mowder, Widerstrom, & Sandall, 1989). In particular, this series of legislation led school psychologists to adopt a wider range of roles, although most practitioners still were involved primarily in conducting evaluations, meeting with parents and teachers, and planning educational programs (Ramage, 1979).

Advances in Training and Practice

Graduate Programs and Professional Accreditation

As mentioned earlier, the growth of professional literature (including journals and books) in school psychology coincided with the proliferation of graduate training programs. By 1968, there were 96 school psychology training programs, and over the next 3 years, this number rose to more than 150 (Fagan, 1986b). The increased capacity for training that resulted from program development directly impacted the number of practicing school psychologists, which rose to more than 5,000 nationwide by 1970 (Fagan & Wise, 2007).

Just as it impacted the roles of school psychologists, the advent of federal disability legislation affected the development of graduate programs. As school districts scrambled to meet the requirements imposed by this legislation, the demand for school psychologists increased, as did the demand for school psychology programs. By the late 1970s, there were more than 200 school psychology training programs and more than 10,000 school psychologists practicing in schools nationwide (Fagan, 1988).

As the number of graduate programs grew throughout the 1970s, national organizations representing the field of school psychology began to accredit programs that aligned with their standards for training and practice. APA began credentialing psychology graduate programs in 1971, during which time the University of Texas at Austin's PhD program became the first APA-accredited school psychology program in the nation. In 1976, NASP partnered with the National Council for Accreditation of Teacher Education (NCATE) to offer program approval in tandem with NCATE accreditation (Fagan & Wise, 2007). The emergence of these accreditation bodies and procedures resulted in the increased standardization of school psychology training, as many programs attempted to align with guidelines provided by national organizations.

The Spring Hill Symposium and Olympia Conference

In response to legislation and litigation throughout the 1970s, leaders in school psychology recognized the need to provide guidance on the evolving roles and functions of school psychologists. With funding provided by the U.S. Department of Education, the National School Psychology Inservice Training Network (NSPITN) was launched in 1978. This network had two primary goals: (1) to train school psychologists in innovative assessment and intervention practices consistent with those mandated by PL 94-142 and (2) to clarify the long-term goals, training needs, and roles of school psychologists. As part of its efforts, the NSPITN disseminated training modules on topics such as unbiased assessment, non–test-based assessment, and consultation for classroom teachers (Davis, Reynolds, Weinberg, & Ysseldyke, 1984).

Collectively, the NSPITN and school psychology's two major national associations (APA's Division 16 and NASP) coordinated the *Spring Hill Symposium*, which took place in 1980 in Wayzata, Minnesota. At this symposium, 69 key constituents from 22 states, the District of Columbia, and Canada came together to discuss directions for the future of school psychology. As summarized by Ysseldyke (1982), participants at this conference raised issues related to the goals of school psychology practice, ethical and legal issues, the professionalization of school psychology, the content of training programs, and accountability for practice. The Spring Hill Symposium identified the broad overarching issues that needed to be addressed in the field, but specific details were left for discussion at a later time. One year later, the *Olympia Conference* was held in Wisconsin to develop specific strategies for achieving the vision laid out at the Spring Hill Symposium. The action plan for this conference was to address issues regarding legislation, practice, and the profession (Meyers, Brown, & Coulter, 1982). In addition, participants at the conference were encouraged to identify larger societal issues and their potential impact on future services (Brown & Cardon, 1982).

The NSPITN integrated many of the ideas generated during the Spring Hill Symposium and Olympia Conference in its subsequent publication of *School Psychology: A Blueprint for Training and Practice* (Ysseldyke et al., 1984) and the companion volume to this publication, *School Psychology: The State of the Art* (Ysseldyke, 1984). Together, these documents outlined various domains of competence and training for school psychologists.

Professional Regulation

In response to the changing landscape of schools throughout the 1960s and 1970s, professional regulation became a major priority for NASP. In 1974, NASP adopted its first professional code of ethics, the *Principles for Professional Ethics*. The purpose of this code was to protect recipients of school psychological services by ensuring that practitioners would implement empirically sound practices, respect the dignity of all parties involved in service delivery, and monitor their own behavior (NASP, 2010). By the end of its first decade (1979), NASP had issued standards for training, credentialing, practice, and field placements. These standards included the *Guidelines for the Provision of School Psychological Services* (1978). The guidelines were revised in 1984, 1992, 1997, 2000, and 2010. The *Model for Comprehensive and Integrated School Psychological Services* (i.e., the NASP Practice Model described in Chapter 1) represents the most recent iteration of these guidelines. The adoption of various standards ultimately allowed the profession to take ownership of its own regulation (Batsche et al., 1989; Curtis & Zins, 1989). As a result, external agencies (i.e., state and federal agencies) began to look to NASP and the broader profession for guidance on legislation and regulations.

One of NASP's landmark achievements was the establishment of its national credentialing system for practitioners. The National School Psychology Certification System (NCSP) was established in 1989 and approved the certification of more than 14,000 school psychologists in its first 2 years. Standards set forth by NASP for the NCSP were frequently adopted by state education agencies for credentialing purposes. The advent of the NCSP is one example of how the profession began to drive its own regulation, rather than simply reacting to government requirements; (Rossen & Williams, 2013).

The APA also remained involved in the regulation of school psychology, although its professional positions sometimes clashed with those of NASP. Although the majority of school psychologists practiced at the non-doctoral level during the 1970s, APA contended that the doctoral degree should be the entry-level degree for any individual using the title of *psychologist*. In 1977, the APA Council passed a resolution affirming this position, which fueled tensions between the two organizations. In 1978, APA and NASP established an Inter-Organizational Committee to resolve their differences. Although tensions between APA and NASP abated in the 1990s, the Inter-Organizational Committee eventually was disbanded in 2002 due to a reprise of conflict (Fagan & Wise, 2007).

SOCIAL JUSTICE CONNECTIONS

How did the emergence of multicultural scholarship influence school psychology?

During the Thoroughbred Years, multicultural scholarship became increasingly prominent in the school psychology literature. Although psychological research addressed racial differences during the beginning of the 20th century, not all of this literature was beneficial for diverse youth. During the first few decades of the 20th century, a considerable body of psychological research centered on testing hypotheses of genetic inferiority, which proposed that minority racially and ethnic groups were inherently inferior to Whites in a number of intellectual and psychosocial domains (Newell & Chavez-Korell, 2017). Toward the middle of the century, theories of cultural deprivation began to take hold. From this perspective, racial and ethnic minorities were believed to have poor academic, psychosocial, and economic outcomes due to inadequate exposure to European American values and norms (Newell & Chavez-Korell, 2017). Generally, individual differences among school-age youth were seen as a problem to be remedied rather than an asset to be embraced.

As social movements of the 1950s, 1960s, and 1970s emphasized respect for the rights and dignity of all children, psychologists began to recognize a need for multicultural competence. The **Vail Conference** of 1973, which examined the role of applied psychologists, was the first conference to directly address issues of diversity in psychology (Korman, 1974). Conference participants acknowledged a need for cultural diversity training among psychologists to promote ethically sound practice. When the National Association of School Psychologists (NASP) published its first standards for school psychology training, it, too, addressed cultural issues related to service delivery.

Throughout the 1980s and 1990s, multicultural scholarship in psychology gained increasing momentum. Psychologists and others were beginning to embrace a cultural difference perspective, which acknowledged the legitimacy and value of diverse lifestyles, norms, beliefs, and customs (Newell & Chavez-Korell, 2017). Particularly in the 1990s, most of this scholarship focused on assessment practices, with relatively fewer articles addressing multicultural considerations for intervention (Miranda & Gutter, 2002). In school psychology, notable scholars who contributed to the field's emerging multicultural agenda included Ena Vazquez-Nuttall and Chieh Li. The work of these pioneers and many others would serve as the foundation for a subsequent wave of 21st century scholarship dedicated to social justice issues.

School Psychology's Evolving Agenda

The 1990s represented a period of quiet yet stable growth for school psychology (Fagan & Wise, 2007). Two additional school psychology organizations were established (the Society for the Study of School Psychology [SSSP] and the American Academy of School Psychology [AASP]), and the profession continued to enjoy increasing legitimacy. Despite this stability, the shortages in the number of available school psychologists became increasingly worrisome. Moreover, since the 1980s, it had been apparent that the demographic makeup of the school psychology workforce (which was predominantly White) did not reflect that of the U.S. student population. NASP leaders such as Deborah Crockett initiated efforts to remedy this problem through proactive efforts to recruit more minorities into school psychology. Crockett became the first African American president of NASP in 1997, and she continues to advocate for the recruitment of minority school psychologists today (Crockett, 2004).

By the mid- to late 1990s, school psychologists began to fill a new role: **crisis intervention**. Crisis intervention refers to the provision of immediate, short-term psychological services to assist an individual in restoring problem-solving skills and employing coping strategies following an extremely or unusually stressful life event (Brock, Reeves, & Nickerson, 2014). A series of high-profile school shootings occurred in various locales. including Jonesboro, Arkansas; Paducah, Kentucky; and Columbine. Colorado. These incidents drew attention to the need for schools to be able to deal with school violence, other traumatic events, and their aftermath.

Following the Oklahoma City bombing in 1995, NASP created the National Emergency Assistance Team (NEAT), which was composed of nationally certified school psychologists who had formal training in and direct experience with crisis situations (Heath, Ryan, Dean, & Bingham, 2007). Scott Poland, Stephen Brock, and Bill Pfohl are notable school psychologists who served on NEAT during that time. Throughout the end of the decade and into the 2000s, school psychologists became more relied upon to assist students, teachers, parents, and administrators through various crisis events (NASP, 2012).

After several years of serving as a crisis resource for the nation, NASP decided to create a school crisis and intervention training for school-based professionals. The result was the PREPaRE training, which was developed in 2006 and continues to expand (NASP, 2012). The advent of PREPaRE and increased emphasis on crisis training at the graduate level has resulted in more school psychologists incorporating crisis prevention and intervention into their roles in schools.

The provision of crisis intervention services was just one indicator that the role of the school psychologist needed to undergo change. In the early 2000s, many school psychology leaders believed the field was at a crossroads. Whereas national associations and leaders emphasized roles in consultation, prevention, and intervention, many practitioners continued to find themselves mired in special education assessment activities (Cummings et al., 2004). Authors such as Sheridan and Gutkin (2000) cautioned that school psychologists were not actualizing their potential to fill a wider range of roles and that traditional models of assessment hindered school psychologists' ability to effectively meet the needs of all children. Specifically, many scholars advocated for the field to move away from the traditional medical model of assessment and diagnosis and toward an ecological model of service delivery. The traditional **medical model** focuses on identifying inherent "problems" within children through extensive diagnostic and assessment procedures. The **ecological model**, in contrast, focuses on person–environment interactions that give rise to academic and behavioral problems as well as emphasizes assessment for the purpose of designing interventions (rather than making diagnoses).

More than 20 years after the Spring Hill Symposium and Olympia Conference, the **2002 Conference on the Future of School Psychology** was held. Sponsored by several of school psychology's major associations (e.g., NASP), the conference was motivated in part by a growing desire to reflect on the momentous changes in the profession and schools that took place during the previous two decades. At the 2002 Futures Conference, a number of broad themes emerged, including (a) a need to focus on prevention and early intervention, (b) a focus on evidence-based interventions, (c) a reduced emphasis on traditional assessment, (d) a greater emphasis on assessment for the purposes of intervention and accountability, and (e) an emphasis on systems-level functioning via the incorporation of public health approaches (Dawson et al., 2004).

The ***public health model*** is a population-based approach to addressing academic, health, and social problems that incorporates environmental factors as well as comprehensive, multilayered prevention and intervention efforts. This model served as the foundation for what eventually came to be known as the multitiered system of support (MTSS), which is described extensively in Chapter 7. Ultimately, the themes of the 2002 Futures Conference provided clear directions for the field's continued development. They also reflected trends in contemporary educational legislation, as described in the following subsection.

Legislation of the 1990s and 2000s

The 1990s saw two reauthorizations of the EAHCA. In 1990, this legislation was reauthorized as the Individuals with Disabilities Education Act (IDEA). Among other changes, autism and traumatic brain injury were recognized as areas of disability. Moreover, the renaming of this act represented a shift away from the term *handicap* and toward the less pejorative and more widely accepted term *disability* (Bicehouse & Faieta, 2017). Subsequently, IDEA was reauthorized in 1997 and again in 2004. The 2004 reauthorization renamed this legislation the Individuals with Disabilities Education Improvement Act (IDEIA) as well as introduced other important changes. One of these changes was the requirement that states permit the use of Response to Intervention (RtI) methods for disability identification purposes. RtI is a form of MTSS that incorporates environmental and instructional factors in educational decision making. Core features of these models include an emphasis on meeting the needs of all learners, an increased focus on prevention and intervention services in general education settings, and data-based decision making. This legislation is discussed in further detail in Chapter 5.

The No Child Left Behind (NCLB) Act of 2001 was another critical piece of legislation that impacted the role of school psychologists. The goal of this legislation was to implement robust accountability systems that would hold schools responsible for measuring and supporting students' progress toward meeting rigorous academic standards. This focus on accountability meant that schools needed to aggregate and interpret large amounts of data. With the implementation of this legislation, schools increasingly called on school psychologists to support their data collection and accountability efforts. As explained in Chapter 5, NCLB is no longer in effect and was replaced by the Every Student Succeeds Act (ESSA) in 2015. Nevertheless, both the 2004 reauthorization of IDEIA and the 2001 implementation of NCLB were critical in supporting school psychology's emerging focus on evidence-based intervention and accountability for student outcomes.

Organizational Conflict in the 21st Century

While relations between APA and NASP were cordial throughout the 1990s, long-simmering issues became inflamed in 2007. In particular, APA and NASP continued to disagree regarding the appropriate entry-level degree for school psychologists. Tensions arose largely due to impending revisions to APA's ***Model Licensure Act*** (MLA), which represents the organization's formal recommendations to states regarding requirements for licensure in psychology. In its 1987 revision of the MLA, APA had included an exemption for non–doctoral-level school psychologists, which allowed these practitioners to retain the title of "school psychologist" when practicing in the context of schools and under the authority of a state certificate (NASP, 2009). In 2007, however, the MLA was revised and the exemption for school psychologists was removed in the initial draft. Advocacy efforts from school psychologists in both NASP and APA's Division 16 led to the subsequent revision of the MLA draft to include an exemption for non-doctoral school psychologists practicing in school settings. The collaborative efforts of NASP and APA's Division 16 during this time represent a milestone in the history of their relationship (Duncan & Bohmann, 2010; Nastasi, 2010).

Transitioning From the Past to the Present

In 2012, school psychology leaders held another conference to discuss future directions for the field. Like the 2002 conference, the **2012 School Psychology Futures Conference** was sponsored jointly by a variety of professional organizations including NASP, APA's Division 16, AASP, and SSSP. The 2012 School Psychology Futures Conference was held in a virtual environment, which allowed for participation worldwide via live webinars. Its mission was to join school psychologists together to support the academic success and mental health of children and adolescents. The 2012 Conference had three themes: *leadership*, *critical skills*, and *advocacy*. Its emphasis on advocacy for school-age youth from diverse backgrounds was consistent with the field's emerging focus on social justice issues, which continues to permeate its work (Jarmuz-Smith, Harrison, & Cummings, 2013).

SUMMARY AND CONCLUSIONS

The field of school psychology has undergone significant changes since its inception in the 1890s. As the public education system evolved to meet the needs of an increasingly diverse student population, so did the profession of school psychology. One recurrent theme throughout school psychology's history is an emphasis on consciousness raising in regard to a wide range of social, academic, and mental health issues that impact school-age youth. Reflecting on these changes, Ysseldyke (1982) commented, "Society increasingly expects schools to function as the major agent of social change. Society today does not place small demands on its schools. Schools are expected to bring about social equality and to eliminate poverty, unemployment, racism, and war" (pp. 547–548). Indeed, schools have become central institutions for addressing social issues and supporting diverse youth. As the future of the field begins to take shape, school psychologists should continue to make schools a primary venue for social change.

DISCUSSION QUESTIONS

1. How do the techniques used by Lightner Witmer in the United States' first psychological clinic reflect current practices in school psychology?

2. Which legislation or court cases do you believe had the largest impact on the development of the field? Why?
3. The formation of NASP is believed to have marked the transition from the Hybrid Years to the Thoroughbred Years. Why was the formation of NASP such a monumental event in school psychology's history?
4. The professionalization of school psychology was greatly assisted by the formation of national organizations. What role did these organizations play in shaping the profession? What role do these organizations continue to play in shaping the profession?
5. Over time, a variety of social movements (e.g., civil rights movement) have influenced the field of school psychology. How did these movements influence the field's development? How do contemporary social concerns and values continue to shape school psychology's agenda?

REFERENCES

Angell, J. R. (1911). William James. *Psychological Review, 18,* 78–82.

Baker, D. B. (1988). The psychology of Lightner Witmer. *Professional School Psychology, 3,* 109–121.

Baker, D. B., & Benjamin, L. T. (2000). The affirmation of the scientist-practitioner: A look back at Boulder. *American Psychologist, 55,* 241–247.

Batsche, G. M., Knoff, H. M., & Peterson, D. W. (1989). Trends in credentialing and practice standards. *School Psychology Review, 18,* 193–201.

Benjamin, L. T., & Crouse, E. M. (2002). The American Psychological Association's response to *Brown v. Board of Education*: The case of Kenneth B. Clark. *American Psychologist, 57,* 38–50.

Benjamin, L. T., Henry, K. D., & McMahon, L. R. (2005). Inez Beverly Prosser and the education of African Americans. *Journal of the History of the Behavioral Sciences, 41,* 42–62.

Bicehouse, V., & Faieta, J. (2017). IDEA at age forty: Weathering Common Core Standards and data driven decision making. *Contemporary Issues in Education Research, 10,* 33–44.

Boake, C. (2002). From the Binet-Simon to the Wechsler-Bellevue: Tracing the history of intelligence testing. *Journal of Clinical and Experimental Neuropsychology, 24,* 383–405. doi:10.1076/jcen.24.3.383.981

Braden, J. S., DiMarino-Linnen, E., & Good, T. L. (2001). Schools, society, and school psychologists. *Journal of School Psychology, 39,* 203–219. doi:10.1016/S0022-4405(01)00056-5

Brock, S. E., Reeves, M. A. L., & Nickerson, A. B. (2014). Best practices in school crisis intervention. In A. Thomas & J. Grimes (Eds.), *Best practice in school psychology* (Vol. 3, pp. 211–230). Bethesda, MD: National Association of School Psychologists.

Brown, D. T., & Cardon, B. W. (1982). Synthesis and editorial comment. *School Psychology Review, 11,* 195–198.

Colby, S. L., & Ortman, J. M. (2014). *The baby boom cohort in the United States: 2012 to 2060. Current Population Reports, P25-1141.* Washington, DC: U.S. Census Bureau.

Crockett, D. (2004). Critical issues children face in the 2000s. *School Psychology Review, 33,* 78–82.

Cummings, J. A., Harrison, P. L., Dawson, M. M., Short, R. J., Gorin, S., & Palomares, R. S. (2004). The 2002 Conference on the Future of School Psychology: Implications for consultation, intervention, and prevention services. *Journal of Educational and Psychological Consultation, 15,* 239–256.

Curtis, M. J., & Zins, J. E. (1989). Trends in training and accreditation. *School Psycology Review, 18,* 182–192.

Cutts, N. E. (1955). *School psychologists at mid-century : A report of the Thayer Conference on the functions, qualifications, and training of school psychologists.* Washington, DC: American Psychological Association.

Davis, T. F., Reynolds, M. C., Weinberg, C. A., & Ysseldyke, J. E. (1984). The National School Psychology Inservice Training Network (USA): A resource for change. *School Psychology International*, 5, 67–70.

Dawson, M., Cummings, J., Harrison, P., Short, R. J., Gorin, S., & Palomares, R. (2004). The 2002 multisite conference on the future of school psychology: Next steps. *School Psychology Review*, 33, 115–125.

Duncan, B., & Bohmann, J. (2010). APA Council of Representatives approves MLA, which retains the exemption for all school psychologists. *Communique*, 38(6), 7.

Evans, R. B. (1990). William James, "The Principles of Psychology," and experimental psychology. *American Journal of Psychology*, 103, 433–447.

Fagan, T. K. (1985). Sources for the delivery of school psychological services during 1890–1930. *School Psychology Review*, 14, 378–382.

Fagan, T. K. (1986a). School psychology's dilemma reappraising solutions and directing attention to the future. *American Psychologist*, 41, 851–861.

Fagan, T. K. (1986b). The historical origins and growth of programs to prepare school psychologists in the United States. *Journal of School Psychology*, 24, 9–22. doi:10.1016/0022-4405(86)90038-5

Fagan, T. K. (1987). Gesell: The first school psychologist. Part II. Practice and significance. *School Psychology Review*, 16, 399–409.

Fagan, T. K. (1988). The historical improvement of the school psychology service ratio: Implications for future employment. *School Psychology Review*, 17, 447–458.

Fagan, T. K. (1992). Compulsory schooling, child study, clinical psychology, and special education. Origins of school psychology. *American Psychologist*, 47, 236–243.

Fagan, T. K. (1996). Witmer's contribution to school psychological services. *American Psychologist*, 51, 241–243.

Fagan, T. K. (2000). Practicing school psychology: A turn-of-the-century perspective. *American Psychologist*, 55, 754–757.

Fagan, T. K., Hensley, L. T., & Delugach, F. J. (1986). The evolution of organizations for school psychologists in the United States. *School Psychology Review*, 16, 127–135.

Fagan, T. K., & Jack, S. L. (2012). A history of the founding and early development of the *Journal of School Psychology*. *Journal of School Psychology*, 50, 701–735. doi:10.1016/j.jsp.2012.11.002

Fagan, T. K., & Wise, P. (2007). Historical development of school psychology. In *School psychology: Past, present, and future* (3rd ed., pp. 25–70). National Association of School Psychologists.

Fancher, R. E. (1990). *Pioneers of psychology* (2nd ed.). New York, NY: W. W. Norton & Company.

Farling, W. H., & Agner, J. (1979). History of the National Association of School Psychologists: The first decade. *School Psychology Digest*, 8, 140–152.

Field, A. J. (1976). Educational expansion in mid-nineteenth century Massachusetts: Human capital formation or structural reinforcement? *Harvard Educational Review*, 46, 521–552.

French, J. L. (1986). Books in school psychology: The first forty years. *Professional School Psychology*, 1, 267–277.

French, J. L. (1992). *The influence of school psychologists in APA on APA*. Washington, DC: American Psychological Association.

Gesell, A. (1921). *Exceptional children and public school policy*. New Haven, CT: Yale University Press.

Gibbons, W., & Van Nort, S. C. (2009). Mamie Phipps Clark: The "other half" of the Kenneth Clark legacy. *Encounter: Education for Meaning and Social Justice*, 22(4), 28–32.

Graves, S. (2009). Albert Sidney Beckham: The first African American school psychologist. *School Psychology International*, 30, 5–23.

Graves, S., & Mitchell, A. (2011). Is the moratorium over? African American psychology professionals' views on intelligence testing in response to changes in federal policy. *Journal of Black Psychology*, 37, 407–425. doi:10.1177/0095798410394177

Heath, M. A., Ryan, K., Dean, B., & Bingham, R. (2007). *History of school safety and psychological first aid for children. Brief Treatment and Crisis Intervention*, 7, 206–223. doi:10.1093/brief-treatment/mhm011

Hildreth, G. H. (1930). *Psychological services for school problems* (1st ed.). Yonker-On-Hudson, NY: World Book Company.

Jackson, J. P. J. (1998). Creating a consensus: Psychologists, the Supreme Court, and school desegregation, 1952–1955. *Journal of Social Issues, 54,* 143–177.

Jarmuz-Smith, S., Harrison, P. L., & Cummings, J. A. (2013). The 2012 School Psychology Futures Conference: Accomplishments and next steps. *Communique, 41*(5), 6, 8.

Kaplan, M. S., & Kaplan, H. E. (1985). School psychology: Its educational and societal connections. *Journal of School Psychology, 23,* 319–325.

Kaufman, A. S. (2000). Intelligence tests and school psychology: Predicting the future by studying the past. *Psychology in the Schools, 37,* 7–16.

Kehle, T. J., Clark, E., & Jenson, W. R. (1993). The development of testing as applied to school psychology. *Journal of School Psychology, 31,* 143–161.

Korman, M. (1974). National conference on levels and patterns of professional training in psychology. *American Psychologist, 29,* 441–449.

Kuriloff, P. (1975). Law, educational reform, and the school psychologist. *Journal of School Psychology, 13,* 335–348.

McLinden, S. E., & Prasse, D. P. (1991). Providing services to infants and toddlers under PL 99-457: Training needs. *School Psychology Review, 20,* 37–48.

McReynolds, P. (1996). Lightner Witmer: A centennial tribute. *American Psychologist, 51,* 237–240.

Meyers, J., Brown, D. T., & Coulter, W. A. (1982). Analysis of the action plans. *School Psychology Review, 11,* 161–185.

Miranda, A. H., & Gutter, P. B. (2002). Diversity research literature in school psychology: 1990–1999. *Psychology in the Schools, 39,* 597–604.

Mowder, B. A., Widerstrom, A. H., & Sandall, S. (1989). School psychologists serving at-risk and handicapped infants, toddlers, and their families. *Professional School Psychology, 4,* 159–171.

Mullen, F. A. (1981). School psychology in the USA: Reminensces of its origin. *Journal of School Psychology, 19,* 103–119.

Nastasi, B. K. (2010). Life after MLA: Message from Division 16 President. *Communique, 38*(6), 7–8.

National Association of School Psychologists. (2009). Proposed APA Model Act for state licensure of psychologists: Implications for school psychological services. *Communique, 37*(7).

National Association of School Psychologists. (2010). *Principles for professional ethics.* Bethesda, MD: Author.

National Association of School Psychologists. (2012). *School safety and crisis preparedness and response NASP leadership: 1996–2011.* Bethesda, MD: Author.

Newell, M. L., & Chavez-Korell, S. (2017). Multiculturalism: An interdisciplinary perspective. In E. C. Lopez, S. G. Nahari, & S. L. Proctor (Eds.), *Handbook of multicultural school psychology* (pp. 3–17). New York: NY: Routledge.

Noltemeyer, A., Mujic, J., & Mcloughlin, C. S. (2012). The history of inequity in education. In A. Noltemeyer & C. S. Mcloughlin (Eds.), *Disproportionality in education and special education: A guide to creating more equitable learning environments* (pp. 3–15). Springfield, IL: Charles C. Thomas Publisher.

Ramage, J. C. (1979). National survey of school psychologists: Update. *School Psychology Digest, 8,* 153–161.

Reynolds, C. R., & Clark, J. H. (1984). Trends in school psychology research: 1974–1980. *Journal of School Psychology, 22,* 43–52.

Ross, D. (1972). *G. Stanley Hall: The psychologist as prophet.* Chicago, IL: University of Chicago Press.

Rossen, E., & Williams, B. B. (2013). The life and times of the National School Psychology Certification System. *Communique, 41*(7), 1, 28–30.

Routh, D. K. (1996). Lightner Witmer and the first 100 years of clinical psychology. *American Psychologist, 51,* 244–247.

Rury, J. L. (2016). *Education and social change: Contours in the history of American schooling* (5th ed.). New York, NY: Routledge.

Samelson, F. (1978). From "race psychology" to "studies in prejudice": Some observations on the thematic reversal in social psychology. *Journal of the Behavioral Sciences, 14,* 265–278.

Sattler, J. M. (2001). *Assessment of children: Cognitive applications* (4th ed.). San Diego, CA: Author.

Sheridan, S., & Gutkin, T. (2000). The ecology of school psychology: Examining and changing our paradigm for the 21st century. *School Psychology Review*, 29, 485–502.

Siegel, A. W., & White, S. H. (1982). The child study movement: Early growth and development of the symbolized child. *Advances in Child Development and Behavior*, 17, 233–285.

Slater, R. (1980). The organizational origins of public school psychology. *Educational Studies*, 11(1), 1–11.

Trachtman, G. M. (1987). Bootstrapping it in the big apple: A history of school psychology at New York University. *Professional School Psychology*, 2, 281–296.

Tulchin, S. H. (1956). In memoriam: Lightner Witmer. *American Journal of Orthopsychiatry*, 27, 200–201.

Urban, W. J. (1989). The black scholar and intelligence testing: The case of Horace Mann Bond. *Journal of the History of the Behavioral Sciences*, 25, 323–334.

Wallin, J. E. W. (1920). Problems confront a psycho-educational clinic in a large muncipality. *Mental Hygiene*, 4, 103–136.

White, S. H. (1992). G. Stanley Hall: From philosophy to developmental psychology. *Developmental Psychology*, 28, 25–34.

Witmer, L. (1897). The organization of practical work in psychology. *Psychological Review*, 4, 116–117.

Ysseldyke, J. E. (1982). The Spring Hill Symposium on the future of psychology in the schools. *American Psychologist*, 5, 547–552.

Ysseldyke, J. E. (Ed.). (1984). *School psychology: The state of the art*. Minneapolis, MN: National School Psychology Inservice Training Network.

Ysseldyke, J. E., Reynolds, M. C., Weinberg, R. A., Bardon, J., Heaston, P., Hines, L., . . . Taylor, J. (1984). *School psychology: A blueprint for training and practice*. (1st ed.). Minneapolis, MN: National School Psychology Inservice Training Network.

CHAPTER 3

Graduate Preparation and Credentialing

ERIC ROSSEN ■ NATALIE N. POLITIKOS ■ JOSEPH S. PRUS

CHAPTER OBJECTIVES

- Identify differences in degree types among school psychology graduate preparation programs
- Describe the national context and value of program approval and accreditation
- Specify specific aspects of relevant accreditation/approval bodies
- Differentiate among various credentials relevant to school psychology
- Identify different credentialing pathways based on degree or setting

Because school psychologists care for the well-being of our nation's most vulnerable youth and families, it is critical that they deliver high-quality and ethically sound psychological services. A number of organizations work to ensure that school psychologists are appropriately qualified to provide psychological and educational services to youth and families. These entities include both professional organizations (e.g., American Psychological Association [APA] and National Association of School Psychologists [NASP]) and government organizations (e.g., state education agencies and licensing boards). Collectively, guidelines delineated by professional organizations and government agencies help to ensure that our nation's school psychologists receive high-quality graduate preparation, demonstrate appropriate qualifications when entering the workforce, and pursue continuing education on a regular basis. To illustrate these concepts, this chapter describes pathways of graduate preparation and credentialing for school psychologists.

PROFESSIONAL STANDARDS

To ensure the quality of service delivery, professional psychology organizations (e.g., NASP and APA) develop professional standards or benchmarks that delineate expectations for preparation, practice, and continuing education among professionals. Standards may govern a wide range of professional preparation and practice activities, including graduate education, field experiences, professional practice, ethical behavior, and continuing education. Moreover, they serve as an important tool for communicating and advocating among stakeholders, policy makers, and other professional groups at the national, state, and local levels. Overall, standards help define contemporary practices and lay the foundation for future advancements and directions in a field.

As noted in Chapter 1, the professional organizations that generate standards most relevant to the practice of school psychology include APA, the International School Psychology Association (ISPA), and NASP. Of these three organizations, NASP maintains standards most directly tailored to the diverse roles of school psychologists practicing in the United States. NASP's standards for school psychology consist of four official documents: (1) *Standards for Graduate Preparation of School Psychologists* (NASP, 2010a; graduate education); (2) *Standards for the Credentialing of School Psychologists* (NASP, 2010b; certification and licensure); (3) *Model for Comprehensive and Integrated School Psychological Services* (NASP Practice Model; NASP, 2010c; practice); and (4) *Principles for Professional Ethics* (NASP, 2010d). These four sets of standards are developed concurrently and provide a comprehensive, cohesive, and unified set of national principles to guide the field. The first three of these documents are described in this chapter. The fourth document (*Principles for Professional Ethics*) is discussed in further detail in Chapter 5.

Similar to NASP, APA maintains related but independently developed standards, such as the *Ethical Principles of Psychologists and Code of Conduct* (APA, 2010a), *Standards of Accreditation for Health Service Psychology* (SoA; APA, 2015), and the *Model Act for State Licensure of Psychologists* (APA, 2010b). Unlike NASP's professional standards, these documents are designed to address all practice specialties within psychology (e.g., clinical, counseling, and pediatric psychology). Thus, they are written broadly and are less tailored for the practice of school psychology specifically. Moreover, as noted in Chapter 1, APA differs from NASP in that it considers the doctoral degree to be the entry-level degree for professional psychologists; therefore, its standards for graduate program accreditation and professional and ethical practice primarily address doctoral-level psychologists.

Finally, ISPA maintains a code of ethics for school psychologists internationally (ISPA, 2011) as well as the *International Guidelines for the Preparation of School Psychologists* (Cunningham & Oakland, 1998). These graduate preparation guidelines are described in further detail later in this chapter. Although ISPA accreditation has been pursued by some U.S. programs that emphasize an international focus, these standards are likely to be more beneficial to programs located in countries that do not possess separate standards at the national level.

Standards confer a number of benefits on a field. Specifically, they offer a consistent set of expectations for the profession as well as widely accepted benchmarks for quality. Consistency in professional expectations is highly important (especially for the field of school psychology), as variability in the quality and types of services provided would create substantial challenges for ensuring that all youth have equal access to appropriate supports. However, the need for consistency is also problematic in some ways. For example, standards development teams often grapple with the challenge of crafting language that is adequately specific to ensure clarity while also accommodating potential future directions for the field. At times, the desire to foster professional consistency may result in standards that inadvertently undermine innovation or stifle potential advances in the profession.

Furthermore, given the time- and labor-intensive nature of their development, approval, and implementation processes, standards documents are updated relatively infrequently. For example, current NASP and APA standards generally have not kept up with the rapidly expanding role of technology in psychology and education over the past decade. Final drafts of the 2010 NASP standards began development in 2007 with the next anticipated revision process first beginning in 2017, and the last APA guidelines for accreditation were in effect from 2006 through the end of 2016. Due to relatively infrequent updating, standards are sometimes less responsive to emerging needs of practitioners, youth, and families and can even become outdated.

As noted previously, both professional standards and state legislation shape pathways to becoming a school psychologist. Generally, these pathways involve completing a graduate preparation program, obtaining relevant credentials, and maintaining credentials through ongoing professional development. The next few sections of this chapter describe procedures and requirements for graduate preparation, credentialing, and continuing education in school psychology. Standards documents relevant to each section are described or referenced throughout.

GRADUATE PREPARATION IN SCHOOL PSYCHOLOGY

Degree Types

In the United States, there are approximately 240 universities with established school psychology programs (SPPs) that offer a variety of degrees. Different types of degrees are associated with different preparation requirements, employment outcomes, and credentialing standards. Generally, school psychology degrees can be divided into two broad categories: *non-doctoral* (e.g., specialist-level) *degrees* and *doctoral degrees*.

Non-doctoral Degrees

According to NASP standards, the **specialist-level degree** is the entry-level degree for school psychologists, meaning that it represents the minimum level of education required to become a practitioner. Generally, these types of degrees require a *minimum* of 3 years of full-time graduate study (or the equivalent) beyond the bachelor's degree, involving at least 60 graduate semester or 90 graduate quarter hours. In addition to coursework, these degrees require a yearlong internship consisting of at least 1,200 clock hours of supervised practice, 600 of which must be completed in a school setting (NASP, 2017).

Different institutions or programs may refer to non-doctoral school psychology degrees by different names. For example, some SPPs grant a specialist degree (e.g., Educational Specialist [EdS] or Specialist in Psychology [PsyS]), while others award a 60-credit-hour master's degree or some combination of a master's degree *and* certificate of graduate study. For example, in some parts of the country, students obtain both a master's degree in school psychology (approximately

30 credits) and a Certificate of Advanced Graduate Study/Studies (CAGS; approximately 30 credits). Conversely, master's degree programs in school psychology that constitute fewer than 60 graduate credit hours generally have been phased out by U.S. graduate institutions. In a few states, terminal master's degrees of fewer than 60 credit hours may allow individuals to obtain a credential as an educational or psychoeducational diagnostician (who provides a limited range of assessment services), but rarely as a school psychologist.

This variation in degrees and certificates can cause confusion among prospective program applicants. Most important, however, candidates ideally complete a program of at least 60 graduate hours with curriculum and internship requirements consistent with national standards. It is also important to be properly supervised by a credentialed school psychologist or, for any setting outside of the schools, a psychologist who has obtained the appropriate credential for practice in that particular setting. Notably, specialist-level programs may be accredited by NASP and/or ISPA but not APA (as APA accredits doctoral-level programs only).

The majority of school psychologists (55%) hold a specialist degree or CAGS, and 20% hold a master's degree (many of whom possess a master's degree that required 60 graduate credit hours or more; Walcott, Charvat, McNamara, & Hyson, 2016). Thus, overall, 75% of school psychologists practice at the non-doctoral level. Individuals may opt to pursue a specialist-level degree for a variety of reasons, including the desire to become school-based practitioners who work directly with children, families, and educational systems; the desire for a broad, generalist training; and the freedom to pursue employment sooner (i.e., sooner than doctoral-level candidates). However, in many states, practitioners with non-doctoral degrees have fewer employment opportunities, especially in nonschool settings, than those with a doctoral degree.

Doctoral Degrees

Approximately 25% of school psychologists hold a doctoral degree (Walcott et al., 2016). The number of necessary credits hours for a doctorate varies by program (although NASP requires 90 semester hours), as does the specific emphasis. For example, some doctoral programs emphasize clinical preparation over research preparation, and vice versa. Moreover, some programs provide options to pursue an area of specialization, such as school neuropsychology or pediatric school psychology. Doctoral programs may be accredited by NASP, APA, and/or ISPA.

Doctoral programs in school psychology may confer several different degree types, such as Doctor of Philosophy (PhD), Doctor of Education (EdD), or Doctor of Psychology (PsyD) degrees. The PsyD degree tends to be geared more toward practice than research. As such, it tends to be accepted more in practice settings than in higher education settings that emphasize research (despite findings suggesting that the two degree programs do not have significant differences in their research-related coursework; Rossen & Oakland, 2008). For doctoral programs approved or accredited by NASP, candidates must accrue a minimum of 90 graduate semester hours and complete a 1,500-hour internship (NASP, 2010a). Faculty positions in higher education institutions and, in some instances, research and policy jobs within school psychology typically require candidates to have earned a doctoral degree. Factors that may contribute to an individual's decision to pursue a doctoral degree include aspirations to enter academia, the desire for "prestige," and the desire to pursue increased expertise and skill level (often in a specialized area of practice; Laurent, Steffey, & Swerdlik, 2008).

Content and Structure

The content and structure of graduate preparation programs is often linked closely to standards issued by professional organizations. This alignment is largely attributable to efforts by many programs to achieve accreditation, which is described later in this chapter. As already noted, three primary organizations provide guidance on the content and structure of SPPs: NASP, APA, and ISPA. Standards for program content for each of these organizations are listed in Table 3.1 and described in further detail in this section.

NASP Graduate Preparation Standards

NASP has been developing graduate preparation standards since its 1972 *Guidelines for Training Programs in School Psychology*. Since that time, the organization has revised its standards approximately every 10 years, and each successive revision has introduced several changes. The most recent revision of NASP's (2010a) *Standards for Graduate Preparation of School Psychologists* retains much of the structure that was already present and organizes the standards into four main areas:

1. School Psychology Program Context/Structure
2. Domains of School Psychology Graduate Education and Practice
3. Practica and Internships in School Psychology
4. School Psychology Program Support/Resources

Notably, the 10 domains of practice in the NASP (2010c) Practice Model (described in Chapter 1) are the same as those described in the Domains of School Psychology Graduate Education and Practice. These domains describe the necessary content to be taught and reinforced in graduate preparation programs. The 10 domains are reiterated in Table 3.1. NASP anticipates approving updated standards in 2020.

APA Standards for Health Service Psychology

In 2015, APA (2015) adopted the *Standards of Accreditation of Health Service Psychology* (SoA), which came into effect on January 1, 2017. These standards continue to be outcome oriented, allowing each program to define its model of preparation, goals, competencies, and student outcomes. Each program also must monitor individual student performance and conduct ongoing program evaluation. The SoA includes five broad standards:

1. Institutional and Program Context
2. Aims, Competencies, Curriculum, and Outcomes
3. Students
4. Faculty
5. Communication Practices

TABLE 3.1 Areas of Competency for Program Accreditation

NASP	APA	ISPA
Domain 1: Data-Based Decision Making and Accountability	1. Research	*Goal 1: Core Knowledge in Psychology and Education*
	2. Ethical and legal standards	1.1 Cognition and Learning
Domain 2: Consultation and Collaboration		1.2 Social and Emotional Development
	3. Individual and cultural diversity	1.3 Individual Differences
Domain 3: Interventions and Instructional Support to Develop Academic Skills		*Goal 2: Professional Knowledge and Skills in Assessment and Intervention*
	4. Professional values, attitudes, and behaviors	2.1 Evidence-Based Decision Making and Accountability
		2.2 Prevention, Mental Health Promotion and Crisis Intervention
Domain 4: Interventions and Mental Health Services to Develop Social and Life Skills	5. Communication and interpersonal skills	2.3 School and Systems Organization, Policy Development and Implementation
		2.4 Home–School–Community Collaboration
	6. Assessment	*Goal 3: Transnational/Multicultural School Psychology*
Domain 5: School-wide Practices to Promote Learning	7. Intervention	3.1 Role and functions of school psychologists nationally and internationally
	8. Supervision	3.2 Working with children and families from culturally diverse communities
Domain 6: Preventive and Responsive Services	9. Consultation and interprofessional/ interdisciplinary skills	*Goal 4: Professional Practice of School Psychologists*
Domain 7: Family–School Collaboration Services		4.1 Legislation that impacts on education policy and practice
		4.2 Ethical issues in professional practice
		4.3 Report writing
Domain 8: Diversity in Development and Learning		*Goal 5: Interpersonal Skills*
		5.1 Self-awareness and reflexivity
		5.2 Interviewing
Domain 9: Research and Program Evaluation		5.3 Consultation
		Goal 6: Research Methods
Domain 10: Legal, Ethical, and Professional Practice.		6.1 Research design and implementation
		6.2 Analysis and interpretation of research findings

APA, American Psychological Association; ISPA, International School Psychology Association; NASP, National Association of School Psychologists.

Sources: American Psychological Association. (2015). *Standards of Accreditation for Health Service Psychology.* Retrieved from http://www.apa.org/ed/accreditation/about/policies/standards-of-accreditation.pdf; International School Psychology Association. (2017). *The accreditation of professional training programs in school psychology.* Retrieved from https://www.ispaweb.org/accreditation/; National Association of School Psychologists. (2010a). *Standards for the graduate preparation of school psychologists.* Bethesda, MD: Author.

Each of these standards has specific requirements that need to be addressed by the program. Several structural items (e.g., residency requirements), program processes (e.g., annual written evaluation of all students), program assessment and quality improvement mandates (e.g., systematic program self-assessment), and public disclosure issues are also required. Additionally, Standard II (B) includes nine distinct areas that must be addressed in the program's curriculum. These nine areas are listed in Table 3.1.

ISPA Training Standards

ISPA's Professional Development and Practice Committee initially developed key standards for accreditation in 2001, which were substantially updated in 2014 (ISPA, 2017). ISPA identifies six broad goals and standards for SPPs. These goals designate skills and competencies that emerging professionals should attain to become successful school psychologists (ISPA, 2017). The goals and standards listed in Table 3.1 have many similarities to the NASP's standards, with the exception of Goal 3 (i.e., transnational/multicultural standard).

SOCIAL JUSTICE CONNECTIONS

How can school psychology programs (SPPs) prepare effective agents of social justice?

Over time, the National Association of School Psychologists (NASP) and SPPs across the United States have increasingly recognized the importance of teaching social justice advocacy skills to preservice school psychologists. The 2010 NASP graduate preparation standards (NASP, 2010a) describe the need for school psychologists to reflect an "understanding and respect for human diversity and promote effective services, advocacy, and social justice for all children, families, and schools" (p. 4). Since the development of these standards, there has been a greater demand for graduate preparation that emphasizes social justice principles. In line with this shift, NASP has identified the promotion of social justice as one of its strategic priorities. Other professional organizations also address social justice issues in their mission statements and professional standards. For example, the American Psychological Association's (APA's) Standards of Accreditation (SoA) for Health Service Psychology call for programs and their constituents to engage in actions that promote respect for cultural diversity and individual differences.

How can SPPs teach skills in social justice advocacy? As noted by Shriberg (2012), "best practices" in preparing future social justice advocates are still emerging; however, scholars in school, clinical, and counseling psychology have made attempts to tackle this question. For example, Goodman et al. (2004) identified six core competencies related to the practice of social justice advocacy: (1) engaging in ongoing self-examination; (2) sharing power (i.e., among practitioners, students, families, and others); (3) giving voice (i.e., empowering students and families to share their perspectives and participate in educational decision making); (4) facilitating consciousness raising (e.g., helping children and families become more aware of social injustices in society); (5) building on strengths; and (6) leaving clients with the tools to work toward social change. Notably, several of these competencies center on empowering clients to actively participate in service delivery and educational decision-making processes. Others are more practitioner centered and require the psychologist to reflect meaningfully on their own personal beliefs and attitudes. Principles such as those described by Goodman et al. (2004) provide a strong foundation for preparing effective social justice advocates and have slowly begun to permeate the curricula of SPPs across the nation (e.g., Grapin, 2017; Miranda, Radliff, Cooper, & Eschenbrenner, 2014; Moy et al., 2014).

GRADUATE PROGRAM ACCREDITATION

Broadly, higher education accreditation is "a system for recognizing educational institutions and professional programs affiliated with those institutions for a level of performance, integrity, and quality which entitles them to the confidence of the educational community and the public they serve" (Chernay, 1990, p. 1). Generally, government regulations related to accreditation focus on institutional/ university or program infrastructure and student outcomes, and rely on professions to more specifically dictate the skills and knowledge required for competency in that field. In other words, the profession itself determines an appropriate set of standards and behaviors that govern the field, and private, nonprofit organizations (e.g., NASP, APA) conduct external reviews of program quality (Eaton, 2012). One of the main goals of accreditation is to provide the public with assurance that the institutions or programs under scrutiny are meeting or exceeding established professional standards.

Importantly, accreditation is "voluntary," meaning that universities may or may not choose to pursue this marker of program quality (Prus & Strein, 2011). However, some state departments of education require applicants for school psychology state certification or licensure to be graduates of NASP-approved programs or to hold the Nationally Certified School Psychologist (NCSP) credential (described in the following section). This means that programs in those states must secure NASP approval to produce candidates who are qualified to practice within the state. Likewise, some state licensing boards either require or encourage applicants for the title of "licensed psychologist" to be graduates of APA-accredited programs. This incentivizes doctoral programs in these states to seek APA accreditation. In general, accreditation in a specialized professional field increases the legitimacy of the credentials awarded to program graduates. Moreover, accreditation signals to prospective applicants that a program is subject to quality control by an independent, external agency (Prus & Strein, 2011).

Over time, there has been a shift in higher education accreditation from focusing on program operations to focusing on accountability for student outcomes (Nelson & Messenger, 2003). Essentially, in addition to asking, "Do programs contain the necessary components determined by organizational and national standards?" accreditation agencies are increasingly asking the question "Are students actually learning what they are supposed to be learning?" As a result, there is relatively less emphasis on scrutinizing program structure and supports (i.e., inputs) and greater emphasis on assessing candidate performance (i.e., outcomes). The question "Are students actually learning what they are supposed to be learning?" can be answered through performance assessments (e.g., measures of skills in psychological service delivery) throughout the various stages of graduate preparation. It is for this reason that programs often must have at least one full student cohort complete all coursework and requirements in their entirety prior to consideration for approval or accreditation. As noted previously, APA accredits only doctoral-level programs in various areas within psychology (including school psychology), while NASP accredits both specialist and doctoral-level SPPs. ISPA is a relatively new accrediting body in school psychology, as it began accrediting specialist-level and doctoral programs in 2011.

CREDENTIALING IN SCHOOL PSYCHOLOGY

Credentialing generally describes the process of establishing qualifications and authorizing individuals to practice professionally. In the context of school psychology, a credential is a generic, umbrella term that includes both *certification* and *licensure*. From a national perspective in school psychology, the terms are generally interchangeable, as they both refer to a process of a state agency (typically the state department of education) granting permission to practice under that agency's authority. Certification is often mistakenly assumed to refer only to school-based practice, whereas licensure is sometimes considered a term exclusively dedicated to credentialing for psychological services provided outside of school settings, such as independent practice, hospitals, and clinics. Indeed, many states use those terms in this manner (i.e., certification for school practice; licensure for independent practice). However, in some states, credentials for school-based practice are officially called licenses or endorsements; therefore, such global distinctions in terminology are potentially misleading. Ultimately, each state agency will identify the title of any credentials it may oversee.

Additional differences exist between practice and nonpractice credentials. *Practice credentials* are awarded by a government agency (e.g., state education agency [SEA]) and are required for an individual to practice psychology legally in a specified range of settings (e.g., K–12 schools). For example, in the state of New Jersey, school psychologists employed in the K–12 public schools must hold a valid "School Psychologist Standard Certificate" to provide services. This credential also identifies settings where services can be provided (e.g., K–12 school settings, early childhood and pre-K settings, private and charter schools) and the scope of practice (i.e., the range of allowable services) in these settings. Individuals who do not hold this credential are not permitted to serve in the role of school psychologist in schools.

By comparison, *nonpractice credentials* are issued by nongovernment agencies (e.g., professional organizations such as NASP). These credentials are desirable because they are markers of high-quality or specialized training. Returning to our earlier example in New Jersey, many school psychologists who are permitted to practice under law via their state-issued credential also hold the NCSP credential. However, holding the NCSP credential alone without a credential from the state agency would not be sufficient to provide services. While the NCSP is not required for school psychologists to practice legally in New Jersey, it is recognized in New Jersey for automatic issuance of the state credential. Additionally, it signals to employers that the individual has met NASP's rigorous graduate preparation standards and maintains a commitment to ongoing professional growth. Ultimately, it is common for practitioners to hold more than one credential (although usually not required by law within the United States).

Practice Credentials at the State Level

As already described, credentialing for the purposes of professional practice in school psychology is a state-level function. In other words, each state maintains independent credentialing laws, regulations, and requirements. In nearly every state and territory, the credential for school psychological practice is issued by the state department of education or SEA; Texas and Hawaii represent the only exceptions. The Texas State Board of Examiners of Psychologists (i.e., board of psychology) oversees the credentialing of school psychology practitioners in Texas. As of the writing of this chapter, in Hawaii, no state-level agency has oversight over the credentialing of school psychologists, though the state board of education offers general descriptions and minimum qualifications for districts to use in the hiring process. Given that SEAs largely oversee the credentialing of school psychologists, the requirements and expectations are generally more impacted by educational rather than psychological norms. Updated information on state requirements can be found at www.nasponline.org/standards-and-certification/state-school-psychology-credentialing-requirements.

Credentialing for Practice in Schools

States vary considerably in their credentialing requirements with respect to a range of factors. including (a) basic eligibility requirements (e.g., graduate preparation, supervised field experiences, exams); (b) title (e.g., "school psychologist"); (c) setting where services can be provided (e.g., schools, hospitals); and (d) scope or range of services. As of the writing of this chapter, no states maintain an official reciprocity agreement for school psychologists; in other words, holding a school psychology credential in one state does not automatically qualify an individual to work in another state (though some states consider out-of-state credentials or the NCSP as part of their application process). Thus, any school psychologist who is considering work in more than one state, at any point in time, should become familiar with the various requirements and pursue experiences that allow for eligibility in as many states as possible. Unfortunately, a study of 216 school psychology doctoral students found that only 34% of those who had planned to pursue multiple credentials had actively researched the requirements to obtain them (Hall, Wexelbaum, & Boucher, 2007).

Eligibility and Education

Although eligibility requirements for the practice of school psychology vary by state, they typically include criteria related to education (e.g., degree), supervised field experiences, and, in some states, examination. Generally, these requirements should be completed as part of a school psychology degree or program of study. Most states require a degree specifically in school psychology and a minimum of a specialist-level degree as the entry-level requirement. A specialist-level degree is typically defined as 60 semester hours (or 90 quarter hours) of graduate study packaged under various degree titles including, but not limited to, EdS, PsyS, Master of Arts (MA), Master of Science (MS), MA with Certificate of Advanced Graduate Study/Studies, or MA with Certificate of Advanced Study (CAS). Some, however, allow for degrees in fields other than school psychology or for fewer credit hours; for example, Washington, D.C., requires only 42 graduate semester hours in school, educational, or clinical psychology. Some state requirements are broader or more inclusive, such as those upheld by Oregon, which requires a "master's or higher degree in the behavioral sciences or their derivative therapeutic professions" (Oregon Teacher Standards and Practices Commission, 2011, p. 1). Others specify unique requirements within their degree criteria, such as North Dakota, which requires candidates to complete a three-credit course in Native American and multicultural studies. Notably, *no state requires a doctoral degree for the school psychology credential for practice in schools*, and there is no indication that we will see any significant trend toward requiring a doctoral degree in the foreseeable future.

Additionally, some states require that candidates come from a school psychology graduate program that held NASP or APA approval/accreditation at the time of their graduation (or that the individual hold the NCSP). Thus, an individual who has worked as a practitioner for many years in one state could potentially not be eligible to work in another state if he or she did not attend an approved or accredited program.

Supervised Field Experiences

Supervised field experiences in SPPs comprise both practicum and internship experiences. Although terminology varies across graduate programs, a **practicum** (plural: *practica*) is a field-based experience that generally occurs during the early-to-middle years of graduate preparation, exposes students to professional settings, and builds skills in psychological and educational service delivery through close supervision. Very few states have specific requirements related to practica, though some exist (e.g., Illinois requires 250 hours of practica in a school setting or child study center and California requires 450 hours of practica, of which 300 must be in preschool through grade 12).

In SPPs, an **internship** is a culminating field experience that typically requires the integration of skills developed during practica and, in many cases, greater independence (although interns continue to be closely supervised by their appointed field-based and university-based supervisors). The internship is the culminating experience in school psychology graduate preparation and thus typically occurs in the final year of the program. Many states require a 1,200-hour internship experience, and some go on to stipulate that at least 600 of those hours take place in a school setting, which aligns with the NASP (2010b) credentialing standards. No state requires *more* than 1,200 hours of internship. However, some states require certain types of experiences (e.g., working with minority students or students with emotional/behavioral disabilities) or specify requirements for intern supervisors.

Exams

Approximately half of all states require candidates to achieve a passing score on the School Psychologist Praxis exam (#5402), which is administered by the Educational Testing Service (ETS). To qualify for the NCSP credential, candidates must earn a score of 147 or higher (as recommended by ETS), and most states utilizing this exam have adopted this criterion as well. Some states, however, utilize different exams that assess basic skills in reading, writing, and math or have adopted a school psychology exam administered by other test publishers. In addition, albeit rarely, a state may require a state-specific exam; for example, Nevada requires an exam demonstrating knowledge of both the U.S. and Nevada constitutions. No SEA requires the Examination for Professional Practice in Psychology for a school psychology credential (although this exam is often a requirement for a general psychology credential from a state board of psychology). This exam is described briefly later in this chapter.

Title

A credential identifies a professional title and/or a scope of practice. With the exception of Texas and Arkansas, the school psychology credential allows for use of the title "school psychologist" in professional settings. Some states may have expanded titles; for example, Maine's credential specifies whether the school psychologist holds a specialist or doctoral degree. Other states do not have "school psychologist" in the name of the credential and instead confer titles such as School Specialist License (e.g., Kansas). The majority of these states, however, do not prohibit use of the title "school psychologist" among individuals who have obtained these credentials. The exceptions are Arkansas and Texas, as explicit restrictions within these states prohibit the use of "psychologist" in any title without a general psychologist credential (reserved for doctoral-level psychologists only). Thus, the Texas credential confers the title of Licensed Specialist in School Psychology (LSSP), and the Arkansas credential confers the title of School Psychology Specialist (SPS).

Setting and Scope of Services

Credentials may also specify the services that can be provided, the recipients of those services, and the settings in which service delivery can take place. Most state regulations allow qualified practitioners (i.e., those who hold the school psychology credential) to provide a general, nonspecific range of school psychological services. In other words, states rarely restrict specific psychological services or techniques and instead define the practice of school psychology broadly. Broad language allows for the continuous improvement and evolution of practice and the provision of services based on contextual need. This broad language also allows school psychologists to provide services within the scope of their competencies.

Some SEA credentials may restrict service delivery to students from pre-K to grade 12 only, whereas others extend these parameters to include college students and children ages birth through 5 years. Such distinctions are not made clear in many states. Credentials may also identify the settings in which services can be provided. For those with the SEA school psychology credential, the majority of states restrict service delivery to schools, which typically include public, charter, and private schools (including contractual services). Sometimes, states do not specify which agency has regulatory authority over the credentialing of school psychologists employed in private/independent schools (i.e., schools privately funded that are not administered by local, state, or federal governments), leaving hiring decisions to the independent schools themselves.

A school psychologist with the SEA credential working outside of an approved setting may be considered as operating outside of the scope of his or her credential. However, some exceptions exist. For example, in Pennsylvania, school psychologists with the SEA credential can provide independent services outside of schools (e.g., private practice) as long as they are employed by a school in Pennsylvania in good standing and do not provide private practice services to students within the district of employment.

Alternative or Temporary Credentialing

The field of school psychology has faced workforce shortages for decades, such that the supply of personnel has not met the demand (Bocanegra, Grapin, Nellis, & Rossen, 2017). Some settings or areas of the country experience more severe shortages than others do; for example, many rural districts report difficulties filling vacant positions, particularly in states where very few school psychology graduate programs exist. As a result, some states have created alternative credentialing practices that allow for temporary or emergency credentials (e.g., a 2-year temporary credential while fulfilling other requirements) or more narrowly defined credentials (e.g., credentials that allow only for testing for special education evaluations) in an effort to fill gaps in service delivery. Often, these credentials have less strict criteria related to graduate preparation, field experiences, and exams, which, in turn, may undermine the quality and consistency of services provided. Some states also require school psychology interns to obtain a provisional or temporary credential to complete an internship in the schools.

Credentialing for Practice Outside of Schools

The majority (96%) of NASP members maintain an active SEA credential, whereas few hold credentials with the state board of psychology (11%) or other credentials (fewer than 10%) (Walcott et al., 2016). Despite this minority, some have anticipated a rise in the number of school psychologists pursuing secondary employment outside of schools, either due to burnout or due to the need to supplement income (Rossen, 2011). Generally, to practice psychology outside of schools, one must obtain a credential from the state board of psychology (though specific names of state boards or agencies vary) or other relevant agencies. Credentials to practice independently (i.e., outside of schools without supervision) typically require a doctoral degree in either school, clinical, or counseling psychology; however, there are many states that allow for non-doctoral-level practitioners to practice outside of schools in some capacity.

Doctoral Practice

In most states, practicing psychology outside of schools requires a doctoral degree in school, clinical, or counseling psychology, a passing score on the Examination for the Professional Practice of Psychology (EPPP; described below), and the completion of supervised field experiences. Some states also require a state-level jurisprudence exam or oral exam, postdoctoral supervision hours (i.e., field supervision *after* the completion of doctoral studies and formal internship), a doctoral degree from an APA-accredited graduate program , and/or the completion of an APA-accredited or **Association of Psychology and Postdoctoral Internship Center (APPIC)** internship. APPIC is an organization that sets quality standards for internships, postdoctoral positions, and fellowships in professional psychology and facilitates matches between applicants and approved training sites. As of the writing of this chapter, most states do not require candidates to complete accredited degree programs or internships to qualify for the psychology license (meaning that candidates may graduate from nonapproved or nonaccredited programs and complete internships outside of the APPIC network).

As noted earlier, many states require that candidates achieve a passing score on the EPPP exam. Developed by the Association of State and Provincial Psychology Boards (ASPPB), the EPPP is a knowledge-based exam of a variety of areas pertinent to the practice of professional psychology, including topics such as biological, social, and cultural bases of behavior; growth and life-span development; assessment, diagnosis, prevention, and treatment practices; research methods; and legal and ethical issues. The ASPBB also has announced the development of a second, related exam, the EPPP Step 2, which will serve as a competency-based skills exam and a complement to the knowledge-based EPPP. The ASPPB anticipates that this exam will be ready for use in January 2019; however, it remains to be seen how state boards will utilize the exam.

Non-Doctoral Practice

Some states allow for the delivery of psychological services by non-doctoral school psychologists outside of schools. In many instances, separate credentials have been developed for which school psychologists may qualify, though often the credential does not include "school psychologist" as a professional title. For example, Massachusetts confers the title of *Educational Psychologist*, and South Carolina and California confer the titles of *Licensed Psycho-Educational Specialist* and *Licensed Educational Psychologist*, respectively. An even greater number of states have credentials for non-doctoral professionals that allow for practice under the supervision of a licensed psychologist. The requirements, scope of practice, titles, and agencies that maintain oversight over all of these credentials vary significantly across states.

Finally, depending on their preparation and supervised experience, school psychologists often qualify for other credentials in related professions that may allow for practice outside of schools. These may include, but are not limited to, *Licensed (Clinical) Professional Counselor*, *Licensed Mental Health Counselor/Therapist*, or *Licensed Marriage and Family Therapist*. As already discussed, each credential defines preparation requirements, the professional title to be used when operating under that credential, the scope of practice, and the settings in which services can be provided.

Maintenance and Renewal of Credentials

The majority of credentials (both practice and nonpractice credentials) require some form of periodic renewal, although a few exceptions exist where no renewal or maintenance is required. Those requiring renewal typically mandate a process for continuing education or continuing professional development in the form of a certain number of clock or credit hours (e.g., 75 clock hours) over a specified period of time (e.g., 3 years). Some states require that a portion of those hours cover specific topics (e.g., ethics, legal regulation, or diversity) or be obtained from specific types of providers (NASP- or APA-approved providers). As with all components of credentialing, the specific requirements vary from state to state and often evolve over time.

Nonpractice Credentials

Recall that the conferral of practice credentials is primarily a state-level function, such that one must possess an appropriate state-level credential to legally provide services. Nonpractice credentials (as described earlier), however, often are conferred at the national level. Although nonpractice credentials alone do not afford regulatory authority to provide services, they can provide a great deal of professional benefit to practitioners. To name a few, these credentials include the Diplomate in School Psychology, Diplomate in School Neuropsychology, and NCSP (as mentioned toward the beginning of this chapter). Of particular relevance among nonpractice credentials, is the NCSP.

Nationally Certified School Psychologist Credential

The NCSP credential, while considered a nonpractice credential, does provide a number of benefits. First, the credential is recognized by more than 30 states as either partially or fully meeting the criteria to earn an SEA credential. This means that, although holding the NCSP alone does not allow for legal practice, possession of this credential provides a facilitated path to obtaining the state credential. Such reciprocity allows for greater mobility among school psychologists who wish to relocate or practice in more than one state. As of the writing of this chapter, some states require candidates to either hold the NCSP or complete a NASP-approved or APA-accredited program to obtain a state practice credential.

Some school districts, and a few states, offer an additional annual stipend to any school psychologists holding the NCSP credential. Aside from the more tangible benefits, the NCSP also provides professional credibility and demonstrates that the individual has met national standards for practice. Two thirds of all NASP members presently hold the NCSP (Walcott et al., 2016), and there are more than 15,000 active NCSPs. To qualify for this credential, one must meet the NASP credentialing standards (NASP, 2010b) and basic eligibility requirements, including the following:

- Completion of an organized program of study that is officially titled "School Psychology" that consists of at least 60 graduate semester/90 quarter hours
- Completion of a sequence of supervised experiences that occurred prior to and exclusive of the internship is required (i.e., practica)
- Successful completion of a 1,200-hour internship in school psychology, of which at least 600 hours must be in a school setting
- A passing score on the Praxis School Psychologist exam

The NCSP credential also requires completion of a NASP-approved program or the equivalent (i.e., a program that does not have NASP approval but upholds the graduate preparation standards set forth for the NCSP). Graduates of programs *not* approved or accredited by NASP are eligible to apply for the NCSP, but they must demonstrate that they have attained the knowledge and skills represented in the NASP standards by providing more extensive documentation of their preparation. Graduates of NASP-approved programs submit relatively less documentation because their programs have already been deemed aligned with NASP standards and have documented candidate outcomes. The NCSP credential also has an NCSP-Inactive status (e.g., those on a leave of absence) as well as an NCSP-Retired status. More information can be found at www.nasponline.org/certification.

SUMMARY AND CONCLUSIONS

Regulation of professional preparation and practice in school psychology are critical for ensuring that students, families, and other stakeholders in schools receive high-quality services. A number of organizations and agencies, including both government and nongovernment organizations, confer credentials for school psychologists that attest to the quality and depth of their preparation for practice. As the field of school psychology continues to evolve in response to the ever-changing landscape of education and mental health service delivery, regular review and revision of professional standards and credentialing requirements must be undertaken. These revisions should be responsive to changes in the field (e.g., use of technology, virtual service delivery) as well as the social context in which youth live. This ongoing process of responsive reflection allows for the continuous improvement of approaches to preparing and supporting highly qualified and effective professionals.

DISCUSSION QUESTIONS

1. What are the benefits of having standards related to school psychology provided by multiple organizations? What are the drawbacks?
2. NASP and all U.S. states view the specialist-level degree as the entry-level degree for school psychology, as opposed to the doctoral degree. What might be some consequences for the field of shifting to a doctoral-only profession?
3. States largely maintain oversight of school psychology credentialing, despite the existence of a national certification procedures. Why is state oversight important?
4. As noted in the chapter, some states choose not to allow specialist-level school psychology practitioners to use the title "school psychologist" (e.g., Texas, Arkansas). Do you agree with these restrictions? Why or why not?
5. What are some advantages and disadvantages of alternative and temporary credentialing options?

REFERENCES

American Psychological Association. (2010a). Ethical principles of psychologists and code of conduct. Retrieved from http://apa.org/ethics/code/index.aspx

American Psychological Association. (2010b). Model act for state licensure of psychologists. Retrieved from https://www.apa.org/about/policy/model-act-2010.pdf

American Psychological Association. (2015). Standards of Accreditation for Health Service Psychology. Retrieved from http://www.apa.org/ed/accreditation/about/policies/standards-of-accreditation.pdf

Bocanegra, J. O., Grapin, S. L., Nellis, L. M., & Rossen, E. (2017). Remediating the shortages crisis through the creation of a resource guide. *Communique*, *45*(6), 16–18.

Chernay, G. (1990). *Accreditation and the role of the Council on Postsecondary Accreditation.* Washington, DC: Council on Postsecondary Education.

Cunningham, J., & Oakland, T. (1998). International School Psychology Association guidelines for the preparation of school psychologists. *School Psychology International*, *19*, 19–30.

Eaton, J. (2012, August). An overview of U.S. accreditation. Retrieved from http://www.chea.org/pdf/Overview%20of%20US%20Accreditation%202012.pdf

Goodman, L. A., Liang, B., Helms, J. E., Latta, R. E., Sparks, E., & Weintraub, S. R. (2004). Training counseling psychologists as social justice agents: Feminist and multicultural principles in action. *Counseling Psychologist*, *32*, 793–837.

Grapin, S. (2017). Social justice training in school psychology: Applying principles of organizational consultation to facilitate change in graduate programs. *Journal of Educational and Psychological Consultation*, *27*(2), 173–202.

Hall, J. E., Wexelbaum, S. F., & Boucher, A. P. (2007). Doctoral student awareness of licensure, credentialing, and professional organizations in psychology: The 2005 National Register International Survey. *Training and Education in Professional Psychology*, *1*, 38–48. doi:10.1037/1931-3918.1.1.38

International School Psychology Association. (2011). *Code of ethics.* Retrieved from http://www.ispaweb.org/wp-content/uploads/2013/01/The_ISPA_Code_of_Ethics_2011.pdf

International School Psychology Association. (2017). The accreditation of professional training programs in school psychology. Retrieved from https://www.ispaweb.org/accreditation

Laurent, J., Steffey, L., & Swerdlik, M. (2008). *Why students pursue a specialist or doctoral degree in school psychology.* Poster presented at 40th annual convention of the National Association of School Psychologists, New Orleans, LA.

Miranda, A. H., Radliff, K. M., Cooper, J. M., & Eschenbrenner, C. R. (2014). Graduate student perceptions of the impact of training for social justice: Development of a training model. *Psychology in the Schools*, *51*(4), 348–364.

Moy, G., Briggs, A., Shriberg, D., Jackson, K., Smith, P., & Tompkins, N. (2014). Developing school psychologists as agents of social justice. *Journal of School Psychology*, *52*, 323–341.

National Association of School Psychologists. (2010a). *Standards for the graduate preparation of school psychologists.* Bethesda, MD: Author.

National Association of School Psychologists. (2010b). *Standards for the credentialing of school psychologists.* Bethesda, MD: Author.

National Association of School Psychologists. (2010c). *Model for comprehensive and integrated school psychological services.* Bethesda, MD: Author.

National Association of School Psychologists. (2010d). *Principles for professional ethics.* Bethesda, MD: Author.

National Association of School Psychologists. (2017). Becoming a school psychologist. Retrieved from http://www.nasponline.org/about-school-psychology/becoming-a-school-psychologist

Nelson, P. D., & Messenger, L. C. (2003). Accreditation is psychology and public accountability. In E. M. Altmaier (Ed.), *Setting standards in graduate education: Psychology's commitment to excellence in accreditation* (pp. 7–37). Washington, DC: American Psychological Association.

Oregon Teacher Standards and Practices Commission. (2011). *Application instructions for an Oregon initial school psychologist license.* Salem, OR: Author.

Prus, J., & Strein, W. (2011). Issues and trends in the accreditation of school psychology programs in the United States. *Psychology in the Schools*, *48*(9), 887–900. doi:10.1002/pits.20600

Rossen, E. (2011). Essential tools for prospective and early career school psychologists: Credentialing for school and independent practice. *NASP Communique*, *40*(1), 30.

Rossen, E., & Oakland, T. (2008). Graduate preparation in research methods: The current status of APA-accredited professional programs in psychology. *Training and Education in Professional Psychology*, *2*(1), 42–49.

Shriberg, D. (2012). Graduate education and professional development. In D. Shriberg, S. Song, A. Miranda, & K. Radliff. (Eds.), *School psychology and social justice: Conceptual foundations and tools for practice* (pp. 311–326). New York, NY: Routledge.

Walcott, C. M., Charvat, J., McNamara, K. M., & Hyson, D. M. (2016, February). School psychology at a glance: 2015 Member Survey results. Presentation at the annual convention of the National Association of School Psychologists, New Orleans, LA.

CHAPTER 4

Multicultural Foundations

SHERRIE L. PROCTOR

CHAPTER OBJECTIVES

- Describe the demographics of school psychologists in the United States
- Describe the importance of diversity in the profession
- Describe the demographics of school-age youth
- Discuss how the use of multiculturalism can guide school psychological service delivery
- Describe recommendations for multiculturalism and social justice orientations to school psychology practice

No book on school psychology would be complete without a comprehensive discussion of factors related to human diversity and multicultural competence. In this chapter, ***diversity*** is defined broadly as a spectrum of individual differences related to factors such as age, disability status, gender or gender identity, race, ethnicity, national origin, religion, sexual orientation, language, and socioeconomic status (SES). Competent school psychologists consider human diversity in all aspects of their psychological service delivery.

The U.S. population is rapidly becoming more diverse in a number of ways. This rapid diversification has implications for pre-K–12 schools as well as for society at large. Diversity within the student population provides educators with an important opportunity to teach students how to live in a pluralistic U.S. society and an increasingly global world (Proctor & Meyers, 2014; Proctor & Simpson, 2016). Nevertheless, shifting demographics of the United States and school-age populations also present challenges for educators, including school psychologists, regarding the provision of culturally responsive and competent services in diverse schools and communities (Proctor & Meyers, 2014). This chapter explores the importance of valuing and incorporating diversity in the delivery of school psychological services.

MULTICULTURALISM, INTERSECTIONALITY, AND SOCIAL JUSTICE FOUNDATIONS

As discussed in Chapter 1, **multiculturalism** is a worldview that recognizes and values diverse learners, including their intersecting dimensions of individual identity and cultural backgrounds (Carroll, 2009). Many individuals who have attended public schools in the United States have experienced some aspect of "multicultural" education. **Multicultural education** refers to a wide variety of programs and practices designed to facilitate educational equity for individuals from all genders, racial and ethnic groups, language backgrounds, social classes, exceptionalities, and cultures (Banks, 2010). Banks (2010) underscores that multicultural education extends beyond curricular reform (e.g., including representation of diverse populations in the curriculum) to transforming all aspects of a school including its culture, policies and politics, staff perceptions and beliefs, assessment and testing procedures, instructional materials, community participation, and so forth. Indeed, multiculturalism is a "practice movement" that has its roots in education, counseling, psychology, and the behavioral sciences (Carroll, 2009, p. 3).

In its most effective manifestation, multiculturalism permeates a school and results in educational policies, procedures, and practices that take into account the needs of students with a range of backgrounds and talents (Carroll, 2009). Proctor and Meyers (2014) have noted the importance of school psychologists understanding, valuing, and engaging a multicultural practice orientation as well as developing multicultural competence. Newell et al. (2010) describe **multicultural competence** as the display of knowledge, attitudes, and behaviors that result in successful interactions with diverse students and populations. Carroll (2009) explains that educators who apply a multicultural orientation to their practice "see learners, their families, and communities within the context of culture, race, ethnicity, gender, sexual orientation, and all those other cultural lenses that give meaning to students' daily learning experiences" (p. 5).

Some school psychologists who use multiculturalism to guide their practice may believe that providing culturally responsive psychological services is sufficient to support diverse learners. However, a more comprehensive view of multiculturalism in school psychology practice refers to (a) examining and challenging personal attitudes, perceptions, and beliefs about diverse students and populations; (b) acquiring knowledge about diverse populations; (c) understanding how systemic, school-wide issues (e.g., curriculum, policies, assessment and counseling practices) impact diverse student populations; (d) engaging in advocacy for policies that promote equity for diverse student populations; and (e) acting in proactive ways that promote and proliferate the core values of multiculturalism (Carroll, 2009; Proctor & Meyers, 2014).

Another critical concept is intersectionality. **Intersectionality** can be defined as the simultaneous experience of social categories such as race, gender, class, and nationality. This term highlights the ways in which social categories interact to create systems of privilege, power, discrimination, and oppression (Cooper, 2016). It is important to consider intersectionality because identity is complex and multidimensional and students can have different school experiences, including the experience of bias and/or prejudice, based on either one or a combination of their identities (Suárez-Orozco et al., 2015).

DEMOGRAPHICS OF SCHOOL PSYCHOLOGISTS

Since its beginning, school psychology has been a predominantly White profession, with few individuals from racially, ethnically, or linguistically diverse backgrounds represented in its workforce (Castillo, Curtis, & Gelley, 2013; Proctor & Romano, 2016). To ascertain the demographics of school psychologists, Walcott, Charvat, McNamara, and Hyson (2016) surveyed a sample of National Association of School Psychologists (NASP) members during the 2014–2015 school year. Of the 2,654 respondents, 16% identified as male, 83% as female, and 1.0% as agender. Regarding the racial and ethnic backgrounds of respondents, 87% identified as White, 5.0% as Black or African American, 2.8% as Asian, and 6.0% as Hispanic. The majority (86%) of school psychologists were monolingual English speakers, although the school psychologists surveyed reported fluency in a total of 27 different languages. Spanish was the most commonly endorsed language among participants (7.0% of respondents), followed by American Sign Language (1.3% of respondents); the remainder of participants who identified as bilingual or multilingual spoke a variety of other languages (5.3% of participants). Notably, although 14% of respondents reported fluency in a language other than English, many did not utilize these talents in their practice. Of the respondents who endorsed speaking a second language, only 7.9% indicated that they provided bilingual or multilingual psychological or educational services.

As becomes evident later in this chapter, there is a significant demographic mismatch between school psychologists and the student populations they serve. Yet, diversity in the school psychology workforce is critical for a number of reasons, some of which are described in the following text. Although NASP, the American Psychological Association (APA), and other stakeholders and organizations have striven to increase diversity in the profession for decades, the demographic composition of the field has remained stagnant (Castillo et al., 2013; Proctor, Simpson, Levin, & Hackimer, 2014). Given these difficulties, all school psychologists must be well versed in principles of multiculturalism to effectively meet the needs of their diverse clientele.

CHALLENGES ASSOCIATED WITH A HOMOGENEOUS WORKFORCE

The longstanding lack of racial, ethnic, and linguistic diversity in the school psychology workforce has resulted in a number of challenges both within and outside the profession itself. For example, it has had repercussions for both scholarship and innovations in school psychology. In both areas, a dearth of diverse school psychologists may partially explain the profession's delayed focus on how school psychological practices impact diverse student populations (Newell et al., 2010; Proctor & Truscott, 2013). Although studying multicultural issues is not, nor should be, the responsibility of racially, ethnically, and linguistically diverse scholars, a historical scarcity of diverse scholars (and other scholars interested in multicultural issues) undoubtedly has impeded the field's development of a multicultural research base and its articulation of a social justice agenda (Miranda & Gutter, 2002; Newell et al., 2010; Shriberg et al., 2008; Speight & Vera, 2009).

Deficits in workforce diversity also have presented challenges in relation to practice. Notably, school psychology practitioners are key psychological service providers to students from diverse backgrounds (Curtis, Castillo, & Gelley, 2012; Proctor & Truscott, 2012). A recent national survey of school psychologists noted that 86% are employed in public schools (Walcott et al., 2016). These school psychologists reported spending much of their time engaged in activities such as conducting evaluations to determine special education eligibility and participating in the development of Individualized Education Programs. Other primary job roles included collecting and interpreting student data as part of school-based problem-solving teams and providing mental and behavioral health services to students (Walcott et al., 2016). All of the job roles in which school psychologists engage require attention to multicultural issues, especially given that most practitioners report serving diverse students (Curtis et al., 2012). Ultimately, a lack of diversity among school psychologists (in combination with a slowly emerging repository of multicultural scholarship) raises serious concerns regarding the field's preparedness to address the needs of diverse students, their families, and communities (Castillo et al., 2013; Proctor & Truscott, 2013).

DEMOGRAPHICS OF U.S. PUBLIC SCHOOL STUDENTS

The U.S. public school student population also is becoming increasingly racially, ethnically, and linguistically diverse. During the 2013–2014 school year, the U.S. pre-K–12 public schools served approximately 50 million students, of whom 50% were White, 25% were Hispanic, 16% were African American, 1% were Asian/Pacific Islander, 1% were American Indian/Alaska Native, and 3% were two or more races or ethnicities (National Center for Education Statistics [NCES], 2016a). During this same time, Hispanic students accounted for the largest percentage of the public school population in the West (41.6%) and the second largest percentage in the Northeast (18.7%) and South (24.2%), with White students representing the largest percentage of this population in the latter two regions. Although Black students have traditionally been one of the largest student demographics in the South, these data indicated that they were the third largest percentage in this region (23.6%). Asian/Pacific Islanders represented 9.1% of students in the West, 6.7% in the Northeast, and 3.2% in both the Midwest and South (NCES, 2016a). By 2020, Hispanic student representation is expected to increase by 25%, whereas Asian/Pacific Islander representation is predicted to increase by 36% and Native American/Alaskan Native by 17% nationally (Husser & Bailey, 2011).

Linguistic diversity is also abounding, with more than 400 languages spoken in U.S. public schools (NCES, 2016a). Approximately 4.5 million students, or 9.3% of the total public school population, are English learners (ELs) (NCES, 2016a). ELs, or students who are in the process of developing English language proficiency, are a protected class of students under Title VI, a federal law that prohibits any organization that receives federal funding from discriminating on the basis of race, color, or national origin (Hakuta, 2011). While Spanish is the most common home language spoken by ELs in the United States, other commonly used languages include Arabic, Chinese, Vietnamese, Hmong, Haitian/Haitian Creole, Somali, Russian, and Korean (NCES, 2016a). During the 2013–2014 school year, the EL population in six states (i.e., Alaska, California, Colorado, Nevada, New Mexico, and Texas) represented at least 10% of the student population in each of these states (NCES, 2016a). Nationally, ELs represent 14.1% of the student population in city schools, 8.7% in suburban schools, 6.1% in town schools, and 3.5% in rural schools (NCES, 2016a). These trends highlight the prevalence of racially, ethnically, and linguistically diverse students in communities and public schools across the United States.

Students who attend U.S. public schools are also diverse in regard to SES and family structure (Lopez & Bursztyn, 2013). As compared with Asian and White children, higher percentages of Black, American Indian/Alaskan Native, Hispanic, Pacific Islander, and children of two or more races live in poverty (NCES, 2016a). In fact, the prevalence of Black and American Indian/Alaska Native children living in poverty is approximately three times that of their Asian and White peers (NCES, 2016a). Moreover, data suggest that children who live in mother-only households have a higher rate of poverty than those who live in two-parent households (NCES, 2016a). Among children who live in mother-only households, poverty rates are higher for Blacks (52%), Hispanics (50%), and American Indian/Alaska Natives (50%) than they are for Whites (35%) and Asians (28%).

In terms of understanding diverse students' intersectional identities, school psychologists and other educators must also take into account how students identify in terms of religious affiliation and sexual orientation. According to Lopez and Bursztyn (2013), approximately 78% of Americans identify as Christian; however, the influence of immigrant populations who are Buddhist, Catholic, Hindu, Islamic, and Jewish is expanding the range of religions and belief systems observed among public school students. Lopez and Bursztyn (2013) underscore the importance of understanding that differences exist within religious subgroups as well (e.g., the Protestant faith includes evangelical, mainline, and Black congregations). Finally, lesbian, gay, bisexual, transgender, and queer (LGBTQ) youth account for 4% to 5% of the U.S. student population. As discussed later in this chapter, many students who identify as LGBTQ face unique challenges in U.S. public schools (Graybill & Proctor, 2016; Hackimer & Proctor, 2014).

CHALLENGES DIVERSE STUDENTS FACE IN U.S. PUBLIC SCHOOLS

Students from diverse racial, ethnic, linguistic, and socioeconomic backgrounds may face many challenges in their respective school environments. More specifically, they may encounter a range of barriers (some of which are readily apparent and others, which are seemingly "hidden") to academic, social, emotional, and behavioral success. The following describes several of these challenges.

Achievement Gap

National data have long captured a discrepancy in academic outcomes, or achievement gap, between Black and Hispanic students and their White peers (Castillo et al., 2013). For example, in 2015, 48% of Black and 45% of Hispanic fourth graders scored below the basic level on the National Assessment of Educational Progress (NAEP) reading assessment, as compared to 21% of White fourth graders (NCES, 2016b). This racial achievement gap is evidenced in higher grade levels as well. Specifically, 42% and 34% of Black and Hispanic eighth graders, respectively, scored below the basic level on the NAEP reading assessment as compared to 15% of White eighth graders. NAEP math achievement scores evidence similar racial gaps in achievement for Black, Hispanic, and White students in both the fourth and eighth grades. Further, findings from this assessment indicate that high percentages of students from American Indian/Alaska Native and Native Hawaiian/Other Pacific Islander backgrounds also perform below basic levels in reading and math at both the fourth and eighth grades (NCES, 2016b). Here, it is important to note that achievement gaps are also evident between fourth- and eighth-grade students from lower socioeconomic backgrounds and their peers from higher-income families. This is a particularly salient observation because children from many traditionally marginalized racial and ethnic groups (e.g., Black, Hispanic, American Indian/Native Alaskan) experience higher rates of poverty (Albritton, Anhalt, & Terry, 2016).

These data highlight the need for school psychologists and other educators to acknowledge and understand how intersectionality of racial and socioeconomic identities can influence educational outcomes. Racial and socioeconomic achievement gaps can result in specific groups of students (a) experiencing higher rates of grade retention, (b) having less access to higher level classes, and (c) dropping out of school (Ford, Wright, Washington, & Henfield, 2016; Miranda, 2014; U.S. Department of Education, 2016).

Representation in Special Programming

Other concerning issues include the over-representation of racially and ethnically diverse students in special education and, conversely, the under-representation of these students in gifted education (Ford et al., 2016; Proctor, 2016; Sullivan & Proctor, 2016). Inaccuracies in special education identification in both directions (i.e., over-identification and under-identification) can be problematic for several reasons. For example, failure to identify students who truly have a disability may limit access to needed educational services. Conversely, identifying students with a disability who, in fact, do not have a disability may result in dire consequences, such as removal from inclusive settings and restricted access to the appropriate academic services. For example, some students who receive special education services receive limited preparation for college admissions and future employment (Proctor, Graves, & Esch, 2012).

Specifically, studies frequently indicate that Black students are over-identified as having emotional disturbance and intellectual disability, whereas Native American students are over-identified as having learning disabilities (Sullivan & Proctor, 2016). Conversely, Hispanic and Asian students often are disproportionately under-identified in most educational disability categories (Sullivan &

Proctor, 2016). Unfortunately, years of research has suggested that Black students, in particular, often are identified in disability categories whose core criteria involve more subjective judgments (e.g., emotional disturbance, learning disabilities) rather than objective judgments (e.g., vision and hearing impairments) (Sullivan & Proctor, 2016). To complicate matters further, when Black and Hispanic students are deemed eligible for special education services, they often are placed in more restrictive environments than their White peers (NASP, 2013; Proctor et al., 2012). Consequently, they may have less access to the general education curriculum and population.

Regarding gifted education, Black and Hispanic students represent only 10% and 16%, respectively, of those enrolled in gifted and talented programs nationally. White students, by comparison, represent 62% of those in gifted programs (Ford et al., 2016). Additionally, fewer than 3% of students enrolled in gifted and talented programs nationwide are ELs (U.S. Department of Education, 2016). In light of the fact that Black and Hispanic students are enrolled in gifted programming at lower rates than they are enrolled in public schools altogether, it is clear that they are under-represented in these programs. Conversely, White students (who, as noted previously, account for only 45% of the public school population) are over-represented in gifted programs. The systematic under-representation of certain student populations in gifted education is highly problematic, as these students are deprived of academic enrichment, a gateway to higher education classes, and preparation for college (Ford et al., 2016).

Discipline

Research indicates that racially and ethnically diverse students are subject to more severe disciplinary practices for exhibiting similar or the same behaviors as their White peers. These disparate discipline practices (e.g., office disciplinary referrals, corporal punishment, and suspensions and expulsions) have been documented at the national level for American Indian/Alaska Native, Black, and Hispanic students (Blake, Gregory, James, & Hasan, 2016; Skiba et al., 2011). Reliance on teacher, administrator, and school psychologists' subjective judgments about these behavioral infractions presents the opportunity for bias to be introduced in disciplinary procedures (Skiba, Michael, Nardo, & Peterson, 2002; Skiba et al., 2011). Researchers have hypothesized that such bias occurs because of a cultural mismatch between majority White educators and ethnically and racially diverse students (Skiba et al., 2002, 2011).

For example, research indicates that many Black students are more likely to be disciplined for minor, subjective infractions classified as disruptive or insubordinate behavior (Skiba et al., 2002). Black students' suspension rates exceed their representation in the student population by twofold and for American Indian/Alaskan Native students, by fourfold (Blake et al., 2016). Researchers have also investigated other potential student variables (e.g., SES, disability status) that might relate to disparities in school-based discipline; however, they have found that these variables do not account for these differences (Blake et al., 2016). Thus, they have concluded that students' race is a significant predictor of over-representation in school-based discipline (Blake et al., 2016; Skiba et al., 2011).

Recent data indicate that disparate discipline practices along racial lines begin as early as pre-kindergarten. In 2013–2014, Black children made up 19% of all preschoolers, but 47% of those receiving one or more out-of-school suspensions. Conversely, White children accounted for 41% of the preschoolers, but only 28% of those receiving one or more out-of-school suspensions (U.S. Department of Education, 2016). Overall, Black female preschoolers were represented at a higher percentage (54%) than Black males (45%) among preschoolers receiving one or more out-of-school suspensions (U.S. Department of Education, 2016).

Disparate disciplinary practices constitute a major educational and social justice issue in U.S. public schools (Blake et al., 2016; NASP, 2013). These practices negatively impact individual students (e.g., loss of instructional time, academic failure, school dropout, involvement with juvenile justice system) as well as overall school climates (by rendering them less inviting, more alienating, and less welcoming and appreciative of racial diversity) (Skiba et al., 2011).

SOCIAL JUSTICE CONNECTIONS

How can school psychologists work to eliminate racial disparities in student disciplinary practices?

As noted in this chapter, racial disparities in school-based disciplinary practices are alarming and undoubtedly call for urgent systems-level reform in schools (as described in Chapter 12). Clearly, traditional models of discipline that rely heavily on in-school and out-of-school suspension practices are ineffective approaches to fostering student success. What, then, are promising alternatives to these practices?

One such model is *school-based restorative justice (SBRJ)*. Broadly defined, SBRJ is a systemic approach to discipline that engages all parties affected by a behavioral incident in proactive conflict resolution. The goals of SBRJ include teaching students to take responsibility for their actions; fostering positive relationships among students, school personnel, and community members; and teaching alternatives to inappropriate and/or aggressive behaviors in an effort to prevent their recurrence. For example, one commonly employed mechanism of SBRJ is mediation. Through mediation, school psychologists and other educators can encourage students to consider questions such as the following (developed by Zehr, 2002, and recapitulated by Song & Swearer, 2016):

1. Who was harmed? What is the extent of the harm? (By contrast, a punitive approach asks whichlaws/rules were broken.)
2. What are the needs that gave rise to the event? (By contrast, a punitive approach asks who did it.)
3. How do we make this right? How do we ensure that harm is repaired, relationships are restored, and future harm is prevented? (By contrast, a punitive approach asks which punishments the perpetrator deserves.) (Song & Swearer, 2016, pp. 317–318)

One reason that restorative justice may mitigate racial disparities in disciplinary practices is that it prevents disciplinary problems from escalating to the point of suspension, expulsion, and other severe consequences (which disproportionately impact racial minorities). It also interrupts the harmful cycle of "offend, suspend, and reoffend" by helping students understand the consequences of their behaviors and encouraging them to engage in adaptive conflict resolution skills (von der Embse, von der Embse, von der Embse, & Levine, 2009). For these reasons, SBRJ serves as a mechanism of both *prevention* and *intervention*.

(continued)

The implementation of SBRJ has been associated with a variety of positive student outcomes, including reductions in student suspensions and missed school days (e.g., Ashworth et al., 2008). Nevertheless, research on SBRJ practices is still emerging, and its implications for promoting racial justice have yet to be fully clarified. For example, Song and Swearer (2016) pose the following pressing questions regarding SBRJ:

> Does RJ (restorative justice) need to incorporate practices that are explicit about race issues for it to be effective at promoting racial equity? Are there other benefits to being explicit about race that we have not thought about? What is compromised, if anything, when RJ is nonexplicit and indirect about race issues in schools? (p. 320)

Answering each of these questions and others will be necessary for better understanding outcomes associated with SBRJ. Overall, these practices warrant further exploration and may be a promising alternative to traditional disciplinary practices.

Poverty

Poverty may also have a significant impact on the experiences and performance of diverse public school students. Again, this observation is particularly salient, as Black, Hispanic, American Indian/Alaska Native, and Native Hawaiian/Pacific Islander children are disproportionately represented in lower-income households (NCES, 2016a). For instance, students from lower-income backgrounds often begin school with less developed academic skills than their peers from middle- to upper-income backgrounds. As a result, academic achievement gaps between these groups of students often persist throughout schooling (Albritton et al., 2016; Miranda, 2014; Proctor & Meyers, 2014). Regarding disciplinary outcomes, research findings documenting the experiences of students from low-socioeconomic backgrounds are less robust. Although students from lower-income backgrounds are more likely to receive school-based discipline sanctions, research suggests that, even after controlling for SES, Black students are disciplined at a disproportionately higher rate as compared with students of other races (Skiba et al., 2011).

School Climate

Recent research has yielded concerning findings (e.g., increased levels of absenteeism, depression, and consideration of dropping out of school as well as lower self-esteem, grade-point average [GPA], and feelings of school belonging) regarding the experiences of students who identify as minorities with respect to sex or gender (Kosciw, Greytak, Giga, Villenas, & Danischewski, 2016). These findings are particularly relevant for LGBTQ students who attend unsafe schools in which they experience discrimination and victimization due to their sexual orientation and/or gender expression (Graybill & Proctor, 2016). A national examination of the experiences of middle and high school students who identify as sexual minorities found that 85.2% experienced verbal harassment based on their sexual orientation and gender expression. Moreover, 27% and 20.3% were physically harassed due to sexual orientation and gender expression, respectively (Kosciw et al., 2016).

Overall, 57.6% of the students sampled felt unsafe at school due to their sexual orientation, and 43.3% felt unsafe because of their gender expression. Results of this study also indicated that students who identify both as ethnic or racial minorities *and* sexual minorities may face additional challenges. For instance, students of color who identified as LGBTQ reported higher frequencies of victimization (due to race or ethnicity) than White students who identified as LGBTQ (Kosciw et al., 2016). These findings underscore the salience of understanding how students' intersecting identities with respect to race, sexual orientation, and gender expression can impact their daily school experiences.

Unfortunately, research exploring school-based experiences of diverse youth (including youth who are diverse with respect to race, ethnicity, linguistic background, SES, gender, and sexual orientation) often engenders a deficit-oriented perspective rather than a strengths-based perspective (Baker & Rimm-Kaufman, 2014). In other words, these research findings are framed in a manner that attributes students' difficulties to within-person deficits, thereby deemphasizing the contributions of environmental pressures and obstacles. While the data presented here are certainly concerning, the intent is not to suggest that diverse students have inherent deficits; in fact, they have a plethora of inherent strengths that enrich school environments. Rather, these data provide a foundation for understanding the variety of individual and systemic issues and injustices that diverse students and families may encounter in U.S. public schools. Ultimately, these issues highlight the need for multicultural perspectives to guide school psychological service delivery in rapidly diversifying school systems. Thus, the following section offers practice recommendations that are grounded in a multicultural and social justice–oriented approach.

RECOMMENDATIONS FOR ENHANCING MULTICULTURALISM AND SOCIAL JUSTICE IN SCHOOL PSYCHOLOGY PRACTICE

Develop Personal Awareness and Knowledge of Self as Intersectional

One of the first steps to implementing a multicultural framework is to acknowledge and understand one's own culture and recognize how it influences one's worldview (Miranda, 2014). It is also important to identify salient facets of one's identity (e.g., gender, gender identity, race, ethnicity, sexual orientation, religious affiliation) and the ways in which these facets intersect to influence one's view of the world.

Self-examination with respect to cultural beliefs and worldview can be a difficult and arduous task. It involves, for example, considering one's own experiences with oppression and/or *privilege*. **Privilege** refers to the set of unearned benefits, advantages, and opportunities that are afforded to an individual simply due to his or her membership in a particular social group. In other words, while the oppression of some traditionally marginalized social groups (e.g., racial minorities) may be acknowledged, the corresponding advantages afforded to non-victimized groups (e.g., Whites) typically go unrecognized. Generally, these privileges manifest in seemingly inconspicuous ways. Individuals from many types of social groups may hold privilege, including those who identify as White, male, and heterosexual. In her seminal work, *White Privilege: Unpacking the Invisible Knapsack*, Peggy

McIntosh (1989) provides numerous examples of White privilege. Writing from the perspective of a White individual, McIntosh states the following:

1. I can be sure that my children will be given curricular materials that testify to the existence of their race.
2. I am never asked to speak for all the people of my racial group.
3. I can take a job with an affirmative action employer without having coworkers on the job suspect that I got it because of race.

While these privileges often go unrecognized on a daily basis, they play an important role in maintaining oppressive social structures and interpersonal dynamics that negatively impact the lives of racial and ethnic minorities.

Although a trying and, at times, daunting task, examining one's own experiences with marginalization and privilege is key to becoming an effective school psychologist. This may be a challenge for some individuals who are not necessarily inclined to view themselves through a diversity lens. Nevertheless, all humans possess personal identity features that influence their life experiences and the ways in which they make sense of the world. For example, most school psychologists identify as White and female. These two intersecting identities influence how many practitioners experience life in the United States (both inside and outside of schools) and can be associated with both privilege (as a White individual) and marginality (as a female).

How a White female school psychologist views the world is also influenced by other identity features, such as social class, religious affiliation, sexual orientation, immigration status, and so forth. Developing personal awareness of one's own identity features and how they intersect to influence personal assumptions, beliefs, and values can facilitate understanding of diverse students and their experiences, perspectives, and behaviors. Gaining awareness and knowledge of self as an intersectional being requires self-reflection and can help school psychologists examine personal biases that might impact their service delivery, as described in the next section.

Identify and Challenge Biases

Although often difficult, and sometimes painful to admit, all people hold biases for and against certain groups. Such biases often arise as a result of our backgrounds, firmly held beliefs, life experiences, and exposure (or lack thereof) to those outside of our own groups. These biases have the potential to impede school psychologists' effective engagement with youth, families, and educators, thereby impacting the quality of services delivered. Moreover, harboring potential biases reduces the likelihood that the school psychologist will engage in advocacy behaviors at the systems level (e.g., school level). Personal biases can impact the way school psychologists approach virtually all job functions and areas of practice (e.g., disability identification, gifted identification, and disciplinary practices)

For instance, consider a school psychologist who is asked to provide counseling services to a student who identifies as bisexual. This school psychologist would need to critically examine any conscious or subconscious personal beliefs and/

or biases about sexual-minority youth, and in particular, bisexual youth. Using a multicultural approach to guide his or her practice, the school psychologist would attend to issues related to sexual orientation (if brought up and considered relevant by the student) and seek to understand how the student's experiences impact his or her overall well-being. In turn, the school psychologist would empower the individual to employ appropriate coping strategies, and when applicable, self-advocacy strategies. In considering the potentially larger social justice issues at play, the school psychologist may also advocate for school policies that seek to prevent victimization of and discrimination against LGBTQ students. Overall, identifying and challenging personal biases is an imperative and foundational step toward applying principles of multiculturalism and social justice.

Increase Knowledge of Diverse Populations

School psychologists must also be knowledgeable about the challenges facing diverse students and seek up-to-date information about educational and social issues that permeate school environments (Lopez & Bursztyn, 2013; Proctor & Meyers, 2014). This is importantbecause it is difficult to provide culturally competent school psychological services and/or to advocate for diverse populations without a clear understanding of issues that impact their access to quality educational experiences, safe school environments, and appropriate mental health supports. School psychologists can increase their knowledge about diverse student groups by (a) attending professional development sessions focused on diverse populations at local and national conferences, (b) critically consuming current research about diverse students and populations and (c) seeking out community resources that enhance their multicultural knowledge (Newell et al., 2010). Notably, accessing local community resources can afford school psychologists invaluable insights into the cultural values, beliefs, and inherent strengths of the specific population(s) they serve. Further, Proctor and Meyers (2014) recommended that school psychologists join professional organizations dedicated to uplifting diverse student populations (e.g., the National Black Child Development Institute), develop supportive networks with other professionals who are engaged in social justice work, and access resources (e.g., books, websites, videos) that address education and diversity issues. Table 4.1 provides resources that may assist practitioners in increasing their knowledge of diverse student populations.

Share and Improve Skills Related to Working With Diverse Students

School psychologists have a responsibility to enhance their skills in serving diverse student populations and, when appropriate, to share these skills with other school professionals. For instance, school psychologists are sometimes called upon to help school-based problem-solving teams analyze and interpret school-wide data. In line with a social justice orientation, school psychologists participating in these teams can teach their colleagues how to examine data to determine whether educational injustices (e.g., racial disparities in discipline referrals) are present. If findings reveal that such disparities exist, school psychologists can share with staff

TABLE 4.1 Resources for Increasing Knowledge About Diverse Student Populations

Name of Resource	Source	Content
Civil Rights Project at UCLA	civilrightsproject.ucla.edu	Effective educational practices for ELLs, long-term implications of U.S. demographic shifts, racial disparities in school discipline and special education
EdChange	www.edchange.org	Diversity awareness activities; diversity climate assessments for schools and organizations; journal articles, books, and essays on multicultural education and social justice
Gay, Lesbian, and& Straight Education Network (GLSEN)	www.glsen.org	Research and evaluation on LGBT issues in K–12 education
National Center for Cultural Competence	www.nccc.georgetown.edu	Cultural competence checklists, cultural competence curricula for mental health providers, content related to specific subgroups
National Association of School Psychologists	www.nasponline.org	Information on marginalized students, social justice, disability rights, and school psychology roles and responsibilities
Southern Poverty Law Center	www.splcenter.org	Information on children at risk, immigrant justice, LGBTQ rights, and teaching tolerance

ELL, English language learner; LGBTQ, lesbian, gay, bisexual, transgender, and queer; UCLA, University of California, Los Angeles.

skills they have developed in areas such as culturally responsive classroom management strategies, restorative justice practices (described in further detail in the section of this chapter), and collaborative problem solving.

The development of multicultural competence is a lifelong pursuit (Miranda, Radliff, Cooper, & Eschenbrenner, 2014), so school psychologists should continually strive to improve their own skills in serving diverse students. In addition to employing the strategies described in the preceding text, school psychologists can seek consultation from other professionals who have expertise in working with particular populations. When and if it becomes apparent that school-wide professional development is needed, school psychologists can work with administrators to coordinate such activities.

SUMMARY AND CONCLUSIONS

In conclusion, school psychologists should consider diversity in all aspects of their service delivery. The use of multicultural and social justice frameworks provides a practice foundation for engaging diverse clients. The ever-increasing diversity of the U.S. population necessitates school psychologists' critical attention to providing culturally relevant, competent, and effective service delivery to diverse children, families, and schools.

DISCUSSION QUESTIONS

1. How has the historical under-representation of diverse school psychologists impacted the field?
2. What are some of the challenges diverse students experience in U.S. public schools? How might the challenges diverse students experience in U.S. public schools be impacted by their intersecting identities?
3. How does the use of multiculturalism guide school psychologists' service delivery to diverse students?
4. If you were a school psychologist, what are some of your intersecting identities that might influence, either positively or negatively, your service delivery to diverse students? How might these identities influence your practice?
5. What are some actions school psychologists can take to increase their knowledge of and skills in working with diverse student populations?

REFERENCES

Albritton, K., Anhalt, K., & Terry, N. P. (2016). Promoting equity for our nation's youngest students: School psychologists as agents of social justice in early childhood settings. *School Psychology Forum: Research in Practice, 10*, 237–250.

Ashworth, J., Van Bockern, S., Ailts, J., Donelly, J., Erickson, K., & Woltermann, J. (2008). An alternative to school detention. *Reclaiming Children & Youth, 17*(3), 22–26.

Baker, C. E., & Rim-Kaufman, S. E. (2014). How homes influence schools: Early parenting predicts African American children's classroom social–emotional functioning. *Psychology in the Schools, 51*, 722–735. doi:10.1002/pits.21781

Banks, J. A. (2010). Multicultural education: Characteristics and goals. In J. A. Banks & C. A. M. Banks (Eds.), *Multicultural education: Issues and perspective* (5th ed., pp. 3–26). Hoboken, NJ: Wiley.

Blake, J. J., Gregory, A., James, M., & Hasan, G. W. (2016). Early warning signs: Identifying opportunities to disrupt racial inequities in school discipline through data-based decision making. *School Psychology Forum: Research in Practice, 10*, 289–306.

Carroll, D. W. (2009). Toward multicultural competence: A practical model for implementation in the schools. In J. M. Jones (Ed.), *The psychology of multiculturalism in schools* (pp. 1–16). Bethesda, MD: National Association of School Psychologists.

Castillo, J. M., Curtis, M. J., & Gelley, C. D. (2013). Gender and race in school psychology. *School Psychology Review, 42*, 262–279.

Cooper, B. (2016). Intersectionality. In L. Disch & M. Hawkesworth (Eds.), *The Oxford handbook of feminist theory* (pp. 385–406). New York, NY: Oxford University Press.

Curtis, M. J., Castillo, J. M., & Gelley, C. (2012). School psychology 2010: Demographics, employment, and the context for professional practices-part 1. *Communiqué, 40*(7), 1, 28–29.

Ford, D. Y., Wright, B. L., Washington, A., & Henfield, M. S. (2016). Access and equity denied: Key theories for school psychologists to consider when assessing Black and Hispanic students for gifted education. *School Psychology Forum: Research in Practice, 10*, 265–277.

Graybill, E., & Proctor, S. L. (2016). Lesbian, gay, bisexual, and transgender youth: Limited representation in school support personnel journals. *Journal of School Psychology, 54*, 9–16.

Hackimer, L., & Proctor, S. L. (2015). Considering the community influence for gay, lesbian, bisexual, and transgender youth. *Journal of Youth Studies, 18*, 277–290.

Hakuta, K. (2011). Educating language minority students and affirming their equal rights: Research and practical perspectives. *Educational Researcher, 40*, 163–174.

Husser, W. J., & Bailey, T. M. (2011). *Projections of education statistics to 2020* (NCES 2011-026). Washington, DC: National Center for Education Statistics.

Kosciw, J. G., Greytak, E. A., Giga, N. M., Villenas, C., & Danischewski, D. J. (2016). *The 2015 National School Climate Survey: The experiences of lesbian, gay, bisexual, transgender, and queer youth in our nation's schools*. New York, NY: GLSEN. Retrieved from https://www.glsen.org/article/2015-national-school-climate-survey

Lopez, E. C., & Bursztyn, A. M. (2013). Future challenges and opportunities: Toward culturally responsive training in school psychology. *Psychology in the Schools, 50*, 212–228. doi:10.1002/pits.21674

McIntosh, P. (1989). White privilege: Unpacking the invisible knapsack. *Peace and Freedom*, 10–12.

Miranda, A. H. (2014). Best practices in increasing cross-cultural competency. In P. Harrison & A. Thomas (Eds.), *Best practices in school psychology: Foundations*. (pp. 9–19). Bethesda, MD: National Association of School Psychologists.

Miranda, A. H., & Gutter, P. B. (2002). Diversity research literature in school psychology: 1990–1999. *Psychology in the Schools, 39*, 597–604. doi:10.1002/pits.10051

Miranda, A., Radliff, K. M., Cooper, J., & Eschenbrenner, C. (2014). Graduate student perceptions of the impact of training for social justice: Development of a training model. *Psychology in the Schools, 51*, 348–365. doi:10.1002/pits.21755

National Association of School Psychologists. (2013). *Racial and ethnic disproportionality in education* [Position statement]). Bethesda, MD: Author.

National Center for Educational Statistics. (2016a). *Condition of education 2016*. Washington, DC: Author.

National Center for Educational Statistics. (2016b). *The nation's report card 2015: Mathematics and reading assessments*. Retrieved from https://www.nationsreportcard.gov/reading_math_2015/#mathematics?grade=4

Newell, M. L., Nastasi, B. K., Hatzichristou, C., Jones, J. M., Schanding, G. T. Jr., & Yetter, G. (2010). Evidence on multicultural training in school psychology: Recommendations for future directions. *School Psychology Quarterly, 25*, 249–278. doi:10.1037/a0021542

Proctor, S. L. (2016). Introduction to the special issue: Encouraging racial and social justice throughout the pre-K to graduate school pipeline. *School Psychology Forum: Research in Practice, 10*, 233–236.

Proctor, S. L., Graves, S. L. Jr., & Esch, R. C. (2012). Assessing African American students for specific learning disabilities: The promises and perils of response to intervention. *Journal of Negro Education, 81*, 268–282. doi:10.7709/jnegroeducation.81.3.0268

Proctor, S. L., & Meyers, J. (2014). Best practices in primary prevention in diverse schools and communities. In P. Harrison & A. Thomas (Eds.), *Best practices in school psychology: Foundations*. (pp. 33–47). Bethesda, MD: National Association of School Psychologists.

Proctor, S. L., & Romano, M. (2016). School psychology recruitment research characteristics and implications for increasing racial and ethnic diversity. *School Psychology Quarterly, 31*, 311–326. doi:10.1037/spq0000154

Proctor, S. L., & Simpson, C. (2016). Improving service delivery to ethnic minority youth through improved program training. In S. L. Graves & J. Blake (Eds.). *Psychoeducational assessment and intervention for ethnic minority children: Evidence-based approaches* (pp. 251–265). Washington, DC: American Psychological Association.

Proctor, S. L., Simpson, C. M., Levin, J., & Hackimer, L. (2014). Recruitment of diverse students in school psychology programs: Direction for future research and practice. *Contemporary School Psychology*, 117–126. doi:10.1007/s40688-014-0012-z

Proctor, S. L., & Truscott, S. D. (2012). Reasons for African American student attrition from school psychology programs. *Journal of School Psychology, 50*, 655–679. doi:10.1016/j.jsp.2012.06.002

Proctor, S. L., & Truscott, S. D. (2013). Missing voices: African American school psychologists' perspectives on increasing professional diversity. *Urban Review, 45*, 355–375. doi:10.1007/s11256-012-0232-3

Shriberg, D., Bonner, M., Sarr, B. J., Walker, A. M., Hyland, M., & Chester, C. (2008). Social justice through a school psychology lens: Definitions and applications. *School Psychology Review, 37*, 453–468.

Skiba, R. J., Horner, R. H., Chung, C-G., Rausch, M. K., May, S. L., & Tobin, T. (2011). Race is not neutral: A national investigation of African American and Latino disproportionality in school discipline. *School Psychology Review, 40*, 85–107.

Skiba, R. J., Michael, R. S., Nardo, A. C., & Peterson, R. (2002). The color of discipline: Sources of racial and gender disproportionality in school punishment. *Urban Review, 34,* 317–342. doi:10.1023/A:1021320817372

Song, S. Y. & Swearer, S. M. (2016). The cart before the horse: The challenge and promise of restorative justice consultation in schools. *Journal of Educational and Psychological Consultation, 26*(4), 313–324. doi:10.1080/10474412.2016.1246972

Speight, S. L., & Vera, E. M. (2009). The challenge of social justice for school psychology. *Journal of Educational and Psychological Consultation, 19,* 82–92. doi:10.1080/10474410802463338

Suárez-Orozco, C., Casanova, S., Martin, M., Katsiaficas, D., Cuellar, V., Smith, N. A., & Dias, S. A. (2015). Toxic rain in class: Classroom interpersonal microaggressions. *Educational Researcher, 44,* 151–160. doi:10.3102/0013189X15580314

Sullivan, A., & Proctor, S. L. (2016). The shield or the sword? Revisiting the debate on disproportionality in special education and implications for school psychologists. *School Psychology Forum: Research in Practice, 10,* 278–288.

U.S. Department of Education. (2016). 2013–2014 civil rights data collection: A first look. Retrieved from http://www.attendanceworks.org/research/u-s-department-education-civil-rights-data-collection

von der Embse, N., von der Embse, D., von der Embse, M., & Levine, I. (2009). Applying social justice principles through school-based restorative justice. *NASP Communique, 38*(3), 18–19.

Walcott, C. M., Charvat, J., McNamara, K. M., & Hyson, D. M. (2016, February). *School psychology at a glance: 2015 member survey results.* Special session presented at the annual meeting of the National Association of School Psychologists, New Orleans, LA.

Zehr, H. (2002). *The little book of restorative justice.* Intercourse, PA: Good Books.

CHAPTER 5

Ethical and Legal Foundations

BARBARA BOLE WILLIAMS ■ LAURA W. MONAHON

CHAPTER OBJECTIVES

- Define and differentiate between law, ethics, and applied professional ethics
- Understand the similarities and differences between various codes of ethics in professional school psychology
- Describe the four broad principles encompassed in the National Association of School Psychologists' *Principles for Professional Ethics*
- Describe the impact that legislation, including federal and state education and civil rights laws, has had on professional school psychology, both historically and currently
- Illustrate applications of a problem-solving model to solve ethically challenging situations or dilemmas

As described in Chapter 1, Domain 10 of the National Association of School Psychologists (NASP, 2010a) Practice Model dictates that school psychologists should be knowledgeable about ethical, legal, and professional standards for practice. Moreover, they must be competent in delivering services in accordance with these standards and engage in responsible ethical and legal decision making. As described previously, Domain 10 is one of three domains in the NASP Practice Model that is identified as a foundational area of practice, meaning that professional knowledge and skills in this area are essential for supporting practice in all other domains. Indeed, legal and ethical issues underlie all types of service delivery in school psychology, and practitioners must be mindful of whether they are operating within the parameters of state and federal laws as well as professional codes of ethics. This chapter describes the nature of legal and ethical codes that govern school psychology service delivery. Moreover, it presents models for ethical decision making and describes their applications.

DEFINING LAW AND ETHICS

One might ask, *How are law and ethics related?* and *Why should law and ethics be studied in tandem?* To answer these questions, one must first consider the definitions of the terms *law*, *ethics*, and *applied professional ethics*. According to Williams, Armistead, and Jacob (2008), **law** is defined as "a body of rules of conduct prescribed by the state that has binding legal force" (p. 10). These same authors define **ethics** as "a system of principles of conduct that guide the behavior of an individual" (p. 1). Finally, **applied professional ethics** refers to the application of such broad ethical principles and specific rules to problems that arise in professional practice (Beauchamp & Childress, 2001). More simply stated, *laws* are rules of conduct prescribed by the government that have binding legal force, and *ethics* comprises a range of acceptable (or unacceptable) social and personal behaviors, from rules of etiquette to more basic rules of society (Armistead, Williams, & Jacob, 2011). In the context of this chapter, we focus primarily on *applied professional ethics* in school psychology, meaning the ways in which professional codes of ethics are applied in practice.

Returning to our earlier question, why should ethics and law be studied in tandem? One answer is that ethics and law are closely related and both provide a form of quality control over school psychologists' professional interaction with others, including students, parents and guardians, teachers, principals, and other school personnel. In essence, ethics and law comprise procedures for school psychology practice and, therefore, guide school psychologists' behavior.

The relationship between ethics and law becomes particularly evident when situations arise that require a school psychologist to look to both areas for guidance in problem solving. Situations like these are often referred to as **dilemmas**, which implies that the presenting problem does not have one clear-cut solution but rather many alternatives that should be considered carefully before arriving at a plan of action. In these situations, a school psychologist must look to both ethical and legal guidelines to solve the problem. According to Jacob, Decker, and Lugg (2016), professional codes of ethics are "generally viewed as requiring decisions that are 'more correct or more stringent' than required by law" (p. 22). Further, Jacob and colleagues recommend that if ethical responsibilities of school psychologists conflict with law, school psychologists should clarify the nature of the conflict and attempt to resolve it in a responsible manner.

One of the hallmarks of a profession is the development of a code of ethics that helps to guide the behavior of professionals. A **code of ethics** is a body of principles and guidelines (typically developed and endorsed by a professional organization or other entity) for engaging in equitable and morally sound professional behaviors that ensure the well-being of affected parties. Additionally, in school psychology, Williams et al. (2008) posit that codes of ethics are developed for the purposes of (a) protecting the public and maintaining public trust, (b) showing the profession's commitment to self-regulation, (c) enhancing the prestige of the profession, (d) educating professionals and assisting them in monitoring their own behavior, and (e) providing guidelines for adjudicating complaints.

For school psychologists, three primary ethical codes may govern the practice of school psychology: the American Psychological Association's (APA, 2002)

Ethical Principles of Psychologists and Code of Conduct; the NASP's (2010b) *Principles for Professional Ethics* (NASP-PPE), and the International School Psychology Association's (ISPA, 2011) *Code of Ethics*. Whereas the ethical codes of the APA apply to professional psychologists in many areas (e.g., clinical psychologists, counseling psychologists, school psychologists), the ethical codes of ISPA and NASP focus exclusively on the practice of school psychology. Each of these ethical codes is described in the following sections.

ETHICAL GUIDELINES OF THE APA

The *Ethical Standards of Psychologists* was adopted by the APA initially in 1952 and subsequently has been revised and amended 10 times (Fisher, 2017). The APA's current code of ethics, ***Ethical Principles of Psychologists and Code of Conduct*** (heretofore referred to as the **APA Ethics Code**), includes both aspirational goals and enforceable rules for conduct (APA, 2002). The code's aspirational principles (i.e., broad, guiding principles) mirror those developed by Ross (1930) and include (a) beneficence and nonmaleficence, (b) fidelity and responsibility, (c) integrity, (d) justice, and (e) respect for people's rights and dignity (Knapp & VandeCreek, 2005). The enforceable rules for conduct provide more specific guidelines for behavior across a variety of professional activities.

While the adoption of the original APA Ethics Code in 1952 represented a breakthrough in the field of psychology in terms of ethical standards and codes of conduct, it soon became clear that there was a need for specific disciplines within the field of professional psychology to develop specialized ethical guidelines and codes of conduct. In 1974, NASP addressed emerging ethical and legal issues in school psychology in a special issue of *School Psychology Digest* (now *School Psychology Review*; Kaplan, Crisci, & Farling, 1974). Proponents of a specialized code of ethics and conduct for school psychology felt that the existing APA Ethics Code (which, at that time, had been most recently revised in 1963) could not be readily applied to practitioners who worked within a school system (Trachtman, 1974). In addition, the existing APA Ethics Code did not address issues that were critical to professional school psychologists. These issues included balancing the interests of children with the rights of parents, including students in educational and mental health decision-making processes, defining boundaries of confidentiality within a school setting, and ensuring fair and valid assessments of students from diverse cultural and linguistic backgrounds (Jacob, 2008). In addition to these issues, another topic central to decision making in the profession of school psychology remained largely unaddressed—namely, the resolution of conflicts that resulted from serving in the dual roles of child advocate and school employee (Armistead et al., 2011; Bersoff, 1983; Trachtman, 1974). In an effort to address these issues, NASP developed and adopted the first iteration of its ***Principles for Professional Ethics (NASP-PPE)*** in 1974. Since that date, the NASP code of ethics has been revised five times, most recently in 2010. As of the writing of this chapter, revisions to the existing NASP-PPE are under way. It is anticipated that these revisions will be completed and approved by the NASP leadership by 2020.

THE NASP PRINCIPLES OF PROFESSIONAL ETHICS

As previously described, the APA Ethics Code was developed for psychologists trained in a variety of specialty areas and settings, including private practice, industry, hospitals and clinics, public schools, postsecondary institutions, and research settings (APA, 2002; Williams & Armistead, 2010). NASP developed and adopted its *Principles for Professional Ethics* to address specifically the practice of school psychology (NASP, 2010b). *Williams and Armistead (2010) describe the NASP-PPE as the ethical guidelines most school psychologists use as a resource to guide their practice.*

When a school psychologist joins NASP, he or she agrees to abide by the guidelines set forth in the NASP-PPE in all professional interactions with consumers of school psychological services (e.g., students, parents, school personnel, and colleagues) (NASP, 2010b). Some school psychologists may seek membership in both NASP and APA, in which case they are beholden to apply both the NASP-PPE and the APA Ethics Code. Jacob (2005) further notes that school psychology students and practitioners should be familiar with both ethics codes, as doing so will likely bolster the individual's knowledge of ethical principles and standards more generally. This knowledge can, in turn, increase the practitioner's ability to anticipate and possibly prevent ethical problems from occurring, and if a challenging situation does arise, prepares the practitioner to make ethically and legally sound choices (Jacob, 2005).

Like the APA's Code of Ethics, the NASP-PPE encompasses and endeavors to codify the "moral duties" outlined by Ross (1930), including nonmaleficence, fidelity, beneficence, justice, and autonomy (NASP, 2010b). The NASP-PPE also provides a framework (i.e., a code of conduct) for the application of these moral duties within the scope of professional duty (i.e., applied professional ethics). The NASP-PPE includes two fundamental underlying principles that are introduced at the outset of the document. First, school psychologists must act as advocates for their clients (i.e., students). Second, they must, at the very least, do no harm (NASP, 2010b). The NASP-PPE also addresses four broad ethical themes with regard to professional ethical competence: (1) respecting the dignity and rights of all persons, (2) professional competence and responsibility, (3) honesty and integrity in professional relationships, and (4) responsibility to schools, families, communities, the profession, and society (NASP, 2010b). Each of these areas is further discussed as follows.

Respecting the Dignity and Rights of All Persons

As outlined in the NASP-PPE, a fundamental responsibility of school psychology practitioners is to engage only in those practices that promote and maintain the dignity of all individuals. Inherent in this principle is the need for school psychologists to consider the constructs of personal autonomy, self-determination, and privacy when working with individuals and their families (Armistead et al., 2011). Additionally, all professional school psychologists have an ethical responsibility to uphold "a commitment to just and fair treatment of all persons" (NASP, 2010b, p. 3).

Informed consent is one method by which school psychologists seek to maintain a client's self-determination and autonomy. Put simply, professional school psychologists must ensure that individuals with whom they work have a "voice and a choice" in all decision-making processes (Armistead et al., 2011, p. 6). Not all professional services provided by a school psychologist, however, require informed consent. For example, if a school psychologist is serving on a multidisciplinary team or making recommendations to a classroom teacher regarding an intervention that is within the scope of a typical classroom intervention, he or she is not required to obtain informed consent from the parent(s) of the child or children who may be recipient(s) of the consultative services (Armistead et al., 2011; Burns, Jacob, & Wagner, 2008; Corrao & Melton, 1988). This example underscores the need for an ethical code of conduct specific to school psychologists, as their professional duties frequently are shaped by their work settings. It also reinforces the notion that practicing school psychologists must be knowledgeable about their code of professional ethics and its application in a variety of situations.

NASP recognizes that school psychologists often are required to advocate for students within the school system in which they are employed. Similarly, it is important to acknowledge that school psychologists must maintain relationships with a variety of individuals, groups, and systems across the scope of their professional duties. Generally speaking, school psychologists must strive to develop relationships that improve the quality of the life of children, their families, and the school community (Williams & Armistead, 2010). At times, however, negotiating the best interests of all parties can be a challenging task. For example, when school psychologists employed by a school board make professional decisions regarding students in their district, they are obligated to maintain knowledge and respect for these students' rights under both state and federal law (NASP, 2010b, p. 2). While, on the surface, this task seems straightforward, school psychologists must be able to balance the authority of parents to participate in educational decision making with the needs and rights of children. To complicate matters further, all decisions must be made in light of the "purposes and authority" of the school system (NASP, 2010b, p. 2). Although the NASP-PPE recognizes that it can be difficult to balance the wishes of involved parties while observing school, state, and federal policies, the responsibility to resolve these types of situations in an ethically and legally sound manner clearly rests on the school psychologist. To illustrate this point, the introductory section of the NASP-PPE states, "It is expected that school psychologists will make careful, reasoned, and principled ethical choices based on knowledge of [the] code, recognizing that responsibility for ethical conduct rests within the individual practitioner" (NASP, 2010b, Introduction).

Professional Competence and Responsibility

Beneficence, or responsible caring, is a common theme across many professional ethical codes of conduct. In the field of school psychology, beneficence is achieved through engaging in actions that are likely to benefit others, practicing within the boundaries of professional competence, using evidence-based knowledge to guide decision making, and accepting responsibility for professional decisions (Armistead et al., 2011; Welfel & Kitchener, 1992).

The NASP-PPE further stipulates that school psychologists act as advocates for children across every facet of their practice (NASP, 2010b). This requires school psychologists to be knowledgeable about best practices across the various types of services they provide. For example, consider a case in which a school psychologist is asked to evaluate a student and share assessment results with relevant stake-holders (i.e., the student, his or her parents, and appropriate school personnel). Under the guidelines of the NASP-PPE, the practitioner must select appropriate, empirically supported, valid, and reliable assessment measures as well as admin-ister them in the standardized manner outlined in the test materials. Next, the school psychologist must report assessment results using language that is under-standable and meaningful, rather than presenting unedited computerized reports as his or her own (NASP, 2010b). Moreover, according to the NASP-PPE, all rel-evant data must be reported in a manner that best serves the school psychologist's primary client (i.e., the student) and must be shared only with those individuals who will be actively involved in the development, delivery, and monitoring of sub-sequent interventions (e.g., parents/guardians and appropriate school personnel). As illustrated in this example, the NASP-PPE not only provides aspirational goals for professional service delivery, but also delineates the proper procedures for specific activities (NASP, 2010b).

Honesty and Integrity in Professional Relationships

In addition to beneficence, school psychologists must demonstrate fidelity in all professional duties (Armistead et al., 2011). Bersoff and Koeppl (1992) define fidelity as continuing faithfulness to the truth and to one's professional duties. As such, school psychologists must be honest about the boundaries of their compe-tence and must accurately represent the services they are able to provide, based on their training and credentials (NASP, 2010b). They also must be able to explain the scope of their services to clients and families in a clear and straightforward manner. In the same vein, school psychologists must be respectful of the partici-pation and competencies of other professionals who are involved with clients and their families (NASP, 2010b).

Included in the principle of honesty and integrity is the directive that school psychology practitioners abstain from any activity in which their own personal problems might interfere with their professional effectiveness (Williams & Armistead, 2010). In the event that such a situation should arise, school psycholo-gists should seek assistance from supervisors and/or colleagues and make every effort to resolve conflicts in an ethically sound manner (Armistead et al., 2011). Finally, to maintain the highest standards of professional competence, the NASP-PPE indicates that school psychologists must be responsible for knowing and actively applying the code within their practice (NASP, 2010b). As Williams and Armistead (2010) summarize, "Ignorance of the ethical code is no excuse" (p. 18).

Responsibility to Schools, Families, Communities, the Profession, and Society

As members of a helping profession, school psychologists must promote healthy school, family, and community environments (Armistead et al., 2011). In addition to acting in ways that maintain safe and healthy environments for all clients and families, the NASP-PPE further charges school psychologists with the duty of assuming a proactive role in counteracting social injustices that affect children and schools (NASP, 2010b). While school psychologists can work on an individual level to ensure that the students and families under their direct care are treated fairly and justly, they also should strive to be a part of systems-level change to secure socially just environments for all.

CODE OF ETHICS OF ISPA

ISPA, founded in 1982, adopted an international code of ethics in 2011 (ISPA, 2011). *ISPA's Code of Ethics* contains six principles that constitute aspirational behaviors. The six principles that form the basis of ISPA's Code of Ethics are (1) beneficence and nonmaleficence, (2) competence, (3) fidelity and responsibility, (4) integrity, (5) respect for people's rights and dignity, and (6) social justice. In addition, the ISPA Code of Ethics contains four professional standards: (1) professional responsibilities, (2) confidentiality, (3) professional growth, and (4) professional limitations, as well as three professional practices describing (1) professional relationships, (2) assessment, and (3) research. As written, the ISPA Code of Ethics is not intended to supersede national codes of ethics but rather to reflect principles and standards from an international perspective.

PUBLIC LEGISLATION RELEVANT TO THE PRACTICE OF SCHOOL PSYCHOLOGY

To trace the influence of legislation relevant to the practice of school psychology, one must begin with the U.S. Constitution. Considered the "supreme law of the land" and adopted in 1787, the U.S. Constitution outlines the federal government's role as the protector of the rights and liberties of the people. The U.S. Constitution does not guarantee the provision of education to U.S. citizens; however, the 10th Amendment to the Constitution indicates that this responsibility rests within individual states. Moreover, the U.S. Constitution and the 14th Amendment provide the basis for contemporary special education law through the *equal protection clause* and *due process rights* (Jacob, Decker, & Lugg, 2016). The **equal protection clause** prohibits states from denying any individual in its territory equal protection under the law. **Due process** requires government officials to afford all individuals fair and equal treatment through the judicial system. So, while the provision of education is a matter of individual states' rights, the Supreme Court of the United States becomes involved in and arbitrates states' jurisdiction over public education when it is believed that civil rights guaranteed under the Constitution have been violated.

Individuals With Disabilities Education Improvement Act

In 1975, the U.S. Congress passed legislation titled *Public Law 94-142*, which, among other mandates, ensures that all children with disabilities are entitled to a *free and appropriate public education (FAPE).* The legislation also mandates that such an education must be provided in the *least restrictive environment* appropriate to meet students' needs. The **least restrictive environment (LRE)** refers to the environment, educational setting, or placement in which the child is educated with peers without disabilities to the maximum extent possible. In 1977, Congress reauthorized this legislation under the new title of the Education for All Handicapped Children Act (EHA). In 1990, EHA was again reauthorized under the Individuals with Disabilities Education Act (IDEA; 1990, 1997), which was subsequently revised and reauthorized under the **Individuals with Disabilities Education Improvement Act (IDEIA) of 2004** (IDEIA, 2004). Under Part B of IDEIA (2004), the federal government allocates funds to those states that provide assurances that all students with disabilities ages 3 to 21 years are provided FAPE. According to the Institute for Education Sciences' (IES) National Center for Educational Statistics (NCES), in 2013 through 2014 (the most recently reported data available), there were more than 6,464,000 students with disabilities between the ages of 3 and 21 years in the United States who received services through an Individualized Education Program (IEP).

This series of statutes forms the basis for federal education law that governs special education and directly impacts the professional practice of school psychology. Murdick, Gartin, and Crabtree (2007) outline six basic principles of special education legislation. These principles require that a child with a disability be provided (1) an FAPE for all children with disabilities; (2) the guarantee of a non-discriminatory assessment process for identifying any potential disabilities; (3) an IEP (defined in the following text) to ensure the entitled instruction and services are provided to the student with a disability; (4) the right to be educated within the LRE (e.g., inclusion in general education classes to the greatest extent possible); (5) the right to procedural due process, should there be a disagreement between parties; and (6) the assurance of parents' rights and procedural safeguards to facilitate their participation in educational decision making. As already mentioned, an **Individualized Education Program (IEP)** is a comprehensive plan detailing the specific disability services to which a student is entitled to support his or her access to the curriculum and participation in the school community. Such services may include psychological counseling, speech and language therapy, occupational therapy, academic support services, and testing accommodations. IEPs also document goals for student growth and are developed jointly by parents, teachers, special services staff (e.g., school psychologists), and students (when they are old enough to participate in the process).

Section 504 of the Rehabilitation Act of 1973

Section 504 of the Rehabilitation Act of 1973 is a civil rights legislation that prohibits discrimination against individuals with disabilities (Jacob et al., 2016). This law applies to all schools that receive federal funding. Jacob et al. (2016) assert that a contemporary interpretation of Section 504 requires schools to address three types of potential discrimination. First, it prohibits public schools from excluding students from participating in school programs solely on the basis of their disability. Second, it requires schools to take steps to prevent harassment on the basis of students' disability. Third, it requires schools to provide "reasonable" accommodations for students with disabilities, such that they have equal opportunity to benefit from programs that are also provided to students without disabilities. Thus, under this civil rights law, students who are identified as having a disability (as interpreted by Section 504) are entitled to an accommodation plan, often referred to as a **504 Plan**. Similar to an IEP, a 504 Plan stipulates the services and accommodations to which a student with a disability is entitled in school. Unlike under IDEIA, however, the federal government does not contribute funds to assist with the cost of services provided under Section 504.

Differences Between IDEIA and Section 504

One important distinction between Section 504 of the Rehabilitation Act and IDEIA concerns the way in which these two laws define the term *disability*. Under IDEIA, Part B, students suspected of having a disability must be evaluated in accordance with procedures outlined in Part B and, subsequently, must be deemed eligible for special education and related services under 1 of 13 categories of disability. These 13 IDEIA categories (in alphabetical order) are as follows: autism spectrum disorders, deaf–blindness, deafness, emotional disturbance, hearing impairment, intellectual disability, multiple disabilities,orthopedic impairment, other health impaired, specific learning disability,; speech or language impairment, traumatic brain injury, and visual impairment including blindness (34 CFR & 300.S). Under IDEIA, determining special education eligibility requires a two-pronged approach; in addition to meeting criteria for 1 of the 13 disability categories, the student must demonstrate a *need* for special education services (i.e., the disability impedes the student's access to the general curriculum; Reschly, 2000).

Under Section 504, the definition of a *disability* is broader and more open-ended than under IDEIA (Jacob et al., 2016). This legislation defines a disability as a "physical or mental impairment that substantially limits one or more of major life activities" (Source 28 CRF § 35.104). Major life activities include, but are not limited to, caring for oneself, performing manual tasks, seeing, hearing, eating sleeping, walking, standing, lifting, bending, speaking breathing, learning, reading, concentrating, thinking, communication, and working (Source 28 CRF § 35.104). Overall, from a school psychologist's perspective, understanding the eligibility requirements for receiving services under either IDEIA or Section 504 is important for daily assessment and intervention activities.

Family Educational Rights and Privacy Act of 1974

Another piece of federal legislation that governs the provision of educational services to students in U.S. public schools is the **Family Educational Rights and Privacy Act of 1974 (FERPA)**. Also known as the Buckley Amendment, FERPA protects and safeguards the rights of parents by guaranteeing privacy and confidentiality of student educational records. **Educational records** are defined under FERPA as records, files, documents, and other materials that contain information directly related to a student or are maintained by an educational agency

(34 C.F.R. § 99.3). Such records may include report cards, class schedules, psych-oeducational reports, and attendance records, among other student information. Under FERPA, any educational agency (e.g., school) that receives federal funds must develop policies and procedures that require written parental consent to release education records. The only potential exceptions to this include release of information to employees in the student's school system who have "legitimate edu-cational interest," authorized officers of state or federal agencies, and/or members of certain judicial and law enforcement agencies (FERPA, 20 U.S.C. § 1232g; 34 CFR Part 99). An educator or other school employee has "legitimate educational interest" in reviewing a student's education records when, for example, access to such data is necessary for carrying out essential job assignments or the individual is called upon to provide direct or indirect services to benefit the student.

No Child Left Behind Act and the Every Student Succeeds Act

In 2001, Congress passed legislation known as the **No Child Left Behind Act (NCLB)**. These statutes mandated the implementation of accountability and statewide student performance assessment systems. Specifically, NCLB required each state to adopt academic content standards for mathematics, reading or lan-guage arts, and science. Additionally, states were required to develop and adminis-ter yearly statewide achievement tests to gauge students' progress toward meeting academic standards. School districts or individual schools whose standardized test results did not meet the predetermined levels of acceptable performance were labeled as *low performing* or *failing* and consequently subject to remedial sanc-tions (Jacob et al., 2016).

In December 2015, President Barack Obama signed into law the **Every Student Succeeds Act (ESSA)**, which replaced NCLB. According to Jacob et al. (2016), ESSA attempts to maintain an emphasis on high-performance expectations for students while also correcting the over-reliance on statewide achievement test scores to determine school effectiveness. As its name implies, ESSA emphasizes the provision of high-quality educational services to *all* students. NASP (2016b) has identified several essential school-based practices that school psychologists should strive to implement and that are consistent with ESSA's goals:

1. Use of data in an effective, coordinated manner that informs instruction, student and school outcomes, and school accountability
2. Provision of comprehensive, rigorous curricula to all students
3. Coordination of effective services across systems and within schools
4. Provision of evidence-based comprehensive learning supports
5. Integration of comprehensive school mental and behavioral health services into learning supports
6. Integration of school climate and safety efforts into school improvement efforts
7. Provision of high-quality, relevant professional development
8. Implementation of comprehensive accountability systems (NASP, 2016b, p. 1)

ESSA emphasizes high-quality instruction, professional development for edu-cators, and comprehensive learning supports that are responsive to the unique needs of school communities (NASP, 2016b). Furthermore, ESSA provides states and districts with greater flexibility to blend federal funding streams so as to achieve these goals and encourages states and districts to use these funds to implement multi-tiered systems of supports (MTSS). Broadly defined, an MTSS is a multilevel framework of evidence-based prevention and intervention services for supporting the academic, behavioral, social, and emotional well-being of all students (NASP, 2016a). MTSS is explored in greater detail in Chapter 7.

With the advent of ESSA, advocates for school psychological services (e.g., NASP) have highlighted the "goodness of fit" between the goals of this legislation and the skills of school psychologists. ESSA language uses two terms whose definitions explicitly reference school psychologists: **school-based mental health services providers**, or professionals who are qualified under state law to provide mental health services to children and adolescents, and **specialized instructional support personnel**, or school-based professionals who are qualified to provide assessment, diagnosis, counseling, educational, therapeutic, and other related services. As outlined in the NASP Practice Model, school psychologists are highly qualified to guide schools in meeting the goals of ESSA, as they have expertise in improving academic achievement, facilitating effective instruction, supporting behaviorally and socially successful students, supporting diverse learners, and creating safe, positive school climates (NASP, 2010a).

A MODEL FOR LEGAL AND ETHICAL DECISION MAKING

Returning to our earlier discussion of law and ethics, school psychologists must be able to integrate and apply legal and ethical principles to their professional practice so as to make morally sound decisions. Although critical to effective practice, this process can be trying. To guide school psychologists in resolving potential dilemmas, Williams et al. (2008) advocate for the use of a decision-making model in which ethical and legal issues are examined in a critical and logical fashion. Based on the earlier work by Koocher and Keith-Spiegel (2008), this decision-making model employs a sequential, step-by-step approach to evaluating dilemmas and formulating an action plan. These steps are described in Table 5.1 and are as follows: (1) State objectively the problem situation and its controversies; (2) carefully define the potential ethical–legal issues from multiple perspectives; (3) consult with available ethical–legal guidelines; (4) consult with supervisors and valued colleagues; (5) evaluate the rights, responsibilities, and welfare of all affected parties; (6) consider alternative solutions and consequences of making each decision; and (7) make a decision and take responsibility for it.

Williams et al. (2008) contend that following this decision-making model may increase the likelihood that actions taken to resolve ethical dilemmas will be principled and reasoned (as well as potentially applicable to other similar situations). Rather than relying on intuition, it is imperative that school psychologists use critical–evaluative decision making, especially when faced with complex and sometimes emotionally charged dilemmas. Overall, the decision-making model of Williams et al. may assist school psychologists in arriving at more proactive and reflective solutions to ethical issues.

TABLE 5.1 Ethical and Legal Decision-Making Model

Model of Ethical and Legal Decision Making in School Psychology
1. Describe the problem situation.
Focus on available information and attempt to gather and objectively state the issues or controversies. Breaking down complex, sometimes emotionally charged situations into clear, behavioral statements is helpful.
2. Define the potential ethical—legal issues involved.
Enumerate the ethical and legal issues in question. Again, state these as clearly and accurately as possible, without bias or exaggeration.
3. Consult available ethical—legal guidelines.
Research the issues in question using reference sources, such as NASP's *Principles for Professional Ethics*, IDEA 2004, state guidelines governing special education, textbooks on ethics and legal issues in school psychology (e.g., Jacob et al.'s [2016] *Ethics and Law for School Psychologists* [7th ed.], Harrison & Thomas's [2014] *Best Practices in School Psychology: Foundations*), job descriptions, school board policies, and other appropriate sources.
4. Consult with supervisors and colleagues.
Talk with your supervisor and trusted colleagues who are familiar with the legal and ethical guidelines that apply to school psychology. On a need-to-know basis, share information specifically about the issues you have identified. Brainstorm possible alternatives and consequences, and seek input from those whose opinions you value.
5. Evaluate the rights, responsibilities, and welfare of all affected parties.
Consider the "big picture" rather than focusing on the isolated details of the controversy. Consider implications for students, families, teachers, administrators, other school personnel, and yourself. How will the various alternative courses of action affect each party involved? Remember two basic assumptions underlying NASP's *Principles for Professional Ethics*: (1) school psychologists act as advocates for their student-clients and (2) at the very least, school psychologists will do no harm.
6. Consider alternative solutions and the consequences of making each decision.
Carefully evaluate in a step-by-step manner how each alternative solution will impact the involved parties. Who will be affected and how will they be affected? What are the positive and negative outcomes of each alternative? Weigh the pros and cons. Step back and carefully consider the information you have gathered.
7. Make the decision and take responsibility for it.
Once all the steps are completed, make a decision that is consistent with ethical and legal guidelines and one that you feel confident is the best choice. Take responsibility for following through on that decision, attend to the details, and attempt to bring closure to the scenario.

IDEA, Individuals with Disabilities Education Act; NASP, National Association of School Psychologists.

Source: Williams, B. B., Armistead, L., & Jacob, S. (2008). *Professional ethics for school psychologists: A problem-solving model casebook.* Bethesda, MD: National Association of School Psychologists, Bethesda, MD. Copyright (as applicable) by the National Association of School Psychologists, Bethesda, MD. Reprinted/Adapted with permission of the publisher. www.nasponline.org

SOCIAL JUSTICE CONNECTIONS

How can practitioners advocate for social justice in their legal and ethical decision making?

Social justice, legal, and ethical issues regularly intersect. Thus, models of ethical decision making may assist practitioners in bringing school-based social issues to light and advocating for marginalized populations. The following case example illustrates the the application

(continued)

of the Williams et al. (2008) model of decision making in an ethical dilemma concerning the rights and opportunities of students with disabilities.

1. **Describe the problem situation.**

   Mr. Jones is a special education teacher who teaches secondary-level science to students with learning disabilities. Mr. Jones is finding it challenging to provide these students with science instruction that follows the goals and objectives outlined in the students' Individualized Education Programs (IEPs) and would like to enhance the students' exposure to hands-on science experiments. He consults with the school psychologist to consider what additional options are available to his students to accommodate their learning differences. Mr. Jones and Ms. Green, the school psychologist, confer and decide that one option would be to schedule a period each day in one of the school's science labs. When Mr. Jones contacts the administrator responsible for scheduling the science lab, he is told that, according to school policy, special education classes are not permitted to use the science lab because the students may damage the expensive science equipment. What should Mr. Jones and Ms. Green do?

2. **Define the potential legal and ethical issues involved. Review guidelines. Consult others as needed.**

   Ms. Green offers to research both legal and ethical guidelines related to this problem situation. She recalls from her *Professional School Psychology* course in graduate school that there are several laws that might pertain to this issue. She refers to Jacob et al. (2016) and finds that, under Section 504 of the Rehabilitation Act of 1973 (a civil rights law), public schools are prohibited from excluding students from participating in school programs and activities solely on the basis of a disability (Jacob et al., 2016, p. 151). Ms. Green believes this school policy of prohibiting students with disabilities from using the science lab is a violation of Section 504.

   Ms. Green now must consider how to approach the school administrator who cited school policy as a reason to not allow students with disabilities to use the science lab. Ms. Green reviews the National Association of School Psychologists' *Principles for Professional Ethics* (NASP-PPE) and finds that it is her ethical responsibility to advocate for these students to have access to the science lab. According to the NASP-PPE, "School psychologists consider the interests and rights of children and youth to be their highest priority in decision making and act as advocates for all students" (NASP-PPE, p. 2). Furthermore, Ms. Green reads the following: "To best meet the needs of children, school psychologists cooperate with other professionals in relationships based upon mutual respect" (Principle III.3, p. 10).

   Contemplating both the legal and ethical guidelines relevant to this issue, Ms. Green confers with her supervisor, who is an experienced school psychologist, to discuss her options. How should she approach the school administrator who conveyed the school policy regarding students with disabilities being prohibited from using the science lab? Ms. Green and her supervisor discuss various strategies and options.

3. **Evaluate the rights, responsibilities, and welfare of all affected parties.**

   Based upon review of legal and ethical guidelines, the *students with disabilities* have a right to use the science lab (i.e., have equal opportunity to gain the same benefit as other students) as part of their science instruction. *Parents of students with disabilities* also have the right for their children to benefit from equal opportunity to be instructed in the science lab. Mr. Jones, the *special education teacher*, has the responsibility to provide students with disabilities with the same benefit as general education students in having access to the hands-on experiences in the science lab so as to help students meet the objectives outlined in their IEPs.

4. **Consider alternative actions and the consequences of each action.**

   Ms. Green has several alternative actions to consider:

   a. Meet with her union representative to gain the association's support in her fight to overturn the school policy of not allowing students with disabilities access to the science lab (Consequence: The situation may quickly become adversarial.)

(continued)

b. Attend a Board of Education meeting to testify during the public portion of the session to express her disagreement with the school policy that prevents students with disabilities from accessing the science lab (Consequence: The Board of Education members have an expectation that these types of issues would have been discussed previously with the administrative staff, including the school superintendent.)

c. Make an appointment to meet with the school administrator to discuss her concerns related to the policy and express her willingness to work on a draft of the school policy to bring it in line with Section 504 (Consequence: This action is consistent with the *NASP-PPE, which* recommends that school psychologists approach problem solving with mutual respect.)

d. Inform parents of the students with disabilities of this injustice and ask for their support to protest this school policy (Consequence: This action may become necessary if the option of working within the system with school administrators is not effective.)

e. Do nothing and comply with the school administrator's interpretation of the school policy (Consequence: Nothing will change.)

5. **Make the decision and take responsibility for it. Monitor outcomes.**
Ms. Green decides to begin by requesting a meeting with the school administrator to discuss her concerns related to the school policy of not allowing students with disabilities access to the science lab. She plans to discuss the legal implications of the policy and explain her ethical obligation to advocate for these students. Fortunately, her supervisor agreed to accompany her to this meeting to offer her support. Ms. Green is hopeful that, by working within the system to correct the misinterpretation of this legislation, the school's policy can be revised. She believes she has "done her homework" and is well prepared to openly discuss the issues. She is willing to volunteer to work with a committee of her colleagues to draft a proposal to the school superintendent and ultimately to the Board of Education to formally revise the existing policy. Fortunately, during her meeting with the school administrator and her supervisor, the three are able to agree that the school policy with regard to the use of the science lab should be reviewed and revised to be compliant with both legal and ethical standards. As a result of their discussion, an action plan is developed to begin the process. If Ms. Green had not been able to effect change via this approach, she was prepared to consider other methods to attempt to resolve the issue.

CONSEQUENCES OF ETHICAL VIOLATIONS

While consequences of legal violations fall under the purview of the government, consequences of ethical violations are addressed by the organizations that develop and enforce professional codes of ethics. As noted earlier, school psychologists are beholden to the ethical codes of professional organizations in which they are members. Thus, for example, members of NASP and/or those who hold the organization's hallmark credential of Nationally Certified School Psychologist (NCSP) are responsible for abiding by the NASP-PPE. Likewise, APA members are responsible for upholding the APA Ethics Code, and members of both NASP and APA are beholden to both codes.

As part of their organizational structure, NASP, APA, and other professional organizations (e.g., state school psychology associations) typically establish a standing committee for ethics and professional practices that provides ongoing support and education for organizational members. These committees also respond to informal inquiries regarding ethical dilemmas and assist members in resolving them. State-level ethics committees often provide an educative function and may serve as the first-level contact for members inquiring about ethical and professional matters. The majority of state school psychology associations adopt the NASP-PPE rather than a state-specific code of ethics. Through the local application of these principles, many ethical concerns and legal questions are resolved at the state level and without further escalation to the national level.

The NASP-PPE provides valuable guidance for school psychologists who believe that colleagues in the profession are acting in an unethical manner. Before filing a formal complaint, NASP members are encouraged to consider this guidance. In its *Principle IV.3. Maintaining Public Trust by Self-Monitoring and Peer Monitoring*, the NASP-PPE suggests potential responses to these situations: "When a school psychologist suspects that another school psychologist or another professional has engaged in unethical practices, he or she attempts to resolve the suspected problem through a collegial problem-solving process, if feasible" (NASP, 2010b).

This standard recommends an informal approach to resolving potential problems and puts the onus on the school psychologist to broach these issues in an unofficial manner with the colleague in question. If, however, this action is not successful, Standard IV.3.3 states that the following action is appropriate:

> If a collegial problem-solving process is not possible or productive, school psychologists take further action appropriate to the situation, including discussing the situation with a supervisor in the employment setting, consulting state association ethics committees, and, if necessary, filing a formal ethical violation complaint with state associations, state credentialing bodies, or the NASP Ethical and Professional Practices Committee in accordance with their procedures. (NASP, 2010b)

When necessary, and presumably following interaction with the state school psychology association, a school psychologist who is also a member of NASP may refer a concern to the NASP Ethical and Professional Practices Committee (EPPC) for formal consideration and possible adjudication. Specific procedures are available on the NASP website at www.nasponline.org/standards-and-certification/professional-ethics/resolving-complaints. Once a complaint is heard by the EPPC, possible sanctions of the committee may include mandated professional development or peer supervision and, in more severe cases, probation, suspension, or termination of NASP membership or revocation of the NCSP credential.

Ultimately, problems may be less likely to arise when school psychologists are knowledgeable about relevant legal and ethical codes and, therefore, able to adhere to them closely. Engaging in best practices in promoting ethical behavior involves remaining abreast of new developments in ethics and law through activities such as reading professional publications and attending state and national conferences. By becoming well versed in ethical and legal issues, school psychologists can strive for excellence in this area, rather than merely meeting minimum standards for acceptable behavior.

SUMMARY AND CONCLUSIONS

Within the NASP Practice Model, Domain 10 requires school psychologists to be knowledgeable about ethical, legal, and professional standards of practice. Armed with this knowledge, school psychologists are better equipped to deal effectively with professional dilemmas that arise in the delivery of school-based services. These dilemmas may involve a school psychologist's interactions with students, parents and guardians, teachers, administrators, and other school personnel. School psychologists rely upon codes of ethics (e.g., NASP-PPE), educational laws (e.g., ESSA), and other types of regulations to guide their behavior. For example, two important fundamentals underlying ethical principles embedded within the NASP-PPE are (a) school psychologists must act as advocates for their clients (i.e., students) and (b) they must, at the very least, do no harm (NASP, 2016b). When implemented effectively, the legal and ethical decision-making model outlined in this chapter helps school psychologists examine issues on a critical–evaluative level to arrive at ethically and legally sound decisions.

DISCUSSION QUESTIONS

1. Best practices suggest that coursework in ethics and law should be introduced to students early on in their school psychology graduate preparation. Why is early exposure to this content important?
2. Unlike the APA Ethics Code, the NASP-PPE specifically addresses school-based practice. Provide examples of how each of the four broad ethical themes of the NASP-PPE relate to school-based practice for school psychologists.
3. PL 94-142 (now known as IDEIA) was the first legislation to mandate educational services for students with disabilities throughout the United States. How do you think this legislation has affected the practice of school psychology?
4. How does ESSA specifically address the role of the school psychologist?
5. What are some of the advantages of using a decision-making model when examining ethical and legal dilemmas?

REFERENCES

American Psychological Association. (2002). Ethical principles of psychologists and code of conduct. *American Psychologist, 57,* 1060–1073.

Armistead, L. D., Williams, B. B., & Jacob, S. (2011). *Professional ethics for school psychologists: A problem-solving model casebook* (2nd ed.). Bethesda, MD: National Association of School Psychologists.

Beauchamp, T., & Childress, J. (2001). *Principles of biomedical ethics* (5th ed.). New York, NY: Oxford University Press.

Bersoff, D. N. (1983). Children as participants in psychoeducational assessment. In G. B. Melton, G. P. Koocher, & M. J. Sakes (Eds.), *Children's competence to consent* (pp. 149–177). New York, NY: Plenum Press.

Bersoff, D. N., & Koeppl, P. M. (1992). The relation between ethical codes and moral principles. *Ethics & Behavior, 3,* 345–357. doi:10.1080/10508422.1993.9652112

Burns, M. K., Jacob, S., & Wagner, A. R. (2008). Ethical and legal issues associated with using response-to-intervention to assess learning disabilities. *Journal of School Psychology, 46,* 263–279.

Corrao, J., & Melton, G. B. (1988). Legal issues in school-based behavior therapy. In J. C. Witt, S. N. Elliot, & F. M. Gresham (Eds.), *Handbook of behavior therapy in education* (pp. 131–144). Bethesda, MD: National Association of School Psychologists.

Family Educational Rights and Privacy Act of 1974, 20 U.S.C. § 1232g (1974).

Fisher, C. B. (2017). *Decoding the ethics code* (4th ed.) Thousand Oaks, CA: Sage.

Harrison, P. L., & Thomas, A. (Eds.). (2014). *Best practices in school psychology: Foundations.* Bethesda, MD: National Association of School Psychologists.

Individuals with Disabilities Education Act, Pub. L. No. 101-476, 104 Stat. 1142 (1990).

Individuals with Diasabilties Education Act of 1997, Pub. L. No. 105-17, 105 Stat. 37 (1997).

Individuals with Disabilities Education Improvement Act of 2004, Pub. L. No. 108-446 (2004).

Institute for Education Sciences (IES), National Center for Educational Statistics (NCES). Retrieved from https://nces.ed.gov/fastfacts/display.asp?id=64

International School Psychologists Association. (2011). *International School Psychologists Association code of ethics.* Retrieved from http://www.ispaweb.org/wp-content/uploads/2013/01/The_ISPA_Code_of_Ethics_2011.pdf

Jacob, S. (2005). *Ethics and law update for school psychologists.* Presentation at the NASP 2005 Summer Conference, Philadelphia, PA.

Jacob, S. (2008). Best practices in developing ethical school psychological practice. In A. Thomas & J. Grimes (Eds.), *Best practices in school psychology: V.* Bethesda, MD: National Association of School Psychologists.

Jacob, S., Decker, D. M., & Lugg, E. T. (2016). *Ethics and law for school psychologists* (7th ed.). Hoboken, NJ: Wiley.

Kaplan, M. S., Crisci, P. E., & Farling, W. (1974). Editorial comment [Special issue]. *School Psychology Digest, 3.*

Knapp, S. J., & VandeCreek, L. D. (2005). *Practical ethics for psychologists: A positive approach.* Washington, DC: American Psychological Association.

Koocher, G. P., & Keith-Spiegel, P. (2008). *Ethics in psychology and the mental health professions: Standards and cases.* New York, NY: Oxford University Press.

Murdick, N. L., Gartin, B. C., & Crabtree, T. L. (2007). *Special education law* (2nd ed.). Columbus, OH: Merrill Publishing.

National Association of School Psychologists. (2010a). *National Association of School Psychologists model of comprehensive and integrated school psychological services.* Bethesda, MD: Author.

National Association of School Psychologists. (2010b). *National Association of School Psychologists principles for professional ethics.* Bethesda, MD: Author.

National Association of School Psychologists. (2016a). ESSA and multitiered systems of supports for school psychologists. Retrieved from http://www.nasponline.org/research-and-policy/current-law-and-policy-priorities/policy-priorities/the-every-student-succeeds-act/essa-implementation-resources/essa-and-mtss-for-school-psychologists

National Association of School Psychologists. (2016b). *Leveraging essential school practices, ESSA, MTSS, and the NASP practice model: A crosswalk to help every school and student succeed* [Policy brief]. Bethesda, MD: Author.

Reschly, D. J. (2000). Assessment and eligibility determination in the Individuals with Disabilities Education Act of 1997. In C. F. Telzrow & M. Tankersley (Eds.), *IDEA amendments of 1997* (pp. 65–104). Bethesda, MD: National Association of School Psychologists.

Ross, W. D. (1930). *The right and the good.* New York, NY: Claredon Press.

Trachtman, G. M. (1974). Ethical issues in school psychology. *School Psychology Digest, 3*(1), 4–5.

Welfel, E. R., & Kitchener, K. S. (1992). Introduction to the special section: Ethics education: An agenda for the '90s. *Professional Psychology: Research and Practice, 23,* 179–181. doi:10.1037/0735-7028.23.3.179

Williams, B. B., & Armistead, L. (2010). Applying law and ethics in professional practice. In T. M. Lionetti, E. P. Snyder, & R. W. Christener (Eds.), *A practical guide to building professional competencies in school psychology* (pp.209–225. New York, NY: Springer Science+Business Media.

Williams, B. B., Armistead, L., & Jacob, S. (2008). *Professional ethics for school psychologists: A problem-solving model casebook.* Bethesda, MD: National Association of School Psychologists.

Service Delivery in School Psychology

CHAPTER 6

Assessment

NICHOLAS F. BENSON ■ ASHLEY DONOHUE

CHAPTER OBJECTIVES

- Define assessment in the context of school-based service delivery
- Describe essential features of assessment
- Describe purposes and applications of assessment in school settings
- Describe commonly used assessments in school psychology
- Describe integration and reporting of assessment results

In psychology and education, ***assessment*** is a methodical process that involves the collection, evaluation, integration, and application of information to guide decision making and to achieve professional objectives (e.g., instructional decision making, diagnosis, and treatment planning). One common misconception about the process of assessment is that it is synonymous with tests and testing. Although tests are typically an integral part of this process, tests are only one of several types of assessment methods. Moreover, assessment often focuses on multiple domains of functioning (e.g., academic, behavioral, and emotional domains), occurs on multiple occasions, and includes collection of information from multiple sources.

There is a strong demand for assessment in school settings. In fact, most of the assessment practices utilized in other settings originated from applications in schools (Fagan, 1996). Assessment is routinely used to help promote desired outcomes and address problems that hinder students' psychological and educational functioning. This chapter highlights the importance, foundations, and applications of assessment in the practice of school psychology.

IMPORTANCE OF ASSESSMENT IN THE PRACTICE OF SCHOOL PSYCHOLOGY

People display individual differences in the extent to which they successfully execute various tasks (e.g., reading and writing) and participate in life activities (e.g., interacting with peers and engaging in daily routines). Understanding individual differences in students' functioning is essential for providing appropriately matched services and, ultimately, to the educational process. Thus, information gleaned from assessments is invaluable for fostering students' strengths and preventing and/or remediating difficulties.

Assessments conducted by school psychologists have traditionally focused on determining students' eligibility for special education and related services. While there continues to be a need to identify students in need of these services, the role of the school psychologist has broadened. For example, many school psychologists are now involved in universal screenings of academic skills and behavior to identify students in need of early interventions (Albers, Glover, & Kratochwill, 2007). To help ensure that students make adequate progress in meeting academic and behavioral expectations, school psychologists must engage in assessment *for* intervention (i.e., assessment aimed at evaluating the need for and focus of an intervention), assessment *during* intervention (i.e., assessment that monitors a student's progress during intervention), and assessment *of* intervention (assessment that evaluates the outcomes of the intervention) (Albers, Elliott, Kettler, & Roach, 2015). The purpose of these assessment activities is to develop customized interventions for individual students and to guide decisions regarding whether these interventions should be continued, terminated, or modified.

OVERVIEW OF ASSESSMENT PROCESSES

Assessments typically involve interactions between a person or an agency (e.g., caregiver or school) that arranges for an assessment, one or more professionals with competency in testing and assessment (e.g., school psychologist), and an individual or group (e.g., all students in a classroom or school) that is the subject of the assessment. For example, a parent or teacher may refer a student for an assessment, and a variety of school-based professionals may engage in assessment activities to identify the student's strengths and weaknesses. The assessment process is often interdisciplinary, meaning that it involves a team of professionals who possess complementary areas of expertise. This interdisciplinary assessment team assumes varied roles in the collection, evaluation, and utilization of data. In schools, school psychologists may collaborate with a number of individuals, including school social workers, behavior interventionists, guidance counselors, teachers, and others, to coordinate assessment activities.

The collection process involves gathering historical data as well as data regarding current functioning. This information is used to clarify a referral question and refine assessment goals. The referral question, or **reason for referral**, indicates the reason or purpose for which an assessment is undertaken. Theoretically, there can never be too much information collected during an assessment; however, it is important for practitioners to be efficient in their data collection practices. Excessive data collection can detract from students' instructional time, which can ultimately interfere with their learning.

ESSENTIAL FEATURES OF TESTS: PSYCHOMETRIC PROPERTIES

For school psychologists to hone competencies in assessment, they must first understand the features of high-quality assessments. As previously noted, the assessment process is often interdisciplinary. Nonpsychological staff may have minimal training in measurement and assessment issues (Reynolds, 1986); thus, it is imperative that school psychologists immerse themselves in this literature to ensure the quality of assessment services.

Psychometrics refers to the study of psychological measurement. Psychometricians (and ultimately, school psychologists) are concerned with the extent to which psychological instruments accurately and consistently measure the phenomenon, or *construct*, they are designed to measure. **Constructs** are conceptual abstractions of phenomena that are not directly observable (MacCorquodale & Meehl, 1948). For example, some constructs that school psychologists may evaluate among youth include intelligence and self-esteem. While these attributes may not be observable to the human eye, they can be measured through the use of psychological tests. A comprehensive review of psychometrics and measurement is beyond the scope of this chapter; however, some key concepts are reviewed here.

Validity

Validity is the most fundamental consideration in selecting and evaluating tests and other assessment techniques. Broadly defined, **validity** refers to the "degree to which evidence and theory support the interpretation of test scores for proposed uses of tests" (American Educational Research Association, American Psychological Association, & National Council on Measurement in Education, 2014, p. 11). Validity is not a property of a test per se; rather, it pertains to specific interpretations and uses of test scores. In other words, the validity of an instrument cannot be evaluated without considering the purpose and context of the instrument's use and interpretation. For example, a test of reading comprehension cannot be deemed either universally "valid" or "invalid" across all contexts; rather, it may have some degree of established validity for a particular purpose or interpretation (e.g., measurement of third-grade students' end-of-year reading competence). Evidence of validity is needed to support the interpretation and use of test scores, and tests should not be administered in the absence of sufficient evidence to support proposed interpretations or uses.

Test developers, school psychologists, and others can evaluate validity evidence in a number of ways. For example, experts in a particular domain can examine the content of the assessment (e.g., whether it addresses the full range of reading comprehension skills targeted for measurement). They can also evaluate the internal structure of the test (e.g., relations among test items) as well as its relations with other similar and dissimilar tests (e.g., correlations with other measures of reading comprehension). Importantly, school psychologists should also consider the ***consequential validity*** of assessments, meaning the intended or unintended consequences of test use. Although evidence may suggest that a test is an excellent measurement tool, it is inappropriate to use test scores to drive policy unless there is sufficient evidence to indicate that this use leads to acceptable outcomes. For example, while there is ample evidence to support the reliability and validity of scores from most statewide achievement tests, research suggests that teacher identity explains less than 20% of variance in student achievement outcomes (e.g., Hanushek, Kai, & Rivken, 1998). Although student achievement data are commonly used to evaluate teachers and inform policy decisions such as the provision of merit pay, little to no evidence exists to support the consequential validity of such practices (Welner, 2013).

Reliability

Classical test theory posits that an examinee's scores on a particular test or measure will inevitably have some degree of error. This implies that the examinee's ***true score***, or the score that best represents his or her true skills or abilities, is masked by some degree of error. Error in scores arises for a number of reasons, including mistakes in administration or scoring, chance distractions during the testing process, or guessing on the part of the examinee. Because error is pervasive and unavoidable, test administrators can never know an examinee's true score definitively; they can only observe the score that the examinee obtains during test administration, known as the ***observed score***.

Reliability refers to the extent to which measures yield consistent scores and are free from these types of error. The goal of estimating reliability is to determine how much of the variability in test scores reflects meaningful individual differences as opposed to measurement error. When considering a test's psychometric properties, school psychologists should consider several types of reliability, including internal consistency and test–retest reliability. ***Internal consistency*** refers to the average inter-item correlation among test items—in other words, the interrelatedness of items. Reliability coefficients range from .00 (perfectly unreliable) to 1 (perfectly reliable). ***Test–retest reliability*** refers to the temporal stability of test scores, or the extent to which scores can be replicated across measurement occasions. For example, a test that generally yields highly similar scores when administered to the same individuals at different points in time may be considered to have high test–retest reliability.

FORMATIVE AND SUMMATIVE ASSESSMENT

Traditionally, assessments of student learning have been categorized as formative or summative based on their purpose and actions. ***Formative assessment*** refers to the collection and use of information to monitor students' progress over the course of intervention. This type of assessment aims to improve students' learning and attainment of intervention objectives by providing ongoing information that can be used for instructional decision making (Black & William, 1998; Shepard, 2006). **Summative assessment** also focuses on the collection and use of information to evaluate students' learning and attainment of instructional objectives, but it is conducted after the curricular content addressing these objectives has already been delivered. That is, it provides a summary of the students' outcomes in the intervention.

The distinction between formative and summative assessments is important but is not always clear, as some argue that assessments can serve both formative and summative functions. For example, results from end-of-year, statewide achievement tests are commonly used for summative accountability purposes. Such results are used to evaluate the effectiveness of instructional practices and to hold school districts accountable for student outcomes. However, these results also assist with the identification of students who fail to meet academic proficiency standards and students who do not display adequate yearly progress. Thus, end-of-year results can be used formatively to plan instruction for the upcoming school year. Such dual functions (i.e., using results to both evaluate instructional effectiveness and monitor student progress) have blurred the distinction between formative and summative assessment (Dixson & Worrell, 2016; Hattie & Leeson, 2013).

PURPOSES OF ASSESSMENT IN SCHOOLS

There are multiple financial, pragmatic, legal, ethical, and professional reasons for providing assessment services in schools. Assessment procedures most commonly utilized in school settings are those that "address student learning, psychoeducational interventions, and intervention implementation mediated via consultation" (Braden, 2003, p. 262). As previously noted, school psychologists may engage in assessment for intervention, during intervention, and of intervention (Albers et al., 2015).

Assessment for Intervention

Assessing for intervention centers on several goals. including (a) identifying students who may require further assessment and intervention services and (b) clarifying areas of need and potential targets for intervention. These assessments reveal information that allows school psychologists to target students' needs efficiently and effectively. Two ways that school psychologists typically assess for intervention are through screening and disability identification. Both of these types of services are described in further detail in the following subsections.

Screening

Many schools conduct **universal screening** of academic skills and behavior, meaning that an entire population of students (e.g., all students at a grade level within a school or school district) are assessed to identify individuals in need of additional academic or mental health supports (Albers et al., 2007). Universal screening is a prevention-oriented assessment technique, because it involves identifying students who show early warning signs of academic and behavioral difficulties. Students who do not meet the performance criterion on a school's screener(s) may receive additional interventions to prevent their difficulties from escalating into more severe problems.

Because screening measures are administered to all students for the purpose of identifying individuals who are at risk for various types of difficulties, they must be both efficient and psychometrically defensible. Thus, screening procedures rely on brief tests and other assessment procedures to provide information regarding students' academic and behavioral functioning. A variety of tests, rating scales, and other procedures can be used in screening systems aimed at identifying students who are at risk for problems in a wide range of areas (e.g., early reading skills, early numeracy skills, social functioning, or emotional functioning). Screening systems typically include decision criteria for taking action. For example, school personnel may decide that students identified on a screener as experiencing "some risk" will receive moderately intensive services, whereas students identified as experiencing "high risk" will receive the most intensive services. In this manner, screeners can guide schools in utilizing their limited resources more efficiently.

Diagnosis/Eligibility Determination

Classification involves assigning things to categories based on common features. **Diagnosis** is a special case of classification that involves grouping individuals using **nosology**, the taxonomies of proposed syndromes, diseases, or disabilities. Diagnoses are made based on properties that provide meaningful distinctions, such as etiology (i.e., cause), pathogenesis (i.e., onset, course, and underlying mechanisms), or syndromes (i.e., patterns of signs and symptoms). Diagnoses and disability identifications, which are discussed in further detail in the following text, often provide valuable information that sets the stage for intervention and treatment planning.

It is important to note that non-doctoral school psychologists employed in pre-K–12 settings do not diagnose students per se. Rather, they identify students as eligible or ineligible to receive special education and related services based on criteria associated with 13 broad disability categories (e.g., emotional and behavioral disabilities, specific learning disabilities, and autism spectrum disorders). These broad disability categories derive from the Individuals with Disabilities Education Improvement Act (IDEIA) of 2004 (described in Chapter 5) as well as specific eligibility criteria developed by individual states. Evaluations must be sufficiently comprehensive to identify the need for any special education or related services and must utilize a variety of technically sound assessment tools and strategies (34 C.F.R. § 300.304). Eligibility determinations must be made by a multidisciplinary team that includes a parent or guardian, teachers, a school administrator, an assessment specialist who assists with the interpretation of assessment data (e.g., a school psychologist), and other relevant educational professionals. A student is considered eligible for special education and related services if the team determines the student is a child with a disability (as defined by one or more of the 13 disability categories) and, as a result of his or her disability status, needs special education and related services (34 C.F.R. § 300.306).

School psychologists who have secured the appropriate state-level credentials and who are employed in settings other than K–12 schools (e.g., private practice and hospital settings) often make mental health diagnoses. Mental health professionals in the United States utilize the **Diagnostic and Statistical Manual of Mental Disorders**, which is currently in its fifth edition (*DSM-5*; American Psychiatric Association, 2013), to diagnose mental disorders. The *DSM-5* contains descriptive text and diagnostic criteria for each disorder, as well as diagnostic codes used for billing service providers and data collection purposes. In school settings, *DSM-5* classifications are often used to gain third-party (e.g., Medicaid or private health care insurers) reimbursement for psychological services (Tobin & House, 2016). *DSM-5* diagnoses are used ubiquitously in the United States to determine the need for and allow access to mental health and rehabilitation services.

Assessment During Intervention

It is critical that school psychologists assess not only *prior to* and *following* intervention, but also *during* intervention. These types of assessments allow school personnel to monitor student growth in response to interventions as these services are being delivered. Failure to periodically monitor student progress may result in the continued delivery of interventions that are not accomplishing their intended objectives. This wastes valuable instructional time as well as coveted school resources. Conversely, having more regular data available allows school psychologists to make more immediate adjustments to interventions that can enhance their efficiency and impact.

Progress monitoring involves measuring the student's rate of change using a time-series design (i.e., data are collected at several successive, equally spaced measurement occasions). Progress monitoring may focus on an array of academic, social, and emotional behaviors, although in schools it is most commonly associated with the assessment of academic development (Fuchs & Fuchs, 2010). Progress monitoring involves formative assessment, meaning that the results are used to inform instructional or interventional efforts. Specifically, frequent (e.g., weekly or biweekly) measurements are collected at the level of individual students with verified academic problems and the resulting time-series data are analyzed to guide decisions regarding responsiveness to intervention. Responsiveness to intervention is evaluated relative to the expected rate of change (improvement) and informs decisions regarding the continuation, modification, or discontinuation of intervention.

Assessment of Intervention

Assessment of intervention, or **outcome assessment**, refers to the assessment that takes place following an intervention. Unlike progress monitoring, it involves summative assessment. Outcome assessment focuses on change in students' skills and functioning that occurs after instruction or intervention. Broadly, such assessments are used to inform evaluations of efficacy (i.e., how well an intervention works under ideal circumstances) and effectiveness (i.e., how well the intervention works when replicated across implementers, populations, and settings). Outcome assessment can occur at a variety of levels (e.g., national, statewide, school-wide, classroom, or individual students). Academic achievement is undoubtedly the most commonly measured outcome in school settings, although a variety of systems-level (e.g., school climate) and individual (e.g., social–emotional adjustment) outcomes may be measured.

Statewide assessments of academic achievement are among the most common types of outcome assessments. The Every Student Succeeds Act (ESSA; described in Chapter 5) mandates that state achievement tests align with state content and performance standards. This allows student achievement to be evaluated relative to these standards. More generally, these assessments focus on the extent to which learning objectives or performance standards were attained. Attainment may be judged relative to norm-referenced or criterion-referenced standards. Norm-referenced and criterion-referenced standards are discussed in more detail in the next section of this chapter. Numerous outcomes can be assessed beyond academic outcomes. For example, outcome assessment may focus on the results of interventions aimed at improving emotional, social, or other behavioral outcomes. These measures are discussed in greater detail in Chapter 9.

ASSESSMENT TECHNIQUES

Testing

Testing can be defined as a method used to examine the presence of some phenomenon (VandenBos, 2015). This method involves the observation and measurement of behavioral samples. The aim of testing may be to measure manifest behaviors (e.g., behaviors that are easily observed, such as skills in complete single-digit addition problems) or to make inferences about traits that are not directly observable (i.e., intelligence or personality). Performance on formal tests can be evaluated using norm-referenced, criterion-referenced, or qualitative interpretations. Informal tests also may be used to collect supplemental information. For example, teachers will sometimes create informal tests to measure attainment of classroom learning objectives. Notably, there are many informal procedures that are not tests (e.g., school records and referral documents).

Norm-Referenced and Criterion-Referenced Comparisons

School psychologists commonly administer tests that use two types of comparisons: norm-referenced comparisons (NRCs) and criterion-referenced comparisons (CRCs). A test that uses **NRCs** is one in which an individual's test performance is compared to that of a larger reference group or normative sample. The **normative sample** typically comprises a large number of individuals who have previously taken the test and who are similar to the examinee in some way (typically same-age peers or same-grade peers). For example, the Woodcock Johnson, Fourth Edition, Tests of Achievement (WJIV-TA; Schrank, Mather, & McGrew, 2014) is a widely administered norm-referenced test of academic achievement that includes both age-based and grade-based norms. It allows the examiner to identify the **percentile rank** at which the examinee scored, or the percentage of individuals in the normative sample who achieved an equal or lower score.

Norm-referenced tests are standardized, meaning that procedures for administering (e.g., giving directions and delivering test items) and scoring the test are precisely delineated and must be executed in a consistent manner. Standardization ensures the validity of assessment results by providing equal opportunities for test takers to display the construct being assessed. To minimize the possibility of administration and scoring errors (e.g., Hopwood & Richard, 2005; Ramos, Alfonso, & Schermerhorn, 2009), it is important to become proficient in administering and scoring a test before using it in practice. Having an experienced practitioner who is deeply familiar with a particular test observe administration and provide corrective feedback is one strategy that is effective in reducing administration and scoring errors (Roberts & Davis, 2015).

Unlike NRCs, CRCs (Glaser, 1963) use a content domain as a frame of reference, focusing on what an examinee can do rather than where the examinee's performance ranks relative to a normative comparison group. Often, performance levels are compared to specific and absolute standards, or criteria, that demonstrate mastery of a content domain. For example, performance on state-mandated tests of academic achievement may be interpreted relative to cut scores that reflect preestablished criteria for grade-level proficiency within a particular academic content area (e.g., reading or mathematics). Like norm-referenced tests, many criterion-referenced tests are standardized (e.g., curriculum-based measures, which are discussed in greater detail in Chapter 8).

Qualitative Interpretations

Qualitative interpretations of test performance can focus on a variety of behaviors, including test-taking strategies, patterns of error, and behaviors that are likely to facilitate or hinder test performance (e.g., attention/inattention, compliance/resistance, interest/indifference, and persistence/unresponsiveness). Observations of test session behavior provide insights into how an examinee approached and responded to test stimuli. Moreover, test session behavior can provide a means of cross-checking the validity of score interpretations (Glutting, Oakland, & McDermott, 1989). Specifically, observations can be used to judge the appropriateness of the testing conditions and the extent to which test session behaviors suggest that observed test scores are likely to provide accurate estimates of an examinee's true scores.

Reviews of Historical Records

A student's current functioning must be evaluated against the backdrop of his or her history. Knowledge of the incidence of physical and mental illness and other genetically linked diseases in first- and second-degree relatives is important, given familial-related proclivity for these conditions. Other records that tend to be useful include those from medical, psychiatric, neurological, neuropsychological, psychological, legal, and educational sources. In reviewing students' educational records, school psychologists may be particularly interested in previous intervention data, previous psychoeducational reports, attendance records, course grades, standardized test scores, and, if applicable, records from special education services (e.g., Individualized Education Plan documents). On many occasions, practitioners will find that historical records are less comprehensive than desired and need to be supplemented with interview data.

Historical information may be particularly important for students who have experienced disease or trauma that negatively impacts their current functioning. In fact, premorbid functioning is best established by review of historical records (Reynolds, 1997). Of course, school psychologists must make determinations about the relative value of historical records for informing the assessment process. For example, relying on course grades as indicators of academic achievement can be problematic due to variability in grading criteria, which often incorporate non-academic criteria (e.g., class participation). Moreover, assessments used to determine course grades (e.g., unit tests and quizzes) are often informal, tend to be unstandardized, and rarely apply principles of good measurement (Allen, 2005).

School psychologists should consider both strengths and weaknesses in assessing the skill sets of their clients. **Strength-based assessments** focus on personal competencies (e.g., emotional and behavioral skills) that enhance coping, promote development in domains such as academic achievement and social functioning, and allow individuals to set and accomplish goals (Jimerson, Sharkey, Nyborg, & Furlong, 2004). Thus, when reviewing historical records, it is important to focus on past accomplishments and identify assets and skills that facilitated success. Moreover, numerous measures have been developed to measure assets and skills such as optimism, gratitude, empathy, prosocial behavior, student engagement, and life satisfaction (Furlong, Gilman, & Huebner, 2014).

Behavioral Observations

Observations are used to elucidate patterns of behavior. Observations may be indirect or direct. **Indirect observation** relies on the observations of others and includes methods such as rating scales (described in further detail in the following text), whereas direct observations require assessors to directly view and record the behaviors themselves. **Direct observation** "requires careful attention to specifying what and how long the behaviors are observed, where and how observations are made, and how they are recorded" (Benson, 2010, p. 74).

Behavioral observations can be qualitative or quantitative. For example, a practitioner may use qualitative observations, such as writing a narrative of behavioral and classroom events, to form a general impression of cooperation and motivation during testing. When quantifying behaviors, school psychologists can attend to a number of observable characteristics of the behavior (Salvia, Ysseldyke, & Witmer, 2017), including its frequency and duration. To illustrate the concepts of duration and frequency, consider a school psychologist who wishes to observe a student's tantrum behaviors. The school psychologist could measure the **frequency**, or number of occurrences of a behavior during a fixed period of time, by counting the number of tantrums that occur in one class period. The frequency of a behavior can be measured only if the target behavior has a clear beginning and end and does not occur at such a high frequency that it is difficult to count. The school psychologist could also quantify the behavior's **duration**, or the length of time for which a behavior occurs, by measuring the number of minutes during which the tantrum lasts.

School psychologists often use behavioral observations to identify environmental events that predict and maintain behaviors. For example, ***antecedents*** (i.e., stimuli that precede a target behavior) and ***consequences*** (i.e., behaviors that occur subsequent to a target behavior) are controlling variables that maintain behavior. In the case of a student experiencing tantrums, one or more antecedents may trigger the behavior (e.g., receiving a poor grade on a test), while consequences can impact whether a behavior continues and/or is likely to occur again in the future (e.g., receiving teacher and peer attention as a result of the tantrum). Observations can be used to identify controlling variables that can be manipulated to promote the desired behavior and reduce the problem behavior, as well as to monitor changes in the target behaviors that occur as a result of manipulating environmental variables.

Rating Scales

Rating scales are commonly used as part of the assessment process because they are an efficient way to acquire information. ***Behavior rating scales*** contain a limited set of items that measure the frequency with which relevant behaviors are displayed. (These types of rating scales are discussed in further detail in Chapter 9.) Ratings are an indirect measure that summarize the behaviors an informant observes over an extended period. The professional administering the rating scale (e.g., school psychologist) typically discusses the directions for completion with the respondent (e.g., teacher or parent) and explains why the information is needed as well as how it will be used. Benefits of rating scales include efficiency, ease of administration and scoring, and relatively low cost. Moreover, although it is not feasible to observe more than a few students at once when conducting direct behavioral observations, rating scales feature normative samples that allow comparisons with representative samples of same-age peers.

Numerous rating scales are available for a large range of problems. Some rating scales are ***narrow-band*** instruments, meaning that they measure a specific construct (e.g., depression, attention, and anxiety); others are ***broad-band*** instruments, meaning that they measure several constructs. A broad-band rating scale that is widely used in educational settings is the Behavior Assessment System for Children, Third Edition (BASC-3; Reynolds & Kamphaus, 2015). The BASC-3 system includes self-report forms as well as parent and teacher rating forms, each of which measures several areas (e.g., adaptive skills, externalizing problems, internalizing problems, school problems, clinical scales measuring specific constructs such as anxiety and aggression). A commonly used narrow-band rating scale is the Revised Children's Manifest Anxiety Scale (RCMAS; Reynolds & Richmond, 2008), which measures various signs and symptoms associated with anxiety (e.g., physiological anxiety, worry, social anxiety).

School psychologists often request multiple raters, or ***informants*** (e.g., students, teachers, and parents), to complete rating scales so that they can gain multiple perspectives on behavior. In many cases, raters may not agree in their scoring. Likely causes of disagreement between raters include systematic differences in (a) what is observed, (b) access to information other than observations of performance (e.g., conversations with parents and staff), and (c) expertise in interpreting what is observed (e.g., knowledge of developmental milestones) (Achenbach,

McConaughy, & Howell, 1987). When using information from multiple informants (i.e., parents, teachers, and student), it is important to examine assessment results for discrepancies among raters. Nevertheless, it remains beneficial to administer assessment tools to multiple informants to gain valuable information on the student in varying settings (i.e., within school and outside of school) (De Los Reyes et al., 2015).

Interviews

Interviews are purposeful and planned encounters intended to obtain information about a person's behaviors, preferences, strengths, and areas of difficulty (e.g., symptoms). They also offer an opportunity for the clinician to observe the interviewee's verbal and nonverbal behavior. In addition, interviews can help build rapport and trust with the interviewee. In educational assessments, interviews are most commonly conducted with students, teachers, and parents. Like rating scales, interviews can be used to gather information from multiple informants.

The content of interviews varies depending on the interviewer's goals. Practitioners may use a variety of interview instruments, including structured, semistructured, and unstructured interviews. **Structured diagnostic interviews** are characterized by standardized formats and explicit guidelines on how responses are to be scored and followed up (Frick, Barry, & Kamphaus, 2009). They provide relevant information regarding symptom presentation and functional impairments associated with these symptoms (Loney & Frick, 2003). This information closely relates to *DSM-5* criteria and typically is not obtained using other assessment methods such as rating scales. **Semistructured interviews** are similar to structured interviews in that they comprise a predetermined list of questions; however, responses may be open-ended and can be followed up with clarifying questions as deemed appropriate by the interviewer. Finally, **unstructured interviews** are open-ended interviews that lack a specific set of questions and afford the interviewer full flexibility in following up on the interviewee's responses. When compared to unstructured interviews, semistructured and structured interviews demonstrate superior reliability (McCellan & Werry, 2000). However, structured interviews are, by definition, considerably more rigid and do not allow the interviewer to deviate from the preset question list.

INTEGRATING AND REPORTING ASSESSMENT RESULTS

Integration of assessment results is essential to accomplishing professional objectives. Given that school psychologists typically use a number of different techniques to evaluate students' functioning in several domains, the assessment process often yields a plethora of data. These data often conflict, as information is typically acquired using multiple methods, from multiple settings on multiple occasions, and from multiple informants. Thus, it is necessary to (a) assign relative weights to data based on evidence of reliability, validity, and utility; (b) look for themes and patterns in assessment data; (c) develop testable alternative hypotheses and the means of testing these hypotheses when possible; and (d) determine the probability that various inferences and impressions are accurate.

Further, when describing an examinee, it is important to provide a balanced discussion of strengths (i.e., positive characteristics that might be built upon and contribute to success) and weaknesses that ostensibly contribute to problems. As Weiner (2013) notes, "Psychological assessment has often addressed mainly what is wrong with people while giving insufficient attention to their adaptive capacities, positive potentials, and admirable qualities" (p. 20).

Assessment results are typically reported to others both orally and in written format. Typically, reports are written first, then shared, summarized orally, and discussed with stakeholders (e.g., students, parents, teachers, multidisciplinary teams). Psychoeducational reports contain integrated assessment information that describes the examinee, informs the question that led to referral for assessment, and informs planning of instruction and intervention. Psychoeducational reports generally include the following components: identifying information (e.g., student's name and chronological age), description of the referral question, a list of the assessment procedures utilized, background information, observations of test session behavior, assessment results, summary, and recommendations. However, the components of reports vary depending on the purpose of the assessment.

MULTICULTURAL CONSIDERATIONS IN ASSESSMENT

As always, it is important for school psychologists to ensure that their practices are culturally responsive. **Cultural responsiveness** involves appreciating differences in language, values, customs, and experiences, and implementing practices that are sensitive to these differences (Sullivan, 2010). According to Klingner et al. (2005), culturally responsive practice encompasses the following components: (a) affirmation of diversity, (b) sociocultural consciousness, (c) critical reflection, (d) critical appraisal of cultures that shape schools, (e) advocacy, and (f) continuous professional development.

Affirmation of diversity involves acknowledgment and appreciation of differences, as well as demonstrations of respect for these differences, when serving students and their families as well as when interacting with colleagues. **Sociocultural consciousness** involves acknowledgment of the effects that social factors have on behavior and achievement, including the potentially strong influence of the classroom environment. School psychologists with sociocultural consciousness examine the curriculum, instructional practices, and behavior management strategies to understand the impact of these factors on the development of students' academic, emotional, and social functioning (Sullivan, 2010).

Critical reflection emphasizes the appropriateness of assessment practices and ensures that these practices address students' strengths and needs. rather than focusing primarily on psychopathology and meeting criteria for diagnosis or eligibility determination (Sullivan, 2010). Critical appraisal of cultures that shape schools involves identifying cultural influences that shape schools and the effects of these influences on behavior and achievement. As described in Chapter 1, advocacy entails the promotion of change. School psychologists may advocate for change when states, school systems, or individual practitioners utilize inappropriate assessment practices or interpret and use test scores in unfair ways. According to Sullivan (2010), school psychologists "have an ethical responsibility to speak up against practices that are potentially biased, not based on research, and/or that contribute to undesirable outcomes" (p. 26). Finally, continuous professional development involves acquiring and maintaining knowledge of legislation relevant to assessment in school settings (e.g., IDEIA 2004), ethical codes and professional standards of the National Association of School Psychologists (NASP) and the American Psychological Association (APA), and relevant professional literature. This component also involves receiving supervision and feedback as needed to ensure competency in the delivery of assessment services.

SOCIAL JUSTICE CONNECTIONS

How can school psychologists promote socially just assessment practices?

Generally, the field of school psychology has generated a considerable amount of literature related to test bias as well as culturally responsive and nondiscriminatory assessment practices. Even so, there is a need for more scholarship that explores assessment processes through a social justice lens. Many of the challenges that racial, ethnic, and linguistic minority students face (e.g., inappropriate educational placements and excessively harsh discipline) can be addressed, in part, by promoting socially just assessment practices.

As described in this chapter, it is imperative that school psychologists employ culturally responsive assessment practices. However, in and of itself, displaying cultural sensitivity is not sufficient to rectify deep-rooted injustices in school-based practices. The following general recommendations are appropriate when employing a social justice approach to the broad process of assessment.

1. *Assume an ecological, strength-based approach.* As noted in Chapter 2, a traditional *medical model* of assessment and diagnosis posits that evaluators should seek to identify "problems" within individuals and subsequently propose solutions for eliminating those problems. For school psychologists, this approach is problematic for two reasons. First, it assumes that problems reside solely within individuals rather than in the person–environment interactions that shape their experiences. Second, it implores practitioners to focus on clients' "inherent problems" and weaknesses at the expense of recognizing their strengths. A more constructive approach to assessment is one that proactively seeks to identify both the within-person and environmental variables that impact student functioning as well as strengths that are likely to serve as the foundation for future successes. This type of approach can provide clear avenues for effective intervention as well as reduce the likelihood that teachers and other personnel will perceive children as "problem students."

2. *Advocate for holistic and comprehensive assessment practices.* Recognize that test scores alone cannot provide a comprehensive picture of a child's strengths and weaknesses. Multimethod approaches that incorporate test scores, parent and teacher interviews, classroom observations, and other sources of data will provide the most well-rounded information about students' and their school experiences.

3. *Advocate for valid assessment practices.* It is easier for schools to default to discriminatory assessment practices (often unintentionally) when time, money, and resources are scarce. In some cases, school psychologists may need to find creative ways to access the right assessment tools and training opportunities. For example, many academic progress monitoring measures are available to users online free of charge. Connecting with colleagues in neighboring districts and local professional organizations may allow practitioners to share or borrow resources when necessary. Finally, connecting with nearby universities and scholars who are involved in high-quality research can afford access to training opportunities and assessment procedures that might not be otherwise feasible (although school psychologists should ensure that the practices to be implemented have some established evidence base).

SUMMARY AND CONCLUSIONS

School psychologists spend much of their time conducting assessments. While the identification and implementation of effective interventions are essential to student outcomes, the efficiency and effectiveness of instruction and intervention are unquestionably enhanced by assessment. Assessment allows educators and other professionals to engage in data-based decision making (described in Chapter 7). It also informs many important decisions such as eligibility for and allocation of services, instructional planning, and selection and implementation of intervention services. Ultimately, assessment is a critical function of school psychologists, as is demonstrated throughout the remaining chapters of the book.

DISCUSSION QUESTIONS

1. As noted in this chapter, school psychologists conduct assessments *for* intervention, *during* intervention, and *of* intervention. What are the purposes of each of these types of assessments?
2. For classroom observations, which types of student behaviors are best quantified by measuring frequency? Why? Which types of behaviors are best quantified by measuring duration? Why?
3. A school psychologist administers a broad-band rating scale (i.e., BASC-3) to a student, two of her teachers, and one of her parents. Upon scoring the protocols, it is found that the student's and teachers' results indicate elevated levels of anxiety and depression; however, results from the parent's rating scale do not indicate that the student is experiencing any anxiety or depression. Why might this situation arise? In this situation, what steps might the school psychologist take next? What other data might he choose to collect?
4. What are some advantages and disadvantages of using each of the three types of interviews described in this chapter (i.e., structured, semistructured, and unstructured interviews)?
5. Describe at least three important considerations for communicating assessment results to parent and teachers.

REFERENCES

Achenbach, T. M., McConaughy, S. H., & Howell, C. T. (1987). Child/adolescent behavioral and emotional problems: Implications of cross-informant correlations for situational specificity. *Psychological Bulletin, 101*, 213–232. doi:10.1037/0033-2909.101.2.213

Albers, C. A., Elliott, S. N., Kettler, R. J., & Roach, A. T. (2015). Evaluating intervention outcomes within problem-solving–based assessment. In R. Brown-Chidsey, K. J. Andren, R. Brown-Chidsey, & K. J. Andren (Eds.), *Assessment for intervention: A problem-solving approach* (2nd ed., pp. 344–360). New York, NY: Guilford.

Albers, C. A., Glover, T. A., & Kratochwill, T. R. (2007). Where are we, and where do we go now? Universal screening for enhanced educational and mental health outcomes. *Journal of School Psychology, 45*, 257–263.

Allen, J. D. (2005). Grades as valid measures of academic achievement of classroom learning. *Clearing House: A Journal of Educational Strategies, Issues and Ideas, 78*(5), 218–223.

American Educational Research Association, American Psychological Association, & National Council on Measurement in Education. (2014). *Standards for educational and psychological testing.* Washington, DC: American Educational Research Association.

Benson, N. (2010). Types of tests and assessments. In E. Mpofu & T. Oakland (Eds.), *Assessment in rehabilitation and health* (pp. 72–90). Boston, MA: Allyn & Bacon.

Black, P., & William, D. (1998). Assessment and classroom learning. *Assessment in Education, 5,* 7–74.

Braden, J. P. (2003). Psychological assessment in school settings. In J. R. Graham, J. A. Naglieri, J. R. Graham, & J. A. Naglieri (Eds.), *Handbook of psychology: Assessment psychology* (Vol. 10, pp. 261–290). Hoboken, NJ: Wiley.

De Los Reyes, A., Augenstein, T. M., Wang, M., Thomas, S. A., Drabick, D. A. G., & Rabinowitz, J. (2015). The validity of the multi-informant approach to assessing child and adolescent mental health. *Psychological Bulletin, 141,* 858–900.

Dixson, D. D., & Worrell, F. C. (2016). Formative and summative assessment in the classroom. *Theory into Practice, 55,* 153–159. doi:10.1080/00405841.2016.1148989

Every Student Succeeds Act, Pub. L. No. 114-95, § 1177 (2015).

Fagan, T. K. (1996). Witmer's contribution to school psychological services. *American Psychologist, 51,* 241–243. doi:10.1037/0003-066X.51.3.241

Frick, P., Barry, C., & Kamphaus, R. (2009). *Clinical assessment of child and adolescent personality and behavior* (3rd ed.). New York, NY: Springer Publishing.

Fuchs, L. S., & Fuchs, D. (2010). Progress monitoring. In P. Peterson, E. Baker, & B. McGaw (Eds.), *Encyclopedia of education* (3rd ed., Vol. 4, pp. 102–111). Oxford, UK: Elsevier.

Furlong, M. J., Gilman, R., & Huebner, E. S. (2014). *Handbook of positive psychology in schools* (2nd ed). New York, NY: Routledge.

Glaser, R. (1963). Instructional technology and the measurement of learning outcomes: Some questions. *American Psychologist, 18,* 519–521. doi:10.1037/h0049294

Glutting, J. J., Oakland, T., & McDermott, P. A. (1989). Observing child behavior during testing: Constructs, validity, and situational generality. *Journal of School Psychology, 27,* 155–164. doi:10.1016/0022-4405(89)90003-4

Hanushek, E. A., Kai, J. F., & Rivken, S. J. (1998). Teachers, schools, and academic achievement. NBER working paper 6691. Cambridge, MA. Retrieved from http://www. cgp.upenn.edu/pdf/Hanushek_NBER.PDF

Hattie, J., & Leeson, H. (2013). Future directions in assessment and testing in education and psychology. In K. F. Geisinger, B. A. Bracken, J. F. Carlson, J. C. Hansen, N. R. Kuncel, S. P. Reise, & M. C. Rodriguez (Eds.), *APA handbook of testing and assessment in psychology, Vol. 3: Testing and assessment in school psychology and education* (pp. 591–622). Washington, DC: American Psychological Association.

Hopwood, C. J., & Richard, D. C. S. (2005). Graduate student WAIS-III scoring accuracy is a function of Full Scale IQ and complexity of examiner tasks. *Assessment, 12,* 445–454.

Individuals with Disabilities Education Improvement Act, Pub. L. No. 108-446 (2004).

Jimerson, S. R., Sharkey, J. D., Nyborg, V., & Furlong, M. J. (2004). Strength-based assessment and school psychology: A summary and synthesis. *California School Psychologist, 9*(1), 9–19. doi:10.1007/BF03340903

Klingner, J. K., Artiles, A. J., Kozleski, E., Harry, B., Zion, S., Tate, W., . . . Riley, D. (2005). Addressing the disproportionate representation of culturally and linguistically diverse students in special education through culturally responsive educational systems. *Education Policy Analysis Archives, 13*(38). Retrieved from http://epaa.asu.edu/ojs/article/view/143

Loney, B. R., & Frick, P. J. (2003). Structured diagnostic interviewing. In C. R. Reynolds, R. W. Kamphaus, C. R. Reynolds, & R. W. Kamphaus (Eds.), *Handbook of psychological and educational assessment of children: Personality, behavior, and context* (2nd ed., pp. 235–247). New York, NY: Guilford.

MacCorquodale, K., & Meehl, P. E. (1948). On a distinction between hypothetical constructs and intervening variables. *Psychological Review, 55,* 95–107. doi:10.1037/h0056029

McCellan, J., & Werry, J. S. (2000). Introduction to special section: Research psychiatric diagnostic interviews for children and adolescents. *Journal of the American Academy of Child and Adolescent Psychiatry, 39*, 19–27.

Ramos, E., Alfonso, V. C., & Schermerhorn, S. M. (2009). Graduate students' administration and scoring errors on the Woodcock-Johnson III Tests of Cognitive Abilities. *Psychology in the Schools, 46*, 650–657.

Reynolds, C. R. (1986). The elusive professionalism of school psychology: Lessons from the past, portents for the future. *Professional School Psychology, 1*, 41–46. doi:10.1037/h0090499

Reynolds, C. R. (1997). Postscripts on premorbid ability estimation: Conceptual addenda and a few words on alternative and conditional approaches. *Archives of Clinical Neuropsychology, 12*, 769–778. doi:10.1016/S0887-6177(97)00051-6

Reynolds, C. R., & Kamphaus, R. W. (2015). *Behavior assessment system for children, third edition (BASC-3)*. New York, NY: Pearson.

Reynolds, C. R., & Richmond, B. O. (2008). *Revised children's manifest anxiety scale, second edition (RCMAS-2) manual*. Torrance, CA: WPS Publishing.

Roberts, R. M., & Davis, M. C. (2015). Assessment of a model for achieving competency in administration and scoring of the WAIS-IV in post-graduate psychology students. *Frontiers in Psychology, 6*, 641. doi:10.3389/fpsyg.2015.00641

Salvia, J., Ysseldyke, J. E., & Witmer, S. (2017). *Assessment: In special and inclusive education* (13th ed.). Boston, MA: Cengage Learning.

Schrank, F. A., Mather, N., & McGrew, K. S. (2014). *Woodcock-Johnson IV tests of achievement*. Rolling Meadows, IL: Riverside.

Shepard, L. A. (2006). Classroom assessment. In R. L. Brennan (Ed.), *Educational measurement* (pp. 623–646). Westport, CT: Praeger.

Sullivan, A. L. (2010). Preventing disproportionality: A framework for culturally responsive assessment. *NASP Communiqué, 39*, 1.

Tobin, R. M., & House, A. E. (2016). *DSM-5 diagnosis in the schools*. New York, NY: Guilford.

VandenBos, G. R. (2015). *APA dictionary of psychology* (2nd ed.). Washington, DC: American Psychological Association.

Weiner, I. B. (2013). The assessment process. In I. B. Weiner, J. R. Graham, J. A. Naglieri, J. R. Graham, J. A. Naglieri, & I. B. Weiner (Eds.), *Handbook of psychology: Assessment psychology* (pp. 3–25). Hoboken, NJ: Wiley.

Welner, K. G. (2013). Consequential validity and the transformation of tests from measurement tools to policy tools. *Teachers College Record, 115*(9), 1–6. Retrieved from www.tcrecord.org

CHAPTER 7

Intervention Planning and Implementation

SUSAN G. FORMAN ■ PHILIP OLIVEIRA

CHAPTER OBJECTIVES

- Describe the multi-tiered systems of support framework for service delivery
- Describe how screening, assessment, and progress monitoring are used in data-based decision making
- Define a data-based problem-solving model for use in decision making about services and programs
- Discuss the importance of research evidence in selecting interventions
- Introduce the process of implementation and the importance of using implementation strategies to support successful intervention use

The primary goal of schools is to provide students with the educational services that they need to become well-adjusted and productive members of society. This means that schools should provide high-quality services that promote students' academic development as well as their social, emotional, and behavioral (SEB) well-being. Ultimately, these services are designed to ensure that students are meeting appropriate milestones and to prevent problems from arising. When problems do arise, school personnel must take action to remediate them before they escalate further.

Prevention refers to those services that foster student competencies (e.g., academic and social skills) so as to promote healthy development and to avoid the onset of long-term problems. **Intervention** refers to services that address problems that have already become apparent. Schools can deliver prevention and intervention services in a number of ways, and both types of services are fundamental for supporting the success of all students. The goal of this chapter is to discuss broadly how prevention and intervention services may be structured, delivered, and evaluated in schools. In subsequent chapters, we address specific types of prevention and intervention services in academic and SEB domains.

MULTI-TIERED SYSTEMS OF SUPPORT

Among other organizations, the National Association of School Psychologists (NASP, 2016) endorses a framework of service delivery commonly referred to as multitiered systems of support. Broadly defined, **multi-tiered systems of support (MTSS)** are comprehensive service delivery frameworks that provide a continuum of prevention and intervention services to meet the needs of all students. The goal of MTSS is to promote successful academic or SEB development for all students in a school building. The framework is predicated on the assumption that all students can learn when provided with the appropriate instruction. Prevention and intervention services represented in this continuum must be evidence-based, meaning that they must have acceptable levels of research support. MTSS can be implemented at various organizational levels, including the individual school, district, and state levels. For consistency and clarity, this chapter describes MTSS implementation at the individual school level.

One of the core features of MTSS is its ecological (i.e., environmentally focused) approach to conceptualizing and addressing student problems. In MTSS, student problems are conceptualized as a mismatch between student variables (e.g., previous knowledge and motivation) and environmental variables (e.g., instructional strategies and classroom routines), rather than as inherent problems that lie within students themselves. Thus, the primary mechanism by which academic and behavioral skill problems are resolved is the alteration of environmental and intervention variables to better match individual students' needs. This ecological approach is beneficial because it requires educators to move away from "blaming" students for academic and behavioral problems and instead to focus on environmental variables that impact instruction.

Overview of the Tiered System

In MTSS, a continuum of supports is provided through a tiered system. While many MTSS models comprise three tiers of support, others include four or even as many as seven tiers. Collectively, tiered services provide an integrated system of school-wide, classroom-wide, and individual learning and behavioral supports for students with a range of needs. As struggling students progress upward through these tiers, the intervention services they receive become increasingly intensive. When and if their difficulties are remediated, students also may progress downward through the tiers, meaning that the services are removed or gradually become less intensive.

Services provided within the tiered system range from school-wide preventive programs for all students to intensive interventions for students with identified problems. One common misconception about MTSS is that it is designed to be a remedial framework for supporting only those students who are struggling behaviorally or academically. In reality, MTSS is a comprehensive service delivery framework for supporting *all* students, including those who are meeting academic and behavioral standards as well as those who are not. Furthermore, this tiered system is based on the assumption that, in many cases, problems in academic and SEB functioning can be prevented if they are identified and addressed early on (Cook, Lyon, Kubergovic, Wright, & Zhang, 2015).

The following subsections provide an overview of MTSS. The descriptions presented here are based on a three-tiered model, as such models are mostly commonly referenced in the school psychology literature. Figure 7.1 depicts the three tiers and their core features.

Tier 1

Tier 1 services and interventions are also called *primary, universal,* or *preventive* services. As already noted, MTSS is designed to support the progress of all students in a school. Tier 1 constitutes those services that are provided to *all* students at the classroom, school, or district level. For example, with respect to academic learning, Tier 1 services would consist of an effective, evidence-based core curriculum that is aligned with state and school district learning goals. With respect to SEB learning, Tier 1 interventions may consist of clearly communicated school-wide behavioral expectations (e.g., positively stated school rules) and school-wide instruction in areas such as conflict resolution, bullying prevention, emotional coping, and self-regulation. Because they are designed to reach all students, Tier 1 interventions tend to be large-group programs conducted with whole classrooms or in multiple classrooms. Moreover, they may be implemented by a variety of personnel who interact regularly with students, including teachers, guidance counselors, and school psychologists. For example, Tier 1 academic interventions are implemented by classroom teachers, since they deliver the whole-group instruction that all students receive in their classrooms on a daily basis. Tier 1 interventions in the SEB domain may be implemented by teachers

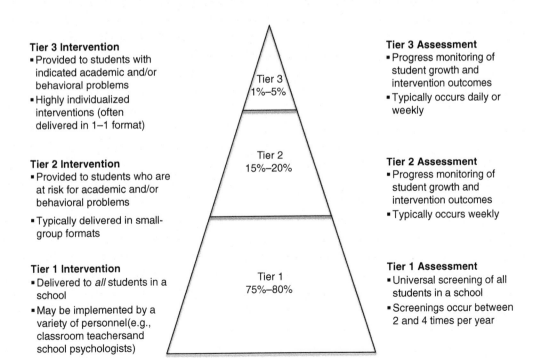

Tier 3 Intervention
- Provided to students with indicated academic and/or behavioral problems
- Highly individualized interventions (often delivered in 1–1 format)

Tier 3
1%–5%

Tier 3 Assessment
- Progress monitoring of student growth and intervention outcomes
- Typically occurs daily or weekly

Tier 2 Intervention
- Provided to students who are at risk for academic and/or behavioral problems
- Typically delivered in small-group formats

Tier 2
15%–20%

Tier 2 Assessment
- Progress monitoring of student growth and intervention outcomes
- Typically occurs weekly

Tier 1 Intervention
- Delivered to *all* students in a school
- May be implemented by a variety of personnel(e.g., classroom teachersand school psychologists)

Tier 1
75%–80%

Tier 1 Assessment
- Universal screening of all students in a school
- Screenings occur between 2 and 4 times per year

FIGURE 7.1 ASSESSMENT AND INTERVENTION IN MULTI-TIERED SYSTEMS OF SUPPORT (MTSS).

or, alternatively, by school psychologists or school counselors in collaboration with the classroom teacher.

One of the goals of providing Tier 1 services is to decrease the need for students to accelerate to higher tiers for further, more intensive interventions. Generally, it is expected that the majority of students in a school will be able to meet academic standards when receiving Tier 1 services only. More specifically, Tier 1 services aim to comprehensively meet the needs of between 75% and 80% of students (Stoiber & Gettinger, 2016). If fewer than 75% to 80% of students are meeting performance expectations while receiving Tier 1 supports alone (meaning that more than approximately 20% of students demonstrate need of higher tiers of intervention), there is likely a problem with the design or delivery of the school's universal supports. This observation would suggest a need for teachers, school psychologists, and other personnel to consider the design and delivery of core instruction and to make necessary changes such that the majority of students will be successful in response to these supports.

Tier 2

One critical assumption of the MTSS framework is that not all students learn in exactly the same way and that some will require more intensive instruction than others do to meet academic and behavioral standards. Students who struggle, despite access to Tier 1 services, may demonstrate need of **Tier 2** services, which are also called *secondary*, *targeted*, or *selective* interventions. Interventions in this tier are provided to students who are deemed to be at risk for academic or SEB problems. Further information about how these students are identified as being "at risk" is provided in subsequent sections of this chapter.

Since it is expected that fewer students will demonstrate a need for Tier 2 supports, these interventions tend to be conducted in small groups. Smaller group sizes allow students to receive more frequent and immediate feedback from instructors as well as more individualized attention. It is important to note that Tier 2 services do not replace Tier 1 services, which are consistently delivered to all students. Instead, these secondary services are intended to supplement Tier 1 interventions, thereby accelerating the student's rate of learning. For example, they may involve more exposure to targeted material and more opportunities for guided practice. Tier 2 interventions typically are delivered for 6 to 20 weeks, and sometimes longer. Like Tier 1 interventions, they may be implemented by a variety of school personnel, including teachers, school psychologists, social workers, and others.

Since the majority of learners should be accommodated by Tier 1 services, a relatively smaller number of students will demonstrate a need for Tier 2 services—specifically, approximately 15% to 20% of students. Like Tier 1 services, Tier 2 interventions are designed to prevent students from demonstrating need for even more intensive supports (i.e., Tier 3 interventions).

Tier 3

Tier 3 services are also called *tertiary*, *indicated*, or *intensive* interventions. They are provided to students with identified academic or SEB problems (i.e., students who are considered to have the highest risk for long-term problems). Tier 3 interventions are customized and delivered individually or in small groups (i.e., smaller groups than those seen in Tier 2).

Tier 3 interventions typically require extensive resources, professional involvement, and time beyond what is provided in Tiers 1 and 2. Because students who need Tier 3 interventions have severe difficulties, multicomponent services may be needed. Tier 3 interventions typically are implemented by highly skilled special services staff (e.g., school psychologists) as well as by community-based behavioral health professionals, as necessary. They tend to be longer in duration than Tier 2 programs, sometimes extending to multiple years (Sanetti & Collier-Meek, 2015).

As compared with Tiers 1 and 2, it is expected that an even smaller percentage of students will demonstrate a need for Tier 3 services. Tier 3 services serve approximately 1% to 5% of students who need services beyond what is provided in the first two tiers (Center for Mental Health in Schools, 2011; Stoiber & Gettinger, 2016). Often, students receiving Tier 3 interventions have been identified as individuals in need of special education. Generally, if more than 5% of students in a given school demonstrate a need for Tier 3 supports, it may be necessary for school staff to review and modify the Tier 1 and Tier 2 services, such that the majority of student needs are met at those intervention levels.

Screening, Assessment, and Progress Monitoring in MTSS

After reading these sections, one might wonder: *How do school personnel identify students who are at risk or who have identified problems?* In other words, how do educators determine which students are in need of which tiers of support? Moreover, how do they assess student progress at each tier, and how do they determine whether students should be escalated or de-escalated to and from different tiers of intervention?

Data-based decision making is a critical feature of MTSS implementation and allows personnel to answer these questions in a reliable and valid manner. As described in Chapter 1 (and, more specifically, in Domain 1 of the NASP Practice Model), **data-based decision making** refers to the use of any number of assessment or data collection strategies to inform the design, implementation, and evaluation of services and programs (NASP, 2010). When executed properly, data-based decision making allows school psychologists to accurately identify student- and systems-level needs, match those needs to the appropriate interventions and services, and monitor related outcomes. Thus, it is an essential component of MTSS implementation.

Data-based decision making relies heavily on the use of reliable and valid assessment procedures (as described in Chapter 6). Assessments may be similar or different across tiers, depending on the school's MTSS model and selected procedures. Generally, assessments are administered more frequently at higher tiers of intervention, although assessment schedules vary across schools with different MTSS models. Common assessment procedures implemented at the different tiers are described in further detail in the following subsections.

Tier 1

At Tier 1, assessment objectives are twofold: (a) to determine whether the majority of students (i.e., between 75% and 80% of individuals) are meeting grade-level expectations with Tier 1 supports alone and (b) to identify students who are at risk for academic and behavioral problems and therefore demonstrate need for higher tiers of intervention. These objectives are accomplished through universal screening for all students. *Universal screening* (a concept first introduced in Chapter 6) involves the administration of brief measures of target skills and behaviors. Often, screeners are selected based on their validity for predicting later student outcomes (e.g., state test performance and long-term mental health outcomes).

In MTSS, screenings typically occur between two and four times per year. Some screeners directly measure students' skills (e.g., students complete a brief reading task), whereas others measure skills and behaviors indirectly (e.g., the parent or teacher completes a rating scale reporting the student's behaviors). Often, screening procedures incorporate multiple measures and are supplemented by other types of data, such as grades and attendance records. At times, risk factors or problems identified during screening are followed by more intensive assessment to determine the nature of the problem and to develop appropriate intervention goals. More information about academic and SEB screening is provided in Chapters 8 and 9, respectively.

Universal screening is an essential part of the process for linking students with appropriate services and interventions. Students are identified either as at risk or not at risk based on their screening performance and other factors (e.g., teacher and parent input). School teams may analyze screening data several times per year. In particular, schools analyze data for two primary purposes: (1) to ensure that the majority of students (approximately 75% to 80%) are meeting academic and behavioral expectations with Tier 1 supports alone and (2) to differentiate those students who need additional interventions (i.e., Tier 2 and Tier 3 interventions) from those who do not. In other words, universal screening allows educators to evaluate their school-wide programming and to identify candidates for receiving more intensive interventions.

Tiers 2 and 3

Once students in need of interventions beyond Tier 1 are identified, further data must be collected for decision-making purposes. As described in Chapter 6, *progress monitoring* allows for the periodic assessment of student progress and intervention effectiveness and is essential for ensuring that students are benefiting from interventions. Moreover, progress monitoring data are key for determining whether interventions should be continued, terminated, or changed.

Progress monitoring is a type of formative assessment, meaning that it provides ongoing information about student progress so as to guide instructional decision making. Assessment schedules may vary depending on the characteristics of the intervention, skills and behaviors observed, and the progress monitoring instruments themselves. For example, progress monitoring may occur on a monthly, weekly, or daily basis. In many cases, more intensive interventions are associated with more frequent progress monitoring, since they are more resource intensive and intended for higher-risk students. Thus, frequent data must be collected to ensure that instructional resources are used judiciously.

When evaluating progress, students' performance during and following an intervention can be compared to predetermined criteria, or benchmarks, that are based on local or national samples of same-grade or same-age students. Based on these criteria, educators may continue an intervention, provide a modified intervention within the same tier, or escalate or de-escalate to a different tier. For example, if a student were to catch up to same-age or same-grade peers over the course of a Tier 2 intervention, that student might either return to Tier 1 or continue with the Tier 2 intervention, depending on whether the intervention was deemed necessary to sustain skill growth over time. In contrrast, if a student continued to struggle despite receiving Tier 2 intervention services, he or she might be escalated to Tier 3.

Pyle and Vaughn (2012) suggested four decision-making rules for evaluating progress monitoring to determine whether students should be escalated from Tier 2 to Tier 3:

1. If the student has participated in two rounds of Tier 2 intervention and has not made sufficient progress, he or she should be escalated to Tier 3.
2. If the student has participated in one round of Tier 2, but shows a marked lack of progress, he or she should move to Tier 3.
3. If the student has received less than one round of Tier 2, but intensive intervention is indicated to accelerate skill development and prevent further problem development, he or she should be escalated to Tier 3.
4. If the student has previously received Tier 3 services, he or she should reenter Tier 3 as needed.

PROBLEM-SOLVING MODEL

The preceding sections have provided a number of considerations for selecting interventions and monitoring student progress. School psychologists and others must consider a number of factors in their decision making about service delivery within and across tiers. These pieces of information allow them to identify student needs, select appropriate intervention services, determine whether those services should be continued and/or modified, and evaluate the intervention's effectiveness in achieving predetermined goals.

School psychologists may implement a ***problem-solving model*** to gather and synthesize information in a logical manner and, subsequently, to make educational decisions that best serve students and school systems. The problem-solving model is a systematic process used "to make decisions about continuously improving educational programs and services" (Pluymert, 2014, p. 25). Problem solving relies heavily on data-based decision-making procedures. Typically, a problem-solving model is conceptualized as involving four primary steps. Each of these steps is described in the following text and depicted in Figure 7.2.

1. *Problem identification.* In this stage, the school psychologist develops a clear and measurable definition of the problem to be remediated. ***Gap***

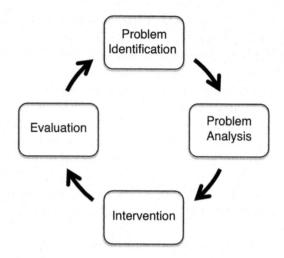

FIGURE 7.2 PROBLEM-SOLVING MODEL.

analysis seeks to quantify the difference between current performance and targeted (desired) performance. For example, simply identifying a student as being a "slow reader" would not constitute a clear and measurable definition of a reading problem. Instead, a school psychologist might measure the student's reading rate and accuracy by calculating the number of words he or she can read correctly in 1 minute. Subsequently, the school psychologist would identify a target reading rate for the student based on grade-level standards and local or national norms. By comparing these two quantities, the school psychologist is able to more clearly and concisely state the problem. An example of a clear, well-defined problem statement is as follows: "Suzanne reads 84 words correct per minute from grade-level passages. On average, Suzanne's same-grade peers read 123 words correct per minute from the same passages." This statement suggests that Suzanne must increase her reading rate by 39 words correct per minute and paves the way for the development of clear and concrete reading intervention goals.

2. *Problem analysis.* Problem analysis involves identifying the causes of the student's or system's difficulties. One of the key assumptions of this stage is that identifying the cause of the problem facilitates the development of appropriate and successful interventions (Burns & Gibbons, 2008; Pluymert, 2014). Through various assessment methods (e.g., observation, brief testing, and record review), the school psychologist may seek to clarify a number of questions. For example, is Suzanne's slow reading attributable to a deficit in core reading skills (a *skill problem*)? Or is Suzanne's reading hindered by other factors, such as attention difficulties or shyness (a *performance problem*)? Knowledge of the various factors contributing to Suzanne's slow reading would assist school personnel in developing the intervention best suited to her needs. The problem analysis phase culminates in the formation of a hypothesis that describes the root cause of the problem.

3. *Plan development and implementation.* This third step involves the development of an intervention plan to remediate the problem defined in the first step. First, the school psychologist must define clear intervention goals or clear criteria for desirable performance. These criteria must be easily measured (e.g., by counting Suzanne's number of words read correctly in 1 minute). The intervention itself should be aligned with the hypothesized cause of the problem identified during problem analysis. Moreover, the intervention should be research based, and procedures for progress monitoring and measuring achievement outcomes should be clearly delineated.

4. *Plan evaluation.* The final phase of the problem-solving process involves determining whether the intervention has successfully remediated the problem at hand. This involves reviewing progress monitoring data and comparing the student's level of performance at the end of the intervention to the performance criteria stated in the intervention goals. Based on this information, the school psychologist and others can determine whether the intervention should be continued, modified, terminated, or replaced by a different intervention.

The four phases of the problem-solving model are intended to be recursive rather than linear, meaning that the school psychologist may revert to previous stages as necessary. For example, if the school psychologist reaches the plan evaluation phase only to find that the problem has not been remediated, it may be necessary to return to previous steps to reformulate the problem definition or hypothesis and, ultimately, the intervention plan. Overall, the problem-solving model allows the school psychologist to assume a methodical and practical approach to addressing student- and systems-level problems.

SELECTING INTERVENTIONS: THE IMPORTANCE OF EVIDENCE

As described in the MTSS framework and problem-solving models, selecting interventions that are likely to be effective in addressing student-specific and school-wide problems is an essential role of the school psychologist. Key considerations for selecting an appropriate intervention are the goals for the client(s) and the evidence base for the intervention. ***Evidence-based interventions (EBIs)*** are interventions that are likely to produce positive outcomes for clients because they are supported by high-quality research indicating that such outcomes are probable. Various authors, federal agencies, and professional associations have offered different definitions of the term *evidence-based*, though these definitions all share some commonalities. Generally, EBIs are interventions that are supported by an appropriate number of well-designed research studies, such that they meet Kazdin and Weisz's (2010) six criteria:

1. The support includes two or more research studies in which there has been specification of the target population.
2. Random assignment of participants to conditions (e.g., treatment and control groups in the experiment) is utilized in these supporting studies.

3. Supporting studies report utilizing intervention manuals that specify intervention procedures in detail (which facilitates the replicability of the intervention).
4. Supporting studies use multiple outcome measures, including measures of the target problem.
5. These studies report statistically significant differences between the intervention group and a comparison group after treatment.
6. Research findings regarding the intervention have been replicated, ideally, by independent investigators.

In intervention research, the "gold standard" for research design is the randomized controlled trial. A *randomized controlled trial* (**RCT**) involves the comparison of at least two groups of participants: an experimental group (i.e., a group of participants who receive the intervention under investigation) and a control group (i.e., a comparison group of participants who do not receive the intervention). Although RCTs share a number of core features, one quintessential feature is random assignment. *Random assignment* refers to the process of sorting participants into treatment comparison groups based on chance (i.e., each participant is equally likely to be assigned to any one particular group). Researchers can use a variety of tools for carrying out random assignment, including random number generators (i.e., electronic mechanisms in which each participant is assigned a number at random that corresponds with membership in a particular group). Random assignment is expected to ensure that participant groups are comparable with respect to both observable and nonobservable characteristics, meaning that treatment effects can be identified in a valid manner.

Many EBIs have been introduced for treating academic and mental health problems among children and adolescents. School psychologists can identify these interventions through individual studies, research reviews published in peer-reviewed journals, and reports from national and international organizations that vet research on academic and SEB prevention and intervention programs. Examples of these organizations include the U.S. Department of Education's What Works Clearinghouse (http://ies.ed.gove/ncee/wwc); the Center for the Study and Prevention of Violence (www.colorado.edu./cspv/blueprints/index.html); the National Institute on Drug Abuse (www.drugabuse.gov); the Substance Abuse and Mental Health Administration's National Registry of Evidence-Based Programs and Practices (www.nrepp.samhsa.gov); the Collaborative for Academic, Social, and Emotional Learning (http://casel.org); and the Effective Child Therapy website (http://effectivechildtherapy.com), developed by the Society of Clinical Child and Adolescent Psychology (Division 53 of the American Psychological Association).

Best practices indicate that an intervention that is supported by well-designed research should be chosen over one that does not have this type of empirical support. Unfortunately, EBIs do not currently exist for all problems and needs. In the absence of strong evidence, it sometimes may be necessary to use an intervention with emerging empirical support or to rely on empirical evidence and interventions that are indirectly linked to client and school needs.

SOCIAL JUSTICE CONNECTIONS

How do school psychologists adapt interventions to serve culturally diverse clients?

The children and adolescents with whom school psychologists work are diverse in many respects. In some cases, a student's responsiveness to an intervention may be influenced by the degree to which the intervention aligns with the student's cultural background. *Cultural adaptation* describes the process of modifying an intervention to ensure that it is congruent with the patterns, meanings, and values of a client's culture.

When an intervention is modified from its original form as described in research studies, client outcomes may also be different (i.e., the outcomes documented in previous research may not be reproduced). On the one hand, while cultural adaptations can be key for maximizing client–intervention fit, practitioners must be careful that these adaptations do not disrupt key intervention mechanisms that are believed to lead to positive client change. On the other hand, when executed properly, cultural adaptation can enhance the success of an intervention (see Barrera, Castro, Strycker, & Toobert, 2013). There is considerable debate in the literature regarding the types and degree of adaptation that are appropriate, although there is general agreement that core components of an intervention should not be violated.

Typical adaptations to an intervention include additions, deletions, or modifications of intervention components; changes in the manner of delivery or intensity of components; and cultural modifications based on local circumstances (McKleroy et al., 2006). Language translations and use of culturally relevant examples are frequently employed to enhance the match between interventions and clients. Other types of adaptations may include involving families and other significant individuals, changing the setting of the intervention, and incorporating cultural values in intervention content (Barrera et al., 2013). Ultimately, successful cultural adaptation requires practitioners to consider the individual characteristics and needs of their clients as well as to demonstrate knowledge of intervention design principles.

INTERVENTION IMPLEMENTATION

Selecting an appropriate intervention based on research evidence is only an initial step in the process of successful intervention use. The process of incorporating a program or practice at the individual, group, or organizational level is called *implementation*. Implementation involves a set of strategies and activities designed to put a program into use in a specific setting, such as a classroom or school. The mere act of selecting EBIs will not necessarily lead to successful implementation. Rather, specific steps must be taken to ensure that the individual receiving the intervention (client), those who are invested in the intervention (stakeholders), and the larger organizational setting are supportive. Good intentions related to delivering an intervention will not guarantee its success unless appropriate measures are taken during planning and implementation. The larger systems change process in schools is discussed in depth in Chapter 12; concepts related to intervention implementation are introduced and described here.

Implementation Components and Stages

The implementation process is characterized by several components and stages. Important components of the implementation process include (a) an *innovation*—a new program or practice to be instituted, such as an intervention; (b) a *communication process*—mechanisms by which those who have knowledge about the intervention exchange information with those who do not; (c) a *social system*—the social/organizational setting in which implementation takes place; (d) a *change agent*—the individual who assumes primary responsibility for the implementation process; (e) *stakeholders*—all individuals who are invested in the delivery and outcome of the intervention; and (f) *implementers*—individuals who either conduct the intervention or play an essential role in its delivery to clients. *Primary implementers* are those who directly conduct the intervention, whereas *secondary implementers* are those who have an essential role in supporting intervention delivery.

For example, consider a school psychologist who is well versed in the Life Skills Training program (Botvin, Baker, Dusenbury, Botvin, & Diaz, 1995) and is interested in implementing this program in her middle school as means of decreasing substance use. In this scenario, Life Skills Training is the *innovation* because although it is not a newly developed program, it is new to the middle school. The *communication process* includes presentations, meetings, and informal discussions between the school psychologist, who is knowledgeable about Life Skills Training, and other staff and administrators who are less familiar with this preventive program. The *social system* for this intervention is the school as well as larger systems that impact educational settings, such as the community and state and federal agencies. The *change agent* is the school psychologist, who is assuming primary responsibility for bringing this new prevention program to the middle school. *Primary implementers* for this program are the health teachers who will conduct the program in their classes, and *secondary implementers* are individuals such as the principal and assistant principal, who will arrange for the purchase of manuals, workbooks, and teacher training. *Stakeholders* include teachers, administrators, counselors, parents, police, and others, all of whom have an interest in school operations and the overall well-being of students. Recognizing each of these components and the roles they play in contributing to the success of the intervention is a fundamental part of the implementation process.

As noted earlier, the implementation process also can be conceptualized as a series of stages or phases in which the intervention is introduced and put into practice. These phases include (a) *dissemination*—the dispersal of information about the intervention to potential users; (b) *adoption*—the collective decision to use the intervention; (c) *implementation*—the delivery of the intervention to clients; and (d) *sustainability*—the continued use of the intervention after its first full implementation (Durlak & DuPre, 2008). During each stage, the change agent must take different steps to support the successful implementation of the intervention. Notably, success in one stage will not necessarily lead to success in a subsequent stage. For example, the decision to use an intervention will not necessarily lead to a successful first full implementation, unless the change agent works to ensure the development of a supportive context. Actions on the part of the change agent that can facilitate a smooth progression through each of the stages include developing implementer and stakeholder support, providing training and technical assistance, developing organizational support, and leveraging external systems (Forman, 2015).

Selecting Interventions: Maximizing Contextual Fit

In addition to examining the evidence base for an intervention (as described previously), it is important to consider other characteristics of an intervention to maximize the fit of the intervention with an implementing organization such as a school. Several intervention characteristics, as perceived by stakeholders, have been identified as influencing implementation success (Durlak & DuPre, 2008; Greenhalgh, Robert, Macfarlane, Bate, & Kyriakidou, 2004; Rogers, 2003): (a) *relative advantage*—the degree to which a new intervention is perceived as better than what currently exists; (b) *compatibility*—the degree to which an intervention is perceived as consistent with the values, beliefs, experiences, and needs of stakeholders; (c) *complexity*—the degree to which an intervention is perceived as difficult to use; (d) *trialability*—the degree to which an intervention may be tried on a limited basis; (e) *observability*—the degree to which results of an intervention are visible; (f) *riskiness*—the perceived degree to which an intervention use may bring about unwanted consequences; (g) *task relevance*—the degree to which the intervention is seen as having the potential to improve the stakeholder's work performance; and (h) *flexibility*—the degree to which the intervention is viewed as adaptable to the unique client and organization aspects and needs.

These intervention characteristics are *perceived* characteristics, meaning that they reflect stakeholders' personal understanding of and beliefs about the intervention. Perceptions of interventions may be based on previous experiences with similar types of programs; beliefs about the capabilities, roles, and responsibilities of oneself and others;, and other personal and individual factors. Notably, perceptions are changeable. As change agents, the school psychologist and leadership team members can take action to establish positive perceptions and dispel negative perceptions of an intervention. Such action can include discussion, consultation, presentations, workshops, and email communications that frame the intervention in positive terms with respect to the characteristics previously described.

Providing Training and Technical Assistance

Implementers must acquire an understanding of the principles, content, and processes of an intervention as well as skill in delivering it. Other stakeholders also need to acquire knowledge about an intervention that will encourage their support for the implementation process. Training and technical assistance are the means through which implementers and other stakeholders learn about an intervention. Training through presentations and workshops can be used to increase knowledge about an intervention, while technical assistance or coaching can increase an individual's skill in delivering the intervention to clients.

Presentations and workshops can provide information about the rationale, philosophy, theory, and research related to an intervention. These methods can introduce stakeholders to the components and key practices of an intervention. They can also provide a venue for implementers to begin to practice new skills. Effective workshop training for implementers takes place over multiple sessions and includes written materials and participant goal setting, modeling, participant practice opportunities, and feedback (Joyce & Showers, 2002). In addition, it is important for workshop training for implementers to focus on acceptable forms of adaptation that can be used to tailor interventions to the characteristics of their clients and organization.

Workshop training alone is rarely sufficient to result in sustainable changes in the skills of those who will be delivering the intervention to clients (Lochman et al., 2009). Thus, technical assistance or coaching after initial training sessions is used to develop sustained implementer skills. This coaching and technical assistance process is well aligned with the school psychologist's role as consultant (described in Chapter 11). In this role, the school psychologist observes the use of the intervention, provides performance feedback that addresses implementation barriers, adapts the intervention to specific client needs and characteristics, and supports the implementer's self-efficacy (Han & Weiss, 2005).

Evaluating Implementation Outcomes: The Importance of Fidelity

In any effort to implement an EBI, it is important to evaluate both implementation and client/student outcomes. When evaluating interventions, psychologists have historically focused on intervention outcomes—that is, the effects of the intervention on the client. For example, in the example presented earlier describing the Life Skills Training program, intervention outcomes measured by the school psychologist and others may center on students' substance use behaviors, self-regulation, and emotional coping skills. (See Chapter 12 for more information about evaluating intervention outcomes.) However, implementation outcomes, which are indicators of whether an intervention is delivered properly and as intended, are also important. Implementation evaluation can provide information about how an intervention is being delivered, so that adjustments can be made, if necessary, regarding the quality or features of the intervention. Implementation evaluation serves to document what is provided to clients and, therefore, can assist in meeting accountability requirements. Implementation evaluation also allows intervention outcomes or client change to be attributed to the intervention. Implementation outcomes include indicators of whether the social and organizational context for the intervention is supportive. The most frequently used implementation outcome is typically related to *fidelity*.

Intervention fidelity (also referred to as program fidelity or treatment integrity) refers to the extent to which an intervention is delivered as planned or conceptualized (Sanetti & Kratochwill, 2009). Positive client outcomes have been consistently associated with high intervention fidelity (Durlak & DuPre, 2008). Fidelity is usually measured using direct observation of the delivery of an intervention. In this process, an observer checks the occurrence (or nonoccurrence) of operationally defined essential components of the intervention. The observation can occur in vivo or through the use of audio or video clips. A percentage of essential components implemented is derived by summing the number of components observed to have been implemented and dividing this number by the total number of components that should have been implemented. Direct observations can be used to measure **adherence** to core intervention components (i.e., the extent to which intervention components are present or not present) as well as **quality of delivery** (i.e., the implementer's skill in delivering each of these core components) (Dane & Schneider, 1998).

SUMMARY AND CONCLUSIONS

School psychologists have an integral role in school-based intervention planning and implementation. Although there are many ways in which school psychologists and other personnel can structure intervention services, MTSS is a particularly promising approach, due to its ecological orientation and its focus on outcomes for all students. Moreover, MTSS promotes early intervention and increases the likelihood that student problems will be remediated in a timely fashion (or avoided altogether). Within MTSS, using EBIs is essential for ensuring the potential for positive student outcomes. Ultimately, considerable planning and action are needed to build competency and support among stakeholders as well as to support the implementation of EBIs in MTSS. The school psychologist has the potential to be a key leader in facilitating this process and in promoting effective and equitable school services for all students.

DISCUSSION QUESTIONS

1. As a school psychologist, which challenges might you face in assisting a school to implement MTSS for the first time?
2. Which methods can be used to determine if Tier 2 or Tier 3 services are appropriate for a student?
3. Which activities does a school psychologist engage in when using a data-based problem-solving model to make educational decisions about students?
4. Which issues should be considered in selecting interventions for students?
5. What are some barriers to implementing EBIs in schools? Which activities does a school psychologist engage in to ensure that an intervention will be implemented successfully?

REFERENCES

Barrera, M. Jr., Castro, F. G., Strycker, L. A., & Toobert, D. J. (2013). Cultural adaptations of behavioral health interventions: A progress report. *Journal of Consulting and Clinical Psychology, 81*, 196–205. doi:10.1037/a0027085

Botvin, G. J., Baker, E., Dusenbury, L., Botvin, E. M., & Diaz, T. (1995). Long-term follow-up results of a randomized drug abuse prevention trial in a white middle-class population. *Journal of the American Medical Association, 273*, 1106–1112. doi:10.1001/jama.1995.03520380042033

Burns, M. K., & Gibbons, K. A. (2008). *Implementing response-to-intervention in elementary and secondary schools.* New York, NY: Routledge.

Center for Mental Health in Schools, University of California, Los Angeles. (2011). *Moving beyond the three tier intervention pyramid: Toward a comprehensive framework for student and learning supports.* Los Angeles, CA: Author. Retrieved from http://smhp.psych.ucla.edu/pdfdocs/briefs/threetier.pdf

Cook, C. R., Lyon, A. R., Kubergovic, D., Wright, D. B., & Zhang, Y. (2015). A supportive beliefs intervention to facilitate the implementation of evidence-based practices within a multi-tiered system of support. *School Mental Health, 7*, 49–60. doi:10.1007/s12310-014-9139-3

Dane, A. V., & Schneider, B. H. (1998). Program integrity in primary and early secondary prevention: Are implementation effects out of control? *Clinical Psychology Review, 18*, 23–45. doi:10.1016/S0272-7358(97)00043-3

Durlak, J. A., & DuPre, E. P. (2008). Implementation matters: A review of research on the influence of implementation on program outcomes and the factors affecting implementation. *American Journal of Community Psychology, 41*, 327–350. doi:10.1007/s10464-008-9165-0

Forman, S. G. (2015). *Implementation of mental health programs in schools: A change agent's guide.* Washington, DC: American Psychological Association.

Greenhalgh, T., Robert, G., Macfarlane, F., Bate, P., & Kyriakidou, O. (2004). Diffusion of innovations in service organizations: Systematic review and recommendations. *Milbank Quarterly, 82*, 581–629.

Han, S. S., & Weiss, B. (2005). Sustainability of teacher implementation of school-based mental health programs. *Journal of Abnormal Child Psychology, 33*, 665–679.

Joyce, B. R., & Showers, B. (2002). *Student achievement through staff development* (3rd ed.). Alexandria, VA: Association for the Supervision and Curriculum Development.

Kazdin, A. E., & Weisz, J. R. (2010). Introduction: Context, background, and goals. In A. E. Kazdin & J. R. Weisz (Eds.), *Evidence-based psychotherapies for children and adolescents* (pp. 3–9). New York, NY: Guilford Press.

Lochman, J. E., Boxmeyer, C., Powell, N., Qu, L., Wells, K., & Windle, M. (2009). Dissemination of the Coping Power program: Importance of intensity of counselor training. *Journal of Consulting and Clinical Psychology, 77*, 397–409. doi:10.1037/a0014514

McKleroy, V. S., Galbraith, J. S., Cummings, B., Jones, P., Harshbarger, C., Collins, C., & ADAPT Team. (2006). Adapting evidence-based behavioral interventions for new settings and target populations. *AIDS Education & Prevention, 18*(suppl), 59–73. doi:10.1521/aeap.2006.18.supp.59

National Association of School Psychologists. (2010). *Model for comprehensive and integrated school psychological services.* Bethesda, MD: Author.

National Association of School Psychologists. (2016). Every Student Succeeds Act opportunities: Multi-tiered systems of supports. Retrieved from https://www.nasponline.org/Documents/Research%20and%20Policy/ESSA_MTSS_Members.pdf

Pluymert, K. (2014). Problem-solving foundations for school psychological services. In P. L. Harrison & A. Thomas (Eds.), *Best practices in school psychology: Data-based and collaborative decision making* (pp. 25–39). Bethesda, MD: National Association of School Psychologists.

Pyle, N., & Vaughn, S. (2012). Remediating reading difficulties in a response to intervention model with secondary students. *Psychology in the Schools, 49*, 273–284.

Rogers, E. M. (2003). *Diffusion of innovations.* New York, NY: Free Press.

Sanetti, L. M. H., & Collier-Meek, M. A. (2015). Data-driven delivery of implementation supports in a multi-tiered framework: A pilot study. *Psychology in the Schools, 52*, 815–828.

Sanetti, L. M. H., & Kratochwill, T. R. (2009). Toward developing a science of treatment integrity: Introduction to the special series. *School Psychology Review, 38*, 445–459.

Stoiber, K. C., & Gettinger, M. (2016). Multi-tiered systems of support and evidence-based practices. In S. R. Jimerson, M. K. Burns, & A. M. VanDerHeyden (Eds.), *Handbook of response to intervention* (pp. 121–141). New York, NY: Springer Publishing.

CHAPTER 8

Academic Assessment and Intervention

SCOTT P. ARDOIN ■ STACY-ANN A. JANUARY

CHAPTER OBJECTIVES

- Describe the nature of academic skills in the areas of reading, mathematics, and written language
- Describe an ecologically oriented approach to academic assessment
- Name and describe the assessments that educators use to measures students' academic skills
- Illustrate academic assessment and intervention procedures within multi-tiered systems of support (MTSS)
- Describe the relevance of social justice in implementing academic MTSS

One of the primary functions of the K–12 education system is to prepare children to be ready for college or a career. Central to college and career readiness is students' proficiency in three key academic skill areas: reading, writing, and mathematics. Although most students acquire the necessary skills taught by teachers, some students need additional support in the form of academic interventions. Given the importance of academic skills, a core skill for school psychologists is the ability to collect and use assessment data that inform an intervention targeting students' academic skills. This chapter reviews the essential components of academic assessment and intervention as well as couches them within a multi-tiered system of support (MTSS).

DEFINITIONS AND PREVALENCE OF ACADEMIC SKILL PROBLEMS

Reading

Many students in grades K–12 in the United States struggle with reading. Data from the National Assessment of Educational Progress (NAEP), an annual assessment of academic achievement that is administered to a nationally representative sample of public and private school students in the United States, indicate that only 36% of fourth-grade students and 34% of eighth-grade students who completed this assessment in 2015 performed at or above the Proficient level (i.e., demonstrated adequate competency) in the subject of reading (U.S. Department of Education, 2017b). These data are alarming and indicate a need for improvements in reading instruction and outcomes nationwide.

Proficient readers are those who read with accuracy, speed, and appropriate expression, as well as comprehend what they read. In the early elementary grades, there is a focus on teaching students to read, as this is fundamental to being able to read for understanding across all content areas (e.g., science, social studies) in late elementary, middle, and high school. The process of reading relies on a number of basic and advanced skills, including phonological awareness, decoding, fluency, vocabulary, and comprehension (National Reading Panel, 2000). **Phonological awareness** refers to the understanding that words are composed of smaller units of sound (e.g., the understanding that the word *cat* comprises three sounds—namely /c/, /a/, and /t/). **Decoding** refers to knowledge and skill in applying sound–letter correspondences (e.g., knowledge that the letter *c* corresponds with the sound /c/). **Reading fluency**, which is discussed later in this chapter, refers to the rate, accuracy, and prosody of an individual's reading. Students who lack fluency because they struggle with reading individual words generally have difficulty comprehending text because they must allocate their attention to reading the words of the text instead of understanding its meaning (LaBerge & Samuels, 1974). **Vocabulary** refers to the student's knowledge of individual words in text, which is important for reading comprehension. Finally, **reading comprehension** refers to the construction of meaning from text. Providing students with effective instruction in each of these five component areas is essential to the development of skilled readers (National Reading Panel, 2000).

Mathematics

Recent results from the NAEP in math are comparable to those in reading, with only 40% of fourth-grade students and 33% of eighth-grade students having performed at or above the Proficient level in this area in 2015 (U.S. Department of Education, 2017b). As in the area of reading, there is a significant need for nationwide improvement in students' math performance.

Proficiency in math is multifaceted and includes the ability to perform basic computations, understand key mathematical concepts, and solve problems. One of the earliest skills that young children must acquire to become competent in math is number sense (Shapiro, 2011). **Number sense** refers to an individual's general facility with numerical concepts. For example, a student who observes two different-size piles of candy and is able to identify the larger pile without counting individual pieces of candy is displaying number sense (and specifically the abstract concepts of *more* and *less*). In the early elementary grades, students must also master basic computational skills, such as addition, subtraction, and multiplication. As in reading, students must develop proficiency in basic math skills to complete complex multistep math problems (Shapiro, 2011).

Written Language

The 2011 results of the NAEP Writing Assessment (the most recent data available) indicated that only 27% of eighth-grade and 12th-grade students performed at or above the Proficient level on this test (U.S. Department of Education, 2017a). Proficient writers are able to plan and compose writing that communicates one or more ideas clearly and in an organized manner. Just as basic addition and subtraction skills are necessary for students to become proficient in complex mathematics, so spelling and handwriting (and potentially typing) are necessary skills to become proficient writers. Students who must exert substantial cognitive resources to write letters and spell words will have fewer cognitive resources to expend on the meaning of the text that they are trying to write (Shapiro, 2011). Other important writing skills that must be taught include generating ideas and topics, producing written text fluently (i.e., producing viable content at an appropriate pace), writing in response to a variety of demands, structuring information, revising, and applying appropriate punctuation and grammar.

OVERVIEW OF ACADEMIC ASSESSMENT

As noted in Chapter 6, assessment for, during, and after intervention is critical for promoting student success. School psychologists use assessment data to learn about students' strengths and needs, progress during intervention, and overall achievement as a result of the intervention. The following subsections review methods commonly used for assessing students' learning in reading, math, and written language.

Assessing the Environment

When evaluating a student's academic skills for the purpose of informing intervention, it is critical to understand the contexts in which the child is functioning. Academic skill deficits are best understood as a mismatch between the child and the environment, as opposed to being characterized as a deficit that lies within the child. According to ecological systems theory (Bronfenbrenner, 1977; Bronfenbrenner & Morris, 1998), children grow and develop within a series of nested contexts, and it is the interaction between the child and these contexts that facilitates the child's learning. Assessing the contexts in which the child functions provides the most complete picture of his or her academic functioning, which better informs intervention strategies. The most proximal of those contexts are the home environment and the classroom environment.

Children spend much of their lives outside of school, at home and with their parents or caregivers. Thus, it is not surprising that features of the home environment may be informative for better understanding the student's functioning at school. For example, parenting practices and the quality of the learning environment predict children's academic skills and functioning in school (Baker & Rimm-Kaufman, 2014; Brennan et al., 2013). To assess the home environment, one can conduct an interview with parents/caregivers. Caregivers can provide information about the resources available at home to support learning, the student's academic strengths, and opportunities for growth. They may also provide information about the child's development that may be relevant for understanding the child's current academic functioning.

Given that there is a direct association between the instructional environment and students' academic skills, it is essential that academic assessment include an assessment of classroom ecology. To assess the academic environment, one would (a) interview the teacher, (b) review the student's work products, (c) conduct one or more direct observations in the classroom, and (d) interview the student. First, it is essential that one obtain an understanding of the curriculum to which the student is exposed. More specifically, one needs to identify the skills that have and have not been taught. Although curriculum standards exist for each grade level, these alone do not provide enough information to discern the specific instructional content to which the student was actually exposed. The second purpose of assessing the classroom environment is to understand the difference between what the child is *able to do* and what the child is *expected to be able to do* at his or her grade level. This information can be obtained via interview with the teacher, with a review of the student's classroom work, or through direct assessment methods (described in the ensuing text).

Measuring Academic Skills

In addition to assessing the academic environment, school psychologists must assess students' academic skill levels. The most common assessments for measuring the academic skills of students are ***curriculum-based measurement (CBM)***, ***computer adaptive tests (CATs)***, ***norm-referenced tests (NRTs)***, ***criterion-referenced tests (CRTs)***, and ***state-mandated tests***. Each type of assessment has its own purpose, strengths, and weaknesses.

Curriculum-Based Measurement

CBM refers to a standardized set of brief, fluency-based assessments that are used to measure student performance in the areas of reading, mathematics, writing, and spelling. It is often described as a ***general outcome measure***, meaning that it requires the integration of several component skills that make up an academic task and, therefore, can be used as a measure of student performance across an academic year (Fuchs & Deno, 1991). There are a number of publishers of CBM assessments, such as AIMSweb (www.aimsweb.com), DIBELS (dibels.uoregon.edu), EasyCBM (easycbm.com), and FastBridge Learning (fastbridge.org). Although the specific materials that each of these companies distributes differ, they share a number of common features—namely, standardized procedures for administration, tasks that measure students' speed and accuracy, and relatively cost-efficient materials (as compared to other measures). They also are quick to administer and allow for a student's gains to be graphed across time so that progress can be assessed. CBM is most commonly used to assess skills in reading, math, writing, and spelling.

Reading CBM

Some of the most commonly used measures are curriculum-based measures of oral reading (CBM-R), maze, and word identification fluency (WIF). CBM-R is a timed, individually administered measure of students' oral reading rate with accuracy. To administer CBM-R, the examiner has two copies of the grade-level passage—one student probe and one corresponding examiner score sheet. After providing the student with a copy of the passage, the examiner reads a set of standardized instructions aloud to the student. These instructions inform the student where to begin reading, to read aloud, to do his or her best reading, and that, if he or she does not know a word, the examiner will provide that word.

After providing the instructions and answering any questions the student may have, the examiner says "Begin," and starts a 1-minute timer when the student reads the first word. While the student is reading, the examiner follows along, noting any errors (e.g., skipped words, substitutions, or misread words), and providing unknown words after the student hesitates for 3 seconds. At the end of 1 minute, the examiner instructs the student to stop reading. The probe is then scored by subtracting the number of words read with errors from the total number of words read. The resulting number is the final score, or the words read correctly per minute (WRCM). Decades of research evaluating the technical characteristics of scores from CBM-R support its reliability and provide evidence that WRCM is a strong indicator of reading achievement and reading comprehension skills (Deno, 1985; January, Ardoin, Christ, Eckert, & White, 2016; Reschly, Busch, Betts, Deno, & Long, 2009).

Since it is important to catch students with academic needs early in their academic careers, and because not all struggling readers can read text, other CBM procedures are available to assess reading skills that are prerequisites to text reading. Two measures frequently used with early readers, or older students who are struggling to read, are nonsense word fluency (NWF) and WIF. NWF assesses a student's ability to identify and blend a list of vowel–consonant and consonant–vowel–consonant nonwords, directly measuring beginning readers' alphabetics and phonics skills (i.e., letter–sound correspondence and decoding skills). In contrast to NWF, WIF is a task in which students read a list of real words. WIF probes include **decodable words**, which are words that can be sounded out (e.g., *cat* and *car*), and/or **high-frequency words**, which are words that appear often in texts (e.g., *the* and *or*). As with CBM-R, administration of NWF and WIF is done individually. As the student completes the task, the examiner makes a slash through incorrect words or sounds. After 1 minute has elapsed, a close bracket is used to mark the student's last word or sound. The number of incorrect sounds or words is then subtracted from the total number of sounds or words read to obtain the correct letter sounds or WRCM.

Math CBM

In mathematics, CBM tools fall into one of two categories: **computation** or **concepts and applications**. CBM math computation probes measure the skills of addition, subtraction, multiplication, and division; they can measure skills in one or more of these areas. For example, a multiple-skill computation probe for second grade may include one- or two-digit addition and subtraction facts with and without regrouping. CBM math concepts and applications probes typically measure a range of skills such as number concepts, money, graphs and charts, and word problems. The specific skills assessed at each grade level vary and are aligned with grade-level expectations for academic performance. Although specific instructions may vary across publishers, when administering CBM math probes, the examiner generally explains the task and asks students to start with the first problem, working in order from left to right and showing their work. Students may skip problems but are encouraged to try to complete each problem. The time allotted for probes varies by publisher and grade level/skills but generally is shorter for computation (e.g., 2–4 minutes) and longer for concepts/applications (e.g., 10–15 minutes or untimed). Math CBM probes are typically scored based on the number and/or percentage of items completed correctly. Research on the technical properties of CBM math generally supports its reliability and relation to mathematics achievement (Christ, Scullin, Tolbize, & Jiban, 2008; Foegen, Jiban, & Deno, 2007; Shapiro, Keller, Lutz, Santoro, & Hintze, 2006).

Writing CBM

Within the area of writing, CBM typically involves asking students to complete a brief writing task in response to a prompt (e.g., "Write about a time you experienced something surprising."). These prompts vary in difficulty by grade level. Students are asked to write a response to the prompt for 3 minutes. There are various ways to score these types of probes, such as counting total words written (TWW), total words spelled correctly (WSC), or total number of correct word sequences (CWS). TWW methods do not account for accuracy of spelling, punctuation, or grammar, whereas WSC methods account for spelling but not grammar, punctuation, or context. CWS methods, however, account for spelling and grammar. A CWS is defined as two adjacent words that are grammatically congruent (e.g., use correct verb tense or exhibit subject–verb agreement) and that are spelled correctly. Often, comparing scores derived via multiple methods can provide useful information about a student's writing skills. For example, using a combination of all three methods may allow the examiner to identify students who produce an appropriate volume of writing but who have difficulty spelling or sequencing words accurately.

Spelling CBM

Spelling CBM differs from other types of written language CBM in that it focuses on writing individual words correctly rather than producing connected text. To conduct a spelling CBM, the examiner provides the student with a blank sheet of lined paper and instructs him or her to write a series of dictated words on the sheet. After reading the instructions, the examiner dictates a list of words to the student at intervals of 7 to 10 seconds (depending on the student's grade level). This occurs for 2 minutes, and the student is instructed to proceed with the next word, even if he or she has not completed the previous one (Shinn, 1989). During this task, the examiner says each word twice. Scoring spelling measures typically involves counting the total number of WSC and/or the number of correct letter sequences (CLS) in each word. A CLS refers to two adjacent letters (or adjacent initial and final letters and their adjacent spaces) that are written in the correct order (Hosp, Hosp, & Howell, 2016). For example, the word "psychology" would have 11 possible CLS.

Computer Adaptive Tests

CATs are computer-administered assessments that may cover a range of academic skills, but are most often available in the areas of reading and mathematics. CATs present students with a set of multiple-choice test items that are tailored to their skill level. The first item of a CAT is of moderate difficulty, and subsequent items are presented to the students based on their accuracy with the previous item that was presented. That is, if the student gets the item correct, he or she is presented with a more difficult question. Conversely, if the student gets the item incorrect, he or she gets an easier question. As such, items on a CAT are adapted to student performance, with the goal of obtaining a precise estimate of a student's skills in a certain area. Advantages of administering CATs are they typically have a very large bank of items, which results in more precise estimates of the academic skills of lower-performing and higher-performing students, as compared with traditional NRTs. The large item bank also means that CATs can be administered multiple times per year. In comparison to CBM probes, which may be obtained for free, CATs are relatively expensive and require a computer lab for their administration. Independent research on CATs is emerging, and supports their technical adequacy (Clemens et al., 2015; January & Ardoin, 2015; Shapiro, Dennis, & Fu, 2015).

Norm-referenced and criterion-referenced tests

Many schools choose to administer NRTs, such as the Iowa Assessments (Dunbar & Welch, 2015), to students each year. As one might expect, NRTs rely on *norm-referenced comparisons* (described in Chapter 6), meaning that they are useful for understanding a student's relative performance when compared with same-age peers. This information is useful for making decisions about special education eligibility, such as whether a student has a specific learning disability. However, the information provided by these tests does not necessarily allow for monitoring a student's progress or determining which specific skills a student has or has not mastered, which is essential for developing academic interventions. Thus, schools may also choose to administer CRTs to their students. These types of tests rely on *criterion-referenced comparisons* (also described in Chapter 6), meaning that they measure student performance as compared with specific criteria, such as a state's grade-specific content learning standards. Results from CRTs may be useful for understanding the extent to which a student has mastered the skills that were expected to be taught during the academic year. Unfortunately, scores from CRTs cannot be used to inform instruction or monitor students' responsiveness to intervention. This is due in part to the fact that CRTs are typically administered at the end of the year, when it is too late to make changes in the instructional practices to which students are exposed.

State-Mandated Tests

In nearly all states, schools must administer one or more state-mandated tests each year, often beginning in third grade. These state-mandated tests are criterion-referenced and/or norm-referenced, may be computer adaptive (e.g., the Partnership for Assessment of Readiness for College and Careers), and are administered near the end of the academic year. Benefits of these tests are that they are better aligned with students' curriculum than NRTs and are useful for understanding the extent to which a student has mastered the curriculum that was taught during the academic year. Despite these benefits, some limitations weaken their utility when assessing academic skills for the purpose of intervention. First, like NRTs, they are not designed to be administered multiple times per year, so they cannot be used to measure growth. Second, the results do not provide information regarding which skills a student has or has not mastered. Further, since the tests are administered at the end of the year, results are not timely in identifying the skills in which students may need additional support. Despite their limited utility for academic assessment and intervention, state-mandated tests are most useful for accountability purposes. That is, states use results from the tests as part of their accountability systems for identifying schools that may need improvement or may benefit from additional support (Every Student Succeeds Act, 2015).

In summary, each of the assessment tools described here has distinct purposes, benefits, and weaknesses. However, to measure the academic skills of students for the purpose of informing instruction, it is most useful to directly measure students' academic skills in the context of the curriculum. The most appropriate tools withwhich to accomplish this goal are CBM.

ADDRESSING ACADEMIC SKILL PROBLEMS THROUGH MTSS

Chapter 7 broadly described the general framework of MTSS. This section, in contrast, describes the applications of this framework to the delivery of academic assessment and intervention services. MTSS offers a promising model for academic service delivery because it is prevention oriented, focused on outcomes for all students, and heavily reliant on data-based decision making. In particular, the sections that follow provide examples of assessment and intervention procedures at each of the three tiers.

Tier 1 Assessment and Intervention

A properly implemented MTSS process takes into consideration the student's learning environment by assessing Tier 1 instruction (Ardoin, Wagner, & Bangs, 2016). Tier 1 instruction is the instruction to which all students in a building are exposed. As part of the MTSS model, Tier 1 services are evaluated through the universal screening of all students within a school building. Consistent with the MTSS model described in Chapter 7, universal screening at Tier 1 generally involves all students in a school being administered one or more academic assessment measures (e.g., CBM, CAT) three times annually and the comparison of the resulting assessment data to national and/or local norms. **National norms** are estimates of how students at a particular age or grade level perform. They are determined by averaging student performance data for a particular age or grade level across the nation. Testing companies provide these national norms, which are specific to each test. **Local norms** are based on the average performance of students at a specific age or grade level within the individual school or district.

Administration of academic measures multiple times across the school year allows schools to evaluate both the level of performance and the rate of change for both groups and individual students. Prior to the advent of MTSS, few schools conducted universal screening, and even fewer did so on a triannual basis.

To assess the environment in which a student is learning, universal screening data must be evaluated by comparing the performance of groups of students (e.g., students in a specific grade within a specific school). This allows personnel to determine whether the quality of instruction provided to students in the school/district is sufficient for supporting adequate gains. If the environment (i.e., classroom, school, school district) in which a student is receiving instruction does not promote adequate gains for most students, it is unreasonable to expect that any given student will demonstrate achievement at a level commensurate with national norms (Ardoin et al., 2016). Thus, universal screening data should be examined to determine whether the average achievement level and rate of gain of students within the district, individual schools and classrooms are at expected levels. If the answer to any of these questions is "no," then instructional changes must be made (Jimerson, Burns, & VanDerHeyden, 2016). Failure to consider the environment in which a student is receiving instruction and whether that environment is providing quality instruction has the potential for an individual student to be blamed for his or her failure to achieve, when in actuality the student's poor achievement is largely due to the environment. In the absence of Tier 1 universal screening data, schools are more likely to attribute student deficits to a disability within the student than to a deficit in the quality of the instruction being provided by the school.

Tier 2 Assessment and Intervention

After considering the quality of Tier 1 instruction being provided to students, universal screening data should be examined to determine which students might need supplemental or Tier 2 intervention. Recall from Chapter 7 that Tier 2 intervention is instruction that is supplemental to Tier 1 instruction. It should provide students with extra opportunities to practice skills, more explicit instruction, and/or instruction that targets skills the student has failed to learn but that other students within the instructional environment have already learned.

When selecting students in need of Tier 2 intervention services, several factors must be taken into consideration. First, although universal screening data should be used as a primary source of information, it should not be the only source of information used in selecting students for such services (VanDerHeyden, Witt, & Barnett, 2005). It is essential that all reliable and valid data are considered when making decisions regarding the educational services that will or will not be provided to a student. Decisions about the educational services provided to a student should never be made based on a single source of data. Although school psychologists are not always called upon to be part of the MTSS decision-making process at Tier 2, they should work closely with schools to ensure that multiple quality sources of data are used as the basis for making educational decisions. The education that school psychologists receive in regard to test development, test evaluation, and standardized administration procedures makes them uniquely suited for helping schools in evaluating their assessment tools (Fenning et al., 2015).

Another important factor to consider when selecting students for Tier 2 services is that individual student achievement must be evaluated in the context of the environment in which the student has received instruction. Unfortunately, some schools mistakenly select students for Tier 2 services based solely on how each student's scores compare to national norms, thereby failing to take into consideration the context in which students have received instruction. Students should generally be selected for Tier 2 services by comparing their performance to local norms. Selecting students based on national norms can not only result in students being considered as needing Tier 2 instruction when the problem is Tier 1 instruction, but also lead to more students being identified as needing Tier 2 intervention than a school has the resources to provide. For instance, if the performance of 30% of students in a school is in the bottom 15% of students nationally, it is unlikely the school would have the resources to provide quality Tier 2 intervention services to that many students. In such academic situations, the school should (a) consider the changes that need to be made to Tier 1 instruction/behavior management to ensure that more students are making significant gains, (b) make the necessary changes, and (c) provide supplemental Tier 2 intervention to students whose achievement is discrepant from peers within that environment.

A final factor to consider when selecting students for Tier 2 services is that students should be considered for these services when they are discrepant from peers—in other words, when they are performing significantly lower or significantly higher than their peers. Although this chapter focuses on assessment and intervention for students who are struggling academically, universal screening data are useful for assessing whether schools are meeting the instructional needs of all students, including high-achieving students (McCallum et al., 2013).

Tier 2 instructional services vary within and across districts in regard to where and by whom they are provided. Such services also vary within and across school districts in regard to the quality, intensity, and the extent to which the instruction meets the individual needs of the students being provided with Tier 2 intervention. For instance, some schools provide students with what they deem to be Tier 2 interventions but that are, in truth, simply surface-level changes to assessment procedures (e.g., providing students with extra time to complete assignments) or classroom structure (e.g., reducing lengths of assignments, changing a student's seat location) and theoretically would not be expected to improve student learning. When these types of so-called interventions are implemented, it is important that school psychologists inform the school's MTSS team that such interventions would not be expected to change a student's rate of growth and, therefore, cannot be considered a true Tier 2 intervention. Other schools provide students with standardized evidence-based interventions that theoretically could improve students' learning but do not necessarily target specific instructional needs. For instance, in some schools, all students identified as having a reading deficit are provided with the same computer-based reading intervention, despite the fact that the reasons for their deficits vary. For example, whereas some students may lack skills in decoding, others may lack vocabulary skills or specific reading comprehension skills. Providing the same intervention to all students, regardless of the cause of each student's deficits, often occurs when schools lack the resources to provide different interventions or lack the knowledge regarding how to determine which academic deficits a student might have. Although such interventions might prove to be successful when they happen to address a student's needs, students are likely to benefit most when interventions are selected that target their specific skill deficits (Daly, Martens, Barnett, Witt, & Olson, 2007; Martens, Daly, & Ardoin, 2015).

Finally, some schools do their best to successfully provide interventions that match the instructional needs of their students. Schools that match interventions to students' instructional needs must assess those needs, as universal screening data do not generally provide the necessary information. Assessment of a student's instructional needs involves first conducting a task analysis. A **task analysis** is used to determine which skills a student needs to achieve and then to identify the student's proficiency in each of those skills. CBM assessment procedures are generally helpful for these purposes, as they provide information related to both accuracy and fluency. CBM probes must, however, be developed that assess single (as opposed to multiple) skills. For instance, a task analysis of second-grade math word problems would reveal that, to be successful in completing these problems, students must have the skills to do the following: (a) read the words that make up each problem with accuracy and fluency; (b) determine whether the problem requires addition or subtraction of numbers; and (c) add and subtract two-digit by two-digit numbers with accuracy and fluency. CBM reading and math probes composed of each of these skills could be developed and administered to the Tier 2 student using CBM assessment procedures. The same reading and math probes would also be administered to a sample of same-age peers who are considered to be successful in completing the second-grade math word problems. The performance of the student receiving Tier 2 services would then be compared to the average performance of the same-age peers in each skill area to determine skills for which further instruction is needed. Intervention could then be developed to target the skill(s) for which intervention is needed. Subsequently, data regarding the student's response to the developed intervention(s) would provide information regarding the type of intervention the student may need if he or she is deemed eligible for special education.

When examining student data and determining which skills need to be targeted for intervention, it is essential to consider a student's accuracy, fluency, and ability to generalize each skill. Attending to accuracy alone (e.g., percentage of items answered correctly) fails to acknowledge the importance of developing mastery of basic skills that facilitate the learning and mastery of more complex skills (Shapiro, 2011). Haring and Eaton's (1978) Instructional Hierarchy provides schools with a framework for both developing effective intervention and monitoring the effects of intervention. According to the Instructional Hierarchy, accuracy must be targeted before developing students' fluency. **Accuracy interventions** must include modeling of how to complete the skill correctly, multiple opportunities to practice the skill, immediate performance feedback for students regarding response accuracy, and reinforcement for accurate completion. Interventions targeting response accuracy include cover–copy–compare, listening passage preview, and incremental rehearsal (Codding, Eckert, Fanning, Shiyko, & Solomon, 2007; January, Lovelace, Foster, & Ardoin, 2017). The effects of accuracy-based interventions should be measured by assessing the student's response accuracy. Once these data indicate that the student can consistently complete the skill with accuracy, instruction should target response fluency. **Fluent responding** is the performance of a task with both speed and accuracy. When students are able to perform the basic component tasks of a complex skill with fluency, they do not have to dedicate as much attention to its smaller components and can place greater focus on the more complex tasks. *Fluency interventions* must include the provision of multiple opportunities to practice the task, with reinforcement provided for fast and accurate responding. Examples of interventions targeting skill fluency regularly employed within schools include repeated readings, flash card drills, and taped problems (Burns, Codding, Boice, & Lukito, 2010; Therrien, 2004). The effects of fluency interventions should be assessed by measuring the number of problems/items that the student completes in a given time frame.

Throughout the Tier 2 intervention, it is important that generalization of skills be programmed through providing students with the opportunity to respond to multiple exemplars. *Multiple exemplars* offer the opportunity to practice a skill across varying contexts, situations, or variations of the skill. For example, when teaching students sight words, teachers might use flash cards. When developing response accuracy, the teacher might first read (i.e., model) the sight words to the students and then have them immediately practice reading the words aloud. Fluency instruction might then involve timing students' reading of the words for which accuracy was established during the accuracy intervention. Generalization of this skill might then be programmed by having students read previously learned words when presented in texts or by having students read compound words containing previously taught words. In these examples, the students would be required to respond to the same words, but the words are presented in different settings and/or the student must read the words combined with other words (Ardoin, Eckert, & Cole, 2008).

Districts and schools within districts also vary in the level of instructional intensity that they provide to students receiving Tier 2 interventions. In fact, most states require that prior to identifying a student as needing special education services, multiple interventions of increasing intensity be implemented and their impact on student growth be evaluated. *Instructional intensity* is often defined by the amount of intervention time provided to a student (e.g., four 30-minute sessions per week versus five 45-minute sessions per week) or the number of students per intervention group. These two variables are expected to affect the number of opportunities that students have to respond—and number of opportunities to respond is believed to be a key determinant in predicting gains made by students (Haydon, MacSuga-Gage, Somonsen, & Hawkins, 2012).

In addition to using universal screening data to identify students in need of Tier 2 intervention, conducting task analyses to determine for which skills students need to be provided instruction, and developing interventions that appropriately target those skills, schools must monitor the impact of Tier 2 interventions on students' academic progress. Typically, schools use CBM progress monitoring procedures to monitor student gains. These procedures involve administering CBM probes associated with the skill on which instruction is being provided on a regular basis (two to eight times per month) and plotting the resulting data on a graph that has time on the x-axis and student performance on the y-axis. After several weeks of data are collected (a minimum of 8 weeks), schools use those data to determine whether the student's observed rate of growth indicates adequate achievement (Ardoin, Christ, Morena, Cormier, & Klingbeil, 2013;

Christ, Zopluoglu, Monaghen, & Van Norman, 2013). If the rate of growth is not adequate, intervention intensity should be increased and the effects of intervention continually monitored. Should it be determined that the level of intervention intensity necessary for the student to make adequate growth exceeds that which can be provided through regular education services, the resulting data should be used as evidence that the student may need special education services.

When interpreting progress monitoring data and deciding whether a student has achieved adequate growth, it is important to consider that Tier 2 instruction is supplemental to Tier 1 instruction. The majority of instruction that a Tier 2 student receives should be provided in the Tier 1 environment with the student's peers. Thus, when determining what an adequate rate of growth for a specific student is, the rate of growth being made by the student's peers who are receiving the same Tier 1 instruction should be considered (Ardoin, Witt, Connel, & Koenig, 2005; Joseph, Alber-Morgan, & Neef, 2016). Such procedures assure that the assessment properly considers the environment in which instruction is taking place.

Tier 3 Assessment and Intervention

If students are identified as candidates for Tier 3 instruction, it is essential that many of the practices employed during Tier 2 instruction are continued. For instance, Tier 3 services should involve (a) frequent task analyses of the skills a student needs to perform, (b) determination of the level of fluency possessed by Tier 1 students who are proficient in the skills, (c) assessment of the student's level of proficiency in each of the skills, and (d) the matching of instruction to the student's instructional needs. The effects of the intervention on student progress should also be continually evaluated so as to determine whether instructional intensity needs to be modified. Students' instructional needs are not static, but rather are constantly changing; in turn, continual assessment is always necessary. Tier 3 students do not need different types of instruction; rather, they need instruction to be made more explicit and they need more opportunities to respond to stimuli than do students who require only Tier 1 instruction.

SOCIAL JUSTICE CONNECTIONS

How is academic MTSS consistent with a social justice agenda?

The goals and design of academic multitiered systems of support (MTSS) are consistent with social justice principles in a number of ways. For example, a primary aim of academic MTSS is to ensure that all students receive adequate core instruction (i.e., Tier 1 instruction). When schools use universal screening data to evaluate the quality of their Tier 1 instruction, they increase the likelihood that all students will receive a quality education. If Tier 1 data suggest that instruction is not promoting adequate gains for all students, changes to instruction must be made. Thus, these data can be monitored regularly to ensure that students from diverse groups are meeting performance benchmarks.

(continued)

Academic MTSS also promotes social justice in that it helps to increase the probability that students in need of intervention are identified early. The earlier that students are identified as needing intervention, the greater the likelihood that such intervention will be effective (Diamond, Justice, Siegler, & Snyder, 2013). Conversely, failure to build students' foundational academic skills increases the probability that those students will later need special education services (Lonigan, Purpura, Wilson, Walker, & Clancy-Menchetti, 2013). Moreover, students who lack foundational skills may be more likely to engage in disruptive behavior, as they may have difficulty participating in classroom instruction (Darney, Reinke, Herman, Stormont, & Ialongo, 2013; Reynolds, Ou, Mondi, & Hayakawa, 2017). Thus, teaching students the skills they need to succeed academically is key to promoting social justice. Overall, as suggested by Artiles, Bal, and King Thorius (2010), MTSS implementation promises to improve the distribution of school resources by promoting early identification and increasing the quality of universal instruction.

SUMMARY AND CONCLUSIONS

This chapter introduced readers to (a) the importance of evaluating the environment in which a student is receiving instruction, (b) assessment instruments used within schools for identifying and monitoring the progress of students with academic intervention needs, and (c) the three tiers of MTSS. After reading this chapter, readers should better appreciate the importance of the school psychologist not simply asking why a student is not learning, but rather asking whether the student's environment supports learning and which aspects of that environment might need to be altered so that the student can learn and develop the skills necessary for academic and life success.

DISCUSSION QUESTIONS

1. Why is it important to consider both curriculum and instructional variables when designing academic interventions?
2. Why is CBM valuable for monitoring academic outcomes?
3. What are the differences in the purposes for which schools might employ CBM, CRTs, and NRTs?
4. When assessing academic strengths and weaknesses, why is it important to consider the environment in which a student's learning has taken place?
5. How does the MTSS model facilitate the evaluation of both student variables and environmental variables?

REFERENCES

Ardoin, S. P., Christ, T. J., Morena, L. S., Cormier, D. C., & Klingbeil, D. A. (2013). A systematic review and summarization of the recommendations and research surrounding curriculum-based measurement of oral reading fluency (CBM-R) decision rules. *Journal of School Psychology, 51*, 1–18. doi:10.1016/j.jsp.2012.09.004

Ardoin, S. P., Eckert, T. L., & Cole, C. A. S. (2008). Promoting generalization of reading: A comparison of two fluency-based interventions for improving general education student's oral reading rate. *Journal of Behavioral Education, 17,* 237–252. doi:10.1007/s10864-008-9066-1

Ardoin, S. P., Wagner, L., & Bangs, K. E. (2016). Applied behavior analysis: A foundation for response to intervention. In S. R. Jimerson, M. K. Burns, & A. M. VanDerHeyden (Eds.), *Handbook of response to intervention: The science and practice of multi-tiered systems of support* (2nd ed., pp. 29–42). New York, NY: Springer Science+Business Media.

Ardoin, S. P., Witt, J. C., Connel, J. E., & Koenig, J. (2005). Application of a three-tiered response to intervention model for instructional planning, decision making, and the identification of children in need of services. *Journal of Psychoeducational Assessment, 23,* 362–380. doi:10.1177/073428290502300405

Artiles, A. J., Bal, A., & King Thorius, K. A. (2010). Back to the future: A critique of response to intervention's social justice views. *Theory Into Practice, 49,* 250–257. doi:10.1080/00405841.20 10.510447

Baker, C. E., & Rimm-Kaufman, S. E. (2014). How homes influence schools: Early parenting predicts African American childrens' classroom social–emotional functioning. *Psychology in the Schools, 51,* 722–735. doi:10.1002/pits.21781

Brennan, L. M., Shelleby, E. C., Shaw, D. S., Gardner, F., Dishion, T. J., & Wilson, M. (2013). Indirect effects of the family check-up on school-age academic achievement through improvements in parenting in early childhood. *Journal of Educational Psychology, 105,* 762–773. doi:10.1037/a0032096

Bronfenbrenner, U. (1977). Toward an experimental ecology of human development. *American Psychologist, 32,* 513–531. doi:10.1037/0003-066x.32.7.513

Bronfenbrenner, U., & Morris, P. A. (1998). The ecology of developmental processes. In W. Damon & R. M. Lerner (Eds.), *Handbook of child psychology, Vol. 1: Theoretical models of human development* (5th ed., pp. 993–1023). New York, NY: John Wiley and Sons.

Burns, M. K., Codding, R. S., Boice, C. H., & Lukito, G. (2010). Meta-analysis of acquisition and fluency math interventions with instructional and frustration level skills: Evidence for a skill-by-treatment interaction. *School Psychology Review, 39,* 69–83.

Christ, T. J., Scullin, S., Tolbize, A., & Jiban, C. L. (2008). Implications of recent research: Curriculum-based measurement of math computation. *Assessment for Effective Intervention, 33,* 198–205. doi:10.1177/1534508407313480

Christ, T. J., Zopluoglu, C., Monaghen, B. D., & Van Norman, E. R. (2013). Curriculum-based measurement of oral reading: Multi-study evaluation of schedule, duration, and dataset quality on progress monitoring outcomes. *Journal of School Psychology, 51,* 19–57. doi:10.1016/j .jsp.2012.11.001

Clemens, N. H., Hagan-Burke, S., Wen, L., Cerda, C., Blakely, A., Frosch, J., . . . Jones, M. (2015). The predictive validity of a computer-adaptive assessment of kindergarten and first-grade reading skills. *School Psychology Review, 44,* 76–97. doi:10.17105/SPR44-1.76-97

Codding, R. S., Eckert, T. L., Fanning, E., Shiyko, M., & Solomon, E. (2007). Comparing mathematics interventions: The effects of cover–copy–compare along and combined with performance feedback on digits correct and incorrect. *Journal of Behavioral Education, 16,* 125–141. doi:10.1007/s10864-006-9006-x

Daly, E. J. III., Martens, B. K., Barnett, D., Witt, J. C., & Olson, S. C. (2007). Varying intervention delivery in response to intervention: Confronting and resolving challenges with measurement, instruction, and intensity. *School Psychology Review, 36,* 562–581.

Darney, D., Reinke, W. M., Herman, K. C., Stormont, M., & Ialongo, N. S. (2013). Children with co-occurring academic and behavior problems in first grade: Distal outcomes in twelfth grade. *Journal of School Psychology, 51,* 117–128. doi:10.1016/j.jsp.2012.09.005

Deno, S. L. (1985). Curriculum-based measurement: The emerging alternative. *Exceptional Children, 52,* 219–232. doi:10.1177/001440298702000109

Diamond, K. E., Justice, L. M., Siegler, R. S., & Snyder, P. A. (2013). *Synthesis of IES research on early intervention and early childhood education* (NCSER 2013-3001). Washington, DC: National Center for Special Education Research, Institute of Education Sciences, U.S. Department of Education.

Dunbar, S., & Welch, C. (2015). *The Iowa assessments, forms E and F*. Rolling Meadows, IL: Riverside Publishing.

Every Student Succeeds Act, Pub. L. No. 114–95, § 1177 (2015).

Fenning, P., Diaz, Y., Valley-Gray, S., Cash, R. G., Spearman, C., Hazel, C. E., . . . Harris, A. (2015). Perceptions of competencies among school psychology trainers and practitioners: What matters most? *Psychology in the Schools, 52*, 1032–1041. doi:10.1002/pits.21877

Foegen, A., Jiban, C., & Deno, S. (2007). Progress monitoring measures in mathematics: A review of the literature. *Journal of Special Education, 41*, 121–139. doi:10.1177/00224669070410020101

Fuchs, L. S., & Deno, S. L. (1991). Paradigmatic distinctions between instructionally relevant measurement models. *Exceptional Children, 57*, 488–501. doi:10.1177/001440299105700603

Haring, N. G., & Eaton, M. D. (1978). Systematic procedures: An instructional hierarchy. In N. G. Haring, T. C. Lovitt, M. D. Eaton, & C. L. Hansen (Eds.), *The fourth R: Research in the classroom.* (pp. 23–40). Columbus, OH: Merrill.

Haydon, T., MacSuga-Gage, A. S., Simonsen, B., & Hawkins, R. (2012). Opportunities to respond: A key component of effective instruction. *Beyond Behavior, 22*, 23–31. doi:10.1177/107429561202200105

Hosp, M. K., Hosp, J. L., & Howell, K. W. (2016). *The ABCs of CBM: A practical guide to curriculum based measurement* (2nd ed.). New York, NY: Guilford.

January, S.-A. A., & Ardoin, S. P. (2015). Technical adequacy and acceptability of curriculum-based measurement and the Measures of Academic Progress. *Assessment for Effective Intervention, 41*, 3–15. doi:10.1177/1534508415579095

January, S.-A. A., Ardoin, S. P., Christ, T. J., Eckert, T. L., & White, M. J. (2016). Evaluating the interpretations and use of curriculum-based measurement in reading and word lists for universal screening in first and second grade. *School Psychology Review, 45*, 310–326. doi:10.17105/SPR45-3.310-326

January, S.-A. A., Lovelace, M. E., Foster, T. E., & Ardoin, S. P. (2017). A comparison of two flashcard interventions for teaching sight word to early readers. *Journal of Behavioral Education, 26*, 151–168. doi:10.1007/s10864-016-9263-2

Jimerson, S. R., Burns, M. K., & VanDerHeyden, A. M. (2016). *Handbook of response to intervention: The science and practice of multi-tiered systems of support* (2nd ed.). New York, NY: Springer Science+Business Media.

Joseph, L. M., Alber-Morgan, S., & Neef, N. (2016). Applying behavior analytic procedures to effectively teach literacy skills in the classroom. *Psychology in the Schools, 53*, 73–88. doi:10.1002/pits.21883

LaBerge, D., & Samuels, S. J. (1974). Toward a theory of automatic information processing in reading. *Cognitive Psychology, 6*, 293–323. doi:10.1016/0010-0285(74)90015-2

Lonigan, C. J., Purpura, D. J., Wilson, S. B., Walker, P. M., & Clancy-Menchetti, J. (2013). Evaluating the components of an emergent literacy intervention for preschool children at risk for reading difficulties. *Journal of Experimental Child Psychology, 114*, 111–130. doi:10.1016/j.jecp.2012.08.010

Martens, B. K., Daly, E. J. III., & Ardoin, S. P. (2015). Applications of applied behavior analysis to school-based instructional intervention. In H. S. Roane, J. E. Ringdahl, & T. S. Falcomata (Eds.), *Clinical and organizational applications of applied behavior analysis* (pp. 125–150). San Diego, CA: Elsevier.

McCallum, R. S., Bell, S. M., Coles, J. T., Miller, K. C., Hopkins, M. B., & Hilton-Prillhart, A. (2013). A model for screening twice-exceptional students (gifted with learning disabilities) within a Response to Intervention paradigm. *Gifted Child Quarterly, 57*, 209–222. doi:10.1177/0016986213500070

National Reading Panel. (2000). *Teaching children to read: An evidence-based assessment of the scientific research literature on reading and its implications for reading instruction.* (NIH Publication No. 00-4754). Washington, DC: National Institute of Child Health and Human Development.

Reschly, A. L., Busch, T. W., Betts, J., Deno, S. L., & Long, J. D. (2009). Curriculum-based measurement oral reading as an indicator of reading achievement: A meta-analysis of the correlational evidence. *Journal of School Psychology, 47*, 427–469. doi:10.1016/j.jsp.2009.07.001

Reynolds, A. J., Ou, S. R., Mondi, C. F., & Hayakawa, M. (2017). Processes of early childhood interventions to adult well-being. *Child Development, 88*, 378–387. doi:10.1111/cdev.12733

Shapiro, E. S. (2011). *Academic skills problems: Direct assessment and intervention* (4th ed.). New York, NY: Guilford.

Shapiro, E. S., Dennis, M. S., & Fu, Q. (2015). Comparing computer adaptive and curriculum-based measures of math in progress monitoring. *School Psychology Quarterly, 30*, 470–487. doi:10.1037/spq0000116

Shapiro, E. S., Keller, M. A., Lutz, J. G., Santoro, L. E., & Hintze, J. M. (2006). Curriculum-based measures and performance on state assessment and standardized tests: Reading and math performance in Pennsylvania. *Journal of Psychoeducational Assessment, 24*, 19–35. doi:10.1177/0734282905285237

Shinn, M. R. (Ed.). (1989). *Curriculum-based measurement: Assessing special children.* New York, NY: Guilford.

Therrien, W. J. (2004). Fluency and comprehension gains as a result of repeated reading: A meta-analysis. *Remedial and Special Education, 25*, 252–261. doi:10.1177/07419325040250040801

U.S. Department of Education, Institute of Education Sciences, National Center for Education Statistics. (2017a). National Assessment of Educational Progress (NAEP): 2011 writing assessments. Retrieved from https://www.nationsreportcard.gov/writing_2011

U.S. Department of Education, Institute of Education Sciences, National Center for Education Statistics. (2017b). National Assessment of Educational Progress (NAEP): 2015 mathematics and reading assessments. Retrieved from https://www.nationsreportcard.gov/reading_math_2015/#?grade=4

VanDerHeyden, A. M., Witt, J. C., & Barnett, D. W. (2005). The emergence and possible futures of Response to Intervention. *Journal of Psychoeducational Assessment, 23*, 339–361. doi:10.1177/073428290502300404

CHAPTER 9

Social, Emotional, and Behavioral Assessment and Intervention

AMY M. BRIESCH ■ ROBERT J. VOLPE

CHAPTER OBJECTIVES

- Provide an understanding of the need for social, emotional, and behavioral supports in schools
- Describe the most common forms of universal behavioral support (i.e., Positive Behavioral Interventions and Supports; social and emotional learning)
- Highlight available screening approaches for the proactive identification of students who are at risk behaviorally
- Explain how more intensive behavioral intervention and assessment supports may be provided at the Tier 2 level while maintaining efficiency
- Discuss how diagnostic data may be used to develop individualized behavioral supports at the Tier 3 level

Chapter 8 emphasized the important role that school psychologists play in supporting the academic success of students. In recent years, however, there have been notable changes in the way in which schools conceptualize student success. Student success is no longer seen simply as ensuring that students master skills in reading, writing, and math. Rather, schools have taken on the additional responsibility of developing students' social, emotional, and behavioral (SEB) skills and preparing them to become healthy and productive members of society. In this chapter, we describe the types and prevalence of SEB problems that school-age youth may experience. We also describe how these problems affect students in educational settings. Finally, we present a multi-tiered model of service delivery, including intervention and assessment strategies, for supporting students' SEB wellness in schools.

SEB PROBLEMS: DEFINITIONS AND PREVALENCE

Social, emotional, and behavioral (SEB) skills refer to a broad range of inter-related skills in self-regulating emotion and behavior as well as in interacting with others. Social skills are those skills that involve communicating and interacting with others. In schools, students must be able to interact competently with peers, teachers, administrators, parents, and others (e.g., community members) who contribute to educational activities. Emotional skills refer to those skills involved in recognizing, regulating, and expressing one's emotions in a safe and healthy manner. Behavioral skills refer to skills needed to conduct oneself in an appropriate manner (e.g., attending to class instruction and raising one's hand to participate in class). Notably, there is considerable overlap among the definitions and skills associated with each of these areas, which often are addressed jointly in schools. For example, suppressing a tantrum requires a student to exhibit emotional and behavioral regulation skills as well as to consider alternative approaches for interacting effectively with others. Thus, many prevention and intervention programs target a wide range of SEB skills to promote student success.

Students with SEB difficulties may experience problems in a number of domains and daily activities. For example, many students struggle with following directions, managing temper, attending to class instruction, resolving interpersonal conflicts, and expressing emotions. Others struggle with displaying empathy, asking for help, acting responsibly, and ignoring peer distractions.

Students can display SEB problems for a number of reasons. For example, significant life events, such as losing a family member or transitioning to a new school or neighborhood, can precipitate SEB difficulties for shorter or more extended periods of time. In some cases, students experience SEB problems as a result of a mental health disorder. Population surveys have suggested that as many as 25% of youth in the United States may meet diagnostic criteria for a mental health disorder and that roughly 10% of youth may suffer from some type of emotional disturbance (Costello, Mustillo, Keller, & Angold, 2004). Lifetime prevalence rates (i.e., having the problem at any time in one's life) are even higher, indicating that between the ages of 13 and 18 years, 46% of youth experience some mental health disorder, with about 21% of youth experiencing a severe disorder (Merikangas et al., 2010). The most common disorder in school-age children is attention-deficit/hyperactivity disorder (ADHD; between 7% and 9%), followed by anxiety disorders (approximately 3%), conduct problems (approximately 3%), and depression disorders (approximately 4%) (see Perou et al., 2013).

Although these statistics may sound worrisome enough on their own, what makes them even more concerning is the fact that only one in every five youth who exhibit a diagnosable mental health disorder receives mental health care (Burns et al., 1995; Centers for Disease Control and Prevention [CDC], 2004; U.S. Department of Health and Human Services, 1999). The negative impact of behavioral problems, in particular, are far reaching, affecting not only those students who exhibit problems but also their larger communities. For example, when asked about their primary concerns in the classroom, teachers have repeatedly ranked students with emotional and behavioral problems very high on their lists

(Bushaw & Lopez, 2010; Langdon & Vesper, 2000). In fact, many teachers have even cited student behavior problems as a central reason for leaving the teaching profession (U.S. Department of Education, 2004).

MULTI-TIERED SYSTEMS OF SUPPORT FOR SEB FUNCTIONING

A general overview of multi-tiered systems of support (MTSS) was provided in Chapter 7; in Chapter 8, applications of MTSS to academic service delivery were described. In this chapter, we discuss the applications of MTSS for enhancing students' SEB functioning. As described in Chapter 7, one of the primary goals of MTSS is to provide each student with the level of support he or she needs to be successful. As in Chapter 8, both intervention and assessment practices are described for supporting students at Tiers 1, 2, and 3, respectively.

Tier 1

Intervention

As described in Chapter 7, Tier 1 intervention focuses on teaching those skills that *all* students in a given population are expected to demonstrate. Generally, in the academic domain, there is widespread agreement regarding expectations for skill development. These expectations are delineated in learning standards, which explicitly describe the knowledge and skills that students are expected to demonstrate at each grade level. Although the specific content of learning standards varies across the country, every state has a published set of standards for each of the primary academic areas, including language arts, math, science, and social studies.

In contrast, relatively fewer states have adopted standards for students' SEB development (Dusenbury, Weissberg, Goren, & Domitrovich, 2014). This suggests that there is far less consensus regarding the behavioral skills students should be able to demonstrate than the academic skills. As a result, universal instruction within the SEB domain varies considerably across schools.

Universal instruction typically has been conceptualized within either a Positive Behavioral Interventions and Supports framework or a social and emotional learning framework (see Durlak, Weissberg, Dymnicki, Taylor, & Schellinger, 2011); however, these approaches are not necessarily mutually exclusive. Although somewhat different, both are accessible to all students, evidence-based, and grounded in the belief that students learn best in safe and supportive school environments. Moreover, they focus on developing similar types of skill and student competencies.

Positive Behavioral Interventions and Supports

Positive Behavioral Interventions and Supports (PBIS) is a problem-solving framework for providing a continuum of evidence-based behavioral supports that are designed to facilitate the academic and behavioral success of all students (Technical Assistance Center on Positive Behavioral Interventions and Supports, 2010). At the universal level (i.e., Tier 1), one core tenet of PBIS is that all students should receive explicit instruction regarding behavioral expectations. Although school personnel often expect students to know how to act or behave in particular contexts (e.g., classrooms, playgrounds, and cafeterias), the reality is that not all students have been taught how to do so. Just as we would not expect students to teach themselves to read on their own, so we should not expect students to figure out how to behave without clear instruction and expectations. In PBIS, behavioral skills are taught to students in the same manner as academic skills—namely, by explicitly defining the skill, modeling its implementation, and providing practice opportunities and feedback regarding skill application (Sugai & Horner, 2002). Consistent with other forms of Tier 1 instruction, the ultimate goal of teaching and reinforcing appropriate behaviors is to reduce the number of students who develop more severe behavioral problems and, in turn, require additional, more intensive supports.

Although the explicit teaching of behavioral expectations is a critical component of PBIS implementation, scholars and educators do not necessarily agree as to what these expectations should entail. Generally, however, it is recommended that schools establish a set of three to five expectations that meet three criteria: (a) They are positively stated (e.g., "be respectful" as opposed to "don't talk back"); (b) they are easy for students and staff to remember (e.g., not too long or wordy); and (c) they are socially valid (i.e., address those behaviors that the school community believes are important to change) (Warren et al., 2006). School-wide expectations often utilize global or broad wording, such that they are applicable to a wide range of behaviors across school settings (e.g., classroom, lunchroom, playground). For example, common school-wide expectations include the following: Be Responsible (e.g., clean up after self, follow directions, participate in class); Be Respectful (e.g., listen to others, take turns, use kind words); Be Ready/Prepared (e.g., arrive at class on time, come to school with appropriate materials, do your best work); and Be Safe (e.g., keep hands and feet to self, stay in assigned area, walk in the hallways). School staff regularly reference, review, and model appropriate behaviors for students, who are rewarded for engaging in behaviors consistent with the school-wide expectations. Typically, students are awarded tokens or coupons for appropriate behavior, which can be exchanged for prizes and privileges. When possible (and safe to do so), negative behaviors are ignored.

Social Emotional Learning

Whereas PBIS at the universal level focuses on the teaching, practice, and reinforcement of positive behavioral expectations, the aims of social emotional learning are somewhat different. Broadly, *social emotional learning (SEL)* is the process by which individuals acquire the knowledge, attitudes, and skills necessary to recognize, regulate, and express emotions, set positive goals, and maintain positive relationships with others (Collaborative for Academic, Social, and Emotional Learning [CASEL], 2017). CASEL (2017) identifies five core competencies that have been shown to lead to positive life outcomes—namely, self-awareness, self-management, responsible decision making, relationship skills, and social awareness. CASEL (2017) offers the following definitions of each of these five core competencies. *Self-awareness* refers to the individual's skills in recognizing personal strengths, weaknesses, thoughts, and emotions, whereas *self-management* refers to skills in regulating those thoughts and emotions (e.g., impulse control and goal setting). **Social awareness** refers to the individual's recognition of the perspectives of others (e.g., displaying empathy) and social norms that dictate acceptable behaviors. **Relationship skills** are those skills necessary for communicating, cooperating, and interacting appropriately with others. Finally, **responsible decision making** refers to balancing concerns regarding social norms, others' perspectives, ethical considerations, and personal goals to make choices about one's own actions.

Often, SEL competencies are taught explicitly to students within the context of freestanding lessons, such as those that are part of established curricula. For example, elementary-level programs such as Open Circle and Second Step may be used to teach younger students how to identify feelings and make appropriate personal and social decisions. Secondary-level programs such as Responding in Peaceful and Positive Ways can be used to teach older students essential problem-solving and conflict-resolution skills for preventing violent behavior (Weissberg, Goren, Domitrovich, & Dusenbury, 2013). SEL can also be promoted through teachers' use of instructional practices that foster supportive and engaging classroom environments. As one example, the Responsive Classroom program emphasizes the use of 10 teaching practices and strategies (e.g., rule creation, positive teacher language, and collaborative problem solving) to foster a nurturing classroom environment that is responsive to the cognitive, social–emotional, and physical needs of students (Weissberg et al., 2013). Overall, SEL has a strong, well-established evidence base. In reviewing 213 studies in which universal SEL programs were used with K–12 students, Durlak et al. (2011) found that those students who received SEL instruction not only experienced increases in prosocial behaviors and decreases in problem behavior but also made considerable gains in academic achievement.

Class-wide Behavioral Interventions

Regardless of whether a school chooses to implement PBIS, SEL, or both frameworks, Tier 1 behavioral interventions also can be implemented on a class-wide basis by individual teachers. One example of a class-wide behavioral intervention is the Good Behavior Game (GBG), whose use was first reported in the late 1960s (Barrish, Saunders, & Wolf, 1969). In the GBG, the teacher divides the classroom into two teams and explicitly teaches both teams the classroom rules as well as the actions that constitute rule violations. Teams are then given points for any rule violations (e.g., getting out of one's seat at the inappropriate time or talking out of turn). Typically, the team with the fewest points at the end of the game wins some predetermined reward (e.g., extra break time or access to a preferred activity). Alternatively, both teams may earn some privilege if they reach a predetermined point criterion (i.e., fewer than 5 points total). Although punitively awarding points for misbehavior is a typical component of the GBG, several variations have focused on rewarding points for positive behaviors (Crouch, Gresham, & Wright, 1985). The GBG is relatively easy to implement, and it has been demonstrated to have a positive impact on a wide array of classroom behaviors, including oppositional behavior, out-of-seat behaviors, and work completion (Flower, McKenna, Bunuan, Muething, & Vega, 2014). Research indicates that it has a strong impact on disruptive behaviors and on-task behaviors, particularly for students with emotional and behavior disorders (Bowman-Perrott, Burke, Zaini, Zhang, & Vannest, 2016).

Assessment

As you may recall from Chapter 7, the implementation of high-quality, evidence-based Tier 1 intervention should be effective in supporting the academic and behavioral needs of approximately 75% to 80% of the student population. However, regardless of how powerful or well supported Tier 1 interventions may be, approximately 15% to 20% of students are likely to exhibit elevated levels of risk that require additional, more intensive supports. Thus, schools must utilize efficient and effective procedures for identifying these students and ensuring their timely access to needed services. Although many students struggling with SEB problems may exhibit behaviors that are easily identified by personnel (e.g., tantrums and physically aggressive behaviors), others may not be recognized as easily. One factor that may determine how easily or quickly an at-risk behavior is identified concerns its topography, or the manner in which it is expressed. **Externalizing** problems refer to behaviors that manifest outwardly, such as throwing tantrums, hitting, and biting. **Internalizing problems** refer to problems that manifest within individuals, such as elevated levels of anxiety and depression. Generally, students who exhibit externalizing problems are more readily identified as at risk than students who experience internalizing problems.

As in academic MTSS, school personnel who implement social, emotional, and behavioral MTSS (SEB MTSS) conduct universal screenings to identify students with a wide variety of difficulties. These procedures assist personnel in proactively identifying at-risk students, such that Tier 2 and Tier 3 interventions can be implemented to prevent problems from intensifying or becoming more resistant to remediation over time.

Within an SEB MTSS, schools can employ several different screening approaches, depending on their objectives. In some cases, the goal of screening may be to identify those students who currently have—or are at risk for developing—a mental health disorder or emotional/behavioral disorder. To accomplish this goal, the screening instrument selected must be capable of quantifying symptoms or indicators of a particular diagnosis or area of concern. Most typically, this type of screening involves the use of *behavior rating scales* (introduced in Chapter 6), which are designed to assess the perceptions of relevant stakeholders (i.e., teachers, parents, and students themselves) regarding student behaviors. A teacher may be asked, for example, to rate the frequency with which a student has exhibited a particular behavioral indicator (e.g., "easily distracted by peers") over the past month using a 4-point scale (i.e., 0 = *never*, 3 = *almost always*). When used as a universal screening tool, this type of rating scale would be completed for each student in the classroom. Subsequently, students whose scores exceeded an established threshold would be targeted for further assessment and/or intervention.

In other cases, the goal of screening may be to identify those students whose behavior is impeding their success in school, regardless of their diagnostic status. Thus, rather than highlighting the presence of particular symptoms, the screening process is focused on identifying students who exhibit behavioral problems as measured by contextual, school-based indicators. These indicators may include attendance, incidents of suspension or expulsion, and office discipline referrals. Typically, these types of indicators can be examined using existing data (and therefore do not warrant additional data collection). Schools that implement PBIS commonly utilize school-based indicators to screen students for SEB problems. In these settings, a school-based team meets periodically to review attendance, disciplinary, and other records so as to identify students in need of additional supports. General guidelines suggest that students who have received between two and five office discipline referrals may require Tier 2 support, whereas students who have received six or more referrals may need Tier 3 support (McIntosh, Campbell, Carter, & Zumbo, 2009).

Regardless of which screening approach is used to identify those students believed to be at risk, the overarching goal remains the same: to ensure that students receive needed SEB supports in a timely fashion. As such, it is recommended that school-wide screening be conducted between two and three times per year, with the first administration occurring within the first month or two of the school year (Parisi, Ihlo, & Glover, 2014). The data collection process should be followed by an immediate, formal review of data (often by a school-based decision-making team). This immediacy allows the team to act quickly upon the information obtained and to place students who need higher tiers of support as quickly as possible.

Tier 2

Intervention

Tier 2 intervention provides a select group of students who are deemed to be at risk for SEB problems with *supplementary* and *targeted* supports. These supports are *supplementary* because they are provided to students in addition to (rather than in place of) Tier 1 supports, which are provided to all students regardless of their risk status. These supports also are *targeted* because they are matched closely with specific student needs identified through Tier 1 screening.

In some cases, Tier 2 supports may best be provided by specialized personnel (e.g., school psychologists or school social workers) outside of the regular classroom setting. Small-group interventions often are delivered in a pull-out fashion (i.e., outside of the classroom) and can be used to address the needs of students with similar types of difficulties. Often, these interventions are **manualized**, meaning that their content and procedures are both explicit and highly structured. As an example, the Anger Coping Program (Lochman, Nelson, & Sims, 1981) is a manualized program designed to reduce aggressive and disruptive behaviors in elementary and middle school students. Administered to groups of between four and six students across a total of 18 one-hour sessions, the program uses a combination of didactic instruction, group discussion, and activities to teach students skills such as problem solving, recognizing emotions, and managing conflicts. The Social Skills Intervention Guide (Elliott & Gresham, 2008) is another example of a manualized intervention that can be used with small groups of students who struggle with social skills. The 43 scripted lessons in this intervention focus on teaching students skills related to cooperation, assertion, responsibility, empathy, and self-control through a four-step model of *tell* (i.e., explain the skill), *show* (i.e., model the skill), *do* (i.e., role-play use of the skill), and *practice* (i.e., have the student rehearse the skill).

In other situations, it is possible for teachers (rather than specialized staff) to provide supplementary, targeted supports within the regular classroom setting. One example of a Tier 2 classroom intervention is the Daily Behavior Report Card (DBRC). The DBRC serves as both an intervention and a progress monitoring tool and can be used to address a wide array of classroom behavior problems (see Volpe & Fabiano, 2013). In a DBRC intervention, students earn points for working toward a set of predetermined behavioral goals. Typically, the DBRC form itself lists three to five goals (e.g., starts work with fewer than two reminders; follows directions on work assignments; and keeps hands and feet to self), and teachers record whether the student has met each goal at various intervals (e.g., at the end of each class period). Throughout the day, teachers provide feedback and encouragement to the student as he or she works toward the goals. At the end of the day, the teacher tallies the number of points the student earned, and the student receives a reward for reaching an established criterion (as applicable). Ideally, these rewards are provided by caregivers in the home setting but often are provided at school.

Another example of a Tier 2 classroom intervention concerns **self-monitoring** (see Briesch & Chafouleas, 2009). Self-monitoring refers to both a skill and a type of intervention. Broadly, **self-monitoring** (the skill) refers to tracking, management, and regulation of one's own behaviors (Bruhn, McDaniel, & Kreigh, 2015). In self-monitoring (the intervention), a student rates, reflects on, and/or scores his or her own behavior (e.g., proportion of time on task). Typically, some kind of prompt (e.g., timer) is used to indicate to the student when he or should complete the evaluation. Although the only individual who needs to complete the form is the student, often the student is asked to compare his or her evaluation to one completed by the teacher (see Cole & Bambara, 1992). In such cases, students typically are rewarded for rating their behavior accurately (e.g., within a point of the teacher rating). They also may be rewarded for reaching a preestablished criterion for the behavior ratings.

Assessment

As described in Chapter 7, all interventions within MTSS should be evidence-based. However, an intervention or strategy that is identified as *evidence-based* will not necessarily work for *all* students in *all* contexts. As a result, it is necessary to collect ongoing progress monitoring data to examine whether Tier 2 supports have been successful in meeting the needs of individual students. If students do not respond to the services available in Tier 2, they may demonstrate need for the more intensive supports offered in Tier 3. As in academic MTSS, the frequency of assessment in Tier 2 is greater than that in Tier 1. Whereas screening assessments can be likened to a "one-time snapshot" picture of a child's functioning, progress monitoring assessments are better characterized as moving pictures that depict a student's response to intervention. Tier 2 assessments can take many forms; however, given that these assessments involve repeated measurement, they must be carefully vetted for technical adequacy (e.g., reliability and validity) and feasibility (e.g., length of assessment and obtrusiveness; see Briesch & Volpe, 2007).

Systematic Direct Observation

A decade ago, there was heavy reliance on systematic direct observation to track students' response to school-based interventions. **Systematic direct observation (SDO)** is a form of direct behavioral observation (described in Chapter 6) that involves having a trained observer enter the classroom to examine and record in real time the occurrence of a small number of preselected student behaviors. In an SDO, each behavior must have a clear set of defining criteria to ensure the reliability of data recorded. School psychologists commonly conduct SDOs; however, teachers can also conduct them for certain low-frequency, discrete behaviors (e.g., cursing, throwing objects, and biting) that can be tallied easily via a recording sheet or frequency clicker. There are several advantages to using SDOs, as they are sensitive to small or incremental changes in student behavior. Moreover, because they follow a predetermined set of criteria for coding behavior, they are less prone to subjectivity than are other, less structured forms of observation (see Briesch, Volpe, & Floyd, 2018). Although SDO continues to be a common assessment method for monitoring students' intervention response, the extensive training and lengthy, frequent observation sessions needed to obtain reliable and valid data may be barriers to its widespread use.

Rating Scales

Among the progress monitoring methods most commonly used today are brief rating scales that may be completed one or more times per week. Rating scales designed for behavioral screening typically are fairly long (i.e., 30 or more items) because they are administered relatively infrequently (i.e., two to three times per year). Rating scales designed for progress monitoring, however, tend to be much shorter (i.e., 10 or fewer items), because they often are administered on a weekly or biweekly basis. Scale developers or publishers create shorter versions of full-length rating scales by selecting the best (i.e., most psychometrically strong) items from the original, longer measure using statistical procedures.

Direct Behavior Rating

A hybrid of SDO and rating scales, Direct Behavior Ratings are administered one or more times each day (see Briesch, Chafouleas, & Riley-Tillman, 2016). **Direct Behavior Ratings (DBRs)** are teacher ratings of student behavior that are completed at the end of a predetermined observation period (e.g., literacy block) and within a natural context (e.g., classroom). DBR can look very much like rating scales; however, unlike traditional rating scales, they are designed for rating behaviors over a much smaller window of observation (an instructional period or, at most, a school day). A common approach to implementing DBR is to use a single-item scale. In single-item DBR, a definition of the behavior category (e.g., disruptive behavior) is provided to the rater (typically a teacher), who is asked to record the proportion of time that the behavior was exhibited by the target student. To record this information, raters are provided with a line representing the entirety of the observation interval and asked to mark the appropriate proportion (ranging from 0% of the time to 100% of the time). Multi-item approaches to DBR also have received considerable attention. In these approaches, raters record multiple, specific behaviors (e.g., calling out) and can sum item scores to yield measures of broader behavior categories (e.g., disruptive behavior; see Volpe & Briesch, 2012, 2015).

Permanent Products

In some cases, permanent products can be used for progress monitoring purposes. In the context of school-based assessment, **permanent products** are the material entities that result from a given action or task that provide insight into the processes associated with those activities. By their nature, permanent products are naturally occurring sources of data in the classroom. For example, when a teacher takes attendance and records it in a ledger, her notes constitute a permanent product. If the teacher were interested in determining whether her classroom interventions were resulting in improved student attendance, she could use this existing record to monitor changes in attendance. For example, she might track the number of days on which a particular student attended school on time.

Other examples of permanent products include office disciplinary referral forms, completed (or incomplete) work assignments, and records of homework completion. These measures can be useful because they capitalize on existing data rather than burdening teachers with additional data collection responsibilities. At the same time, however, they lack the breadth, depth, and, in many cases, psychometric defensibility of the other measures described in this chapter (e.g., behavior rating scales). Nonetheless, permanent products can be quite useful when their resulting data are well matched with intervention goals.

Tier 3

As described in Chapter 7, Tier 3 intervention and assessment efforts can be differentiated from those at Tier 2 with respect to their degree of intensity and individuation. Tier 3 interventions are more likely to be delivered in individualized (i.e., one-to-one) formats. Moreover, they often are developed after a detailed assessment of the presenting problem has been undertaken. When progress monitoring data indicate that Tier 2 supports are insufficient to meet an individual student's needs, more intensive and individualized assessment is conducted to develop interventions in Tier 3. Generally, this type of assessment is diagnostic in nature, meaning that it is intended to identify the specific strengths and weaknesses in the student's skill set. Because diagnostic assessments often precede intervention in Tier 3, they are described first.

Assessment

Functional Behavior Assessment

Within SEB MTSS, the most typical form of diagnostic assessment is functional behavior assessment. **Functional behavior assessment (FBA)** is a data collection process for developing hypotheses regarding the factors that precipitate, maintain, or deter behavioral problems. Recall from Chapter 6 the terms *antecedents* and *consequences*. Antecedents are events or cues that are believed to trigger or increase the likelihood that a student will exhibit a particular problem behavior. For example, a student may be more likely to engage in a problem behavior when he is asked to complete a task that he does not enjoy (e.g., completing a math worksheet independently) or when seated near a particular peer. *Consequences*, in contrast, are events or cues that follow a problem behavior and either increase or decrease its likelihood of recurring in the future. Identifying the sequences of cues and events that take place both before and after problem behavior occurs can assist school psychologists in better understanding the nature and mechanisms of the behavior.

Reinforcement occurs when consequences lead to the increased recurrence of the problem behavior. For example, consider a student (Molly) who tells a joke during class that prompts her peers to laugh and smile. If Molly comes to class the next day armed with a new arsenal of jokes, the peer attention she received after telling the first joke likely reinforced her behavior. **Punishment**, by comparison, refers to consequences that lead to the decreased recurrence of problem behaviors. Consider Molly's situation again; however, this time, she is verbally reprimanded by her teacher. Following this event, Molly stops telling jokes in class. In this scenario, the teacher's verbal reprimand likely served as a punishing consequence, rendering her behavior less likely to occur in the future.

The goal of conducting an FBA is to identify the most likely antecedents and consequences of a problem behavior and to develop a corresponding intervention plan. A school psychologist may gather this information indirectly by asking a classroom teacher to identify the most likely antecedents and consequences of a student's problem behavior. Semistructured interviews such as the Functional Assessment Checklist for Teachers and Staff (FACTS; March et al., 2000) and rating scales such as the Problem Behavior Questionnaire (PBQ; Lewis, Scott, & Sugai, 1994) can be used to guide this process. Alternatively, information concerning antecedents and consequences may be gathered directly by conducting observations of the student in the classroom or other relevant settings. During these observations, the school psychologist documents problem behaviors and proximal environmental events as they arise, thereby allowing him or her to identify the most probable antecedents and consequences of the target behaviors.

The final step in conducting an FBA is to use the information obtained to develop a hypothesis regarding the **function** of the problem behavior, or the reason why the behavior is occurring. Within the context of an FBA, there are believed to be two primary functions of problem behaviors: () to get or obtain something or (2) to avoid or escape something. Common behavioral functions include obtaining or avoiding items, activities, or attention from peers or adults. Based on the data collected, the school psychologist incorporates his or her best guess as to the likely function of a student's problem behavior into a hypothesis statement. Typically, a hypothesis statement is written in the following form: *When [an antecedent occurs], Student X is likely to [exhibit a problem behavior] so as to [function of behavior].* For example, returning to the example presented earlier, a potential hypothesis statement might be as follows: *When the class is asked to listen quietly during whole-group instruction, Molly is likely to tell jokes so as to* *obtain peer attention.* This hypothesis statement can then be used to guide the selection of appropriate Tier 3 intervention strategies.

Other Forms of Diagnostic Assessment

Although FBAs are commonly used at Tier 3, other assessment tools can provide diagnostic information beyond that related to behavioral function. For example, *narrow-band* rating scales (described in Chapter 6) are instruments designed to obtain a detailed report from a particular informant (e.g., parent, teacher, or the student) of a student's functioning within a specific area. One commonly used narrow-band measure is the Children's Depression Inventory 2 (CDI-2; Kovacs, 2014). The CDI-2 self-report form contains 28 items, all of which are designed to assess symptoms of depression in children and adolescents ages 7 to 17 years. Responses to the items are used to generate both an overall score of depressive symptomatology and four subscale scores that gauge negative mood, negative self-esteem, ineffectiveness, and interpersonal problems.

Clinical interviews may also be used to gather diagnostic information. Whereas rating scales typically ask a respondent to provide a global judgment of a student's behavior over a period of time (e.g., past 2 weeks or past month), interviewing allows the practitioner to obtain more detailed information about particular behaviors, such as when they emerged, how long they have been occurring, and the degree of impairment they have caused. School psychologists most typically use *semistructured interviews* (as described in Chapter 6) to gather information regarding student functioning. In a semistructured interview, the examiner starts with a set of preestablished questions and then generates additional questions during the course of the interview to obtain clarifying information. Unlike semistructured interviews, *structured interview schedules* (also described in Chapter 6) use very specific wording, coding, and item ordering, such that their administration is highly standardized across respondents. Structured interview schedules often are used to determine whether a student meets diagnostic criteria for a particular disorder or disability. One example of a structured interview schedule is the Diagnostic Interview Schedule for Children Version IV (DISC-IV; Shaffer, Fisher, Lucas, Dulcan, & Schwab-Stone, 2000), which can be used to assess more than 30 psychiatric diagnoses in youth ages 6 to 18 years.

Intervention

Whereas multiple students often receive the same intervention at Tier 2, intervention strategies at Tier 3 are highly individualized in nature. Among the most common intervention approaches at Tier 3 are the use of behavior intervention plans and therapeutic interventions. These approaches are described in further detail in the following text.

Behavior Intervention Plans

When an FBA is conducted at Tier 3, the data from this assessment directly inform the development of a behavior intervention plan (see Figure 9.1). A **behavior intervention plan (BIP)** provides strategies for preventing problem behavior from occurring as well as for teaching and reinforcing students for engaging in

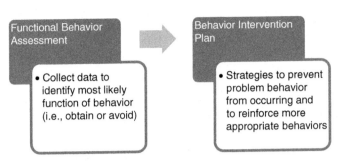

FIGURE 9.1 RELATIONSHIP BETWEEN FUNCTIONAL BEHAVIOR ASSESSMENT AND BEHAVIOR INTERVENTION PLAN.

alternative, more appropriate behaviors. Generally, strategies described in the BIP are integrally linked to each component of the hypothesis statement generated in the FBA. First, ***antecedent strategies*** involve altering the environment in which the behavior typically occurs in an effort to prevent the behavior from occurring. Suppose, for example, that the results of an FBA suggest that the presentation of a particular task demand (e.g., reading aloud to a peer) was the most likely antecedent of a student's (Marco's) verbally aggressive behavior. One possible antecedent strategy for decreasing this behavior might involve modifying the task demand, such as offering Marco a choice between two or more tasks (e.g., reading aloud to peer or reading aloud to a teaching assistant), rather than insisting that he complete one in particular.

The second group of strategies within a BIP are those that aim to teach the student replacement behaviors. ***Replacement behaviors*** are those behaviors that serve the same or a similar function as the problem behavior but are considered to be more appropriate than the current problem behavior. In other words, exhibiting a replacement behavior allows the student to achieve the same outcome (i.e., obtaining or avoiding something) as the problem behavior but in a more appropriate or acceptable manner. For example, returning to our earlier example of the student with verbally aggressive behavior, teaching replacement behaviors may help reduce the recurrence of this problem behavior. If each time the student responds to the peer reading task with verbally aggressive behavior, he is sent out of the classroom (and thus does not have to complete the task), task avoidance would be a likely function of the behavior. One possible replacement behavior for this student might involve telling the teacher privately that he does not want to read aloud in front of a peer and requesting an alternative task (e.g., reading aloud with a teaching assistant). This behavior would be more appropriate than verbal aggression but would achieve the same desired outcome (i.e., avoiding the task).

Finally, ***consequence strategies*** are those that target outcomes and responses to both problem and replacement behaviors. One common and effective consequence strategy for reducing problem behavior is to eliminate the potential reinforcers of that behavior. For example, continuing with the earlier example, it would be important for Marco's BIP to specify that he should not be able to avoid the peer reading task by engaging in verbally aggressive behavior. Instead, the teacher might wait until Marco has calmed down before presenting him with the same task again. Consequence strategies should also be used to reinforce Marco for engaging in the appropriate replacement behavior. Each time that Marco asks politely to read with a teaching assistant, the task demand of reading with a peer should be reliably removed. In addition, Marco may receive other desirable consequences, such as verbal praise, for demonstrating the replacement behavior.

Therapeutic Interventions

Tier 3 interventions may also include manualized interventions to treat individual students with internalizing problems, such as anxiety or depression. One example of a manualized intervention for treating anxiety in children and adolescents is Coping Cat (Kendall & Hedtke, 2006). Coping Cat is an evidence-based cognitive behavioral intervention that helps students recognize and understand their emotional and physical reactions to anxiety as well as critically examine personal thoughts and feelings that arise during anxiety-inducing situations (Kendall, Hudson, Gosch, & Flannery-Schroeder, 2008). It is designed to help students develop plans for effectively coping with anxiety, evaluate the degree to which they use coping strategies, and reward themselves for implementation. Typically, Coping Cat is administered individually in 50-minute weekly sessions over 16 weeks, but it also can be used effectively in small groups of four or five students (Flannery-Schroeder, Choudhury, & Kendall, 2005). During each session, students are introduced to particular concepts and strategies, and in between sessions, they complete related homework assignments. Procedures for implementation are clearly delineated in the Coping Cat manual. These well-defined procedures minimize training demands and increase the likelihood that the intervention will be delivered with fidelity (i.e., as designed).

SOCIAL JUSTICE CONNECTIONS

How can we enhance protective factors for youth who are at risk for mental health problems?

As described in this chapter, a wide range of youth are at risk for mental health problems. Some youth, however, may be at greater risk for mental health problems than others, due to adverse environmental circumstances. For example, Fisher, Wallace, and Fenton (2000) found that perceived discrimination was significantly associated with psychological distress and low self-esteem in a sample of racially and ethnically diverse adolescents. Moreover, individuals who come from economically disadvantaged backgrounds experience disproportionately higher rates of mental health problems than individuals who do not (World Health Organization & Calouste Gulbenkian Foundation, 2014).

Negative social influences, such as discrimination and poverty, can have an indelible impact on mental health outcomes for students. Consistent with a social justice approach, school psychologists should focus on augmenting the strengths, resources, and resilience of students who are affected by these circumstances. The following recommendations are made to assist practitioners in fostering positive mental health outcomes for all students by strengthening their social–emotional competencies, feelings of school belongingness, and networks of support.

1. *Build networks of social support.* Social support refers to the overall sense of being valued and cared for in a network of individuals (Saylor & Leech, 2009). School-age youth may

(continued)

receive social support from a variety of sources, including caregivers, community members, peers, teachers, and other school personnel (e.g., school psychologists). Social support has been commonly identified as a protective factor against social and emotional difficulties. For example, Demaray and Malecki (2002) found that students who reported higher levels of perceived social support exhibited lower levels of depression and higher levels of self-esteem. Moreover, Latino/Latina youth who reported higher levels of *familism* (i.e., a strong sense of closeness and loyalty to immediate and extended family) experienced fewer internalizing problems (Ayón, Marsiglia, & Bermudez-Parsai, 2010).

2. **Foster social emotional learning (SEL).** As described previously, SEL encompasses a range of competences related to self-awareness, self-management, social awareness, relationship skills, and decision making. Generally, children and adolescents who have greater SEL competence are better equipped to deal with adverse circumstances (e.g., stress and social conflict). The implementation of high-quality interventions to build social and behavioral skills has been associated with decreases in both externalizing problems (e.g., aggression) and internalizing problems (e.g., anxiety and depression) among youth (Durlak & Wells, 1997; Greenberg et al., 2003).

3. **Foster a sense of school belonging and connectedness.** School connectedness refers to feelings of being cared for, accepted, respected, and included in school communities (CDC, 2009; Goodenow, 1993). Although similar in some senses to social support, in that it describes students' relationships with others, school connectedness also refers to feelings of safety and involvement in school settings (CDC, 2009). Students who report higher levels of school connectedness generally report more positive mental health outcomes, including lower levels of depression and emotional distress (Shochet, Dadds, Ham, & Montague, 2014). Strategies for increasing students' perceived belongingness may include encouraging their proactive participation in decision-making processes, increasing involvement in extracurricular activities, reducing excessively harsh or punitive disciplinary practices, and implementing positive classroom management strategies (CDC, 2009; McNeely, Nonnemaker, & Blum, 2002; Mitra, 2004).

SUMMARY AND CONCLUSIONS

In this chapter, we described a multi-tiered model of service delivery for supporting students' SEB success in schools (i.e., SEB MTSS). Within a multi-tiered framework, school psychologists and other personnel can provide high-quality, evidence-based supports that are appropriately matched to the type and intensity of students' needs. MTSS also allows schools to make the most efficient use of their potentially limited mental health and behavioral support resources.

Although this chapter has surveyed a variety of common assessment and intervention methods at each tier, specific strategies vary considerably across schools. Notably, the literature on school-based SEB assessment and intervention is expansive, and practitioners should be well versed in this research before selecting procedures for their unique school contexts. Ultimately, there is much work to be done to meet the needs of students who are experiencing SEB problems. Fortunately, schools are an ideal context for identifying students in need of services and for providing them with the supports they need to be successful in a variety of settings.

DISCUSSION QUESTIONS

1. In SEB MTSS, what are some purposes of universal screening?
2. What are some key differences between PBIS and SEL? How are these frameworks alike?
3. Tier 2 SEB interventions may be provided by teachers within the regular classroom setting or in a pull-out fashion by specialized personnel. What might be the advantages of providing such supports in the classroom? What might be the disadvantages?
4. The data gathered through an FBA are used to develop a hypothesis regarding the function of the problem behavior. How does understanding the function of a behavior help us to develop more appropriate interventions for students?
5. As noted in the chapter, Tier 3 assessment procedures tend to be diagnostic in nature and are highly linked to intervention design. Why is this necessary at Tier 3 in particular?

REFERENCES

Ayón, C., Marsiglia, F. F., & Bermudez-Parsai, M. (2010). Latino family mental health: Exploring the role of discrimination and familismo. *Journal of Community Psychology, 38,* 742–756. doi:10.1002/jcop.20392

Barrish, H. H., Saunders, M., & Wolf, M. M. (1969). Good Behavior Game: Effects of individual contingencies for group consequences on disruptive behavior in a classroom. *Journal of Applied Behavior Analysis, 2,* 119–124. doi:10.1901/jaba.1969.2-119

Bowman-Perrott, L., Burke, M. D., Zaini, S., Zhang, N., & Vannest, K. (2016). Promoting positive behavior using the Good Behavior Game: A meta-analysis of single-case research. *Journal of Positive Behavior Interventions, 18,* 180–190. doi:10.1177/1098300715592355

Briesch, A. M., & Chafouleas, S. M. (2009). Review and analysis of literature on selfmanagement interventions to promote appropriate classroom behaviors (1988–2008). *School Psychology Quarterly, 24,* 106–118.

Briesch, A. M., Chafouleas, S. M., & Riley-Tillman, T. C. (2016). *Direct behavior rating: Linking assessment, communications, and intervention.* New York, NY: Guilford Press.

Briesch, A., & Volpe, R. J. (2007). Selecting progress monitoring tools for evaluating social behavior. *School Psychology Forum, 1,* 59–74.

Briesch, A. M., Volpe, R. J., & Floyd, R. G. (2018). *School-based observation: A practical guide to assessing student behavior.* New York, NY: Guilford Press.

Bruhn, A., McDaniel, S., & Kreigh, C. (2015). Self-monitoring interventions for students with behavior problems: A systematic review of current research. *Behavioral Disorders, 40,* 102–121. doi:10.17988/BD-13-45.1

Burns, B. J., Costello, E. J., Angold, A., Tweed, D., Stangl, D., Farmer, E. M., & Erklani, A. (1995). Children's mental health service use across service sectors. *Health Affairs, 14,* 147–159. doi:10.1377/hlthaff.14.3.147

Bushaw, W. J., & Lopez, S. J. (2010). Highlights of the 2010 Phi Delta Kappa/Gallup Poll. *Phi Delta Kappan, 92,* 8–26. Retrieved from http://www.pdkintl.org/kappan/docs/2010_Poll_Report.pdf

Centers for Disease Control and Prevention (CDC). (2004). *National Center for Health Statistics: National health interview survey.* Washington, DC: Author.

Centers for Disease Control and Prevention (CDC). (2009). *School connectedness: Strategies for increasing protective factors among youth.* Atlanta, GA: U.S. Department of Health and Human Services.

Cole, C. L., & Bambara, L. M. (1992). Issues surrounding the use of self-management interventions in schools. *School Psychology Review*, *21*, 193–201.

Collaborative for Academic, Social, and Emotional Learning. (2017). What is SEL? Retrieved from http://www.casel.org/what-is-sel

Costello, E. J., Mustillo S., Keller G., & Angold, A. (2004). Prevalence of psychiatric disorders in childhood and adolescence . In B. L. Levin, J. Petrila, & K. D. Hennessy (Eds.), *Mental health services: A public health perspective* (pp. 111–128). Oxford, UK: Oxford University Press.

Crouch, P. L., Gresham, F. M., & Wright, W. R. (1985). Interdependent and independent group contingencies with immediate and delayed reinforcement for controlling classroom behavior. *Journal of School Psychology*, *23*, 177–187. doi:10.1016/0022-4405(85)90008-1

Demaray, M. K., & Malecki, C. K. (2002). The relationship between perceived social support and maladjustment for students at risk. *Psychology in the Schools*, *39*, 305–316. doi:10.1207/s15374424jccp3502_1

Durlak, J. A., Weissberg, R. P., Dymnicki, A. B., Taylor, R. D., & Schellinger, K. B. (2011). The impact of enhancing students' social and emotional learning: A meta-analysis of school-based universal interventions. *Child Development*, *82*, 405–432. doi:10.1111/j.1467-8624.2010.01564.x

Durlak, J. A., & Wells, A. M. (1997). Primary prevention mental health programs for children and adolescents: A meta-analytic review. *American Journal of Community Psychology*, *25*, 115–152. doi:10.1023/A:1024654026646

Dusenbury, L., Weissberg, R. P., Goren, P., & Domitrovich, C. (2014). *State standards to advance social and emotional learning.* Chicago, IL: Collaborative for Academic, Social, and Emotional Learning.

Elliot, S., & Gresham, F. (2008). *Social Skills Improvement System (SSIS) intervention guide.* San Antonio, TX: Pearson.

Fisher, C. B., Wallace, S. A., & Fenton, R. E. (2000). Discrimination distress during adolescence. *Journal of Youth and Adolescence*, *29*, 679–695. doi:10.1023/A:1026455906512

Flannery-Schroeder, E., Choudhury, M. S., & Kendall, P. C. (2005). Group and individual cognitive-behavioral treatments for youth with anxiety disorders: 1-year follow-up. *Cognitive Therapy and Research*, *29*, 253–259. doi:10.1007/s10608-005-3168-z

Flower, A., McKenna, J. W., Bunuan, R. L., Muething, C. S., & Vega, R. (2014). Effects of the Good Behavior Game on challenging behaviors in school settings. *Review of Educational Research*, *84*, 546–571. doi:10.3102/0034654314536781

Goodenow, C. (1993). The psychological sense of school membership among adolescents: Scale development and educational correlates. *Psychology in the Schools*, *30*, 79–90. doi:10.1002/1520-6807(199301)30:1<79::AID-PITS2310300113>3.0.CO;2-X

Greenberg, M. T., Weissberg, R. P., O'Brien, M. U., Zins, J. E., Fredericks, L., Resnik, H. & Elias, M. J. (2003). Enhancing school-based prevention and youth development through coordinated social, emotional, and academic learning. *American Psychologist*, *58*, 466–474.

Kendall, P. C., & Hedtke, K. (2006). *The Coping Cat workbook* (2nd ed.). Ardmore, PA: Workbook Publishing.

Kendall, P. C., Hudson, J. L., Gosch, E., & Flannery-Schroeder, E. (2008). Cognitive-behavioral therapy for anxiety disordered youth: A randomized clinical trial evaluating child and family modalities. *Journal of Consulting and Clinical Psychology*, *76*, 282–297.

Kovacs, M. (2014). *Children's Depression Inventory* (2nd ed.). North Tonawanda, NY: Multi-Health Systems.

Langdon, C. A., & Vesper, N. (2000). The sixth Phi Delta Kappa poll of teachers' attitudes toward the public schools. *Phi Delta Kappan*, *81*, 607–611. Retrieved from http://www.jstor.org/stable/20439737

Lewis, T. J., Scott, T. M., & Sugai, G. (1994). The problem behavior questionnaire: A teacher-based instrument to develop functional hypotheses of problem behavior in general education settings. *Diagnostique*, *19*, 103–115. doi:10.1177/073724779401900207

Lochman, J. E., Nelson, W. M., & Sims, J. P. (1981). A cognitive behavioral program for use with aggressive children. *Journal of Clinical Child Psychology*, *13*, 146–148. doi:10.1080/15374418109533036

March, R. E., Horner, R. H., Lewis-Palmer, T., Brown, D., Crone, D., Todd, A. W., & Carr, E. G. (2000). *Functional Assessment Checklist: Teachers and Staff (FACTS).* Eugene, OR: Educational and Community Supports.

McIntosh, K., Campbell, A. L., Carter, D. R., & Zumbo, B. D. (2009). Concurrent validity of office discipline referrals and cut points used in schoolwide positive behavior support. *Behavioral Disorders, 34*, 100–113. Retrieved from http://www.jstor.org/stable/43153806

McNeely, C. A., Nonnemaker, J. M., & Blum, R. W. (2002). Promoting school connectedness: Evidence from the National Longitudinal Study of Adolescent Health. *Journal of School Health, 72*, 138–146. doi:10.1111/j.1746-1561.2002.tb06533.x

Merikangas, K. R., He, J. P., Burstein, M., Swanson, S. A., Avenevoli, S., Cui, L., . . . Swendsen, J. (2010). Lifetime prevalence of mental disorders in US adolescents: Results from the National Comorbidity Survey Replication—Adolescent Supplement (NCS-A). *Journal of the American Academy of Child & Adolescent Psychiatry, 49*, 980–989.

Mitra, D. L. (2004). The significance of students: Can increasing "student voice" in schools leads to gains in youth development? *Teachers College Record, 106*, 651–688.

Parisi, D. M., Ihlo, T., & Glover, T. A. (2014). *Screening within a multitiered early prevention model: Using assessment to inform instruction and promote students' response to intervention.* Washington, DC: American Psychological Association.

Perou, R., Bitsko, R. H., Blumberg, S. J., Pastor, P., Ghandour, R. M., Gfroerer, J. C., . . . & Parks, S. E. (2013). Mental health surveillance among children—United States, 2005–2011. *MMWR Surveillance Summaries, 62*(suppl 2), 1–35.

Saylor, C. F., & Leech, J. B. (2009). Perceived bullying and social support in students accessing special inclusion programming. *Journal of Developmental and Physical Disabilities, 21*, 69–80.

Shaffer, D., Fisher, P., Lucas, C., Dulcan, M., & Schwab-Stone, M. (2000). NIMH Diagnostic Interview Schedule for Children, Version IV (NIMH DISC-IV): Description, differences from previous versions, and reliability of some common diagnoses. *Journal of the American Academy of Child and Adolescent Psychiatry, 39*, 28–38. doi:10.1097/00004583-200001000-00014

Shochet, I. M., Dadds, M. R., Ham, D., & Montague, R. (2006). School connectedness is an under-emphasized parameter in adolescent mental health: Results of a community prediction study. *Journal of Clinical Child & Adolescent Psychology, 35*, 170–179.

Sugai, G., & Horner, R. (2002). The evolution of discipline practices: School-wide positive behavior supports. *Child & Family Behavior Therapy, 24*, 23–50.

Technical Assistance Center on Positive Behavioral Interventions and Supports. (2010). *Implementation blueprint and self-assessment.* Washington, DC: U.S. Department of Education, Office of Special Education Programs.

U.S. Department of Education, Policy and Program Studies Service. (2004). *State education indicators with a focus on Title I, 2000–01.* Washington, DC: Author.

U.S. Department of Health and Human Services. (1999). *Mental health: A report of the Surgeon General.* Rockville, MD: U.S. Department of Health and Human Services, Substance Abuse and Mental Health Services Administration, Center for Mental Health Services, National Institutes of Health, National Institute of Mental Health.

Volpe, R. J., & Briesch, A. M. (2012). Generalizability and dependability of single item and multiple item direct behavior rating scales for engagement and disruptive behavior. *School Psychology Review, 41*, 246–261.

Volpe, R. J., & Briesch, A. M. (2015). Multi-item direct behavior ratings: Dependability of two levels of assessment specificity. *School Psychology Quarterly, 30*, 431–442.

Volpe, R. J., & Fabiano, G. A. (2013). *Daily behavior report cards: An evidence-based system of assessment and intervention.* New York, NY: Guilford Press.

Warren, J. S., Bohanon-Edmonson, H. M., Turnbull, A. P., Sailor, W., Wickham, D., Griggs, P., & Beech, S. E. (2006). School-wide positive behavior support: Addressing behavior problems that impede student learning. *Educational Psychology Review, 18*, 187–198.

Weissberg, R. P., Goren, P., Domitrovich, C., & Dusenbury, L. (2013). *2013 CASEL guide: Effective social and emotional learning programs: Preschool and elementary school edition.* Austin, TX: Collaborative for Academic, Social, and Emotional Learning.

World Health Organization & Calouste Gulbenkian Foundation. (2014). *Social determinants of mental health.* Geneva, Switzerland: World Health Organization.

CHAPTER 10

Cognitive Assessment

JOHN H. KRANZLER ■ RANDY G. FLOYD

CHAPTER OBJECTIVES

- Define intelligence
- Describe the structure of intelligence
- Describe how intelligence is measured
- Describe the use of intelligence tests in the schools
- Discuss issues of social justice pertaining to intelligence test use

The "existence of individual differences in cognitive aptitude for learning from instruction is the most longstanding, well-established fact in educational psychology" (Snow & Lohman, 1984, p. 347). Indeed, in virtually every classroom, it is common for teachers to observe that some students struggle to acquire certain knowledge and skills, while others learn that same material quickly and with ease. While at least some academic skill deficits are best viewed as a mismatch between the child and the instructional environment, individual differences in the ability to learn from instruction can also stem from differences in intelligence (Jensen, 1989). Such differences present a tremendous challenge for teachers, because they require teachers to adapt instruction to promote the attainment of common instructional objectives for all students.

Intelligence tests were originally developed to improve educational efficiency by identifying children and youth who were at risk for educational failure (Chapman, 1988). Such tests were used to classify students to fixed educational structures on the basis of general intellectual ability, where they would either succeed or drop out. After the Education for All Handicapped Children Act was passed in 1975 (as described in Chapters 2 and 5), public school systems were mandated to provide an appropriate education for all students, including those with disabilities who had been previously excluded from the education system.

Society's commitment to equal educational opportunity for all necessitates that instructional accommodations be made to address the wide range of aptitudes for learning. As Braden and Shaw (2009) have stated, today intelligence tests are administered "to students who are experiencing academic difficulties in school under the assumption that doing so will help stakeholders (e.g., educators, support services personnel, and parents) find ways to help students overcome their difficulties" (p. 106).

This chapter reviews the current status of intelligence testing in the schools. We begin by defining intelligence, its structure, and distribution. Next, we discuss the origins of individual differences in intelligence and its malleability. We then examine how intelligence is measured and how tests of intelligence are used in the schools. We conclude with a discussion of intelligence and social justice.

WHAT IS INTELLIGENCE?

Despite the fact that tests of intelligence have been used for more than 100 years, a consensus on the definition of ***intelligence*** has not been reached (e.g., Sternberg & Kaufman, 2011). The fact that intelligence can be conceptualized from several different perspectives is one reason why a consensus definition has been so elusive (cf. Eysenck, 1988). One conception of intelligence, *biological intelligence*, refers to the biological functioning of the brain that is involved in all thought and action. Biological intelligence is influenced by genes, because they are related to brain structure and its physiological and biochemical functioning (Haier, 2011; Nisbett et al., 2012). The second conception of intelligence, *psychometric intelligence*, refers to the behaviors that are measured on intelligence tests. Performance on intelligence tests is related not only to one's biological functioning but also to the environment in which one was raised. Important environmental influences on intelligence test performance include family background and level and quality of education, among others (Gottfredson, 2008; Jensen, 1998). The third and final conception of intelligence is *social intelligence*. Social intelligence refers to what is considered "intelligent" behavior in specific contexts, such as school or work. Moreover, the behaviors that are seen as intelligent may differ across cultures (e.g., Gottfredson, 2008). Thus, what is considered "real-world intelligence" is determined in part by one's biological functioning and in part by one's background and experience, as well as by numerous noncognitive factors (e.g., personality, nutrition, and motivation).

Given that intelligence can be defined from these different perspectives, it is perhaps not surprising that a consensus definition is lacking. Despite the lack of consensus, these different conceptualizations of intelligence do overlap in important and meaningful ways. In fact, most researchers vigorously studying intelligence agree that it involves the ability to reason abstractly, solve complex problems, and acquire new knowledge. Intelligence, therefore, reflects more than "book learning" or "test-taking skill"; that is, it incorporates a larger capacity for comprehending and reasoning (Eysenck, 1998; Gottfredson, 2002; Neisser et al., 1996).

THE STRUCTURE OF INTELLIGENCE

One of the most important discoveries in the history of psychology is called the **positive manifold**. The positive manifold refers to the fact that all intelligence tests are positively intercorrelated. Thus, persons who perform well on one kind of test (e.g., a verbal test) tend to do well on every other kind of test (e.g., a spatial test and a reasoning test), and vice versa. The positive manifold indicates that individual differences on all tests of intelligence have something in common. Charles Spearman (1904) developed a sophisticated statistical analysis called **factor analysis** to measure the degree to which different tests of intelligence are related to a common source of individual differences, which he called *the general factor*, or **psychometric g**. In factor analysis, a factor is an underlying variable that accounts for the correlations between test scores. In his two-factor theory, Spearman hypothesized that every test of intelligence measures psychometric g and another factor that is unique to that specific test. Soon after the development of factor analysis, however, Spearman and other pioneers in this method discovered the existence of **group factors**. Group factors are different from *psychometric g* in that they are common only to certain groups of tests that require similar content (e.g., verbal, numerical, or spatial) or cognitive processes (e.g., memory). Factor analysis revealed that intelligence, as measured by intelligence tests, is both general in a sense and specific to subsets of tests.

Over the past 100 years, numerous theories about the number of factors and their relations with one another have been postulated (e.g., Cattell, 1971; Thurstone, 1938). At present, the most widely accepted theory of the structure of factors from intelligence tests is the **Cattell-Horn-Carroll (CHC) theory** (e.g., Schneider & McGrew, 2012). The CHC theory is an integration of two different theories—Carroll's (1993) three-stratum theory and Horn-Cattell's fluid and crystallized (*Gf-Gc*) theory (Horn & Noll, 1997). According to the CHC theory, intelligence is structured hierarchically, with three levels that differ in how general or narrow they are. At Stratum III, the apex of the hierarchy, is psychometric g, the most general factor. At the next level of generality, Stratum II, there are 8 to 10 broad group factors (e.g., Fluid Reasoning, Comprehension–Knowledge, and Short-Term Memory). Finally, at Stratum III, there are more than 80 narrow group factors, including those representing differences in map-reading ability, vocabulary knowledge, and accuracy in learning people's names. What, then, is intelligence? The vast literature on intelligence clearly indicates that it is multidimensional, which means that intelligence cannot be fully captured by any single factor or intelligence test score.

THE MEASUREMENT OF INTELLIGENCE

The measurement of intelligence is viewed by many as one of psychology's greatest contributions to society (Nisbett et al., 2012). When Alfred Binet and Théodore Simon invented the first intelligence test, they began with the assumption that children become more intelligent with age. They developed and administered a set of questions and tasks to children at 1-year intervals between 3 and 15 years of age. Within each age group, Binet and Simon then grouped the test items based on the percentage of children who got each item correct. For example, if the average child at the age of 10 years correctly answered a particular item, then that item had an age level of 10 years. Thus, children who could solve this item were said to have a mental age (MA) of 10 years. At each age level, these researchers selected five items so that they could measure MA in months as well as years. By comparing a child's MA to his or her chronological age (CA), Binet and Simon were able to determine whether a child's intelligence was above or below average in comparison to same-age peers.

Wilhelm Stern was the first to describe intelligence by the ratio of MA by CA to derive a "mental quotient," a term that was later changed to "intelligence quotient" (IQ). When this ratio is multiplied by 100 to remove the decimal point, IQ = MA/CA × 100. Thus, for example, an 8-year-old child with an MA equivalent to that of the average 10-year-old would have an IQ of 125 (10/8 × 100). Despite its appeal, it quickly became apparent that the new IQ scale was not useful after about 16 years of age, given that intellectual skills do not continue to develop steadily after that age. For adults, this method is clearly inappropriate, because their MA would remain relatively constant, while their CA would constantly increase with time. For this reason, all intelligence tests now use a different method for calculating IQs, called a point scale. Using this method, the number of points an individual earned on the test (called a *raw score*) is converted statistically to an IQ based on his or her relative standing in relation to a normative sample of same-age peers. The average score at each age is set at 100, with a standard deviation (*SD*) of 15. The point scale more accurately measures intelligence in comparison to others of the same age.

Intelligence tests have been increasingly developed based on theories as described previously. CHC theory, in particular, has been used in this manner, or it has been referenced as an interpretative option (Keith & Reynolds, 2010). For example, the individually administered intelligence tests such as the Kaufman Assessment Battery for Children, Second Edition (Kaufman & Kaufman, 2004), and the Woodcock-Johnson IV Tests of Cognitive Abilities (Schrank, McGrew, & Mather, 2014) are explicitly based on CHC theory. They were designed to measure five to seven CHC broad group factors in addition to psychometric g. In contrast, the intelligence test called the Wechsler Intelligence Scale for Children, Fifth Edition (WISC-V; Wechsler, 2014) was not explicitly developed based on CHC theory. However, it measures five CHC broad group factors in addition to psychometric g (cf. Canivez, Watkins, & Dombrowski, 2016).

The broad group factors that are measured at Stratum II of CHC theory are not always the same across intelligence tests, so different intelligence tests may not measure all of the same abilities. Nevertheless, all of the most widely used measures of intelligence tests correlate substantially with each other, with the average correlation being approximately +.80. This finding results from the fact that they all largely measure the same thing—psychometric g. Factor analysis has revealed that psychometric g is the largest factor underlying individual differences on intelligence tests, typically explaining a greater proportion of individual differences than all of the group factors that are measured *combined*. On the WISC-V, for example, psychometric g explains more than 80% of all individual differences.

In addition, research has shown that the psychometric *g* measured by different tests of intelligence is essentially the same (Floyd, Reynolds, Farmer, & Kranzler, 2013).

The best measure of psychometric *g* is the overall IQ score on intelligence tests. Many important social outcomes—such as academic achievement, years of education, social status, and income, among others—are predicted better by IQ than they are by any other measurable psychological variable independent of IQ (e.g., Gottfredson, 2008). Nevertheless, despite the fact that IQs are quite predictive of a number of important social criteria, their prediction is far from perfect. As Gottfredson (1997) has noted, "The effects of intelligence—like other psychological traits—are probabilistic, not deterministic. Higher intelligence improves the *odds* of success in school and work. It is an advantage, not a guarantee. Many other things matter" (p. 551, original emphasis). Noncognitive factors such as *conscientiousness*, *ambition*, and *openness to experience*, among others, may be equally as important for real-life success.

THE DISTRIBUTION OF INTELLIGENCE

Like many characteristics in the social and behavioral sciences, individual differences in intelligence closely approximate the **normal distribution**, which is sometimes called a *bell curve*. An idealized normal distribution of intelligence test scores (IQs) is shown in Figure 10.1. In this figure, the mean of the distribution is 100 and the *SD* is 15. The overall score on intelligence tests for most individuals falls near the mean, with increasingly fewer scores at the high and low tails of the distribution. Approximately 68% of all people have IQs that are within one *SD* above and below the mean (i.e., IQs = 85–115), and about 95% have scores that fall within two *SD*s from the mean (i.e., 70–130). For the middle 95% of the population, the normal distribution is a reasonably accurate model of the distribution of intelligence. When the remaining 5% of scores at the extreme tails of the

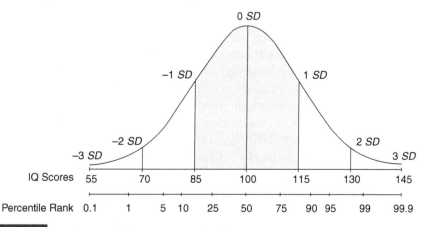

FIGURE 10.1 DISTRIBUTION OF INTELLIGENCE TEST SCORES

Adapted from Kranzler & Floyd (2013).

distribution are included, the normal distribution is not perfectly accurate. One reason is that there is a greater proportion of individuals with very low IQs at the extreme low end of the distribution (i.e., IQs < 50) than on a normal curve.

INTERPRETATION OF INTELLIGENCE TESTS

The first intelligence tests, such as the Stanford-Binet Intelligence Scale (Terman, 1916), yielded only a single score (the IQ) as an estimate of psychometric g. Since the publication of intelligence tests in the 1930s that measured psychometric g and a number of broad and narrow abilities (e.g., Wechsler, 1939), psychologists have conducted *intraindividual analyses* (or *ipsative analyses*) of an individual's test scores to identify cognitive strengths and weaknesses. In intraindividual analyses, the primary focus of clinical interpretation is on the scores that reflect certain group factors, rather than on psychometric g. The aim of this approach is to maximize the effectiveness of instructional interventions by pairing them with particular profiles of intelligence test scores (e.g., Flanagan, Fiorello, & Ortiz, 2010). Despite its potential, intraindividual analysis of intelligence test scores has not been shown to yield the kinds of results that were anticipated. The identified cognitive strengths and weaknesses tend not to be consistent across time, and there is little scientific evidence that links these strengths and weaknesses to more accurate diagnoses of disabilities or effective interventions designed to treat learning problems (see Watkins, 2003). Based on the weak evidence base supporting the utility of intraindividual analysis, some (e.g., Canivez, 2013; Kranzler & Floyd, 2013) have called for a return to a narrower focus on a single score (the IQ).

INTELLIGENCE TESTING IN THE SCHOOLS

In the early 1900s, intelligence tests were initially used in schools to sort students by instructional level or educational track (i.e., vocational or college bound). From then until the 1970s, the practice of testing and grouping students was a common practice in the schools. Throughout this period, however, the use of intelligence tests for "ability grouping" or "tracking" was strongly criticized, resulting in a number of legal challenges related to school admissions, tracking, and determining eligibility for special education. In *Hobson v. Hansen* (1967), for example, the court ruled that the administration of intelligence tests for tracking purposes "deprived students from racial/ethnic minority groups and students from families of low socioeconomic status of educational opportunity, because they were disproportionately placed in lower ability tracks that were substantially different from and inferior to higher ability tracks" (Kranzler, Benson, & Floyd, 2016, p. 277). As a result, the system for tracking students based on intelligence was abolished.

In 1975, the U.S. Congress passed a federal law called the Education for All Handicapped Children Act (PL 94-142), which mandated that all public school systems provide a free and appropriate public education to children and youth with disabilities. PL 94-142 was reauthorized in 2004 as the Individuals with

Disabilities in Education Improvement Act (IDEIA). The IDEIA has explicit guidelines for the use of intelligence tests in the schools to determine eligibility for special education and related services. Under the IDEIA, intelligence tests are mandated in most states for the identification of intellectual disabilities, intellectual giftedness, and specific learning disabilities (as described in more detail in the following sections). Intelligence tests may be used as a benchmark against which to compare students' current academic achievement, but the specific requirements for use of intelligence tests vary across states. IQ tests may be required for the identification of certain disabilities in some states but not in others (e.g., Maki, Floyd, & Roberson, 2015).

Intellectual Disability

Intellectual disability (ID) is defined in IDEIA as "significantly subaverage general intellectual functioning, existing concurrently with deficits in adaptive behavior and manifested during the developmental period that adversely affects a child's educational performance" (Office of Special Education and Rehabilitative Services, Department of Education, 2006, p. 46756). This definition addresses two primary criteria: (1) general intellectual functioning as measured by intelligence tests and (2) adaptive behavior. As of late 2014, in 75% of states, special education eligibility for ID required very low intellectual functioning as reflected in an IQ on a comprehensive intelligence test that is about two *SD*s below the mean when compared to age-based norms (McNicholas et al., 2017). *Adaptive behavior* refers to "the level of everyday performance of tasks that is required for a person to fulfill typical roles in society, including maintaining independence and meeting cultural expectations regarding personal and social responsibility" (VandenBos, 2006, p. 18). Similar deficits in adaptive functioning are also required for ID, but most states do not specify exactly which scores (e.g., total or domains scores) should be used to identify these deficits (McNicholas et al., 2017). Thus, intelligence tests are highly important when identifying children and adolescents with ID.

Intellectual Giftedness

Intellectual giftedness is defined in IDEIA as being present in those persons

> who give evidence of high achievement capability in areas such as intellectual, creative, artistic, or leadership capacity, or in specific academic fields, and who need services or activities not ordinarily provided by the school in order to fully develop those capabilities. (20 U.S.C. Section 7801(22)

At present, most conceptualizations of giftedness view intelligence as a central feature, although all of them expand upon the historical conception of giftedness as an all-purpose, inherited quality of the individual that is identified primarily by an intelligence test (for reviews, see Kranzler & Floyd, 2013; Sternberg & Davidson, 2005). Approximately 90% of states include intelligence as an area or category of giftedness and one third require the assessment of intelligence as part of the identification process for the giftedness (McClain & Pfeiffer, 2012). In addition to other criteria, such as rating scales of gifted characteristics, most states require consideration of IQs, but only 36% of states specify a specific score marker (e.g., IQ > 125). Again, intelligence tests yield vital information in the assessment of giftedness.

Specific Learning Disabilities

Specific learning disability (SLD) is defined in IDEIA as "a disorder in one or more of the basic psychological processes involved in understanding or in using language, spoken or written, which disorder may manifest itself in an imperfect ability to listen, speak, write, spell, or do mathematical calculations" (Pub. L. No. 108–446 § 300.8[c]). There is much disagreement surrounding the definition and diagnosis of SLD, and no consensus definition of SLD exists. Nevertheless, all current definitions of SLD (a) specify that individuals with SLD experience difficulty with school learning and (b) require that certain criteria must be ruled out (e.g., inadequate educational background, sensory impairment, and ID). The biggest point of disagreement among the most widely used definitions of SLD is the need for assessment of intelligence to make the SLD diagnosis (see Kranzler & Floyd, 2013).

SLD was originally conceptualized as unexpected underachievement (Kirk, 1962). In the *IQ–achievement discrepancy* approach, SLD is identified when an individual's level of performance or rate of skill acquisition in a particular academic area falls substantially below the level one would predict based on the person's intelligence. SLD is identified when a significant discrepancy between IQ and academic achievement is observed, after ruling out exclusionary criteria. As late as 2013, more than two thirds of states allowed for the use of the intelligence–achievement discrepancy method for identifying SLD (Maki et al., 2015). Critics of this approach (e.g., Francis et al., 2005) have argued that intelligence tests do not differentiate between students with SLD and slow learners in terms of their cognitive profiles or response to intervention, which makes these tests irrelevant. Some critics (e.g., Vaughn & Fuchs, 2003) refer to the IQ–achievement discrepancy model as supporting a "wait-to-fail" approach, because it is often difficult to determine a severe discrepancy between intelligence and achievement until as late as the third grade.

Given these criticisms, the most recent authorization of IDEIA allows for the identification of SLD on the basis of significant low achievement and lack of *response to intervention (RtI)* within a multitiered service delivery system, as discussed by Kovaleski, VanDerHeyden, and Shapiro (2013). Although methods of identification vary, nonresponders to intervention are defined by academic performance that falls below a predetermined level in comparison to school, district, or national norms and an absence of growth in targeted skills (e.g., oral reading) across time despite intensive interventions. Within a multitiered service delivery system emphasizing RtI, intelligence tests are not typically administered, but they may be included as part of a comprehensive assessment designed to eliminate the hypothesis that ID is the cause of academic problems. Critics of a multitiered service delivery system emphasizing RtI (e.g., Reynolds, 2009) have argued that it represents a fundamental shift in the conceptualization of SLD from unexpected underachievement to a difficulty with academic achievement in general (i.e., slow learners). As of 2013, approximately two thirds of all states allowed for the use of the RtI approach to SLD identification (Maki et al., 2015).

The third approach to SLD identification is referred to as the ***pattern of strengths and weaknesses*** (**PSW**) approach (Flanagan, Ortiz, & Alfonso, 2013; Naglieri & Otero, 2012). The PSW approach defines SLD as unexpected under-achievement as well as corresponding weaknesses in broad or narrow abilities measured by intelligence tests. Although based on the widely accepted CHC theory, very little empirical evidence supports the use of the PSW approaches to SLD identification (e.g., Kranzler, Floyd, Benson, Zaboski, & Thibodaux, 2016a, 2016b). As of 2013, only one fourth of all states allowed for the use of this approach for SLD identification.

INTELLIGENCE AND SOCIAL JUSTICE

Despite more than 100 years of research into intelligence and its measurement, these topics continue to be frequently debated and remain controversial in the fields of psychology and education and in the broader society, including politics. One reason is the frequent finding of group differences, across racial and ethnic groups of children, adolescents, and adults, in average performance on intelligence tests (Nisbett et al., 2012). Another reason is the finding of disproportional repre-sentation of students from minority racial and ethnic groups in special education classes. This disproportionality is particularly prominent in categories for which intelligence tests play a central role. For example, African American and Hispanic students are over-represented in identifications of ID and SLD and under-repre-sented in identifications of giftedness (Musu-Gillette et al., 2016; U.S. Department of Education, 2014; U.S. Department of Education, Office of Special Education and Rehabilitative Services, 2016). The following "Social Justice Connections" box suggests some potential strategies for addressing these systemic problems.

SOCIAL JUSTICE CONNECTIONS

How do school psychologists promote social justice for students from minority racial/ethnic groups and other marginalized groups?

We see five strategies as necessary. First, researchers should continue to conduct research to explain group differences and develop methods to reduce them (e.g., through interven-tions reducing health disparities and early childhood education; Helms, 2007). Second, test authors, test publishers, and independent researchers should continue to evaluate potential bias in intelligence tests at the item level and the score level (Reynolds & Carson, 2005).

Third, professionals who administer intelligence tests (school psychologists and others) should complete assessments that are informed by scientific research and that target not only students' intelligence, knowledge, and skills but also the most salient risk and protec-tive factors predicting success in school and community settings. In particular, they should

---

(continued)

select tests that are likely to minimize measurement error (and presumed bias) while tapping into different facets of intelligence (Kranzler & Floyd, 2013) as well as consider socioeconomic status and richness of early childhood experiences, which intersect with risk and protective factors (Ford, Wright, Washington, & Henfield, 2016).

Fourth, during testing, school psychologists and other professionals should be aware of confounding influences on performance during testing. In particular, students from minority racial and ethnic backgrounds may perform more poorly on intelligence tests due to the influence of **stereotype threat**, which is "being at risk of confirming, as self-characteristic, a negative stereotype about one's group" (Steele & Aronson, 1995, p. 797). Careful planning of, relationship building during, and monitoring of negative emotions, such as anxiety, during testing are important in each individual assessment case and vital for assessing students from minority racial and ethnic backgrounds.

Finally, professionals in psychology and education should carefully examine their own beliefs and expectations that may bias their interactions and lead to harmful or otherwise discriminatory actions. Ford et al. (2016), in referring to assessment for giftedness, stated that

> school psychologists must be self-reflective and consult and collaborate with other educators. It is especially critical to collaborate with educators of color when making gifted education assessments and decisions to decrease cultural misunderstanding in all aspects and phases of assessment and decision making. (pp. 270–271)

SUMMARY AND CONCLUSIONS

In conclusion, we encourage readers to consider the balanced approach offered by Nisbett et al. (2012):

> The measurement of intelligence is one of psychology's greatest achievements and one of its most controversial. Critics complain that no single test can capture the complexity of human intelligence, all measurement is imperfect, no single measure is completely free from cultural bias, and there is the potential for misuse of scores on tests of intelligence. There is some merit to all these criticisms. But we would counter that the measurement of intelligence—which has been done primarily by IQ tests—has utilitarian value because it is a reasonably good predictor of grades at school, performance at work, and many other aspects of success in life. . . . It is important to remain vigilant for misuse of scores on tests of intelligence or any other psychological assessment and to look for possible biases in any measure, but intelligence test scores remain useful when applied in a thoughtful and transparent manner. (p. 131)

DISCUSSION QUESTIONS

1. What is intelligence? Is intelligence one thing or many?
2. What is psychometric g, and why is it particularly important?
3. How are intelligence tests used in the schools today?
4. Describe some of the approaches used to identify SLD in schools. Why do you think that identification of this particular disability has become such a contentious topic in school psychology?
5. Which social justice issues are related to the use of intelligence tests in the schools?

REFERENCES

Braden, J. P., & Shaw, S. R. (2009). Intervention validity of cognitive assessment: Knowns, unknowables, and unknowns. *Assessment for Effective Intervention, 34*, 106–115.

Canivez, G. L. (2013). Psychometric versus actuarial interpretation of intelligence and related aptitude batteries. In D. H. Saklofske, C. R. Reynolds, & V. L. Schwean (Eds.), *The Oxford handbook of child psychological assessments* (pp. 84–112). New York, NY: Oxford University Press.

Canivez, G. L., Watkins, M. W., & Dombrowski, S. C. (2016). Factor structure of the Wechsler Intelligence Scale for Children—Fifth Edition: Exploratory factor analyses with the 16 primary and secondary subtests. *Psychological Assessment, 28*, 975–986. doi:10.1037/pas0000238

Cattell, R. B. (1971). *Abilities: Their structure, growth, and action.* Boston, MA: Houghton Mifflin.

Chapman, P. D. (1988). *Schools as sorters: Lewis M. Terman, applied psychology, and the intelligence testing movement, 1890–1930.* New York, NY: New York University Press.

Eysenck, H. J. (1998). *Intelligence: A new look.* New Brunswick, NJ: Transaction.

Flanagan, D. P., Fiorello, C. A., & Ortiz, S. O. (2010). Enhancing practice through application of Cattell-Horn-Carroll theory and research: A "third method" approach to specific learning disability identification. *Psychology in the Schools, 47*, 739–760.

Flanagan, D. P., Ortiz, S. O., & Alfonso, V. C. (2013). *Essentials of cross-battery assessment* (3rd ed.). Hoboken, NJ: Wiley.

Floyd, R. G., Reynolds, M. R., Farmer, R. L., & Kranzler, J. H. (2013). Are the general factors from different child and adolescent intelligence tests the same? Results from a five-sample, six-test analysis. *School Psychology Review, 42*, 383–401.

Ford, D. Y., Wright, B. L., Washington, A., & Henfield, M. S. (2016). Access and equity denied: Key theories for school psychologists to consider when assessing Black and Hispanic students for gifted education. *School Psychology Forum, 10*, 265–277.

Francis, D. J., Fletcher, J. M., Stuebing, K. K., Lyon, R. L., Shaywitz, B. A., & Shaywitz, S. E. (2005). Psychometric approaches to the identification of LD: IQ and achievement scores are not sufficient. *Journal of Learning Disabilities, 38*, 98–108.

Gottfredson, L. S. (1997). Why g matters: The complexity of everyday life. *Intelligence, 24*, 79–132.

Gottfredson, L. S. (2002). g: Highly general and highly practical. In R. J. Sternberg & E. L. Grigorenko (Eds.), *The general factor of intelligence: How general is it?* (pp. 331–380). Mahwah, NJ: Erlbaum.

Gottfredson, L. S. (2008). Of what value is intelligence? In A. Prifitera, D. Saklofske, & L. G. Weiss, (Eds.), *WISC-IV applications for clinical assessment and intervention* (2nd ed., pp. 545–563). Amsterdam, Netherlands: Elsevier.

Haier, R. J. (2011). Biological basis of intelligence. In R. J. Sternberg & S. B. Kaufman (Eds.), *The Cambridge handbook of intelligence* (pp. 351–370). Cambridge, UK: Cambridge University Pess.

Helms, J. E. (2007). Implementing fairness in racial-group assessment requires assessment of individuals. *American Psychologist, 62*, 1083–1085.

Horn, J. L., & Noll, J. (1997). Human cognitive capabilities: Gf-Gc theory. In D. P. Flanagan, J. L. Genshaft, & P. L. Harrison (Eds.). *Contemporary intellectual assessment: Theories, tests, and issues* (pp. 53–91). New York, NY: Guilford.

Individuals with Disabilities Education Act, Pub. L. No. 108-446 (2004).

Jensen, A. R. (1989). Raising IQ without raising g? A review of "The Milwaukee Project: Preventing mental retardation in children at risk." *Developmental Review, 9*, 234–258.

Jensen, A. R. (1998). *The g factor: The science of mental ability.* Westport, CT: Praeger.

Kaufman, A. S., & Kaufman, N. L. (2004). *Kaufman assessment battery for children* (2nd ed.). Circle Pines, MN: American Guidance Service.

Keith, T. Z., & Reynolds, M. R. (2010). CHC theory and cognitive abilities: What we've learned from 20 years of research. *Psychology in the Schools, 47*, 635–650.

Kirk, S. A. (1962). Diagnosis and remediation of learning disabilities. *Exceptional Children, 29*, 73–78. doi:10.1177/001440296202900204

Kovaleski, J. F., VanDerHeyden, A. M., & Shapiro, E. S. (2013). *The RTI approach to evaluating learning disabilities.* New York, NY: Guilford.

Kranzler, J. H., Benson, N., & Floyd, R. G. (2016). Intellectual assessment of children and youth in the United States of America: Past, present, and future. *International Journal of School and Educational Psychology, 4,* 276–282. doi:10.1080/21683603.2016.1166759

Kranzler, J. H., & Floyd, R. G. (2013). *Assessing intelligence in children and adolescents: A practical guide.* New York, NY: Guilford.

Kranzler, J. H., Floyd, R. G., Benson, N., Zaboski, B., & Thibodaux, L. (2016a). Cross-battery assessment pattern of strengths and weaknesses approach to the identification of specific learning disorders: Evidence-based practice or pseudoscience? *International Journal of School and Educational Psychology, 3,* 146–157. doi:10.1080/21683603.2016.1192855

Kranzler, J. H., Floyd, R. G., Benson, N., Zaboski, B., & Thibodaux, L. (2016b). Classification agreement analysis of cross-battery assessment in the identification of specific learning disorders in children and youth. *International Journal of School and Educational Psychology, 3,* 124–136. doi:10.1080/21683603.2016.1155515

Maki, K. E., Floyd, R. G., & Roberson, T. (2015). State learning disability eligibility criteria: A comprehensive review. *School Psychology Quarterly, 30,* 457–469. doi:10.1037/spq0000109

McClain, M.-C., & Pfeiffer, S. (2012). Identification of gifted students in the United States today: A look at state definitions, policies, and practices. *Journal of Applied School Psychology, 28,* 59–88.

McNicholas, P. J., Floyd, R. G., Woods, I. L., Singh, L. J., Manguno, M. S., & Maki, K. E. (2017). State special education criteria for identifying intellectual disability: A review following revised diagnostic criteria and Rosa's Law. *School Psychology Quarterly.*

Musu-Gillette, L., Robinson, J., McFarland, J., KewalRamani, A., Zhang, A., & Wilkinson-Flicker, S. (2016). *Status and trends in the education of racial and ethnic groups 2016* (NCES 2016-007). Washington, DC: U.S. Department of Education, National Center for Education Statistics. Retrieved from http://nces.ed.gov/pubsearch

Naglieri, J. A., & Otero, T. M. (2012). The cognitive assessment system: From theory to practice. In D. P. Flanagan & P. L. Harrison (Eds.), *Contemporary intellectual assessment: Theories, tests, and issues* (pp. 376–399). New York, NY: Guilford.

Neisser, U., Boodoo, G., Bouchard, T. J. Jr., Boykin, A. W., Brody, N., Ceci, S. J., . . . Urbina, A. (1996). Intelligence: Knowns and unknowns. *American Psychologist, 51,* 77–101.

Nisbett, R. E., Aronson, J., Blair, C., Dickens, W., Flynn, J., Halpern, D. F., & Turkheimer, E. (2012). Intelligence: New findings and theoretical developments. *American Psychologist, 67,* 130–159. doi:10.1037/a0026699

Office of Special Education and Rehabilitative Services, Department of Education. (2006). *Federal Register: Assistance to states for the education of children with disabilities and preschool grants for children with disabilities, final rule.* 34 CFR Parts 300 and 301.

Reynolds, C. R. (2009). RTI, neuroscience, and sense: Chaos in the diagnosis and treatment of learning disabilities. In E. Fletcher-Janzen & C. R. Reynolds (Eds.), *Neuropsychological perspectives on learning disabilities in the era of RtI: Recommendations for diagnosis and intervention* (pp. 14–27). Hoboken, NJ: Wiley.

Reynolds, C. R., & Carson, A. D. (2005). Methods for assessing cultural bias in tests. In C. Frisby & C. R. Reynolds (Eds.), *Comprehensive handbook of multicultural school psychology* (pp. 795–823). Hoboken, NJ: Wiley.

Schneider, W. J., & McGrew, K. S. (2012). The Cattell-Horn-Carroll model of intelligence. In D. P. Flanagan & P. Harrison (Eds.), *Contemporary intellectual assessment* (3rd ed., pp. 99–144). New York, NY: Guilford.

Schrank, F. A., McGrew, K. S., & Mather, N. (2014). *Woodcock-Johnson IV tests of cognitive abilities.* Rolling Meadows, IL: Riverside.

Snow, R. E., & Lohman, D. F. (1984). Toward a theory of cognitive aptitude for learning from instruction. *Journal of Educational Psychology, 76,* 347–376. doi:10.1037/0022-0663.76.3.347

Spearman, C. E. (1904). "General intelligence" objectively determined and measured. *American Journal of Psychology, 15,* 201–293. doi:10.2307/1412107

Steele, C. M., & Aronson, J. (1995). Stereotype threat and the intellectual test performance of African Americans. *Journal of Personality and Social Psychology, 69,* 797–811.

Sternberg, R. J., & Davidson, J. (Eds.). (2005). *Conceptions of giftedness* (2nd ed.). New York, NY: Cambridge University Press.

Sternberg, R. J., & Kaufman, S. B. (Eds.). (2011). *The Cambridge handbook of intelligence*. Cambridge, UK: Cambridge University Press.

Terman, L. M. (1916). *The measurement of intelligence*. Boston, MA: Houghton & Mifflin.

Thurstone, L. L. (1938). *Primary mental abilities*. Chicago, IL: University of Chicago Press.

U.S. Department of Education. (2014). *Civil rights data collection*. Washington, DC: Author. Retrieved from http://ocrdata.ed.gov

U.S. Department of Education, Office of Special Education and Rehabilitative Services. (2016). *Racial and ethnic disparities in special education: A multi-year disproportionality analysis by state, analysis category, and race/ethnicity*. Washington, DC: Author. Retrieved from https://www2.ed.gov/programs/osepidea/618-data/LEA-racial-ethnic-disparities-tables/disproportion-ality-analysis-by-state-analysis-category.pdf

VandenBos, G. R. (2006). *APA dictionary of psychology*. New York, NY: American Psychological Association.

Vaughn, S., & Fuchs, L. S. (2003). Redefining learning disabilities as inadequate response to instruction: The promise and potential problems. *Learning Disabilities Research & Practice, 18*, 137–146. doi:10.1111/1540-5826.00070

Watkins, M. W. (2003). IQ subtest analysis: Clinical acumen or clinical illusion? *Scientific Review of Mental Health Practice, 2*, 118–141.

Wechsler, D. (1939). *The measurement of adult intelligence*. Baltimore, MD: Williams & Wilkins.

Wechsler, D. (2014). *Wechsler intelligence scale for children (5th ed.)*. San Antonio, TX: Pearson Assessment.

CHAPTER 11

Consultation

WILLIAM P. ERCHUL ■ AARON J. FISCHER

CHAPTER OBJECTIVES

- Define consultation within the contemporary practice of school psychology
- Describe several models of consultation practiced by school psychologists
- Consider consultation as fundamentally a problem-solving process
- Present the evidence base for the effectiveness of school consultation
- Describe selected multicultural issues and technological advances within school consultation

Providing consultative services in schools is a fundamental role of the school psychologist. As described in previous chapters, the National Association of School Psychologists (NASP, 2010) identifies *Consultation and Collaboration* as a core domain of practice that "permeates all aspects of service delivery" (p. 2). Whereas previous chapters have described how school psychologists can work directly with children and adolescents to support their well-being, this chapter describes how school psychologists work with parents, educators, and administrators to influence outcomes for youth.

The primary purpose of this chapter is to offer an introduction to many fundamental concepts in consultation as practiced in the field of school psychology. After presenting some widely recognized models of consultation and an overview of the typical process, we turn our attention to its evidence base. To close, we discuss two contemporary issues surrounding consultation: multicultural considerations and the emerging role of technology. By reading this chapter, one should gain an understanding of key aspects of the important role of school psychologists serving as consultants. Furthermore, this chapter illustrates the ways in which school psychologists are uniquely positioned to serve as agents of social justice for their students and other school staff (cf. Li & Vazquez-Nuttall, 2009).

DEFINING CONSULTATION

Given the range of professional settings and contexts in which consultants may deliver services, the term *consultation* has many definitions. Two definitions that are particularly relevant to the field of school psychology, however, are as follows. First, Zins and Erchul (2002) defined **consultation** as

> a method of providing preventively oriented psychological and educational services in which consultants and consultees form cooperative partnerships and engage in a reciprocal, systematic problem-solving process guided by ecobehavioral principles. The goal is to enhance and empower consultee systems, thereby promoting clients' well-being and performance. (p. 626)

In a similar vein, Erchul and Martens (2010) defined *school consultation* as

> a process for providing psychological and educational services in which a specialist (consultant) works cooperatively with a staff member (consultee) to improve the learning and adjustment of a student (client) or group of students. During face-to-face interactions, the consultant helps the consultee through systematic problem-solving, social influence, and professional support. In turn, the consultee helps the client(s) through selecting and implementing effective school-based interventions. In all cases, school consultation serves a remedial function and has the potential to serve a preventive function. (pp. 12–13)

Several key aspects of these definitions should be reinforced. First, the key participants in the consultative process are the consultant, consultee, and client. The **consultant** is an individual (e.g., school psychologist) who provides guidance and expertise to another individual, group, or system (i.e., consultee), which in turn directly delivers the recommended services to a third party (i.e., client). Thus, the **consultee** is the person or entity that implements the action plan resulting from consultation, and the **client** is the recipient of the subsequent services delivered by the consultee. Various models of consultation conceptualize the roles of consultants, consultees, and clients differently; however, this basic constellation generally characterizes the nature of school-based consultation services.

Second, in contrast to the direct service activities described in Section II of this book, consultation is considered an *indirect service* (as defined in Chapter 1). That is, the school psychologist typically works directly with the consultee only, who in turn works directly with the client. In fact, depending on the nature of the case, a consultant may never even meet with the client. One advantage of working in this manner is that the school psychologist's "reach" or sphere of influence is expanded and, as a result, problems occurring throughout schools stand a better chance of being detected earlier (and perhaps prevented altogether). A second advantage is that consultees benefit from the direct support they receive from the consultant. In particular, consultees have opportunities to develop skills that benefit both the target client and future students and families. As emphasized in the preceding definitions, the success of consultation hinges largely on the quality of the relationship that develops between the consultant and the consultee.

MAJOR MODELS OF CONSULTATION

Several models of consultation are commonly employed in schools. Most are grounded in a particular scientific theory (although some are more theory based than others are). The four models described in the following text are mental health consultation, behavioral consultation, conjoint behavioral consultation, and organization development consultation. Additionally, the *I*'''' feature in this chapter presents a fifth model known as advocacy consultation. Although many other consultative models exist (e.g., collaborative, instructional, Adlerian, process, rational–emotive), they are not presented here because they share many key characteristics with the aforementioned models.

Mental Health Consultation

The primary development of ***mental health consultation*** (***MHC***) may be traced to the work of community psychiatrist Gerald Caplan. Caplan (1970) proposed that a consultee's professional effectiveness could be improved through a process involving collegial case discussion and problem solving with a consultant. Importantly, a consultant must never cross boundaries and act as a psychotherapist to the consultee (i.e., the consultant's overt focus clearly should be on professional issues rather than personal problems). Caplan also urged consultants to examine the strengths, weaknesses, capacity, and so forth, of the consultee's organization, as well as to consider the importance of relationships among people in the larger organization. Although Caplan's name is nearly synonymous with MHC, he is credited with broader contributions, including those related to primary prevention, social support, and crisis intervention (Erchul, 2009).

MHC is influenced by Freudian psychoanalytic theory, which accounts for its strong emphasis on more intrapersonal/person-centered issues and unconscious motivations for behavior. Along these lines, a mental health consultant often targets consultee-related factors (e.g., lack of objectivity) as a focus for change (Caplan, 1970). For example, with great finesse and subtlety, a mental health consultant might help a third-grade teacher overcome her difficulty in teaching a student to read by having her make the connection between the present situation and her negative experience with the student's brother, whom she taught 5 years earlier.

There are four overlapping types of MHC: client-centered case consultation, consultee-centered case consultation, program-centered administrative consultation, and consultee-centered administrative consultation (Caplan, 1970). These types differ in regard to whether their focus is on individual cases or programs, and vary in terms of emphasizing prevention or remediation. Consultee-centered case consultation, for instance, is concerned with "elucidating and remedying the shortcomings in the consultee' s professional functioning . . . [so as to] lead to an improvement in the consultee's professional planning and action, and hopefully to improvement in the client" (Caplan & Caplan, 1999, p. 101). Even though MHC offers a rich conceptualization of how to consult, when it is subjected to rigorous standards, it is found to be lacking in empirical support (Gresham & Kendell, 1987). Consultee-centered consultation (Sandoval, 2014), by comparison, holds promise as an updated variation of MHC, as its proponents have adapted many of Caplan's basic principles for specific use in schools.

Behavioral Consultation

Behavioral consultation (**BC**) is based on theories of learning and behavioral psychology, although more recently ecological and social learning theories have been incorporated into the model. Seminal works on BC (e.g., Bergan & Kratochwill, 1990), however, tend to focus on proximal environmental variables that influence learning and behavior and give far less weight to more distal events and systems issues. Considered largely a client-centered approach, BC targets observable client problems (e.g., student frequency of outbursts) as the object of change.

As in the problem-solving model described in Chapter 7, problems most often are defined as a discrepancy between current and desired behavior, and evidence-based interventions (EBIs) are implemented to reduce the observed discrepancy (Erchul & Martens, 2010). In Bergan and Kratochwill's (1990) approach to BC, clearly defined problem-solving steps embedded in structured interviews address problem identification, problem analysis, plan implementation, and problem evaluation. Later in the chapter, we see how an expansion of these four basic steps constitutes a predominant approach to effective consultation within school psychology.

A primary contribution of the BC model is its adherence to methodological rigor and scientific precision. For this reason, the majority of the research on consultation in schools has focused on this model and found it to be effective (e.g., Sheridan, Welch, & Orme, 1996). BC also has been touted as a viable means of delivering psychoeducational services in schools through contemporary multi-tiered systems of support (MTSS) models (Erchul & Ward, 2016).

Conjoint Behavioral Consultation

Conjoint behavioral consultation (**CBC**) is an expansion of BC that is conducted with parents and teachers together, over time, and across settings. CBC is defined as

> a strength-based, cross-system problem-solving and decision-making model wherein parents, teachers, and other caregivers or service providers work as partners and share responsibility for promoting positive and consistent outcomes related to a child's academic, behavioral, and socio-emotional development. (Sheridan & Kratochwill, 2008, p. 25)

CBC considers school, family, and, frequently, community factors, and is therefore an ecologically based model (i.e., one that considers person–environment interactions in understanding development and behavior; Bronfenbrenner, 1977).

CBC often assumes that a child's problem presents similarly both in school and at home. Thus, a CBC consultant typically progresses through a variation of the four stages of BC (Bergan & Kratochwill, 1990) with the child's teacher(s) and parent(s) concurrently. For instance, if a child's problem behavior is identified as frequent tantrums, the consultant would need to identify how specifically the behavior presents itself at school and home (e.g., examine the frequency, duration, and intensity of the behavior), develop goals for improvement in each setting, select and help to implement an EBI in each setting, and evaluate its impact (Sheridan & Kratochwill, 2008). CBC is an excellent example of how school psychologists can coordinate their efforts as consultants to educators, families, and systems.

Organization Development Consultation

Consultation in schools that is intended to have an impact on large groups, targeted layers within a school, an entire school, or a school system (e.g., school district) falls into the category of *organization development consultation* (**ODC**). Some school psychologists utilize ODC because it has the clear advantage of allowing them to share their skills and knowledge with a greater number of individuals and, therefore, to extend their impact. Contemporary examples of situations in which ODC might be applied in schools include systems-level efforts to implement MTSS (Forman & Crystal, 2015) and school-wide mental health screening systems (Dowdy et al., 2015).

ODC draws on many different theoretical perspectives, ranging from general systems theory (von Bertalanffy, 1968) to theories specifically developed for use in human services organizations (e.g., French & Bell, 1999). In general, ODC lacks a unified identity and theoretical basis (Illback, 2014). However, the overall approach to ODC involves a planned, systemic process of introducing new principles and practices into an organization with the goal of effecting organizational improvement, effectiveness, and competence (Castillo & Curtis, 2014).

Despite the promise of ODC for effecting change across systems, the typical school psychologist reports spending only 6% of his or her time on organizational/ system-focused consultation (Castillo, Curtis, & Gelley, 2012). We believe school psychologists could increase their impact on positive outcomes for children if they devoted more time to facilitating systems-level change; however, the role and setting constraints mentioned in earlier chapters may limit opportunities to engage in such activities.

SOCIAL JUSTICE CONNECTIONS

What is advocacy consultation?

In addition to the consultation models previously described, another model holds promise for practitioners who are interested in advancing a social justice agenda: *advocacy consultation* (AC; Conoley, 1981; Conoley & Conoley, 1982). An advocacy consultant is someone who works on behalf of disenfranchised individuals and groups, engaging in roles such as activist, mediator, organizer, negotiator, and, of course, advocate. A common role of an advocacy

(continued)

consultant in schools is to assist parents of children who have been placed in, or are being considered for, special education programming.

An example of AC is as follows: A consultant (Dr. Smith) arrives at a school-based meeting to help the mother (Ms. Gonzalez) of a second-grade student (Guillermo) who has a moderate hearing impairment. Ms. Gonzalez believes that Guillermo has not been receiving adequate help from the school community to address specific goals in his Individualized Education Program (IEP), but his teachers have decided Guillermo will be retained next year due to low achievement scores. At this meeting, three teachers and the assistant principal are present, and Mrs. Gonzalez is understandably nervous about expressing her concerns to this rather large group of educational professionals. Dr. Smith, operating within the role of advocacy consultant, helps the Gonzalez family by seeking clarification, redefining/elaborating on the problem, reinforcing the requirements of federal law, transforming blaming into problem solving, and generating shared goals for moving forward.

According to Conoley and Conoley (1982), advocacy consultants need to develop additional knowledge and skills in the areas of law, community organization, event organization, media utilization, negotiation, and parent partnerships, above and beyond the expected skill set possessed by other human services consultants. Although conceptually appealing, the empirical examination of and support for AC is scarce within the consultation literature at this time. However, the goals and core tenets of AC render it a promising form of service delivery that warrants further investigation.

CONSULTATION AS A PROBLEM-SOLVING PROCESS

To reinforce an earlier point, "Problem-solving is the essence of consultation" (Zins & Erchul, 2002, p. 631). Given this assumption, the consultative process incorporates a sequence of steps that exemplify problem solving. Similar to the problem-solving process described in Chapter 7, this sequence of steps focuses on identifying, analyzing, and addressing problems in a data-driven manner. Specifically, the steps are as follows: (a) relationship development, (b) identification and analysis of the problem, (c) intervention development/selection, (d) intervention implementation, (e) evaluation of intervention effectiveness, and (f) follow-up (Erchul & Martens, 2010). Furthermore, it is necessary for the school psychologist to engage in multiple levels of problem analysis and intervention development during consultation. Because consultation is an indirect service (i.e., focused on delivering services to clients through an intermediary), it requires that changes be achieved on more than just the individual student level. Accordingly, it is essential to monitor the link between changes in the environment or in teachers' behavior and changes in the target student(s) (Truscott et al., 2012). Finally, it should be noted that, although consultation in schools can involve multiple consultants, consultees, and organizational levels, the primary focus here is on the work and contributions of individual consultants, consultees, and students. The following section contains content presented previously by the first author (i.e., Erchul & Martens, 2010; Erchul & Young, 2014; Zins & Erchul, 2002).

Relationship Building/Establishing a Cooperative Partnership

Prerequisites to effective problem solving within consultation include refined interpersonal communication skills and the development of a trusting, cooperative partnership. Relationship building is an essential element of consultation, begin-ning with initial entry into the school and/or classroom and continuing throughout the process. When a school psychologist consultant and a consultee meet initially, each participant tries to become better acquainted with the other, and together they strive to establish an atmosphere of mutual respect and trust. They discuss and negotiate a working contract, which is a mutually agreed-upon oral or written understanding of what will happen during consultation. The contract minimally specifies the roles and responsibilities of each participant, the expected activities, and the anticipated timeline for the consultation (Zins & Erchul, 2002).

Identifying and Clarifying the Problem

Once problem solving begins, the first activity is to identify or clarify the prob-lem and seek agreement on the definition of the problem (Bergan & Kratochwill, 1990). To the greatest extent possible, problems need to be defined in clear, con-cise, objective, and measurable terms so that progress toward solving them can be assessed. It is an unfortunate reality that consultees do not always have clear conceptualizations of problems and, therefore, may describe a problem initially in vague, global terms. Through the consultant's careful questioning and active lis-tening, however, many aspects of the problem can be discussed and subsequently defined in clearer terms. Once a problem is defined satisfactorily, participants can then generate specific goals to address it.

If accurate problem identification does not occur, effort may be wasted in attempts to solve the wrong problem. Conversely, once a problem is identified accurately, this action meets the necessary, but not always the sufficient, condi-tions of solving a problem or promoting some desired goal (Zins & Erchul, 2002).

Analyzing the Problem

During this phase, the consultant and consultee try to understand the forces that are causing and maintaining the problem as well as those resources that may be applied to solve it. They attempt to develop the best possible hypotheses about why the problem exists, collect baseline data (e.g., frequency, duration, and inten-sity), and identify antecedents and consequences that may be contributing to it. Taking a broader ecological systems perspective is important, because problems usually are the result of a complex interaction of multiple factors. Unless a larger array of factors is considered, it is likely that an overly simplistic and unsuccessful solution will be implemented. All resources that potentially could be utilized in the development and implementation of interventions should be explored at this step. These considerations include student strengths, system or setting charac-teristics that help the student be successful in other situations, and material and human resources (e.g., teachers, parents, peer and volunteer tutors, and commu-nity support systems) available for intervention (Zins & Erchul, 2002).

During problem analysis, it has become increasingly important and common for school psychology consultants to employ curriculum-based measurement (described in Chapter 8), functional behavior assessment (described in Chapter 9), and/or brief experimental analysis, rather than depend largely on the verbal reports and observations of consultees (Erchul & Young, 2014). ***Brief experimental*** *analysis* refers to the systematic process of quickly assessing the relative effects of two or more interventions on a target behavior (e.g., computational or oral reading fluency) so asr to determine which approach is likely to be most successful (Burns & Wagner, 2008). These procedures allow the consultant and/or consultee to utilize direct measures of skill and intervention response to inform decision making.

Selecting an Intervention

Moving toward problem resolution, it is important to carefully consider appropriate EBIs. Resources such as comprehensive reviews in scientific journals, *What Works Clearinghouse* , *Intervention Central*, and the *Collaborative for Academic, Social, and Emotional Learning* are helpful in locating EBIs. Once a list of suitable EBIs is generated, participants need to assess each option in regard to its feasibility, acceptability, cost, likelihood of success, consequences, and so forth. In an earlier time, an intervention's *acceptability* (i.e., judgments about whether a treatment is fair, reasonable, or intrusive) was perhaps the top consideration in intervention selection. However, because the hypothesized positive association between acceptability and implementation has not been demonstrated consistently in research (Noell & Gansle, 2014), factors related to intervention effectiveness are now a much higher priority (Erchul & Young, 2014).

A key element in the intervention selection and implementation process is obtaining the consultee's "buy-in" (i.e., commitment to implementing an EBI). Because a consultant holds no administrative authority over a consultee (Martin, 1978), a consultant cannot simply tell the consultee "what to do" and expect results (Erchul & Martens, 2010). Instead, persuasive strategies—drawn, for example, from Raven's (1992) Power Interaction Model of Interpersonal Influence—may be used to secure consultee buy-in. In particular, social influence strategies stemming from the noncoercive, soft bases of expert power and referent power may be effective in achieving consultee behavior change. **Expert power** depends on a consultee's positive perception of the consultant's knowledge and expertise; based on this perception, the consultee may be more willing to commit to intervention selection and implementation. **Referent power** hinges on a consultee's favorable identification with the consultant (e.g., likeability); given this identification, the consultee may be more willing to follow through with intervention implementation (Erchul, Grissom, Getty, & Bennett, 2014). Owens et al. (2017) recently documented the significance of expert and referent power by showing that teachers who needed classroom management consultation and who reported being influenced by soft power bases exhibited better management skills following consultation than other teachers who reported not being influenced by soft bases.

Clarifying Implementation Procedures and Responsibilities

A common obstacle to achieving success in consultation is that intervention implementation procedures are not always specified in sufficient detail. Subsequently, the intervention is carried out inconsistently. In these situations, even a highly recommended EBI may fail to produce the desired results. To remedy this situation, it is advised that the consultant develop a written plan of action that clearly specifies the steps of the intervention, plans for follow-up after intervention implementation is complete, and strategies for monitoring the implementation process. In particular, there should be a plan to monitor intervention fidelity (as defined in Chapter 7, the degree to which the intervention has been implemented as planned; Noell & Gansle, 2014). Finally, it is advised that the consultant model the intervention for consultees and/or directly train them on implementation procedures (Erchul & Young, 2014).

Implementing the Intervention

The selected EBI now can be implemented according to the plans and timelines developed. Although the consultee is typically responsible for intervention implementation, consultants need to be available to assist in the event that unforeseen problems arise or that there are any changes in setting or context. Consultants provide ongoing feedback and support for consultees' efforts (especially in the early stages of intervention, when client improvement may not be particularly discernible). Additionally, the consultant facilitates the assessment of intervention integrity using strategies such as direct observation, self-report, and/or reviews of permanent products (e.g., student work products). It is well established that intervention integrity improves considerably when consultees receive feedback on their performance, and the consistency of this effect is strengthened when data are presented to consultees in graph formats (Noell & Gansle, 2014).

Evaluating Intervention Effectiveness and Follow-Up

The evaluation and follow-up phase involves several interrelated tasks, including determining intervention effectiveness and facilitating the client's generalization of new skills. First, the same data collection procedures that were initially used to measure the client's baseline functioning typically are used again at the end of the intervention to facilitate a pre/post (i.e., before and after) comparison. The results of this evaluation likely will indicate one of two outcomes: (a) The intervention resulted in the client's attainment of desired goals, thereby indicating that follow-up monitoring and/or generalization are needed; or (b) the intended outcomes were not entirely attained, suggesting the need to cycle back through earlier steps of the problem-solving process (Zins & Erchul, 2002).

During this final phase of the consultation process, facilitating client generalization is important. In consultation, **generalization** refers to the student's application of a new skill or behavior learned in one context to other, different contexts. For example, consider a student who receives an intervention designed to increase appropriate class participatory behaviors (e.g., hand raising). This student receives the intervention during math class only. If, during or following the intervention, the student were to demonstrate the target behavior (i.e., hand raising) during other classes (e.g., science or physical education), he or she would be generalizing the learned behavior.

Generalization of new skills and behaviors may be facilitated in several ways. First, when possible, the intervention should take place in a number of settings using multiple tasks and teachers. Second, students (and, when appropriate, parents) should assume an active role in intervention selection and implementation, and efforts should be made to assist them in understanding the intervention's purpose and relevance to their own lives. Moreover, opportunities to confront and deal positively with failure or mistakes should be incorporated into intervention procedures (Zins & Erchul, 2002).

Following the problem-solving model during the consultation process is often necessary, but is rarely sufficient for ensuring favorable outcomes. Effective consultants need not only to include key ingredients in the consultation process (e.g., problem-solving stages) but also to maintain open, collegial, and culturally sensitive consultative relationships. Next, we turn our attention to outcomes of school consultation.

EFFECTIVENESS OF CONSULTATION

Does consultation work? In other words, is there empirical evidence indicating that positive outcomes result when a school psychologist consults with one or more consultees, who then work directly with one or more clients? Before addressing this fundamental question, it is important to step back and recognize that consultation research is difficult to conduct and, unfortunately, many studies are conceptually and methodologically flawed (Erchul & Sheridan, 2014). In other words, because consultation reflects an effort to help a third party (e.g., student client) through assistance of a second party (e.g., teacher consultee), it often is not possible to determine whether client changes have resulted from consultant efforts or other variables. Despite these shortcomings, evidence from literature reviews, meta-analyses, and randomized controlled trial research on consultation indicates it often results in improved outcomes for consultee and client participants.

In regard to literature reviews, Sheridan et al. (1996) completed a thorough analysis of 46 school consultation outcome studies published between 1985 and 1995. They found that consultation resulted in positive effects in 67% of the studies reviewed, while 28% resulted in neutral effects and 5% resulted in negative effects. Moreover, meta-analytic research has yielded positive results in regard to consultation in the school setting. A *meta-analysis* is a study that employs a quantitative method for summarizing the effects of a treatment across large numbers of original research studies that investigated that treatment. Meta-analyses are especially useful for evaluating treatment outcomes, because they allow for the summarization of results across a number of studies, many of which may have divergent findings. Often, results are summarized in the form of an *effect size*, or standardized measure of the magnitude of an effect (*What Works Clearinghouse* [WWC], 2017). With respect to consultation research, Sibley (1986, reported in Gresham & Noell, 1993) found large before–after effect sizes for consultees and even larger effect sizes for clients across 63 studies of school consultation.

Recall from Chapter 7 that randomized controlled trials (RCTs) are considered the "gold standard" of treatment research, as they rely on random assignment of participants to conditions and pay careful attention to experimental control. RCTs of school consultation (e.g., Cappella et al., 2012; Sheridan et al., 2012) have produced positive outcomes, and these types of studies, which employ a more rigorous methodology, support the use of consultation as an evidence-based practice in schools (Erchul & Sheridan, 2014). Taken together, our conclusion is that outcome research on consultation as conducted by school psychologists over many decades has documented its overall effectiveness.

MULTICULTURAL CONSIDERATIONS

Multicultural elements are critical to consider within the realm of school psychology, and particularly within the consultation role. It is essential for a consultant to acknowledge the powerful influence of culture in its many forms (e.g., race, ethnicity, language, socioeconomic status, sexual orientation, age, religious/spiritual beliefs) and to realize the potential impact of these factors on the consultative process (Erchul & Young, 2014).

Multicultural consultation does not constitute a separate model of consultation, but rather is a critical adjunct to the various models of consultation described earlier. It underscores the notion that cultural variables are central aspects of the consultation process and, therefore, must be given the appropriate attention (Ingraham, 2014). Cultural differences may arise between and among the consultant, consultee, and client, and culture can have a significant influence on environmental and interpersonal dynamics (e.g., among family, classroom, school, community). At the same time, it is important for consultants to be able to discern when cultural variables are at play and when they are not. Similarly, the consultant must be able to distinguish between the impact of individual differences and the effects of group cultural variables (Erchul & Young, 2014).

Ingraham's (2000) multicultural consultation framework describes some aspirational competencies for understanding and applying multicultural considerations in consultation. First, as described in Chapter 3, the consultant must have some personal awareness of his or her own cultural background, worldview, and biases. The consultant must also be knowledgeable about the cultural context in which the consultative process will be situated and understand how interpersonal and environmental factors will affect relationships among participants and intervention implementation. Specifically, consultants should consider how values, norms, and traditions permeate relationships and impact consultative dynamics. This often involves reflecting on how privilege and oppression can moderate power dynamics among students, families, and school personnel.

Second, the consultant should consider not only his or her own awareness of personal and contextual variables, but also the consultee's awareness. The consultation process offers an important opportunity to improve the consultee's knowledge, skills, objectivity, and self-confidence in relation to multicultural service delivery. In the consultation relationship, *objectivity* refers to the perception of client problems in a manner that is free from judgment, bias, and other psychological interference. Lack of objectivity on the part of the consultee—sometimes as the result of the consultee's cultural biases—may be a barrier to accurately defining and addressing client problems through consultation (Caplan, 1970). When relevant, the consultant should strive to improve the consultee's understanding of diversity and appreciation of multiculturalism (Erchul & Young, 2014).

INNOVATIONS IN CONSULTATION: CONSULTING FACE-TO-FACE THROUGH VIDEOCONFERENCING

Advances in videoconferencing technology, the increasing availability of high-bandwidth Internet connection, and access to smartphones, tablets, and desktop computers provide school consultants with the ability to interact with teachers and students who are in remote or underserved schools (Fischer, Schultz, Collier-Meek, Zoder-Martell, & Erchul, 2016). **Teleconsultation**, referring to the provision of consultative services through videoconferencing technology, is a contemporary form of traditional face-to-face consultation.

In the past 10 years, the use of teleconsultation in schools has increased, albeit focused primarily on improving outcomes for students with disabilities by training teachers to conduct behavioral assessment procedures (e.g., functional behavior assessments) that inform individualized intervention plans (Frieder, Peterson, Woodward, Crane, & Garner, 2009; Gibson, Pennington, Stenhoff, & Hopper, 2010; Machalicek et al., 2009a, 2009b, 2010). Most recently, studies that applied problem-solving consultation models during teleconsultation have shown this approach to be effective at reducing disruptive behavior, increasing on-task behavior, and reducing body rocking (Bice-Urbach & Kratochwill, 2016; Fischer et al., 2016). Moreover, several studies have found that teachers who participated in teleconsultation found it to be an acceptable modality for receiving consultation services (e.g., Bice-Urbach & Kratochwill, 2016; Fischer et al., 2016).

In a novel application of teleconsultation, Fischer and Erchul (2016) used mobile telepresence robots to conduct problem-solving teleconsultation with special education teachers and paraprofessionals. In that study, consultants provided services to schools 300 miles away and used mobile telepresence robots (https://revolverobotics.com; www.doublerobotics.com) to improve the mobility of the consultant in the school environment. Specifically, teleconsultants were able to determine the functional behavior problems, increase student compliance, and improve expressive number identification skills in students with disabilities. With advances in technology such as mobile telepresence robots and the wider availability of videoconferencing hardware and software, teachers, parents, and other school staff in remote or underserved areas can access consultative services that hold promise for improving student outcomes. Consultants with long commutes can also benefit from teleconsultation due to the reduced travel time and the potential to serve a greater number of teachers and students.

In light of recent shortages of school psychologists (who are primary providers of school consultation services), school districts should take consider carefully the potential benefits of teleconsultation. Further, school psychologists may wish to consider using teleconsultation within their practice, particularly if they work for remote and/or underserved schools. However, practitioners who make use of this modality of service delivery must be well versed in legal and ethical issues and take appropriate measures to ensure student confidentiality and maintain data security, in particular complying with the provisions of legislation such as the Family Educational Rights and Privacy Act (FERPA, 1974).

SUMMARY AND CONCLUSIONS

This chapter emphasized the importance of consultation in school psychology by providing definitions of fundamental concepts, introducing conceptual models of practice, delineating the steps of a problem-solving approach to consultation, reviewing evidence of the effectiveness of consultation, and considering how selected contextual issues frame contemporary practice. One clear message is that consultation provides a vehicle for school psychologists to address client problems by working with consultees to select, implement, and evaluate EBIs. Another message is that school psychologists, acting in a consultant role, are uniquely positioned to serve as agents of social justice. When knowledgeable about foundational aspects of the consultation role, future school psychologists will be better able to serve all children, teachers, and schools.

DISCUSSION QUESTIONS

1. How does consultation differ from traditional direct service delivery models, and what are the benefits of a consultation model?
2. How are the various consultation models described in this chapter similar? How are they different?
3. Why does consultation lend itself well to a problem-solving framework?
4. Which interpersonal skills does a school consultant need to be effective?
5. Recall the discussion of legal and ethical principles presented in Chapter 5. Which ethical and legal issues may be associated with the use of consultation? What are some of the benefits and limitations of using teleconsultation in schools?

REFERENCES

Bergan, J. R., & Kratochwill, T. R. (1990). *Behavioral consultation and therapy*. New York, NY: Plenum Press.

Bice-Urbach, B., & Kratochwill, T. R. (2016). Teleconsultation: The use of technology to improve evidence-based practices in rural communities. *Journal of School Psychology, 56*, 27–43. doi:10.1016/j.jsp.2016.02.001

Bronfenbrenner, U. (1977). Toward an experimental ecology of human development. *American Psychologist, 32*, 513–531. doi:10.1037/0003-066X.32.7.513

Burns, M. K., & Wagner, D. (2008). Determining an effective intervention within a brief experimental analysis for reading: A meta-analytic review. *School Psychology Review, 37*, 126–136.

Caplan, G. (1970). *The theory and practice of mental health consultation*. New York, NY: Basic Books.

Caplan, G., & Caplan, R. B. (1999). *Mental health consultation and collaboration*. Prospect Heights, IL: Waveland Press.

Cappella, E., Hamre, B. K., Kim, H. Y., Henry, D. B., Frazier, S. L., Atkins, M. S., & Schoenwald, S. K. (2012). Teacher consultation and coaching within mental health practice: Classroom and child effects in urban elementary schools. *Journal of Consulting and Clinical Psychology, 80*, 597–610. doi:10.1037/a0027725

Castillo, J. M., & Curtis, M. J. (2014). Best practices in systems-level change. In P. L. Harrison & A. Thomas (Eds.), *Best practices in school psychology—6: Systems-level services* (pp. 11–28). Bethesda, MD: National Association of School Psychologists.

Castillo, J. M., Curtis, M. J., & Gelley, C. D. (2012). School psychology 2010: Part 2: School psychologists' professional practices and implications for the field. *NASP Communique, 40*(8), 4–6.

Conoley, J. C. (1981). Advocacy consultation: Promises and problems. In J. C. Conoley (Ed.), *Consultation in schools: Theory, research, procedures* (pp. 157–178). New York, NY: Academic Press.

Conoley, J. C., & Conoley, C. W. (1982). *School consultation: A guide to practice and training*. New York, NY: Pergamon.

Dowdy, E., Furlong, M., Raines, T. C., Bovery, B., Kauffman, B., Kamphaus, R. W., . . . Murdock, J. (2015). Enhancing school-based mental health services with a preventive and promotive approach to universal screening for complete mental health. *Journal of Educational and Psychological Consultation, 25*, 178–197.

Erchul, W. P. (2009). Gerald Caplan: A tribute to the originator of mental health consultation. *Journal of Educational and Psychological Consultation, 19*, 95–105.

Erchul, W. P., Grissom, P. F., Getty, K. C., & Bennett, M. S. (2014). Researching interpersonal influence within school consultation: Social power base and relational communication perspectives. In W. P. Erchul & S. M. Sheridan (Eds.), *Handbook of research in school consultation* (2nd ed., pp. 349–385). New York, NY: Routledge.

Erchul, W. P., & Martens, B. K. (2010). *School consultation: Conceptual and empirical bases of practice* (3rd ed.). New York, NY: Springer Science+Business Media.

Erchul, W. P., & Sheridan, S. M. (2014). Overview: The state of scientific research in school consultation. In W. P. Erchul & S. M. Sheridan (Eds.), *Handbook of research in school consultation* (2nd ed., pp. 3–17). New York, NY: Routledge.

Erchul, W. P., & Ward, C. S. (2016). Problem-solving consultation. In S. R. Jimerson, M. K. Burns, & A. M. VanDerHeyden (Eds.), *Handbook of response to intervention: The science and practice of multi-tiered systems of support* (2nd ed., pp. 73–86). New York, NY: Springer Science+Business Media. doi:10.1007/978-1-4899-7568-3_6

Erchul, W. P., & Young, H. L. (2014). Best practices in school consultation. In A. Thomas & P. L. Harrison (Eds.), *Best practices in school psychology—6: Data-based and collaborative decision making* (pp. 449–460). Bethesda, MD: National Association of School Psychologists.

Family Educational Rights and Privacy Act of 1974, 20 U.S.C. § 1232g. (1974).

Fischer, A. J., Dart, E. H., Radley, K. C., Richardson, D., Clark, R., & Wimberly, J. (2016). Evaluating the effectiveness of videoconferencing as a behavioral consultation medium. *Journal of Educational and Psychological Consultation*, online first, 1–22. doi:10.1080/10474412.2016.1235978

Fischer, A. J., & Erchul, W. P. (2016, April). *Behavioral teleconsultation in schools through telepresence robots*. Invited presentation at the 2nd annual Miami Association for Applied Behavior Analysis Technology for Behavior Change (Tech B) conference, Coral Gables, FL.

Fischer, A. J., Schultz, B. K., Collier-Meek, M. A., Zoder-Martell, K. A., & Erchul, W. P. (2016). A critical review of videoconferencing software to support school consultation. *International Journal of School & Educational Psychology*, online first, 1–11. doi:10.1080/21683603.2016.1240129

Forman, S. G., & Crystal, C. D. (2015). Systems consultation for multitiered systems of supports (MTSS): Implementation issues. *Journal of Educational and Psychological Consultation, 25*, 276–285.

French, W., & Bell, C. H. (1999). *Organization development: Behavioral science interventions for organization improvement* (6th ed.). Upper Saddle River, NJ: Prentice-Hall.

Frieder, J. E., Peterson, S. M., Woodward, J., Crane, J., & Garner, M. (2009). Teleconsultation in school settings: Linking classroom teachers and behavior analysts through web-based technology. *Behavior Analysis in Practice, 2*, 32–39.

Gibson, J. L., Pennington, R. C., Stenhoff, D. M., & Hopper, J. S. (2010). Using desktop videoconferencing to deliver interventions to a preschool student with autism. *Topics in Early Childhood Special Education, 29*, 214–225.

Gresham, F. M., & Kendell, G. K. (1987). School consultation research: Methodological critique and future research directions. *School Psychology Review, 16*, 306–316.

Illback, R. J. (2014). Organization development and change facilitation in school settings: Theoretical and empirical foundations. In W. P. Erchul & S. M. Sheridan (Eds.), *Handbook of research in school consultation* (2nd ed., pp. 276–303). New York, NY: Routledge.

Ingraham, C. L. (2000). Consultation through a multicultural lens: Multicultural and cross-cultural consultation in schools. *School Psychology Review, 29*, 320–343.

Ingraham, C. L. (2014). Studying multicultural aspects of consultation. In W. P. Erchul & S. M. Sheridan (Eds.), *Handbook of research in school consultation* (2nd ed., pp. 323–348). New York, NY: Routledge.

Li, C., & Vazquez-Nuttall, E. (2009). School consultants as agents of social justice for multicultural children and families. *Journal of Educational & Psychological Consultation, 19,* 26–44.

Machalicek, W., O'Reilly, M., Chan, J., Lang, R., Rispoli, M., Davis, T., . . . Dkidden, R. (2009a). Using videoconferencing to conduct functional analysis of challenging behavior and develop classroom behavioral support plans for students with autism. *Education and Training in Developmental Disabilities, 44,* 207–217.

Machalicek, W., O'Reilly, M., Chan, J. M., Rispoli, M., Lang, R., Davis, T., & Langthorne, P. (2009b). Using videoconferencing to support teachers to conduct preference assessments with students with autism and developmental disabilities. *Research in Autism Spectrum Disorders, 3,* 32–41.

Machalicek, W., O'Reilly, M. F., Rispoli, M., Davis, T., Lang, R., Franco, J. H., & Chan, J. M. (2010). Training teachers to assess the challenging behaviors of students with autism using video tele-conferencing. *Education and Training in Autism and Developmental Disabilities, 45,* 203–215.

Martin, R. (1978). Expert and referent power: A framework for understanding and maximizing consultation effectiveness. *Journal of School Psychology, 16,* 49–55. doi:10.1016/0022-4405(78)90022-5

National Association of School Psychologists. (2010). *Model for comprehensive and integrated school psychological services.* Bethesda, MD: Author.

Noell, G. H., & Gansle, K. A. (2014). Research examining the relationships between consultation procedures, treatment integrity, and outcomes. In W. P Erchul & S. M. Sheridan (Eds.), *Handbook of research in school consultation* (2nd ed., pp. 386–408). New York, NY: Routledge.

Owens, J. S., Schwartz, M. E., Erchul, W. P., Himawan, L., Coles, E. K., Evans, S. W., & Schulte, A. C. (2017). Teacher perceptions of school consultants' social influence: Replication and expansion. *Journal of Educational and Psychological Consultation, 1–26.* doi:10.1080/10474412.2016.1275649

Raven, B. H. (1992). A power/interaction model of interpersonal influence: French and Raven thirty years later. *Journal of Social Behavior and Personality, 7,* 217–244.

Sandoval, J. (2014). Best practices in school-based mental health/consultee-centered consultation by school psychologists. In P. Harrison & A. Thomas (Eds.), *Best practices in school: Data-based and collaborative decision making* (pp. 493–507). Bethesda, MD: National Association of School Psychologists.

Sheridan, S. M., Bovaird, J. A., Glover, T. A., Garbacz, S. A., Witte, A., & Kwon, K. (2012). A randomized trial examining the effects of conjoint behavioral consultation and the mediating role of the parent–teacher relationship. *School Psychology Review, 41,* 23-46.

Sheridan, S. M., & Kratochwill, T. R. (2008). *Conjoint behavioral consultation: Promoting family–school connections and intervention* (2nd ed.). New York, NY: Springer Publishing.

Sheridan, S. M., Welch, M., & Orme, S. F. (1996). Is consultation effective? A review of outcome research. *Remedial and Special Education, 17,* 341–354.

Sibley, S. (1986). A meta-analysis of school consultation research. Unpublished doctoral dissertation. Texas Woman's University, Denton, TX

Truscott, S. D., Kreskey, D., Bolling, M., Psimas, L., Graybill, E., Albritton, K., & Schwartz, A. (2012). Creating consultee change: A theory-based approach to learning and behavior change processes in school-based consultation. *Consulting Psychology Journal: Practice and Research, 64,* 63–82. doi:10.1037/a0027997

von Bertalanffy, L. (1968). *General systems theory.* New York, NY: Braziller.

What Works Clearinghouse. (2017). *Procedures and standards handbook* (3rd ed.). Washington, DC: Author.

Zins, J. E., & Erchul, W. P. (2002). Best practices in school consultation. In A. Thomas & J. Grimes (Eds.), *Best practices in school psychology IV* (pp. 625–643). Bethesda, MD: National Association of School Psychologists.

CHAPTER 12

Systems Change and Program Evaluation

AMITY L. NOLTEMEYER ■ ERIN A. HARPER

CHAPTER OBJECTIVES

- Identify the school psychologist's role within the systems change process
- Describe the primary phases of the systems change process
- Identify skills practitioners need to maximize success in the systems change process
- Define and describe program evaluation
- Describe how systems change and program evaluation can advance a social justice agenda

The field of school psychology has broadened its focus over time, gradually moving toward a systems-focused prevention and intervention orientation. As described in Chapter 1, the National Association of School Psychologists' (NASP) Practice Model (2010) explicitly recognizes systems-level services as critical to the role of the school psychologist. Moreover, legislation such as the Every Student Succeeds Act (ESSA, 2015; described in Chapter 5) further emphasizes the need for systemic approaches to prevention and intervention so as to create effective and equitable learning environments. Despite these and other calls for effective systems-level change, school psychologists report less expertise in systems-based service delivery than in other domains of practice (Noltemeyer & McLaughlin, 2011). When equipped with the proper skills and training, however, school psychologists are uniquely poised to proactively advocate for systems change that enhances school and student functioning.

This chapter seeks to provide school psychologists with information on systems change and the practitioner leader's role within it. We begin by introducing the value of systems change, factors that influence the change process, and prominent models of systems change. Next, we outline considerations for leading systems change and educational reform efforts, including necessary skills for practitioners and considerations for maximizing success. Finally, we define *program evaluation* and describe how school psychologists can engage in process and outcome evaluation of their systems change efforts to drive further improvements. Throughout the chapter, we assume a social justice perspective in which school psychologists are viewed as advocates for equitable service delivery for all children and families.

SYSTEMS-LEVEL CHANGE IN THE SCHOOLS

Castillo and Curtis (2014) define a **system** as "an orderly combination of two or more individuals whose interaction is intended to produce a desired outcome" (p. 13). In an educational context, examples of systems include school districts, schools, grade-level teams, leadership teams, classrooms, professional learning committees, and disciplinary teams. Thus, the term *system* is a relative one and may refer to any one of a number of organizational levels.

A myriad of academic and behavioral indicators suggest that systems-level change is warranted to improve school outcomes in a meaningful way. Regarding the academic realm, recall the National Assessment of Educational Progress (NAEP) results described in Chapter 8. These data indicated that only 40% of 4th graders, 33% of 8th graders, and 25% of 12th graders performed at or above the criteria for proficiency in mathematics on this test in 2015 (U.S. Department of Education, Institute of Education Sciences, National Center for Education Statistics, 2015). In the same year, scores for reading on the same assessment were similarly troubling, with 36% of 4th graders, 34% of 8th graders, and 37% of 12th graders performing at or above the proficiency criteria (U.S. Department of Education, Institute of Education Sciences, National Center for Education Statistics, 2015). With numbers like these, it is clear that efforts to improve achievement at only the individual student level would be inefficient. Rather, system-wide changes to curricula design and delivery are needed to efficiently reach a larger number of students, thereby reducing the need for more individualized supports.

As described in Chapter 9, mental and behavioral health problems are also a concern facing youth in the U.S. school system. For example, 20% of high school students have reported being bullied on school property (Centers for Disease Control and Prevention, 2015), and nearly 20% of youth have been diagnosed with or reported a mental health issue or emotional and behavioral disorder (Merikangas et al., 2010). Furthermore, approximately 2.8 million U.S. students received out-of-school suspensions in the 2013-to–2014 school year (Executive Office of the President, 2016). School climate may also be an important target for systems-level improvement in some settings; for example, of 94,000 staff in 4,844 California schools, only 46% strongly agreed that their school was a supportive and inviting place to learn. Moreover, only 39% of these respondents strongly agreed that their schools were supportive and inviting places to work (WestEd, 2011). Ultimately, a systems-level approach to prevention and intervention is warranted in contexts in which many students are affected by these issues.

All of the problems and circumstances described in the preceding text (i.e., mental health problems, poor school climate, and bullying) are associated with a variety of negative outcomes for students, including conduct problems, increased absenteeism, poor academic achievement, and even school dropout (Fekkes, Pijpers, & Verloove-Vanhorick, 2004; Noltemeyer, Ward, & Mcloughlin, 2015; Thapa, Cohen, Guffey, & Higgens-D'Alessandro, 2013). Even more alarming is the observation that academic and behavioral health problems resulting from these circumstances disproportionately impact some student populations more than others. For example, recall from Chapter 4 that racial disparities in students' disciplinary outcomes have long been documented in public schools (e.g., U.S. Department of Education Office of Civil Rights, 2014). Systems-level reform is critical for eliminating these disparities among diverse groups and promoting equity and fairness for all students. Such systems-level efforts should be guided by a social justice agenda, which highlights treating all individuals and groups with fairness and respect, recognizing and addressing inequities, and ensuring equal access to resources and opportunities offered in schools (North, 2006; Shriberg & Fenning, 2009).

RESEARCH ON SYSTEMS CHANGE AND EDUCATIONAL REFORM

Complex and pervasive challenges in schools require solutions that address entire systems, such as classrooms, grade levels, schools, and/or school districts. Furthermore, successful adoption and implementation of multi-tiered systems of support (MTSS) often require extensive changes in structures, practices, and personal beliefs. Therefore, it is important to consider the research on both systems change and education reform, including factors that influence the change process and its key stakeholders.

Education reform refers to the process of enacting fundamental, deep-rooted changes in the way educators conceptualize and implement school-based services. Not all changes to school practices constitute *reform*, and some are more superficial in nature than others. For example, a school's decision to purchase new technology for its classrooms may increase the range and quality of resources available to students and teachers; however, in and of itself, this change may not constitute deep reform. Rather, this would more likely represent a surface change—in other words, a change that alters school procedures and/or practices in a more superficial manner that is not necessarily guided by a *shared vision*. As described by Fullan (2007), **shared vision** refers to the collective insights, values, goals, and understandings that are synthesized by participants in the change process to guide fundamental shifts in service delivery. In the present example, the introduction of technology into the classroom is not necessarily guided by a mutually agreed-upon, underlying rationale for meaningfully influencing student learning. If this technology were being integrated in learning environments to fundamentally alter the way instruction or curriculum is conceptualized and delivered, however, it might be considered part of a reform process.

The literature on educational reform suggests that it is a difficult and arduous process and that schools often are not successful in achieving sustainable systems change. For example, Datnow and Stringfield (2000) found that only 7 of 13 schools implementing a particular school reform initiative were continuing to implement it by the third year of the initiative. Similarly, in a study of comprehensive school reform, Vernez, Karam, Mariano, and DeMartini (2006) found that none of the participating 350 schools had fully implemented system-wide change. These findings suggest that implementation of systems change is challenging and that it requires intentional planning, implementation, and sustainability methods to support long-term success.

Despite these disappointing findings, research suggests that the outlook for schools seeking to implement systems change is not entirely bleak. First, implementation can be facilitated through systematic efforts to cultivate environments and circumstances that enable change. For example, prior research on implementing Positive Behavioral Interventions and Supports (PBIS; described in Chapter 9) suggests that facilitators of successful systems change include factors such as stakeholder buy-in, a shared vision for the change, administrative leadership, school psychologists as leaders, financial resources, district support, school-level or team-level professional development, and organizational restructuring (George, White, & Schlaffer, 2007; Kincaid, Childs, Blaise, & Wallace, 2007). Furthermore, when implementation of systems change processes *is* strong, results can be powerful. As an example, Ysseldyke et al. (2003) found that students in classrooms whose teachers demonstrated higher implementation integrity of a curricular change (i.e., the addition of a computer-based management system to the regular math curriculum) demonstrated more growth in achievement than students in classrooms with partial implementation or nonimplementation. As a more macro-level example, Durlak and DuPre (2008) conducted a systematic review of more than 500 implementation studies on youth prevention and health promotion programs and found that well-implemented programs were associated with more beneficial outcomes. Overall, research in this area suggests that, although systems change can be challenging, high levels of implementation fidelity can be achieved and are associated with improvements in student outcomes.

FRAMEWORKS FOR SYSTEMS CHANGE

Several frameworks for systems change have been described in the literature. Table 12.1 presents a crosswalk of several prominent frameworks in an attempt to align their phases. Although this information may be a useful heuristic for translating phases from one framework to another, readers should be aware that the alignment of these phases is not precise (due to variations in the definitions and descriptions of phases in each approach). A fundamental assumption of each of the frameworks in Table 12.1 is that implementation of systems change is a complex process; thus, although a framework may includeidentifiable phases, they may not always occur in a perfectly linear or nonrecursive fashion. The remainder of this chapter applies Fixsen, Naoom, Blase, Friedman, and Wallace's (2005) model to guide subsequent discussion.

Fixsen et al.'s (2005) framework for systems change consists of six phases. First, the **exploration and adoption** stage involves determining whether there is a match between the targeted systems change and the needs of the organization or its members. This stage ends with a decision to proceed with the change (if, in fact, the change is deemed to meet organizational needs). The **program installation** stage, which commences following the decision to implement the change, includes several tasks that must be accomplished prior to implementation—for example, ensuring adequate funding and staffing, developing policy and evaluation strategies, and clarifying outcome goals. After these foundations have been established, the **initial implementation** stage begins. This stage constitutes the organization's first attempts at putting the change into practice. During initial implementation, changes may not occur evenly or simultaneously across

TABLE 12.1 Crosswalk of Four Systems Change Frameworks

Fixsen et al. (2005)	Adelman and Taylor (1997)	Fullan (2007)	Kampwirth and Powers (2016)*
1. Exploration and adoption	1. Creating readiness	1. Initiation	1. Determining a need and creating readiness
			2. Determining a long-term vision and desired alternative practices
2. Installation	2. Initial implementation	2. Implementation	3. Installation and initial implementation
3. Initial implementation			
4. Full implementation	3. Institutionalization	3. Institutionalization	4. Institutionalization
5. Innovation	4. Ongoing evolution		5. Ongoing evolution
6. Sustainability			

*Incorporates other models.

Sources: Adelman, H. S., & Taylor, L. (1997). Toward a scale-up model for replicating new approaches to schooling. *Journal of Educational and Psychological Consultation, 8,* 255–271; Fixsen, D. L., Naoom, S. F., Blase, K. A., Friedman, R. M. & Wallace, F. (2005). *Implementation research: A synthesis of the literature.* Tampa, FL: University of South Florida, Louis de la Parte Florida Mental Health Institute, The National Implementation Research Network (FMHI Publication #231); Fullan, M. (2007). *The new meaning of educational change* (4th ed.). New York, NY: Teacher's College Press; Kampwirth, T. J., & Powers, K. M (2016). *Collaborative consultation in the schools: Effective practices for students with learning and behavior problems* (5th ed.). Upper Saddle River, NJ: Pearson Education.

the entire system and may require ongoing refinement through practice opportunities and professional development. **Full operation** occurs when the change becomes completely integrated into the system's practices and procedures, and implementation becomes more skillful and routine. Once the change is fully operational, **innovation** can occur. This phase involves refining, expanding, and adapting implementation in a skillful manner to obtain maximum benefits.[1] Finally, an often overlooked but critical stage of the change process is **sustainability** (also described in Chapter 7), which involves planning for issues that could affect the continued implementation of the change, such as staff turnover, funding changes, and competing initiatives. According to Fixsen et al. (2005), the goal of this stage is "long-term survival and continued effectiveness of the implementation site in the context of a changing world" (p. 17).

School personnel and leadership teams engaged in systems-level work may use these stages as a framework for guiding the planning and implementation of their efforts, thereby ensuring that they do not overlook important considerations. For

---

[1]You may recall the term *innovation* from Chapter 7, in which it was used to describe a new program being implemented in a school or district. In this chapter, the term *innovation* is used to describe a process of refining intervention implementation to suit the contexts and needs of clients. Although related, uses of this term may vary somewhat in the school psychology literature.

example, it is not uncommon for schools to rush through the exploration stage or to fail to plan for sustainability, both of which may diminish the impact and longevity of the initiative.

CONSIDERATIONS FOR LEADING SYSTEMS CHANGE

As already noted, systems-level prevention and intervention are important components of the school psychologist's work. Properly trained and skilled school psychologists are well positioned to collaborate with other stakeholders to initiate and implement change efforts that can enhance school and student functioning. This section reviews key considerations for implementing systems change, with a primary focus on the roles and skills necessary for school psychologists.

As discussed in the previous chapter, a primary role of school psychologists engaged in systems change is that of collaborative consultant. In a school setting, systems-level **collaborative consultation** is a process whereby a trained school consultant enters into a nonhierarchical relationship with a team of consultees to help lead efforts to develop, implement, and evaluate systems-level plans to support student success (Kampwirth & Powers, 2016). Collaborative consultants operate from the perspective that all team members contribute valuable input and expertise to team-based problem solving and decision making based on their previous experiences and talents.

To work successfully with other team members, collaborative consultants first need effective communication and interpersonal skills (Ysseldyke et al., 2006). In the context of school-based consultation, communication often involves an exchange of information between two or more individuals. Critical communication skills include attending, active listening, reframing, and empathy (Kampwirth & Powers, 2016). Other skills necessary for successful communication include the ability to ask clarifying questions in a nonthreatening manner and the ability to maintain a goal-oriented mindset (Kampwirth & Powers, 2016). Strong interpersonal skills facilitate the effective transmission of information and help team members form positive relationships, which effectively position them to work in concert toward meeting organizational goals. Examples of interpersonal skills include the ability to adapt, tolerate ambiguity, and be patient in difficult situations (Ysseldyke et al., 2006).

When implementing systems change in educational settings, collaborative consultants contribute content knowledge and intervention skills, as well as process knowledge during team problem solving. **Content knowledge** refers to knowledge of the programs and changes to be implemented, whereas **process knowledge** refers to expertise in communication, consultation, and systems change processes necessary to support program implementation. Although it is impossible for school psychologists who lead systems change to know everything about each problem they may confront, systems change leaders should have foundational knowledge (i.e., *content knowledge*) of a range of evidence-based strategies and interventions to address various types of student and school issues. As described in Chapter 7, school psychologists should be aware of resources for identifying appropriate evidence-based interventions, such as the What Works Clearinghouse (Institute for Education Sciences, n.d.; www.ies.ed.gov/ncee/WWC), the National Registry for Evidence-Based Programs and Practices (www.nrepp.samhsa.gov), and the

Connecticut Clearinghouse (www.ctclearinghouse.org). Moreover, practitioners must be knowledgeable about principles and research related to resilience and risk factors in learning and mental health, multitiered prevention and intervention, home–school collaboration, and cultural considerations for service delivery.

Also critical for collaborative consultants engaged in systems change and educational reform is *process knowledge*, such as knowledge of systems change frameworks (e.g., the frameworks listed in Table 12.1) and factors that facilitate successful reform. Factors that lcontribute to successful systems change are referred to as **implementation drivers** and can be organized into three categories: competency supports, organization supports, and leadership supports (Fixsen et al., 2005). Competency supports include the selection, training, and coaching of team members who will implement the systems change. Organization supports, which are developed by system administrators, facilitate positive and productive organizational practices and a positive organizational climate. An example of an organization support is the use of high-quality data systems to assure smooth implementation of the intervention over time. Leadership supports include supports that help to resolve both technical and adaptive issues related to factors such as time, funding, and motivation. The National Implementation Research Network (nirn.fpg.unc.edu/learn-implementation) provides a detailed description of each implementation driver and additional implementation resources.

Evaluating School and Student Outcomes Associated With the Change Process

As complex as the change process can be, it is important to realize that implementation is not the end of the process. A critical, but sometimes overlooked, aspect of the systems change process is program evaluation. **Program evaluation** is a form of applied research designed to make a difference in the lives of stakeholders and has been described as a process for evaluating the success of an implemented program (see Royse, Thyer, & Padgett, 2016). Evaluating the implementation and outcomes of a systems change initiative is critical, as the information that emerges can suggest whether the organization should continue, intensify, discontinue, or alter the program implementation. More specifically, program evaluation can inform both formative and summative decisions. (Recall from Chapter 6 that *formative* evaluation occurs during the course of program implementation, whereas *summative* evaluation takes place following implementation.) In formative decision making, ongoing progress monitoring data on fidelity of implementation as well as student outcomes relevant to the particular systems change initiative can be used to drive continuous improvement (Castillo, 2014). In regard to summative decision making, larger spans of periodic data collection can be used to determine whether the outcomes of the systems change initiative justify its continuation (Castillo, 2014).

As an example of the formative–summative distinction, a school implementing PBIS may review monthly data on student office disciplinary referrals (ODRs), positive office referrals, and adult implementation and then make changes in PBIS practices based on areas of need identified through this evaluation. For instance, trends in when and where ODRs are occurring may reveal a need for more modeling, reinforcement, or supervision in those areas or at those times. However, this same school may also perform a more comprehensive annual evaluation that summarizes outcomes over the course of the entire school year, which may be shared with district administrators who make decisions about funding and other supports for PBIS initiatives.

The U.S. Department of Education, Office of Elementary and Secondary Education (2014) proposed a five-step embedded model for planning and implementing evaluations of systems-level initiatives. In Step 1, stakeholders seek to *define* the target program and its scope. Step 2 involves developing a *plan* for program evaluation. In Step 3, stakeholders *implement* selected procedures to evaluate the program, and in Step 4, they seek to *interpret* evaluation results. Finally, in Step 5, evaluation results are used to *inform* and *refine* program efforts and services. Figure 12.1 illustrates each of the five steps of this program evaluation process and identifies key questions that should be considered at each step.

When conducting a program evaluation, there are several important considerations for maximizing the validity and usefulness of the results. For example, evaluators should strive to use multimethod data collection strategies that rely

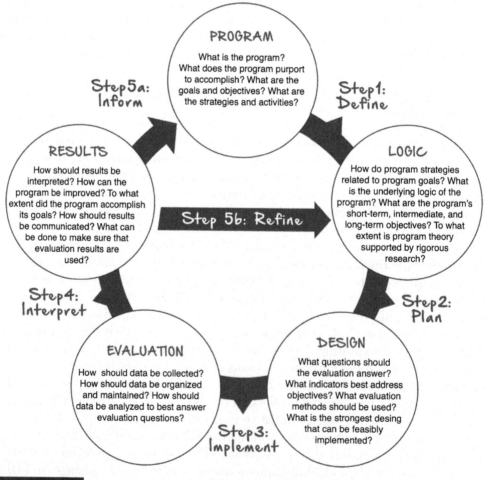

FIGURE 12.1 **FIVE-STEP EMBEDDED EVALUATION MODEL**

Source: U. S. Department of Education, Office of Elementary and Secondary Education, School Support and Rural Programs. (2014). *Evaluation matters: Getting the information you need from your evaluation* (p. 6). Washington, DC: Author. Retrieved from https://www2.ed.gov/about/offices/list/oese/sst/evaluationmatters.pdf

on multiple informants. To continue the PBIS example highlighted earlier, multimethod data collection might be operationalized as collecting several sources of quantitative (e.g., number of ODRs, number of positive office referrals) and qualitative (e.g., stakeholder interviews) information. Multiple informants could be operationalized as collecting information from students, staff, and families, so as to comprehensively understand the impact on diverse groups.

SOCIAL JUSTICE CONNECTIONS

How can program evaluation advance a social justice agenda?

Program evaluation offers important opportunities to advance a social justice agenda. Over the past few decades, scholars have underscored the integral link between program evaluation methodology and social justice (Cooper & Christie, 2005; Greene, 2006; House, 1991). These scholars have contended that because program evaluation is designed to serve the interests of society, it must advance the interests of all constituent groups, especially those that have been traditionally marginalized (e.g., Greene, 2006; Sirotnik, 1990). As stated by Thomas and Madison (2010), "Respect for the rights of others is important to conducting fair and valid evaluations and in engaging in meaningful public discourse" (p. 572).

Based on this literature, the following recommendations may assist school psychologists in undertaking evaluations that are grounded in social justice principles and promote equity in service delivery.

1. Recognize that no evaluation process is entirely value neutral. Evaluators must be mindful of the values, assumptions, biases, and beliefs that impact their methodologies and approaches (Greene, 2006). Moreover, they must account for the cultural, social, economic, and political environments that enshroud the evaluation process. Evaluators should move away from efforts to stress objectivity and instead recognize the importance of acknowledging constituents' multiple perspectives and realities (Thomas & Madison, 2010).
2. Develop and employ high-quality communication skills (e.g., verbal expression and listening skills) as well as interpersonal skills (e.g., conflict resolution and group facilitation skills) (Thomas & Madison, 2010). Building trust with stakeholders is essential for obtaining honest input.
3. Make it a priority to identify and engage the least powerful stakeholder group(s) in the evaluation process. These parties may include families who are recipients of program services or outside groups that are inadvertently affected or marginalized by the implementation process. Evaluators should seek not only to capture the perspectives of these individuals, but also to empower them to participate in the evaluation process (Cooper & Christine, 2005).
4. Ask the important and difficult questions, even when their answers raise difficult and uncomfortable considerations. These questions may include:
   a. Who is accessing program services? In other words, are the intended recipients of services the ones who are benefiting from them? What might be some potential barriers to access?
   b. Are the program's core values and delivery consistent with the cultural values of the populations it is designed to serve?
   c. Are the various subgroups who are accessing the program receiving comparable benefits? Especially among traditionally marginalized groups, are there other needs that could and should be met but have not yet been addressed through program initiatives?

One way to capture the perspectives of diverse stakeholders is to use mixed-methods evaluation designs. Mixed-methods designs incorporate both quantitative data (e.g., numerical data) and qualitative data (e.g., data from focus groups and open-ended interviews). Collecting both of these types of data can yield a much more comprehensive picture of the perspectives, needs, and values of diverse groups.

Another particularly important consideration related to the evaluation of systems change initiatives concerns the assessment of intervention fidelity (also referred to as implementation fidelity, treatment fidelity, implementation integrity, and treatment integrity). Recall from Chapter 7 that *intervention fidelity* refers to the degree to which an intervention or program is implemented as designed or intended. Inherently, systems change initiatives in schools tend to be complex and to require considerable effort, support, and collaborative teamwork from a variety of stakeholders. Thus, many variables can influence program outcomes. To determine whether the outcomes observed are truly related to the systems change itself, it is first necessary to determine whether the systems change was implemented as intended. As described in Chapter 7, widely used methods for assessing implementation integrity include direct observation of implementation, self-report checklists documenting the degree to which key implementation features were put into practice, and review of permanent products from implementation (e.g., student work samples). Ideally, implementation integrity should be assessed using multiple methods (Goss, Noltemeyer, & Devore, 2007).

Given their training in systems-level service delivery, school psychologists are uniquely qualified to facilitate the planning and implementation of the program evaluation processes outlined in the preceding text. As noted in Chapter 1, *Research and Program Evaluation* is one of the 10 domains in the NASP Practice Model (2010), which specifically states that "school psychologists, in collaboration with others, collect, analyze, and interpret program evaluation data in applied settings" (p. 8). School psychologists can use their training in research, program evaluation, and data-based decision making to (a) advocate for the inclusion of embedded evaluation strategies that are systematically identified prior to implementation of the systems change initiative and (b) assist in developing and implementing a plan for applying those strategies, using a framework such as the five-step embedded evaluation model to guide this work.

CASE EXAMPLE

Implementing Systems Change in School Districts

The following case example illustrates the applications of the systems change process in a fictitious school district.

Rushmore Independent School District (RISD) is a rural public school system located near a town that has been impacted by a natural disaster. Although no students in RISD were personally affected, the close proximity of the natural disaster prompted the new superintendent of RISD to explore the district's current policies and procedures for crisis preparedness, response, and recovery. The new superintendent discovered that although the school district had a crisis response plan, the plan was not comprehensive and had not been updated in more than a decade. Moreover, many of the school administrators, teachers, and support staff in the district were unaware that the plan existed.

Realizing the need to develop and implement a more comprehensive plan for crisis preparedness, response, and recovery, the superintendent requested a meeting with the district's director of student support services "to explore the enhancement of crisis response efforts in the district." The superintendent encouraged the support services director to invite others to the meeting who might be good candidates for a district-level planning team devoted to this issue. The support services director then invited the lead school psychologist, social worker, counselor, and nurse to attend the meeting with her.

During the initial meeting, the lead school psychologist shared information about PREPaRE, a crisis prevention and intervention model and training program developed by the National Association of School Psychologists (NASP) to help organizations better prepare for and respond to crisis events (Reeves et al., 2011). Interested in learning more about the program, the superintendent and other team members asked the school psychologist if she would develop a presentation about NASP PREPaRE for other members of the team and present it during a follow-up meeting. After the presentation, each team member was invited to ask questions and was given additional information about the program to review before the next meeting. At the third meeting, all team members reported that they supported implementation of the program, and the superintendent reported that funding was available for training. The team then decided to develop a survey to obtain feedback from other stakeholders, including parents and students. Survey results were presented to the district's Board of Education, and the Board voted unanimously in favor of PREPaRE program training. The district-level planning team worked to develop a systematic plan for initial implementation, informed by local needs and resources. Furthermore, team members met quarterly thereafter to plan for and monitor the degree to which the resulting crisis prevention and intervention strategies were being effectively embedded into school practices, to plan for innovation and sustainability of efforts, and to evaluate outcomes.

SUMMARY AND CONCLUSIONS

As the role of the school psychologist has evolved, systems-level service provision has become an integral aspect of comprehensive school psychology service delivery. This chapter presented an overview of systems change and program evaluation and described the role of school psychologists in these dynamic processes. When implemented from a social justice perspective, systems change and program evaluation may contribute to equitable academic and social outcomes for children and youth.

DISCUSSION QUESTIONS

1. Not all schools that decide to implement a systems change initiative are successful in doing so. Based on the research presented in this chapter, what primary pieces of advice would you give to a school team that is thinking about undertaking a systems change to help the team avoid failures in implementation and sustainability?
2. Consider the roles and skills that are important for school psychologists as they engage in systems-level work. Which of those discussed in the chapter are your personal strengths? Which are areas for continued growth, and how will you develop those over the next 5 years?
3. Why are both content knowledge and process knowledge important to systems-level consultation?
4. What is program evaluation and why is it a critical consideration when implementing a systems change?

5. Why is a social justice perspective important when considering systems-level work? What are some concrete ways that you can infuse a social justice perspective into your systems-level work?

REFERENCES

Adelman, H. S., & Taylor, L. (1997). Toward a scale-up model for replicating new approaches to schooling. *Journal of Educational and Psychological Consultation, 8*, 255–271.

Castillo, J. M., (2014). Best practices in program evaluation. In P. L Harrison & A. Thomas (Eds.), *Best practices in school psychology: Foundations* (pp. 11–28). Bethesda, MD: National Association of School Psychologists.

Castillo, J. M., & Curtis, M. J. (2014). Best practices in systems-level change. In P. L Harrison & A. Thomas (Eds.), *Best practices in school psychology: Systems-level services* (pp. 11–28). Bethesda, MD: National Association of School Psychologists.

Centers for Disease Control and Prevention. (2015). Youth Risk Behavior Survey data. Retrieved from www.cdc.gov/yrbs

Cooper, C. W., & Christie, C. A. (2005). Evaluating parent empowerment: A look at the potential of social justice evaluation in education. *Teachers College Record, 107*, 2248–2274.

Datnow, A., & Stringfield, S. (2000). Working together for reliable school reform. *Journal of Education for Students Placed at Risk, 5*, 183–204. doi:10.1080/10824669.2000.9671386

Durlak, J. A., & DuPre, E. P. (2008). Implementation matters: A review of research on the influence of implementation on program outcomes and the factors affecting implementation. *American Journal of Community Psychology, 41*, 327–350.

Every Student Succeeds Act. Pub. L. No. 114-95, § 1177 (2015).

Executive Office of the President. (2016, December). Report: The continuing need to rethink discipline. Retrieved from https://www.ed.gov/news/press-releases/white-house-report-continuing-need-rethink-discipline

Fekkes, M., Pijpers, F., & Verloove-Vanhorick, S. (2004). Bullying behavior and associations with psychosomatic complaints and depression in victims. *Journal of Pediatrics, 144*, 17–22.

Fixsen, D. L., Naoom, S. F., Blase, K. A., Friedman, R. M., & Wallace, F. (2005). *Implementation research: A synthesis of the literature.* FMHI Publication #231. Tampa, FL: University of South Florida, Louis de la Parte Florida Mental Health Institute, The National Implementation Research Network.

Fullan, M. (2007). *The new meaning of educational change* (4th ed.). New York, NY: Teacher's College Press.

George, M. P., White, G. P., & Schlaffer, J. J. (2007). Implementing school-wide behavior change: Lessons from the field. *Psychology in the Schools, 44*, 41–51. doi:10.1002/pits.20204

Goss, S., Noltemeyer, A., & Devore, H. (2007). Treatment integrity: A necessary component of response-to-intervention. *School Psychologist, 61*, 34–38.

Greene, J. C. (2006). Evaluation, democracy, and social change. In I. F. Shaw, J. C. Greene, & M. M. Mark (Eds.), *The Sage handbook of evaluation* (pp. 118–140). Thousand Oaks, CA: Sage.

House, E. R. (1991). Evaluation and social justice: Where are we? In M. McLaughlin & D. Phillips (Eds.), *Evaluation and education at quarter century: National Society for the Study of Education yearbook* (pp. 233–246). Chicago, IL: University of Chicago Press.

Institute for Education Sciences. (n.d.). What Works Clearinghouse, U.S. Department of Education. Retrieved from http://ies.ed.gov/ncee/WWC

Kampwirth, T. J., & Powers, K. M (2016). *Collaborative consultation in the schools: Effective practices for students with learning and behavior problems* (5th ed.). Upper Saddle River, NJ: Pearson Education.

Kincaid, D., Childs, K., Blaise, K. A., & Wallace, F. (2007). Identifying barriers and facilitators in implementing schoolwide positive behavior support. *Journal of Positive Behavior Interventions, 9*, 174–184.

Merikangas, K. R., He, J., Burstein, M. E., Swanson, S. A., Avenevoli, S., Cul, L., . . . Swendsen, J. (2010). Lifetime prevalence of mental disorders in U.S. adolescents: Results from the National Co-morbidity Study—Adolescent supplement (NCS-A). *Journal for the American Academy of Child and Adolescent Psychiatry, 49*, 980–989. doi:10.1016/j.jaac.2010.05.017

National Association of School Psychologists. (2010). Model for comprehensive and integrated school psychological services. Retrieved from https://www.nasponline.org/assets/Documents/Standards%20and%20Certification/Standards/2_PracticeModel.pdf

Noltemeyer, A., & McLaughlin, C. L. (2011). School psychology's Blueprint III: Knowledge, use, and competence. *School Psychology Forum, 5*, 74–86.

Noltemeyer, A., Ward, R. M., & Mcloughlin, C. S. (2015). Relationship between school suspension and student outcomes: A meta-analysis. *School Psychology Review, 44*, 224–240.

North, C. E. (2006). More than words? Delving into the substantive meaning(s) of "social justice" in education. *Review of Educational Research, 76*, 507–536.

Reeves, M. A., Nickerson, A. B., Connolly-Wilson, C. N., Susan, M. K., Lazzaro, B. R., Jimerson, S. R., & Pesce, R. C. (2011). *PREPaRE: Crisis prevention and preparedness: Comprehensive school safety planning* (2nd ed.). Bethesda, MD: National Association of School Psychologists.

Royse, D., Thyer, B. A., & Padgett, D. K. (2016). *Program evaluation: An introduction to an evidence-based approach* (6th ed.). Boston, MA: Cengage Learning.

Shriberg, D., & Fenning, P. A. (2009). School consultants as agents of social justice: Implications for practice: Introduction to the special issue. *Journal of Educational and Psychological Consultation, 19*, 1–7. doi:10.1080/10474410802462751

Sirotnik, E. A. (Ed.). (1990). *Evaluation and social justice: Issues in public education* (New Directions for Program Evaluation, 45). San Francisco, CA: Jossey-Bass.

Thapa, A., Cohen, J., Guffey, S., & Higgins-D'Alessandro, A. (2013). A review of school climate research. *Review of Educational Research, 83*(3), 357–385.

Thomas, V. G., & Madison, A. (2010). Integration of social justice into the teaching of evaluation. *American Journal of Evaluation, 31*, 570–583.

U.S. Department of Education, Institute of Education Sciences, National Center for Education Statistics. (2015). The nation's report card. Retrieved from http://www.nationsreportcard.gov

U.S. Department of Education, Office of Civil Rights. (2014). Civil rights data collection data snapshot: School discipline (Issue Brief No. 1). Retrieved from http://ocrdata.ed.gov/Downloads/CRDC-School-Discipline-Snapshot.pdf

U.S. Department of Education, Office of Elementary and Secondary Education, School Support and Rural Programs. (2014). *Evaluation matters: Getting the information you need from your evaluation*. Washington, DC: Author. Retrieved from https://www2.ed.gov/about/offices/list/oese/sst/evaluationmatters.pdf

Vernez, G., Karam, R., Mariano, L. T., & DeMartini, C. (2006). Evaluating comprehensive school reform models at scale: Focus on implementation. Retrieved from http://www.rand.org /pubs/monographs/2006/RAND_MG546.pdf

WestEd. (2011). *California School Climate Survey, statewide results, 2008–2010. Report 1. What teachers and other staff tell us about our schools*. San Francisco, CA: WestEd Health & Human Development Program for the California Department of Education. Retrieved from: http://surveydata.wested.org/resources/CSCS_State0810_Main.pdf

Ysseldyke, J. E., Burns, M., Dawson, P., Kelley, B., Morrison, D., Ortiz, S., & Telzrow, K. (2006). *School psychology: A blueprint for training and practice III*. Bethesda, MD: National Association of School Psychologists.

Ysseldyke, J., Spicuzza, R., Kosciolek, S., Teelucksingh, E., Boys, C., & Lemkuil, A. (2003). Using a curriculum-based instructional management system to enhance math achievement in urban schools. *Journal of Education for Students Placed at Risk, 8*, 247–265. doi:10.1207/S15327671ESPR0802_4

Looking Ahead

CHAPTER 13

Future of School Psychology

KATHLEEN M. MINKE ■ ERIC ROSSEN

- Predict the future of the school psychology field through a review of historical trends and contexts
- Identify likely responses of school psychology professional organizations to current challenges, including shortages, standards revisions, and the evolution of professional roles
- Discuss urgent challenges as we move into the future, including diversity, social justice, and technology
- Describe specific action steps for individual school psychologists in creating a robust future for the field

Predicting the future is an intriguing task, but one that is fraught with pitfalls and potential for error. History is replete with failed predictions, such as from those who saw no potential in the possibility of a telephone ("Well-informed people know it is impossible to transmit the voice over wires and that were it possible to do so, the thing would be of no practical value." *The Boston Post*, 1865) or an airplane ("Heavier-than-air flying machines are fantasy. Simple laws of physics make them impossible." Lord Kelvin, president, British Royal Society, 1895). Even within more recent history, industry visionaries can be spectacularly wrong in forecasting advancements ("640 K [of computer memory] ought to be enough for anybody." Bill Gates, founder and CEO of Microsoft, 1981). Therefore, it is with great humility and caution that we undertake the task of discussing the likely future of school psychology.

The purpose of this chapter is to offer predictions regarding future directions for the field. In particular, these predictions pertain to the composition of the workforce, the roles of school psychologists, and professional practices. Recommendations for contributing to the future of school psychology are offered at the end the chapter.

PREDICTIONS OF THE FUTURE'S PAST

School psychology has a long history of self-examination and looking toward a more positive future. Beginning with the Thayer Conference in 1954 and continuing through the most recent Futures of School Psychology Conference in 2012, leaders have come together periodically in efforts not just to predict, but also to influence, future directions in the field. Throughout the years, some issues have been discussed recurrently (e.g., credentialing and scope of practice), while others have become more prominent over time (e.g., multicultural competency and advocacy).

Returning briefly to Chapter 2, recall the Thayer Conference of 1954, in which some of the first organized discussions about the roles and preparation of school psychologists took place (Fagan, 2005). According to Fagan (2005), there were approximately 1,000 school psychologists practicing in the United States at the time of this conference. Moreover, only 20 states (and the District of Columbia) had certification regulations through their State Boards of Education. One of the outcomes of this conference was a broad vision of school psychologists as professionals who serve all children in educational settings. Two levels of training were recommended (i.e., the doctoral and "sub-doctoral" levels), with those practicing at the "sub-doctoral" level envisioned as having a separate title, narrower role, and supervision by doctoral-level school psychologists. Although the two levels of training persisted in the field's subsequent development, visions regarding title and practice did not come to pass. Indeed, later predictions that the field would naturally evolve into a profession centered on doctoral-level preparation and practice were similarly incorrect (e.g., Brown & Minke, 1986).

Several decades later, the Spring Hill (1981) and Olympia (1982) conferences were held jointly by the National Association of School Psychologists (NASP) and the American Psychological Association's (APA's) Division 16 (School Psychology) to provide follow-up to the Thayer Conference and to set directions and strategies for the field. At the time of these conferences, the field was still adjusting to the passage of PL 94-142 (Education for All Handicapped Children Act of 1975; described in Chapters 2 and 5) and considering the impact of large-scale federal intervention in special education. The keynote address, delivered by William Bevan (1981), identified issues that are not terribly different from those we continue to face, such as austerity in government funding, the role of the federal government in education, and the potentially negative effects of far-reaching regulations. The need to define the core identity of school psychology was mentioned repeatedly (Lambert, 1981; Trachtman, 1981). Moreover, there was recognition that remediating the difficulties of one child at a time was not a viable approach to effectively reaching all children (Grimes, 1981; Schaefer, 1982). Nevertheless, practice continued to follow an individualized, deficit model of intervention, which emphasized identifying and remediating problems within children rather than building on strengths (Graden, 2004).

Although change has been slow, there are signs that, as a field, we are beginning to embrace the skills and practices needed to function more proactively in the service of children, families, and schools. The 2002 Future of School Psychology Conference highlighted the need to move toward a population-based strategy of service delivery that emphasizes a continuum of services from the universal, preventive level through the intensive, highly individualized level, as embodied by multi-tiered systems of support (MTSS) (Dawson et al., 2004). In addition, this conference urged the field to assume a problem-solving approach to school psychological services. As described in Chapters 7 and 11, this model emphasizes evidence-based practice and the gathering of data to guide the identification of appropriate interventions and evaluate their effectiveness. Finally, the 2002 conference recognized the need to integrate technology in practice and graduate preparation in ways that enhance service delivery.

As described in Chapter 2, the most recent Futures conference was convened in 2012. This conference was very different from its predecessors because it was conducted virtually (in an effort to actualize the technology goals outlined in 2002). Notably, participants in this conference focused less on defining the profession and more on advancing it through skill development, leadership, and advocacy. As we move into the future, these areas will remain essential to the profession and its continued evolution.

PREDICTIONS FOR SCHOOL PSYCHOLOGY'S FUTURE

> *The real difficulty in changing the course of any enterprise lies*
> *not in developing new ideas but in escaping old ones.*
> —John Maynard Keynes

Forecasting the future of the field is a difficult and elusive task. Nevertheless, knowledge of past predictions, the field's evolution to date, and emerging trends in the field allow for tentative predictions of future directions.

Priorities of School Psychology's Professional Organizations Will Evolve

Several initiatives from APA and NASP likely will affect the field in the immediate future and beyond. The APA recently began exploring a move away from a focus on the traditional specialty areas (e.g., clinical, counseling, and school) and toward a more unified "health service provider" (HSP) designation through the *Professional Psychology in Health Care Services: A Blueprint for Education and Training* (Health Service Psychology Education Collaborative, 2013). Although schools are likely to increasingly serve as venues for both physical and mental health services delivery for youth, it is less clear that the larger community of psychologists understands how the school context differs from other community and clinical settings. Specifically, school psychological services (a) are situated within a different regulatory structure (e.g., credentialing usually through state departments of education rather than boards of psychology; federal and state laws and regulations that apply specifically to schools); (b) are provided to all students, not as "fee for service;" and (c) must address the educational impact of students' concerns, not just the mental health impact (Hughes & Minke, 2014). As such, school psychology practice emphasizes prevention, early intervention, and cross-system collaboration to a larger degree than other specialties do. As the HSP designation becomes more accepted across states, school psychologists will need to be sure that the distinctive aspects of school-based practice are addressed in graduate preparation programs and in state regulations. Because there is far greater need for mental health supports than is currently provided (e.g., Murphey, Vaughn, & Barry, 2013), the development of the HSP designation represents a great opportunity for collaboration among providers of psychological services to better serve all children, provided that school psychologists are integrally involved in shaping the implementation of school-based services.

NASP's focus as an organization is best represented through its strategic plan. Goals include addressing the shortage of school psychologists, implementing the NASP (2010a) *Model for Comprehensive and Integrated School Psychological Services* (i.e., the NASP Practice Model), developing school psychologists' leadership skills, and improving school psychologists' capacity to provide culturally competent and comprehensive mental and behavioral health services. Importantly, a goal was added to the 2017 plan that addresses social justice more explicitly than in the past: "NASP seeks to ensure that all children and youth are valued and their rights and opportunities are protected in schools and communities" (NASP, 2017). As part of this effort, NASP has adopted a definition of *social justice* that will guide this work:

> Social justice is both a process and a goal that requires action. School psychologists work to ensure the protection of the educational rights, opportunities, and well-being of all children, especially those whose voices have been muted, identities obscured, or needs ignored. Social justice requires promoting non-discriminatory practices and the empowerment of families and communities. School psychologists enact social justice through culturally-responsive professional practice and advocacy to create schools, communities, and systems that ensure equity and fairness for all children. (NASP, 2017)

It is expected that school psychologists will become more skilled in implementing nondiscriminatory practices in their work and advocating for equity at the district, state, and national levels.

These goals are ambitious and significant. Achieving them will require commitment from all NASP members, and indeed, all school psychologists, to engage in lifelong professional development and targeted action to improve practice and outcomes for all children and youth. In addition, the field will need to respond thoughtfully and skillfully to the changing contexts of education and mental and behavioral health services.

School Psychology Will Continue to Experience Shortages (Though the Situation Will Improve)

School psychology has never experienced a period in which the supply of practitioners has met the demand (Fagan, 2004), and signs point to the continuation of that trend into the foreseeable future (Castillo, Curtis, & Tan, 2014). Despite the longstanding impact of shortages on the history of the profession, only in 2015 did

NASP first identify remediating shortages in school psychology as one of its strategic goals. This declaration by the NASP leadership provided both a means for enacting coordinated efforts to reduce shortages and a mandate to better understand the mechanisms that have sustained these shortages over time.

Traditionally, school psychology shortages refer to an imbalance in supply and demand or, more specifically, to a lack of sufficient numbers of practitioners to fill available vacancies. However, shortages constitute a much more complex and nuanced issue than previously thought (see Bocanegra, Grapin, Nellis, & Rossen, 2017). In fact, the field has experienced shortages of school psychology practitioners, job openings, graduate preparation programs, graduate educators, internships, internship supervisors, cultural and linguistic diversity, program applicants, and respecialization opportunities. To further complicate this issue, the nature and extent of such shortages depends on geographic location as well as current social and economic influences.

Practitioner Shortages

Practitioner shortages tend to be the most conspicuous and significant type of shortages, as they pose the most immediate obstacles to service delivery and the main mission of school psychologists' work. One method of measuring shortages is to examine ratios of students per school psychologist. National estimates of student-to-school psychologist ratios generally have remained steady over the last decade, being 1,482:1 in 2004–2005 (Charvat, 2011); 1,383 in 2009–2010 (Charvat, 2011); and 1,381 in 2014–2015 (Walcott, Hyson, & Loe, 2017). By comparison, the recommended student-to-practitioner ratio changed from 1,000:1 to 500–700:1 (NASP, 2010a) during the same time period. While the observed student-to-practitioner ratio has improved marginally over the past decade, its distance from NASP's recommended ratio has worsened. Another way to measure practitioner shortages is to examine vacancies and job placement rates. Unfortunately, despite some available data from the Bureau of Labor Statistics (n.d.) on job openings and labor turnover, data specific to school psychology positions have not been collected systematically throughout the United States.

NASP has undertaken several efforts to remediate school psychology shortages. For example, it developed and disseminated the *Shortages in School Psychology Resource Guide* (NASP, 2016b), which provides a range of recommendations for recruiting and retaining school psychologists. Other efforts include the development of the Find-A-Mentor program (www.nasponline.org/membership-and-community/get-involved/find-a-mentor-program) and the 2nd Round Candidate Match Program (www.nasponline.org/about-school-psychology/becoming-a-school-psychologist/2nd-round-candidate-match). The Find-A-Mentor program is designed to help retain school psychologists in the field by providing mentorship and professional supports to early-career school psychologists as well as those professionals who are isolated from other school psychologists in their work settings. The 2nd Round Candidate Match Program connects prospective graduate students with school psychology graduate programs that still have openings after initial rounds of program admissions are complete.

Social influences certainly play a role in the potential outlook for practitioner shortages, such as an increased recognition of integral links between mental health and academic success; federal, state, and local funding priorities; and the oscillation of educational control between federal and local governments. Additionally, it is unclear whether gradual increases in the number of school psychologist practitioners will be able to keep pace with the growing enrollments in the U.S. public school system. In any event, practitioner shortages are likely to continue, though based on graduate student enrollment trends (as described in the next subsection), it is unlikely they will worsen significantly.

Graduate Student Enrollment Shortages

Though it has experienced only modest growth, enrollment in school psychology programs has increased over the last 20 years. In 1997, there were a reported 8,587 total students enrolled (including students working in internships); in 2013, that figure rose to 9,663 students (Rossen & von der Embse, 2014). More recently, an estimated 9,797 total students were enrolled in school psychology programs in 2016 (Gadke, Valley-Gray, & Rossen, 2017). In the same year, the number of new graduates entering the workforce was 2,581 (Gadke et al., 2017), as compared with an estimated 1,900 graduates in 2000 (Curtis, Grier, & Hunley, 2004). Further, despite many reports of the "graying of the field" (i.e., projections that large cohorts of practitioners will retire, leaving significant numbers of job vacancies), recent data suggest current school psychologists have an average of 17.3 years until retirement. These data also suggest that there has been a *decrease* in the average age of school psychologists (42.4 years) for the first time since 1990 (Walcott, Charvat, McNamara, & Hyson, 2016). Nevertheless, observed growth in graduate program enrollments likely will not be sufficient to fill thet existing gaps and meet the new demands associated with the increasing K–12 enrollment in the United States.

Graduate Program and Faculty Shortages

Approximately 240 institutions currently offer school psychology programs in the United States (Rossen & von der Embse, 2014), which represents an 8% increase in the number of these programs over the past 35 years. Many factors may be contributing to this plateau in program growth, including the high costs of program development and maintenance and the considerable challenges associated with achieving program accreditation. Unfortunately, this plateau in programs has capped the number of new practitioners who are entering the field each year.

One potential challenge may concern the accessibility of programs to working professionals. Nearly 43% of school psychology graduate students report having been in the workforce during the year prior to entering a school psychology program (Bocanegra, Rossen, & Grapin, 2017). The challenges associated with relocating and forfeiting a salary to attend school for several years have prompted programs to consider alternative methods for instruction. For example, programs catering to working professionals (i.e., programs that offer primarily weekend and evening courses) as well as distance education programs may emerge as one potential solution to this problem. Nearly one third of school psychology programs report utilizing some form of distance education technology (Hendricker, Saeki, & Viola, 2017), and there is likely to be an increase in the implementation of distance education technology and/or the development of substantially or completely online programs. The ability of such programs to meet accreditation standards remains unclear; however, as technologies improve, programs' capacity to ensure adequate knowledge and skill development via distance education will likely improve as well.

In a related trend, shortages in the number of available school psychology graduate educators may continue to limit the availability of graduate programs. Despite increased enrollment in doctoral programs over time (Rossen & von der Embse, 2014), these programs produce an average of five graduates per year (Gadke, Valley-Gray, & Rossen, 2016). Not all of these doctoral-level graduates will opt to become graduate educators, as many of them will pursue field-based positions. Given the small number of potential candidates for graduate educator positions, developing and sustaining new programs is likely to be difficult, particularly in rural areas that may have trouble recruiting new faculty.

The Specialist-Level Degree Will Remain the Entry-Level Degree for School Psychology

The specialist-level degree, currently defined by NASP as requiring a minimum of 60 graduate semester hours (including internship), has been and remains the entry-level degree for the profession. The availability of doctoral-level programs has grown more rapidly in recent years than that of specialist-level programs (Rossen & von der Embse, 2014), with approximately one third of all programs offering degrees at the doctoral level. However, as noted in Chapter 3, no state agency currently requires a doctoral degree to work as a school psychologist, and no evidence supports the notion that doctoral-level practitioners provide higher-quality services than specialist-level practitioners. Requiring a doctoral degree for school-based practice would essentially decrease an already insufficient workforce by 75% (Walcott et al., 2016), making such a change highly unlikely in the foreseeable future.

School Psychology Will Continue to Diversify (Though at a Slower Pace Than the U.S. Population)

As part of its periodic membership survey, NASP collects data on the racial and ethnic backgrounds of its members (i.e., the data described in Chapter 4). Data from these surveys reflect a slow yet steady increase in the diversity of the profession from 1990 through 2015 (Curtis, Castillo, & Gelley, 2012; Walcott et al., 2016). Specifically, 94% of respondents identified as White in 1990, compared to 87% in 2015 (Walcott et al., 2016). The remaining 13% of respondents identified as Hispanic (6%), Black/African American (5%), and Asian (2.8%). Table 13.1 displays a history of racial and ethnic representation in school psychology.

Despite the relatively slow growth in minority participation in school psychology, data suggest that future school psychologists will be more diverse than those who are currently in the field. Approximately 25% of all school psychology

TABLE 13.1 Racial/Ethnic Representation of School Psychologists Over Time

Ethnicity	Years of Data Collection					
	1980–1981	1989–1990	1999–2000	2004–2005	2009–2010	2014–2015
Black/African American	1.5	1.9	1.9	1.9	3.0	5.0
Caucasian	96.0	93.9	92.8	92.6	90.7	87.0
American Indian/ Alaska Native	<1.0	1.1	0.6	0.8	0.6	
Asian/Pacific Islander	<1.0	0.8	0.6	0.9	1.3	2.8
Hispanic	1.5	1.5	3.1	3.0	3.4	6.0
Other	<1.0	0.9	0.9	0.8	1.0	

Sources: Curtis, M. J., Castillo, J. M., & Gelley, C. (2012, May). School psychology 2010: Demographics, employment, and the context for professional practices: Part 1. *Communique, 40,* 1, 28–30; Walcott, C. M., Charvat, J., McNamara, K. M., & Hyson, D. (2016). *School psychology at a glance 2015: Member survey results.* Paper presented at the Annual Convention of the National Association of School Psychologists, New Orleans, LA.

graduate students during the 2015-to–2016 school year identified as racial and/ or ethnic minorities (Gadke et al., 2017). This percentage was consistent across specialist- and doctoral-level programs.

As described in Chapter 4, the diversification of the school psychology workforce has been far outpaced by that of the student and family populations served in U.S. public schools. To illustrate this discrepancy, the White population as a percentage of the total U.S. population declined from 80% to 66% from 1980 to 2008 (Aud, Fox, & Kewal Ramani, 2010). Some estimates suggest that Whites will account for less than half of the population by 2044, and more than half of all children will identify as members of minority groups by as early as 2020 (Colby & Ortman, 2015).

Similarly, as noted in Chapter 4, only 14% of school psychologists report fluency in a language other than English. Yet among them, only approximately 8% report providing multilingual school psychological services in that language; this represents only 1% of the entire sample of members (Walcott et al., 2016). Current trends suggest that the diversity of school psychologists will increase slowly, but the chasm between the diversity of school psychologists and that of the populations served will widen.

It is also worth noting that school psychology has increasingly become a female-majority profession. In 1990, 65% of NASP members identified as female. This percentage increased with each successive survey through the year 2015, in which 83% of NASP members identified as female (Walcott et al., 2016). Similarly, 85% of school psychology graduate students in 2015–2016 identified as female (Gadke et al., 2017). Notably, this trend is not unique to school psychology: Related professions in psychology (67.5% female), social work (81.5% female), and education (73% female) demonstrate a similar gender imbalance (Bureau of Labor Statistics, 2017a). Unfortunately, gender pay gaps persist, with women's median earnings remaining lower than the median earnings of men (Bureau of Labor Statistics, 2017b). More equity in pay will likely lead to an overall increase in the average salary, thereby improving recruitment and retention of high-quality professionals in the field.

SOCIAL JUSTICE CONNECTIONS

Why is it essential to increase the representation of culturally and linguistically diverse individuals in the field?

The field of school psychology has experienced longstanding shortages of school psychologists who identify as racial, ethnic, and linguistic minorities. In its most recent position statement, the National Association of School Psychologists (NASP, 2016a) recognized the need to increase the number of culturally and linguistically diverse (CLD) school psychologists. Ultimately, advocacy for initiatives that promote the diversification of school psychology are necessary at the local, state, and national levels. The following discussion provides several of the many possible and important answers to the question posed in this box.

1. As described in Chapter 4, the U.S. public school student body is rapidly diversifying. For example, there are approximately 350 languages spoken in the United States (U.S. Census Bureau, 2015). In the New York City (NYC) public schools alone, students speak approximately 180 different languages (NYC Department of Education, 2013). However, among surveyed NASP members, only 27 different languages were reported (Walcott et al., 2016). Increasing diversity among school psychologists will be necessary to provide culturally responsive services (e.g., bilingual assessment services) to an increasingly diverse student clientele.
2. Individuals from CLD backgrounds make critical contributions to identifying, investigating, and meeting the needs of students from these groups. For example, educators from racial, ethnic, and linguistic minority backgrounds bring unique insights to discussions of racism and ethnocentrism, among other issues that may impact the lives of minority students (Quiocho & Rios, 2000; Villegas, Strom, & Lucas, 2012). Moreover, research suggests that matching service providers and clients based on language, race, and ethnicity confers a number of benefits for clients when psychological services are adapted to account for clients' culture and context (Bernal, Jimenez-Chafey, & Domenech Rodriguez, 2009; Griner & Smith, 2006). (This does not mean that White, non-minority practitioners cannot be effective service providers to minority youth. All school psychologists must strive for cultural competence to meet the needs of youth in schools.)
3. CLD scholars have been essential to advancing a multicultural agenda in psychology. For example, Hartmann et al. (2013) estimated that nearly half of authors who contributed the most journal articles in ethnic minority psychology between 2003 and 2009 were ethnic minority scholars themselves. Given that racial and ethnic minority psychologists account for only approximately one fifth of the psychology workforce (APA, 2015), it is clear that scholars from these backgrounds have borne a disproportionate amount of responsibility for advancing this research. As noted in Chapter 4, writing about cultural and linguistic minority issues should not be the sole responsibility of minority scholars, although these scholars have certainly been critical champions of psychology's multicultural agenda. Continuing to make sure their voices are heard will be essential for promoting equity in psychological service delivery.
4. School psychologists from CLD backgrounds are important role models for all students and, in particular, for minority youth. For example, Covarrubias and Fryberg (2015) found that exposure to self-relevant models increased self-reported school belonging among Native American middle school students.
5. Increasing cultural and linguistic diversity in the workplace confers a number of positive benefits for school faculty and staff. For example, research indicates that intergroup contact (i.e., contact between individuals from different racial and ethnic backgrounds) may significantly reduce prejudice among individuals from diverse backgrounds (Pettigrew & Tropp, 2006). Specifically, Pettigrew and Tropp (2006) found that intergroup contact that met Allport's (1954) four optimal conditions was generally most impactful in facilitating prejudice reduction: (1) common goals; (2) equal status; (3) intergroup cooperation; and (4) support from authorities and societal customs. This research suggests that when essential conditions are met, increasing diversity among faculty and staff in school settings may contribute to the establishment of more positive, equitable, and productive work environments.

Professional Standards Will Continue to Evolve (Though at a Significantly Slower Rate Than the Profession)

As described in Chapter 3, professional standards define contemporary practices, promote effective and professional service delivery, and provide a foundation for the future of a field. In addition to NASP, which provides the most relevant standards for school psychology in the United States, the APA and the International School Psychology Association (ISPA) provide standards to help guide the profession.

Professional standards typically go through a significant review, revision, feedback, and approval process on an infrequent basis (e.g., every 10 years). Such infrequency allows for completion of the time-consuming development and implementation process, which can often take several years. However, this infrequency also makes standards less nimble and responsive to the frequent and ongoing changes in society, culture, and the field. As a result, standards typically are written in a way that allows for the profession to evolve without excessive restrictions or specificity. As an example, virtual service delivery methods (e.g., telepsychology and virtual assessments) have emerged in recent years, yet the standards merely maintain that any service provided should be evidence-based and valid for its intended use. It remains unlikely that standards will address such specific issues as whether virtual service delivery is allowed or recommended, as they would run the risk of becoming quickly obsolete given how swiftly the field changes. In addition to standards, the field typically relies on other tools, such as ongoing research, guidance documents, and shifting best practices, to support school psychologists with more specific, emerging trends.

Similarly, standards around practice have changed over time, though slightly. The NASP's (1984) *Standards for the Provision of School Psychological Services* described the need for comprehensive services, including assessment, research, program planning and evaluation, and direct and indirect services to individuals, groups, and organizations. The current practice standards from NASP (2010a), known as the *Model for Comprehensive and Integrated School Psychological Services* (i.e., the NASP Practice Model), include many of the same concepts, though they have been restructured to highlight different elements and expanded from earlier versions incrementally over time.

Despite the general stability of standards, some potential changes are worth monitoring. For example, we may begin to see standards related to program accreditation more directly addressing distance education. The NASP's (2010b) *Standards for the Graduate Preparation of School Psychologists* do not prohibit the use of distance education in any way, though they do make note of the requirement for "face-to-face" (p. 8) field supervision. It remains unclear whether live, synchronous, virtual video communication would be considered as meeting the "face-to-face" requirement, and future standards may address this issue more specifically. Conversely, the APA explicitly notes that its standards for doctoral programs "cannot be met in programs that are substantially or completely online" (APA, Commission on Accreditation, 2015, p. 9). As technology improves over time, and as more evidence emerges to either support or refute its equivalence to more traditional programs, those standards may change.

We may also see standards more directly address social and cultural influences, such as ensuring competency in issues related to cultural and linguistic diversity, social justice, professional advocacy, appropriate behavior and inter-actions on social media, and addressing conflicts between service delivery and personal beliefs (e.g., see Kaplan, 2014). Radical and significant changes to standards can be difficult to implement, however, so future changes are likely to occur in a slow, incremental basis.

The Role of the School Psychologist Will Evolve

Dating back to the early 1980s, school psychologists have struggled to identify a role that balances a focus on the traditional, individualized approach to special education service delivery with the broader range of preventive and early inter-vention services within a public health model of service delivery (as described in models such as MTSS). Although each successive revision of the NASP stand-ards has further emphasized the delivery of a comprehensive range of prevention and intervention services, special education compliance tends to dominate the school psychologist's role. In 2004 –2005, school psychologists reported that they spent more than 80% of their work time engaged in special education activities (Curtis et al., 2008). A decade later (2014–2015), individual evaluations for special education eligibility and participation in Individualized Education Program (IEP) development represented the two most frequent activities of school psycholo-gists (Walcott et al., 2016). The average number of reported special education evaluations dropped slightly during that same time period, from 69 (34.7 initial evaluations, 34.3 reevaluations; Curtis et al., 2008) to 60 (28 initial evaluations, 32 reevaluations; Walcott et al., 2016), though it is clear that a focus on special educa-tion service delivery remains an integral, if not primary, component of the school psychologist's role.

Several factors may help support a more noticeable trend toward comprehen-sive service delivery models. One particularly notable factor is the continued evo-lution of the NASP (2010a) Practice Model. Although NASP has long advocated for comprehensive services, the adoption of the 2010 *Standards* represented the first time that a model of service delivery was specified. This model is designed, in part, to improve the consistent implementation of school psychological ser-vices. Additionally, the Practice Model "delineates what services might reason-ably be expected to be available from most school psychologists and, thus, should help to further define the field" (NASP, 2010a, p. 2). Certainly, gaps continue to exist between the Practice Model and actual service delivery in schools. However, the Practice Model provides important benchmarks and avenues for advocacy to improve services and may serve as a critical tool in moving the needle. Given that the NASP Practice Model is up for review and revision by 2020 (and approxi-mately every 10 years), one could reasonably assume that the it will continue to evolve along with the field.

Every Student Succeeds Act

As described in Chapter 5, the Every Student Succeeds Act (ESSA), which took effect during the 2017–2018 school year, is a federal law that may provide unique opportunities for school psychologists. Some of the major changes most relevant to the field of school psychology include a focus on improved assessment and accountability systems, improved mechanisms for identifying and providing support to struggling schools, and an emphasis on improving students' access to comprehensive learning supports and safe and supportive school climates. Within each of these major areas, the law authorizes the utilization of practices that promote a more comprehensive role for school psychologists. Despite the promise of ESSA for expanding student supports, the law also returns a great deal of control to state and local jurisdictions, which may lead to inconsistency in how school psychologists are utilized across states. Maintaining a consistent set of practices across the United States is important for establishing a professional identity in schools and within the broader fields of psychology and education. Ultimately, assuming that opportunities for role expansion are available in local jurisdictions, school psychologists will need to embrace a more comprehensive repertoire of service delivery activities that expands beyond their traditional focus on assessment.

Contract Services

In a similar vein, the use of contract services to meet special education compliance will likely continue. Contract services are those provided by a third-party agency that is external to and hired by a school district. Typically, such services are limited to discrete, reimbursable, short-term tasks such as special education evaluations or counseling. These services typically do not include more expansive, long-term activities such as systems-level prevention and intervention, program evaluation, ongoing consultation, or crisis planning and response. Some school systems may rely on contract services to compensate for shortages in available school psychologists or to avoid hiring full-time employees. Regardless of schools' reasons for utilizing contract services, the most likely outcome of their continued use is a reduction in the quantity and quality of comprehensive services provided to students and families. Nevertheless, until school psychology shortages are ameliorated, the use of contract services is likely to continue, and perhaps even increase, in the near future.

Virtually Everything Virtual

Enrollments in state-led virtual school settings have grown exponentially in the United States (see Tysinger, Tysinger, Diamanduros, & Kennedy, 2013), with all 50 states and the District of Columbia providing some form of virtual learning opportunities to their students (Watson, Murin, Vashaw, Gemin, & Rapp, 2011). These students, like all others, are entitled to school psychological services. Most school psychologists, however, have little experience or training in applying skills within a virtual setting. More specifically, they know little about the tools available to support this type of work or how to navigate the credentialing issues that may arise when providing services across state lines (Tysinger et al., 2013). At present, those roles are currently filled by contracting school psychologists or those specially assigned to independent online programs (Kennedy, Tysinger, LaFrance, & Bailey, 2012).

In the meantime, new technologies have emerged related to online psychoeducational assessment as well as telepsychology. The APA (2013) defines **tele-psychology** as the delivery of psychological services via telecommunication technologies, which include, but are not limited to, telephone, mobile devices, videoconferencing, texting, and other Internet-based modalities. In fact, telepsychology services (e.g., *teleconsultation*, which is described in Chapter 11) have become a viable and effective option for service delivery. Telephone- and video-based therapy services have been effective in reducing symptoms of anxiety, depression, insomnia, and substance abuse (Lichstein et al., 2013; Rose, Skelly, Badger, Naylor, & Helzer, 2012; Silberbogen, Ulloa, Mori, & Brown, 2012). In addition, telehealth services have allowed individuals who are hampered by their location (e.g., rural settings) to receive services (Bischoff, Hollist, Smith, & Flack, 2004). In fact, one recent study indicated that some adolescents *preferred* online chat or text messaging to in-person or phone hotlines as methods of help seeking (Swearer, Smith, Rossen, & Germanotta, 2014).

In response to the increasing popularity of telepsychology, APA (2013) developed its *Guidelines for the Practice of Telepsychology*. These guidelines address issues related to competence, consent, confidentiality, secure data and record keeping, assessment, and practice across jurisdictions. The emerging trend of providing services at a distance or using technology will likely grow, particularly given its utility in reaching individuals who would otherwise have little to no access to mental health services.

In addition to seeing differences in how psychological services are provided, it is likely that the field will continue to see shifts in how school psychologists obtain their professional development. This change may result from an increase in the number of online professional development opportunities available, which allow for greater convenience and cost saving by eliminating the need to travel. Such online opportunities are likely to become increasingly adaptive and to utilize features such as ongoing discussion, resource sharing, and micro-learning (i.e., learning that occurs in smaller pieces at a time rather than in single, multihour sessions).

Finally, it is anticipated that technology increasingly may be used as a method of networking, providing mentorship and supervision, and even connecting with students and families. These types of connections have become ever more prevalent in social media forums in which school psychologists seek support from one another. Given that such shifts toward more technologically oriented service delivery will require changes in school infrastructure, legal and ethical requirements, knowledge and skills among practitioners, and comfort and trust among families, they are likely to occur gradually over time.

MAKE THE FUTURE: DON'T WAIT FOR IT!

Clearly, school psychology faces many potential challenges and opportunities as it seeks to move forward as a field. School psychologists often fail to recognize them, however, and sometimes feel constrained by current practices. Indeed, change may seem daunting, yet it is possible and often necessary. For example, consider that the 30-semester-hour master's degree was once regarded as the entry-level degree in school psychology. Over the course of merely a decade (beginning in the 1980s), regulations were changed in nearly all states to require the specialist level of training (i.e., approximately 60 semester-hour credits) to enter the field. Clearly, change can happen, and when it does, the ripple effects of those changes can be abrupt and far-reaching.

The change process should be given careful attention. Although change is inevitable, positive changes can lose momentum when we take them for granted or fail to nurture them. School psychologists must seek continuous improvement in their practices, tools, and professional standards to maintain their stake in educational decision making and service delivery. Moreover, they must take measures to embrace positive change while also maintaining practices that have proved effective and relevant over time. Ultimately, the future of our profession will be shaped by the actions (and inactions) of individuals both within and outside of school psychology. Although many of the predicted influences discussed in the preceding text may seem beyond the influence of individuals, the actions of individual school psychologists will significantly influence outcomes for school-age youth and the profession itself. The following recommendations are made to support school psychologists in shaping the future of the field.

1. **Start the year with specific goals for change.**
    At the beginning of each school year, develop at least one professional development goal and one systems-level goal. For example, you might decide to improve your knowledge of single-case designs for documenting student progress, increase your group counseling knowledge and skills, or update your knowledge of the neurobiology of reading disorders. Accomplishing these kinds of goals will invigorate your practice and keep your skills fresh. At the systems level, you might choose to increase the visibility of school psychology services on your school's website, develop a presentation to the Parent–Teacher Association or school board about a contemporary mental health issue (e.g., suicide prevention), or volunteer to coordinate a community group's school-based activities. Such activities increase the positive visibility of the profession within the district and the community, especially when local decision makers are aware of them. They also may increase your professional competence and career satisfaction.

2. **Stop doing things that don't make sense.**
    Solution-oriented counseling approaches adhere to a basic guideline: *If it is working, do it more. If it is not working, do something else* (e.g., Murphy, 2015). At times, school psychologists may find themselves caught in patterns of behavior that are not the most effective or efficient; however, institutional pressures and momentum may deter them from changing. For example, under Delaware regulations for special education, triennial reevaluation procedures do not require school psychologists to perform additional testing unless the IEP team determines that insufficient information is available to make relevant educational decisions. In many cases, reevaluations that involve extensive cognitive and achievement testing are not necessary, yet they often are undertaken (almost as a professional reflex). Alternatively, reevaluations could serve as important opportunities to move away from extensive testing and toward more responsive, problem-solving procedures. Making changes like this requires school psychologists

to be highly aware of their practice habits and the driving forces underlying those habits.

School psychologists can scrutinize many practices and habits in their daily work. For instance, they might ask themselves:

> How "user-friendly" are my psychological reports? Do parents really understand "informed consent" documents? Are my team meetings genuinely directed toward problem solving, or are they simply a vehicle for compliance with regulations? How is my school actively engaging families, especially those who experience the greatest barriers to participating?

Individual school psychologists can and should examine their work with an eye toward improvement and innovation. Such self-examination is an ethical responsibility and may lead to annual goals for change, as already discussed.

Taking these steps may not be easy. By its very nature, advocacy requires individuals to voice their concerns when staying silent may be easier or more comfortable. Advocating for change may be less daunting, however, when undertaken with colleagues, including school psychologists, related professionals (e.g., school counselors, school social workers), and other stakeholders (e.g., parents).

3. **Build alliances with colleagues.**
Many practitioners find that they are the only school psychologists in their building, or even in their district. This does not mean that they are without allies. Once you have a goal in mind, find out who in the school might share that goal. For example, teachers of students with disabilities, speech pathologists, and school social workers are natural allies in prevention and early intervention. Enlisting support from building and district administrators (e.g., principals) is important as well, given that these individuals have the greatest control over funding streams and resource allocation. Build a problem-solving team and then evaluate its success (e.g., through fewer referrals for evaluation, improved attendance, or reduced retentions). Using your knowledge of program evaluation and single-case design, you can both implement evidence-based practices and build practice-based evidence for their success. Align your goals with the interests and goals of those around you, and find common ground. These are the kinds of activities that will demonstrate your worth to administrators and allow you to shape your role in ways that are consistent with the NASP Practice Model.

Becoming active in local, state, and national associations is also essential. There is an oft-repeated saying of unknown source: *If you are not at the table, you are on the menu.* Professional organizations provide a pathway to the proverbial *table* by alerting members to legislative and regulatory initiatives and providing them with opportunities to influence these initiatives before they become law. Similarly, local associations may alert members to important school board meetings and other activities. Staying connected to colleagues through professional associations can build leadership skills, professional knowledge, and support networks. Perhaps most importantly, involvement in professional organizations provides opportunities to directly influence the future of school psychology and the futures of students and families.

SUMMARY AND CONCLUSIONS

School psychology has a rich history of professional self-examination and planning for the future. The field has made great strides in identifying a professional identity, developing and implementing standards that support that identity, and establishing the importance of school psychological services in producing positive outcomes for students. Many changes in school psychology's history can be traced to federal and state legislation (e.g., the Individuals with Disabilities Education Act, state credentialing requirements), changing social and cultural contexts (e.g., increased awareness of the impact of mental health on academic performance), and the evolution of professional standards and best practices. Notably, all of those factors remain interconnected and are likely to continually influence the future. Looking ahead, challenges remain with respect to shortages, adequate diversity among practitioners, and emerging technologies. Individual school psychologists, when working collaboratively with allied professionals and guided by the field's professional organizations, can be effective change agents who facilitate positive outcomes for children, families, and schools.

DISCUSSION QUESTIONS

1. What are some potential barriers to promoting positive change in the field of school psychology? What steps might be necessary to address those barriers?
2. Which components of school psychology practice should *not* be subject to change in the future? In other words, what should stay the same?
3. Shortages have remained a central threat to the school psychology field for decades. What do you see as the most critical step toward alleviating these shortages in the next 5 years?
4. How has your use of technology changed in recent years? In what ways do you see technology affecting your future practice?
5. Identify one professional development goal and one systems-level goal for your future practice (or graduate preparation). What steps do you need to take to begin realizing these goals? How will you know you are making progress?

REFERENCES

Allport, G. W. (1954). *The nature of prejudice*. Oxford , UK: Addison-Wesley.
American Psychological Association. (2013). Guidelines for the practice of telepsychology. *American Psychologist, 68*, 791–800. doi:10.1037/a0035001
American Psychological Association (2015). *Demographics of the U.S. psychology workforce: Findings from the American Community Survey*. Washington, DC: Author.

American Psychological Association, Commission on Accreditation. (2015). *Standards of accreditation for health service psychology.* Retrieved from http://www.apa.org/ed/accreditation/about/policies/standards-of-accreditation.pdf

Aud, S., Fox, M., & Kewal Ramani, A. (2010). *Status and trends in the education of racial and ethnic groups (NCES 2010–2015).* Washington, DC: U.S. Government Printing Office, National Center for Education Statistics, U.S. Department of Education.

Bernal, G., Jimenez-Chafey, M. I., & Domenech Rodriguez, M. M. (2009). Cultural adaptation of treatments: A resource for considering culture in evidence-based practice. *Professional Psychology: Research and Practice, 40,* 361–368. doi:10.1037/a0016401

Bevan, W. (1981). On coming of age among the professions. *School Psychology Review, 10,* 127–137.

Bischoff, R. J., Hollist, C. S., Smith, C. W., & Flack, P. (2004). Addressing the mental health needs of the underserved: Findings from a multiple case study of a behavioral telehealth project. *Contemporary Family Therapy, 26,* 179–198. doi:10.1023/B:COFT.0000031242.83259.fa

Bocanegra, J. O., Grapin, S. L., Nellis, L., M., & Rossen, E. (2017). A resource guide to remediating the school psychology shortages crisis. *Communique, 45,* 16–18.

Bocanegra, J., Rossen, E., & Grapin, S. L. (2017). *Factors associated with graduate students' decisions to enter school psychology* [Research report]. Bethesda, MD: National Association of School Psychologists.

Brown, D. T., & Minke, K. M. (1986). School psychology graduate training: A comprehensive analysis. *American Psychologist, 41,* 1328–1338.

Bureau of Labor Statistics. (2017a). *Labor force statistics from the current population survey.* Retrieved from https://www.bls.gov/cps/cpsaat11.htm

Bureau of Labor Statistics. (2017b). *Women's median earnings 82 percent of men's in 2016.* Retrieved from https://www.bls.gov/opub/ted/2017/womens-median-earnings-82-percent-of-mens-in-2016.htm

Bureau of Labor Statistics. (n.d.). *Job openings and labor turnover survey.* Retrieved from https://www.bls.gov/jlt

Castillo, J. M., Curtis, M. J., & Tan. S. Y. (2014). Personnel needs in school psychology: A 10-year follow-up study on predicted personnel shortages. *Psychology in the Schools, 51,* 832–849. doi:10.1002/pits.21786

Charvat, J. L. (2011). *Ratio of students per school psychologist by state: Data from the 2009–10 and 2004–05 NASP membership surveys.* Bethesda, MD: National Association of School Psychologists.

Colby, S. L., & Ortman, J. M. (2015). *Projections of the size and composition of the U.S. population: 2014 to 2060.* Washington, DC: U.S. Census Bureau. Retrieved from https://www.census.gov/content/dam/Census/library/publications/2015/demo/p25-1143.pdf

Covarrubias, R., & Fryberg, S. A. (2015). The impact of self-relevant representations on school belonging for Native American students. *Cultural Diversity and Ethnic Minority Psychology, 21,* 10–18. doi:10.1037/a0037819

Curtis, M. J., Castillo, J. M., & Gelley, C. (2012, May). School psychology 2010: Demographics, employment, and the context for professional practices: Part 1. *Communique, 40,* 1, 28–30.

Curtis, M. J., Grier, J. E. C., & Hunley, S. A. (2004). The changing face of school psychology: Trends in data and projections for the future. *School Psychology Review, 33,* 49–66.

Curtis, M. J., Lopez, A. D., Castillo, J. M., Batsche, G. M., Minch, D., & Smith, J. C. (2008). The status of school psychology: Demographic characteristics, employment conditions, professional practices, and continuing professional development. *Communiqué, 36,* 27–29.

Dawson, M., Cummings, J. A., Harrison, P. L., Short, R. J., Gorin, S., & Palomares, R. (2004). The 2002 multisite conference on the future of school psychology: Next steps. *School Psychology Review, 33,* 115–125.

Fagan, T. K. (2004). School psychology's significant discrepancy: Historical perspectives on personnel shortages. *Psychology in the Schools, 41,* 419–430. doi:10.1002/pits.10185

Fagan, T. K. (2005). The 50th anniversary of the Thayer Conference: Historical perspectives and accomplishments. *School Psychology Quarterly, 20,* 224–251. doi:10.1521/scpq.2005.20.3.224

Gadke, D. L., Valley-Gray, S., & Rossen, E. (2016). *NASP annual report of graduate education in school psychology: 2014–2015* [Research report]. Bethesda, MD: National Association of School Psychologists.

Gadke, D. L., Valley-Gray, S., & Rossen, E. (2017). *NASP annual report of graduate education in school psychology: 2015–2016*. Manuscript submitted for publication.

Graden, J. L. (2004). Synthesis and commentary: Arguments for change to consultation, prevention, and intervention: Will school psychology every achieve this promise? *Journal of Educational and Psychological Consultation, 154*, 345–359. doi:10.1080/10474412.2004.9669522

Grimes, J. (1981). Shaping the future of school psychology. *School Psychology Review, 10*(2), 206–231.

Griner, D., & Smith, T. (2006). Culturally adapted mental health interventions: A meta-analytic review. *Psychotherapy: Theory, Research, Practice, Training, 43*, 531–548. doi:10.1037/0033-3204.43.4.531

Hartmann, W. E., Kim, E. S., Kim, J. H. J., Nguyen, T. U., Wendt, D. C., Nagata, D. K., & Gone, J. P. (2013). In search of cultural diversity, revisited: Recent publication trends in cross-cultural and ethnic minority psychology. *Review of General Psychology, 3*, 243–254.

Health Service Psychology Education Collaborative. (2013). Professional psychology in health care services: A blueprint for education and training. *American Psychologist, 68*, 411–426. doi:10.1037/a0033265

Hendricker, E., Saeki, E., & Viola, S. (2017). Trends and perceptions of distance learning in school psychology. *Trainers' Forum: Journal of the Trainers of School Psychologists, 34*, 36–68.

Hughes, T. L., & Minke, K. M. (2014). Blueprint for health service psychology education and training: School psychology's response. *Training and Education in Professional Psychology, 8*, 26–30.

Kaplan, D. K. (2014). Ethical implications of a critical legal case for the counseling profession: *Ward v. Wilbanks*. *Journal of Counseling and Development, 92*, 142–146.

Kennedy, K., Tysinger, D., LaFrance, J., & Bailey, C. (2012). Preparing education professionals for K–12 online learning. In M. Orey, S. A. Jones, & R. M. Branch (Eds.), *Educational media and technology yearbook*. New York, NY: Springer Publishing.

Lambert, N. (1981). School psychology training for the decades ahead, or rivers, streams, and creeks: Currents and tributaries to the sea. *School Psychology Review, 10*, 194–205.

Lichstein, K. L., Scogin, F., Thomas, S. J., DiNapoli, E. A., Dillon, H. R., & McFadden, A. (2013). Telehealth cognitive behavior therapy for co-occurring insomnia and depression symptoms in older adults. *Journal of Clinical Psychology, 69*, 1056–1065. doi:10.1002/jclp.22030

Murphey, D., Vaughn, B., & Barry, M. (2013). Adolescent health highlight: Access to mental health care. Retrieved from https://www.childtrends.org/wp-content/uploads/2013/04/Child_Trends-2013_01_01_AHH_MHAccessl.pdf

Murphy, J. J. (2015). *Solution-focused counseling in schools* (3rd ed.). Alexandria, VA: American Counseling Association.

National Association of School Psychologists. (1984). *Standards for the provision of school psychological services*. Washington, DC: Author.

National Association of School Psychologists. (2010a). *Model for comprehensive and integrated school psychological services*. Bethesda, MD: Author.

National Association of School Psychologists. (2010b). *Standards for graduate preparation of school psychologists*. Bethesda, MD: Author.

National Association of School Psychologists. (2016a). *Recruitment and retention of culturally and linguistically diverse school psychologists in graduate education programs* [Position statement]. Bethesda, MD: Author.

National Association of School Psychologists. (2016b). Shortages in school psychology resource guide. Retrieved from: https://www.nasponline.org/resources-and-publications/resources/school-psychology/shortages-in-school-psychology-resource-guide

National Association of School Psychologists. (2017, April). Social justice [Webpage]. Retrieved from http://www.nasponline.org/resources-and-publications/resources/diversity/social-justice

New York City Department of Education, Office of English Language Learners. (2013). Demographic report. Retrieved from http://schools.nyc.gov/NR/rdonlyres/FD5EB945-5C27-44F8-BE4B-E4C65D7176F8/0/2013DemographicReport_june2013_revised.pdf

Pettigrew, T. F., & Tropp, L. R. (2006). A meta-analytic test of intergroup contact theory. *Journal of Personality and Social Psychology, 90*, 751–783. doi:10.1037/0022-3514.90.5.751

Quiocho, A., & Rios, F. (2000). The power of their presence: Minority group teachers and schooling. *Review of Educational Research, 70*, 485–528.

Rose, G. L., Skelly, J. M., Badger, G. J., Naylor, M. R., & Helzer, J. E. (2012). Interactive voice response for relapse prevention following cognitive-behavioral therapy for alcohol use disorders: A pilot study. *Psychological Services, 9*, 174–184. doi:10.1037/a0027606

Rossen, E., & von der Embse, N. (2014). Status of school psychology graduate education in the United States. In A. Thomas & P. Harrison (Eds.), *Best practices in school psychology: Foundations* (pp. 503–512). Bethesda, MD: National Association of School Psychologists.

Schaefer, M. (1982). Improving the shape of school psychology: A practitioner's viewpoint. *School Psychology Review, 11*, 132–135.

Silberbogen, A. K., Ulloa, E., Mori, D. L., & Brown, K. (2012). A telehealth intervention for veterans on antiviral treatment for the hepatitis C virus. *Psychological Services, 9*, 163–173. doi:10.1037/a0026821

Swearer, S. M., Smith, M. H., Rossen, E., & Germanotta, C. (2014, August). Born brave: Mental health help-seeking preferences among youth. In S. M. Swearer (chair), *Born brave bus tour: A mobile youth empowerment experience.* Symposium conducted at the meeting of the American Psychological Association, Washington, DC.

Trachtman, G. (1981). On such a full sea. *School Psychology Review, 10*, 138–181.

Tysinger, P. D., Tysinger, J. A., Diamanduros, T. D., & Kennedy, K. (2013). K–12 online learning and the training needs for school psychology practitioners. *School Psychology Forum: Research to Practice, 7*, 76–88.

U.S. Census Bureau. (2015). Census Bureau reports at least 350 languages spoken in U.S. homes (Release Number: CB15-185). Retrieved from https://www.census.gov/newsroom/press-releases/2015/cb15-185.html

Villegas, A. M., Strom, K., & Lucas, T. (2012). Closing the racial/ethnic gap between students of color and their teachers: An elusive goal. *Equity and Excellence in Education, 45*, 283–301.

Walcott, C. M., Charvat, J., McNamara, K. M., & Hyson, D. (2016). *School psychology at a glance 2015: Member survey results.* Paper presented at the Annual Convention of the National Association of School Psychologists, New Orleans, LA.

Walcott, C., Hyson, D., & Loe, S. (2017). *The state of school psychology: Results from the NASP 2015 member survey.* Manuscript in preparation.

Watson, J., Murin, A., Vashaw, L., Gemin, B., & Rapp, C. (2011). *Keeping pace with K–12 online learning: An annual review of policy and practice.* Evergreen, CO: Evergreen Consulting. Retrieved from http://www. kpk12.com

CHAPTER 14

Preparing for a Career in School Psychology

DIANA JOYCE-BEAULIEU ■ ALEXA DIXON

CHAPTER OBJECTIVES

- Delineate the range of career options in school psychology
- Review considerations in selecting graduate training programs and degree tracks
- Identify strategies for optimizing specialized coursework and supervised clinical experiences aligned with career goals
- Discuss considerations for mentorship that enhances professional skills and scholarly productivity to facilitate acquisition of competitive internships and jobs
- Provide guidance on acquiring preservice social justice advocacy knowledge and skills

As described throughout the preceding chapters, there are several diverse career options within the field of school psychology. Some of these career options involve working in pre-K–12 school settings, whereas others involve working in hospitals, private practice, postsecondary institutions, and other settings. Early awareness of career options in school psychology allows preservice professionals to prepare themselves for the jobs of their choosing. This chapter reviews various career opportunities in school psychology as well as considerations for choosing coursework, field experiences, and other training experiences that are aligned with these paths. Additionally, it presents strategies for representing one's professional qualifications and experiences (i.e., through the development of a résumé or curriculum vitae [CV; plural: curricula vitae]).

CHOOSING A CAREER PATH IN SCHOOL PSYCHOLOGY: GENERAL CONSIDERATIONS

Recall from Chapter 1 that the majority of school psychology practitioners are employed in public school settings. Results from the most recent membership survey of the National Association of School Psychologists (NASP) indicated that 86% of members are practitioners in public schools (Walcott, Charvat, McNamara, & Hyson, 2016). Moreover, in a survey polling early-career NASP members ($N = 688$), 94% identified as school-based practitioners (Guiney, 2010). In addition to working in public schools, school psychologists may be employed in a variety of other educational settings. For example, school psychologists may work in colleges and universities to provide assessment and educational planning services to students with disabilities (Joyce & Grapin, 2012; Joyce-Beaulieu & Grapin, 2014; Sulkowski & Joyce, 2012). They also may be employed in schools on armed forces' military bases, which serve children of personnel. In these roles, they may provide a wide range of services similar to those provided in other pre-K–12 settings.

In addition, professionals with school psychology degrees may have opportunities to work in a variety of nonschool settings (NASP, n.d.). These opportunities typically are available to school psychologists with doctoral-level training and who are eligible for a psychologist's state license (although, as noted in Chapter 3, non-doctoral-level practitioners in some states are permitted to provide a limited scope of services in private practice settings). The psychologist's license offers broader career opportunities within public health agencies, clinics, hospitals, community agencies, and academia. Community agencies employing psychologists can include mental health centers, initiatives for at-risk youth, and some adjudicated youth programs. Positions within hospitals more often involve diagnosis and crisis intervention with an emphasis on short-term service provision, whereas outpatient clinics are treatment oriented and extend services over a longer period of time. Psychologists in private practice may offer a broader range of assessment and intervention services or specialized care for specific populations (e.g., children with autism spectrum disorders and children with chronic and severe medical conditions). Individuals with doctoral training also may hold faculty positions in college and university settings, which focus on teaching and conducting research in school psychology and related disciplines.

Individuals who are interested in a career in school psychology should consider their personal interests, goals, values, and even personality characteristics. Some individuals may gravitate toward more direct service provision roles (i.e., applied practice), whereas others may prefer the more theoretical orientation of research discovery. Alternatively, some individuals may choose to blend research and practice roles, and many change specialization interests and professional positions throughout their career. Given the compelling need for high-quality educational and psychological service providers and innovators, school psychologists fulfill a wide range of roles across many different types of settings.

FIELD-BASED PRACTITIONER CAREERS

General Considerations

Typically, school psychologists with non-doctoral degrees work in K–12 school-based settings. Although there are many similarities among the roles and job characteristics of school psychologists employed nationwide, there is also considerable variability. For example, school psychologists employed in schools exclusively for students with emotional and behavioral disabilities may spend more time implementing school-wide behavioral intervention programs and delivering counseling services than conducting special education eligibility assessments. Conversely, some school psychologists spend a considerable amount of time engaged in special education eligibility activities (although this excessive focus on assessment at the cost of intervention delivery may suggest a need for systems-level reform; Walcott et al., 2016).

Moreover, some school psychologists may work for the duration of the academic year only (e.g., 9 months), whereas others may work year-around (e.g., 12 months). In a survey of school-based practitioners, approximately 50% held a 9-month contract, whereas roughly 25% held a 10- or 11-month contract and the remaining 25% held a 12-month contract (Walcott et al., 2016). As public school systems generally follow a 9-month schedule, school psychologists with 10-, 11-, or 12-month contracts are likely to have additional administrative roles (e.g., professional development preparation and district policy advisement) in the summer months. These may be important considerations for selecting job opportunities.

Like the contract length, the type of contract that school psychologists hold may differ across districts. In some districts, school psychologists work under a teacher union contract; in others, they are employed under an administrative contract. Although seemingly a minor detail, the type of contract may affect the school psychologist's roles, responsibilities, and salary. Generally, school psychologists employed under union contracts have more formalized daily hour guidelines. Conversely, school psychologists employed within a district's administrative track may be expected to work more hours and to remain available for meetings during nontraditional hours (e.g., for on-call emergencies and evening school board meetings). Practitioners employed through administrative contracts also may be more likely to participate in district policy decision making and, ultimately, better positioned to advance to higher-level district administrative positions.

Considerations for Degree Types and Credentials

As described in Chapter 3, school psychologists can practice at the non-doctoral or doctoral level; however, in some states, a doctoral degree is needed to practice outside of primary and secondary school settings. In all states, school psychologists with non-doctoral degrees are permitted to provide services in K–12 schools, and in some states, they are permitted to work in private practice, pending the completion of required postdegree work experiences (e.g., Florida). However, individuals who wish to work in hospitals, clinics, and other nonschool settings may need to obtain a doctoral degree and subsequently pursue licensure as a psychologist. In many cases, degree requirements are determined by the setting in which the practitioner provides services. Chapter 3 provides more information on training and credentialing for non-doctoral and doctoral-level school psychologists.

Considerations for Specialized Coursework

When planning coursework and selecting specializations, awareness of the resources available through universities and graduate programs is critical. Typically, students select a specialty from a list of approved areas and then select course offerings within those areas. Alternatively, some programs allow students to create their own specializations (which are subject to approval by academic advisors). In these cases, students may synthesize a program of study from course offerings across departments, schools, or colleges within their institutions. As students plan their coursework and specialization areas, it is strongly advised that they keep their career goals in mind. For example, students who are interested in working with a specific population (e.g., early childhood or ethnically and racially diverse populations) should pursue coursework relevant to serving these populations (e.g., preschool child development and multiculturalism).

Likewise, if a student desires to work with clients in specific age groups or grade levels, having knowledge of developmental factors, contextual and environmental factors, and risk factors relevant to those groups is important. For example, practitioners who wish to work primarily with middle and high school students should be knowledgeable about important life events and developmental milestones relevant to adolescents. Such milestones may include the onset of puberty and the transition from elementary school (i.e., typically a highly structured environment) to middle and high school (typically less structured environments that afford students greater independence). During this transition, students face new social demands, academic expectations, and daily routines, among other changes. Additionally, half of all lifetime mental health syndromes emerge in childhood or adolescence, and three fourths emerge prior to adulthood (American Psychiatric Association, 2013; Kessler et al., 2005). Each syndrome has very specific developmental windows (e.g., preschool, early childhood, adolescence). Thus, it is important for practitioners working with adolescents to be highly familiar with the prevalent diagnoses and early symptom indicators for this age range (see Joyce-Beaulieu & Sulkowski, 2015, for a thorough review of diagnoses and their prevalence by age and grade level).

In addition to familiarizing themselves with the unique developmental issues that adolescents face, practitioners must be knowledgeable about the legal, ethical, professional, administrative, and systems-level issues that impact middle and high school settings. These issues include matters related to accountability, state testing practices, academic standards and curricula, and postsecondary transition planning. For instance, educational law requires that school personnel develop postsecondary transition plans for adolescents with disabilities—something that is not required for younger children (Joyce & Grapin, 2012; Joyce-Beaulieu & Grapin, 2014). Overall, aligning training experiences and coursework with career aspirations can better prepare individuals to be highly competitive for selective internships and job opportunities.

Considerations for Specialized Field Placements

In addition to coursework, field experiences are critical for preparing students for future employment. Recall from Chapter 3 that students generally complete two types of field experiences: *practica* (early to middle part of graduate preparation) and *internship* (end of graduate preparation). Graduate students typically complete practica within communities surrounding their graduate programs. Through these practica, school psychology graduate students have opportunities to serve children and adolescents across a range of ages and grade levels in the local schools.

Although placement sites ultimately may be assigned by program faculty and/ or practicum coordinators, students may benefit from researching the university's surrounding communities and populations to identify training sites that are an ideal match for their professional interests. For example, surrounding schools may serve a variety of populations (e.g., racially and ethnically diverse populations) and communities (e.g., urban, rural, and suburban communities) and, therefore, may offer different types of training opportunities (e.g., opportunities for bilingual assessment). When students complete their practica in settings with unique characteristics and training experiences, they have opportunities to develop more specialized competencies beyond the range of core competencies required of generalist practitioners.

In addition to considering differences between districts and communities, school psychology graduate students should consider unique opportunities offered within districts. For example, some districts offer highly specialized educational programs for specific populations of students (e.g., early childhood populations and students with low-incidence disabilities). Additionally, resources within the district should be considered. For example, some districts have strong partnerships with community agencies and clinics—which also may open doors to valuable training opportunities.

Typically, graduate students have even more options for internship sites than for practicum sites, as they may leave the university's immediate surroundings to complete this experience. For internship, students may consider seeking sites in the states in which they ultimately intend to hold employment,. so that they can gain familiarity with state-specific practices and requirements. Moreover, if communities surrounding the university are fairly homogeneous or offer few opportunities to achieve the desired training, students can seek these types of experiences elsewhere during their internship. Ultimately, graduate students should strive to identify field experiences that facilitate their achievement of specific career goals.

Considerations for Identifying Mentors and Supervisors

Mentors can provide invaluable supports to school psychology graduate students. Mentorship can be formal or informal, and can be provided by a variety of individuals. Some graduate training programs will assign students a peer mentor (typically an advanced graduate student) who offers guidance or advice on a variety of topics, such as program acclimation, socialization opportunities, potential training routes, and school–life balance. In addition to formally assigned peer mentors, students may seek informal peer mentors. When selecting peer mentors, students should identify individuals who share their interests or professional aspirations.

While these relationships should not replace those with academic advisors and other faculty mentors, they can help support graduate students in many aspects of professional development (Joyce-Beaulieu & Rossen, 2016).

Mentoring relationships with faculty also are important for fostering successful training outcomes. Faculty members are well versed in program requirements and progress expectations, and they often have the resources to connect students with important career opportunities. Faculty members also can guide students in navigating the institution's deadlines, formal processes, and resources. As an example, many universities provide on-campus career centers as a resource. These centers typically offer interview recording and coaching, access to a wide range of employment listservs and resources, and guidance on professional interactions.

Sometimes faculty mentors are assigned by programs; however, students may be encouraged to change advisors as their professional interests evolve. Inquiring about faculty specializations and projects may help inform students' selection of potential mentors. Additionally, it is feasible to connect with faculty mentors both within and outside of the graduate program. Opportunities to network with other faculty and practitioners can be facilitated through professional association memberships, online special-interest groups, and professional conferences. Individuals contacted through these venues can help students build specialized skills and knowledge, particularly if they have expertise in a desirable area. Furthermore, they may be able to provide letters of recommendation, access to early career opportunities, and information about training sites. Ultimately, synthesizing networks of diverse mentors may afford students access to valuable information and expertise.

Additionally, mentorship may be fostered through professional relationships with practica site supervisors, administrators, or other personnel. Throughout practica experiences, these individuals can offer both informal and formal mentorship and supervision. High-quality supervision is essential for professional development, and NASP (2011) encourages school psychologists at all levels, including novice and expert levels, to seek supervision. More specifically, NASP (2011) outlines two types of supervision: professional and administrative. **Professional supervision** focuses on developing the protégé's knowledge and skills in providing professional services (e.g., psychological and educational service delivery to children and families), while **administrative supervision** emphasizes developing skills in maintaining the organizational unit, such as personnel, legal, contractual, and other systems-level issues (NASP, 2011). It is recommended that students in school psychology graduate programs receive both types of supervision from more senior faculty and practitioners in their practicum settings (NASP, 2011).

In general, supervision serves to build and improve skills as well as to promote collaborative relationships that foster the protégé's sense of responsibility and independence (Harvey & Struzziero, 2008). While supervisory relationships are hierarchical by nature, they should also be collaborative (Harvey & Struzziero, 2008). When identifying potential supervisors, graduate students should consider the areas of expertise, interpersonal styles, job roles, and supervision styles of these individuals. For example, supervisees should consider the supervisor's credentials, ability to offer constructive feedback, preferred modalities of supervision (e.g., group, individual, face-to-face, or electronically mediated supervision), and approaches to evaluating performance (Harvey & Struzziero, 2008). Students who are seeking supervision for licensing purposes may need to secure a supervisor who has specific credentials (e.g., doctoral degree and licensure) and who can dedicate a minimum number of hours to individual and/or group supervision. To ensure that both the supervisee and the supervisor have a clear understanding of expectations, both parties should explicitly discuss and agree upon the terms of the relationship at the outset of training (Harvey & Struzziero, 2008).

ACADEMIC CAREERS

General Considerations

Historically, only a small percentage of school psychologists have been employed in academia (Clopton & Haselhuhn, 2009). Presently, there are shortages of graduate faculty in school psychology, and recent estimates indicate that half of the field's current faculty members will retire by 2025 (Castillo, Curtis, & Tan, 2014). If these predictions come true, faculty shortages can beexpected to worsen over the next decade (Castillo et al., 2014). Although concerning for the field as a whole, these conditions make for a promising job market for aspiring academic school psychologists (Little, & Akin-Little, 2004; Merrell, Erwin, & Gimpel Peacock, 2012).

The job responsibilities of most academics comprise three primary activities: teaching, research, and service (e.g., activities that support program and university functioning). A variety of factors may influence the amount of time that faculty members devote to each of these activities. For example, faculty in tenure-track positions typically are expected to devote more time to research activities than non–tenure-track faculty. Traditionally, tenure-track positions require faculty to spend approximately 50% of their time conducting research, approximately 20% to 40% of their time teaching, and approximately 10% of their time engaging in service (Harris & Sullivan, 2012). Conversely, non–tenure-track faculty often are expected to devote greater amounts of time to teaching and program coordination activities.

The percentage of time that academics spend engaged in research, teaching, and service activities also varies by institution type. For example, faculty in doctoral-granting, research-intensive universities often spend large portions of time engaged in research activities. This is, in part, because doctoral students must engage in supervised research activity to meet their degree requirements. Conversely, faculty employed in smaller, less research-intensive institutions may spend more time engaged in teaching and service activities. Recent trends in faculty assignments, however, suggest that roles are becoming increasingly diverse and variable, with higher education institutions employing research faculty, clinical faculty (whose roles are primarily supervisory in nature), lecturers, and program administrators (Harris, Shriberg, Ogg, Newton, & Sullivan, 2012).

To fulfill their teaching obligations, faculty may teach in a variety of modalities, including traditional lecture, group discussion, and online formats. In fact, some school psychology programs (SPPs) offer significant portions of their curricula through distance education classes. Faculty who teach school psychology courses must possess effective communication skills, in-depth knowledge of the content they are teaching, and a firm command of pedagogical techniques. In SPPs, teaching activities also include supervisory responsibilities, wherein the faculty member oversees students' completion of practica or internship experiences. This involves collaborating with field placement supervisors to foster students' skill development in a variety of practice areas. Individuals who aspire to local or national recognition for their teaching may apply for training grants, develop innovative curricula, assume leadership roles in training policy or program accreditation, or produce scholarship (publications and conference presentations) related to best practices in graduate education.

Research also is a major activity for many faculty—and in particular, for those faculty whose job performance is evaluated based on scholarly productivity. The goal of many of these faculty members is to build a program of research that generates innovative knowledge, scholarship, and applications for practice. The type of research pursued by faculty members varies, with some pursuing more theoretical agendas and others, more applied agendas. (Applied agendas generally involve research that has more immediate and direct applications to school psychology practice.) Research-active faculty members usually are expected to mentor undergraduate and graduate students (often doctoral students), who serve as research assistants and facilitate the implementation of research activities. Individuals who wish to develop national recognition for their research may engage in designing and implementing multifaceted or cross-disciplinary research projects, acquiring grants to fund research teams, and publishing journal articles, conference proceedings, books, book chapters, and other scholarship.

The third component of academic appointments is service. Faculty members may engage in service both within their institutions and at the national level. Within the institution, faculty members may engage in service at the program level, department level, college/school level, and university level. Service within institutions typically involves serving as a member or leader on various committees (e.g., curriculum, award, and personnel advisory committees) at one or more organizational levels. Program-level service may involve revising curricula, engaging in academic advising, and preparing for accreditation processes. Individuals who engage in service on a national level may serve in advocacy or policy development roles for national and international associations, such as NASP and the American Psychological Association (APA). Examples of this type of service include significant contributions to the development of national standards, policy position papers, accreditation regulations, and state and national educational or mental health provision law. Other types of service include engaging in editorial work for school psychology journals, such as serving as an editor or reviewing articles. Overall, there is considerable variation in the roles and responsibilities of faculty members, all of which are important for sustaining the future of research and graduate preparation in school psychology.

Considerations for Degree Types and Credentials

Most university academic positions will require the highest terminal degree for a discipline. In school psychology, this is the doctoral degree. Moreover, program faculty with clinical supervision roles may need licensure for practice, which often requires a doctorate. If one's career goal is to obtain an academic position at a research-intensive institution, it is advantageous to pursue a doctoral degree from an institution with a strong research emphasis and considerable grant activity.

Considerations for Specialized Coursework

As for all school psychologists, foundational coursework in the practice and profession of school psychology is critical for aspiring academics (and will be provided in any NASP-approved or APA-accredited program). Regarding specialized coursework, advance consideration of the type of academic position desired (e.g., predominantly teaching or research-intensive position) may be helpful to students in selecting their courses. Generally, for all types of positions, knowledge of adult teaching strategies, clinical supervision skills, statistical and research design methodologies, and writing skills is essential. Moreover, courses that prepare for licensure (e.g., psychopharmacology, assessment, and counseling) and passing the national psychologist's exam (i.e., Examination for Professional Practice of Psychology [EPPP]) may be beneficial for students seeking academic roles that include direct clinical supervision. For individuals with a strong interest in pursuing research or student training grants, a course on grant writing may be informative. Of course, students who plan to pursue research-intensive positions may wish to complete specialized coursework in their anticipated areas of research. Additionally, students who wish to pursue academic positions specific to research and practice with certain populations (e.g., autism spectrum disorders, early childhood), academic needs (e.g., learning disabilities), or mental health challenges (e.g., attention-deficit/hyperactivity disorder [ADHD]) should consider completing specialized coursework in these areas.

Considerations for Specialized Field Placements

Seeking appropriate practica experiences also can strengthen an applicant's résumé (or CV) for competitive internships and career positions. Similar to specialized coursework, practica may allow students to explore service delivery in relation to specific populations, diagnoses, settings, or educational delivery models. Additionally, practica sites may be an ideal source of research data (e.g., dissertation data), especially when the student's clinical and research interests are interrelated. A collaborative discussion with program faculty and field placement supervisors regarding individual training needs may help facilitate practica placements that support the student's career goals. Field placement supervisors also can serve as highly qualified references for internship and job applications.

Considerations for Identifying Mentors and Supervisors

Graduate students who aspire to become faculty members should select their mentors carefully. In particular, they should consider the research, teaching, and clinical skills of potential mentors. For students who wish to pursue research-intensive positions, receiving close mentorship in research design, methods, data analysis, publication, and grant writing is especially important. For individuals interested in pursuing teaching-oriented faculty positions, opportunities for supervised teaching experience and mentorship by highly regarded instructors will be critical. Students who desire faculty positions with clinical supervision responsibilities should seek mentorship from field-based supervisors who can foster the development of specialized practice competencies as well as provide guidance on the pursuit of essential credentials (e.g., licensure). For all students interested in faculty positions (regardless of position type), opportunities to copublish scholarship, copresent at conferences, and collaborate on service activities can be beneficial for preparing for future leadership in the field. Faculty mentors also can provide guidance on locating job listings, corresponding with search committees, and preparing for on- and off-campus interviews. Faculty members with strong professional networks may be able to assist students in connecting with other scholars and practitioners in the field who can advance their careers. Moreover, students who are highly involved in professional organizations and interest groups may be able to seek multiple mentors through these venues.

Research, Publishing, and Conference Presentations

Regardless of the specific type of academic position desired, research, publishing, and conference presentations are likely to play a major role in acquiring that first faculty position and building toward national recognition. Thus, building experience in research, publishing, and presentation during graduate school is important. In strong mentorship relationships, the graduate student's advisor or supervisor is mindful of facilitating these experiences through a scaffolded process. Initially, the graduate student may assist with journal article or presentation development (e.g., through data collection and literature reviews), with the goal of eventually serving as first author on these types of scholarship. Thus, choosing mentors who are open to collaboration with students is essential.

Faculty members may produce a variety of scholarship, including journal articles, books and book chapters, conference presentations, technical reports, and treatment manuals, among other works. Generally, scholarship that undergoes peer review is more highly regarded than work that is not peer reviewed. ***Peer review*** refers to a process in which experts in a particular field vet the scholarly work of others to ensure that it has acceptable quality and scientific rigor. Generally, there are three types of peer review: double-blind review, single-blind review, and open review. In a ***double-blind peer review***, the authors of the work are anonymous to the reviewers, and vice versa. This type of review generally is regarded as the most rigorous type of peer review, as it reduces potential bias in the review process and allows for a more candid dialogue between reviewers and authors. In a ***single-blind peer review***, only one party is anonymous to the other. (Typically, the reviewers are anonymous to the authors, but the reviewers have identifying information about the authors.) Finally, om an ***open peer review***, all parties are mutually aware of the others' identities. Most major scholarly outlets in school psychology (i.e., reputable journals and conference platforms) utilize a double-blind review process.

The number of research projects, publications, and presentations that students must complete during graduate school to be competitive for an academic position is not concretely defined and varies by discipline. Relatively little is known about the average number of publications produced by candidates seeking their first job as a school psychology faculty member; however, there are normative data on faculty productivity in the field. Grapin, Kranzler, and Daley (2013) examined the scholarly output of core faculty members in APA-accredited SPPs between 2005 and 2009. They found that, on average, faculty published

5.8 articles during this 5-year window, meaning that these faculty members published approximately 1.2 articles per year, on average. Assistant professors (who typically are in their first to seventh years of employment) produced an average of 3.9 articles during the 5-year window, which equates to 0.78 article per year. Notably, this study examined only the scholarly productivity of faculty in APA-accredited programs, which are likely to be housed in research-intensive, doctoral-granting institutions (rather than non-doctoral, teaching-focused institutions). To date, little research has explored the productivity of faculty outside of APA-accredited SPPs. It is also worth noting that this study examined only publications in peer-reviewed journals and did not include any other types of scholarship (e.g., book chapters).

Conference presentations also are an important form of scholarship in the field of school psychology. From the perspective of a faculty search committee, the perceived value of conference presentations likely will vary by the breadth of the target audience (e.g., national conferences versus state conferences), the presentation content (original research versus literature review), and the rigor of the conference's review process (e.g., double blind, single blind, or open review). Given the emphasis on research, publishing, and conference presentations as benchmarks for faculty achievement, acquiring experience in developing this type of scholarship during one's graduate education can provide the candidate with a significant advantage during job searches.

Involvement in research and other forms of scholarship requires a considerable amount of work, especially given that graduate students also are expected to balance the demands of practica and coursework at the same time. What can graduate students do to stay productive and to ensure that they are adequately prepared to enter the professoriate? Martínez, Floyd, and Erichsen (2011) surveyed 94 highly productive scholars in the field of school psychology regarding experiences and behaviors that contributed to their success in publishing. Many participants identified their graduate school experiences as critical to their preparation for academia. In particular, these individuals noted that practicing academic writing and advanced statistical methods through their coursework was integral to their success. Many of the participants also noted that connecting with highly productive mentors who encouraged them to publish early on in their graduate education was essential. Other strategies that emerging scholars may find helpful include (a) scheduling time specifically for manuscript writing and adhering to the schedule; (b) becoming well versed in the range and characteristics of publication outlets in school psychology; (c) identifying collaborators with complementary areas of expertise; (d) responding proactively to feedback from colleagues, mentors, and peer reviewers; and (e) remaining abreast of new developments in the field and regularly reading a wide variety of scholarship (Martínez et al., 2011).

ADDITIONAL CAREER OPTIONS

This chapter has noted that the most common career path for school psychologists is geared toward the role of practitioner. Practitioners are mostly likely to work in schools, hospitals/clinics, community agencies/programs, or private practice. Additionally, a smaller, yet significant proportion of school psychologists pursue faculty positions in graduate programs. However, there are other career opportunities within the profession, such as employment in military base schools (i.e., positions acquired through the U.S. Department of Defense), international schools (www.iss.edu; www.internationalschooljobs.com), and incarcerated youth programs through the state prison systems. Additionally, national psychology organizations, such as NASP, offer advocacy and administrative positions within their institutions. Individuals who are interested in these types of employment should seek mentors with similar backgrounds and/or reach out to these organizations for more information about job roles and opportunities.

SOCIAL JUSTICE CONNECTIONS

How can preservice school psychologists prepare to become social justice agents?

Social justice advocacy requires strong foundational knowledge of school-based social issues as well as skills in coordinating systems change. Graduate preparation programs and professional organizations in school psychology offer many opportunities for developing knowledge and skills in social justice principles and advocacy. The following provides suggestions for graduate students who aspire to increase their knowledge and skills in this area.

1. Seek faculty mentors who conduct research designed to identify and meet the needs of traditionally disenfranchised groups. When working with faculty mentors whose scholarship does not directly align with a social justice agenda, consider how social justice principles may be incorporated in this line of work as a direction for future research (e.g., possibly dissertation research).
2. Seek specialized coursework that advances knowledge and skills in social justice advocacy (e.g., courses on multiculturalism, law and ethics, and systems change).
3. Become involved with student groups that promote social justice on campus and within surrounding communities (e.g., multicultural groups; lesbian, gay, bisexual, transgender, and queer [LGBTQ] advocacy groups; community service organizations).
4. Seek training opportunities offered by local and state school psychology organizations. For example, some state school psychology associations offer opportunities for students to visit legislatures, assist with preparing advocacy statements, or organize outreach efforts across similar organizations (e.g., counseling associations).
5. Join special-interest groups in national associations that offer opportunities to network with advocacy leaders (e.g., NASP's Social Justice Interest Group).
6. Seek applied training experiences (e.g., practica, internships, and postdoctoral training) that afford opportunities to work with traditionally marginalized youth and families. When pursuing this training, bear in mind that it is important to engage in ongoing reflection regarding personal beliefs, values, attitudes, and biases.

DEVELOPING A RÉSUMÉ OR CV IN SCHOOL PSYCHOLOGY

Representing one's professional qualifications is an important part of securing training and employment opportunities. One way that professionals and students summarize their experiences and achievements is to develop a résumé or CV. One common question that many people ask is, *What is the difference between a résumé and CV, and which one should I have?*

Both résumés and CVs accomplish a similar goal, which is to outline and highlight an individual's education, experiences, and accolades. More specifically, both delineate education, professional qualifications, practica experiences, research positions, publications, conference presentations, work experience, service, and extracurricular activities. Honors, achievements, and awards as well as special skills also may be highlighted (Jackson, Geckeis, & NetLibrary, 2003). Additionally, both CVs and résumés begin with the individual's most recent information and move backward chronologically. One of the primary differences between a CV and a résumé, however, pertains to length. CVs typically are lengthier than résumés because they contain greater detail. Since CVs generally are discussed less frequently than résumés, they will be the focus of this section.

The first few lines of the CV should provide updated contact information (Bennett, 2014). Next, educational information typically is displayed, including the names of the institutions attended, the dates attended, the degree(s) received, and major or concentrated areas of study. For degrees not yet awarded, it is acceptable to note an expected date of graduation. Grade-point average (GPA) also may be included with the education information (especially if it is high and augments the candidate's qualifications).

In sections describing research experiences, it is important to include project titles, supervising faculty, and a concise, detailed description of roles and responsibilities. Under practicum, employment, and internship experiences, a bulleted list of responsibilities will help the reader conceptualize the depth and breadth of skills acquired. These roles and responsibilities should be presented as action items. In this style, verbs such as "aided" or "provided" are used rather than "I statements" (e.g., "I was in charge of. . ."). Examples are provided in Table 14.1. It is important to avoid making vague statements and instead to use specific examples of job responsibilities (Bennett, 2014).

One of the most important considerations in constructing a CV is to think about how it will be received by the target audience. Descriptions of experiences

TABLE 14.1 Sample Curriculum Vitae Entries Describing Professional Roles

PROFESSIONAL EXPERIENCE	
May 2014–December 2015	**Graduate research assistant** **Success University** *Supervisor: Faculty L. Member, PhD, NCSP*
	• Conducted research and literature reviews • Assisted with development of study design and hypotheses • Presented research findings at national and state conferences
September 2013–April 2014	**Practicum student** **Achievement School District** *Supervisor: Samuel P. Sample, EdS* • Provided group counseling services to middle school students with disabilities • Conducted psychoeducational assessments to inform intervention development • Developed psychoeducational reports for planning of special education services

in CVs should use more sophisticated language rather than conversational phrases or terms. For example, using terms such as "childcare" instead of "babysitting" is likely to give the CV a more professional appearance. While representing oneself in a professional manner is important, it is also important to avoid exaggerating or inflating job responsibilities and experiences. For example, if an individual is only conversationally fluent in a language, the CV should not suggest that he or she is bilingual. Nevertheless, one should not minimize experiences. Overall, the individual should strive to develop relevant, compelling descriptions of work and educational experiences that also are accurate and informative.

One particularly effective strategy for constructing a CV is to emphasize only those experiences most relevant to the position desired. When developing a CV in response to a written internship or job announcement, mirroring the language in the announcement can be helpful. For example, if an internship site describes itself as having a behavioral orientation and a significant emphasis on applied research training, it may be beneficial for the applicant to list all coursework and research experiences with behavioral applications in her or his CV. Including some volunteer or extracurricular activities may be helpful if the activities are related to the individual's professional goals. For example, volunteering in a children's hospital, participating in honor societies in psychology, and sponsoring community activities for children are all relevant to careers in serving youth. Additionally, it may be valuable to include experiences in philanthropic work, leadership positions, or educational service delivery (e.g., peer tutoring or mentoring), as they demonstrate skills in leadership and advocacy.

In summary, preparing a CV is an important way to share professional experiences and achievements with others. Seeking feedback from trusted peers and mentors can facilitate refinement and improvement of the CV. Individuals who are enrolled in postsecondary institutions may have access to career development centers and other institutional services that can assist with CV development. Program advisors, supervisors, and other mentors may also provide valuable guidance in this area. Table 14.2 provides a checklist for CV development.

TABLE 14.2 Checklist for Curriculum Vitae Development

CURRICULUM VITAE CHECKLIST
1. Demographic information: Name, two or more forms of contact information
2. Educational background: Degrees, institution, date obtained or anticipated, minors or areas of concentration, grade-point average (GPA), thesis or honors projects
3. Teaching or research assistantships: Dates, project or course titles, supervisors, role descriptions
4. Publications, professional presentations, grant writing: Related to career goals
5. Work experience: Relevant to graduate school or career goals
6. Extracurricular activities: Leadership roles, clubs/organizations related to professional goals, volunteer experiences related to goals
7. Honors, awards, scholarships: Relevant to career goals
8. Professional organization memberships: Relevant to career goals
9. Specialized skills: Computer/statistical software, language fluency, certifications
10. Writing style: Checked grammar, use of action verbs, sophistication of language

SUMMARY AND CONCLUSIONS

The field of school psychology offers a wide range of important career trajectories that serve the academic and mental health needs of children and youth. Most professionals practice within the pre-K–12 public school systems; however, professional opportunities also abound within public agencies, clinics, hospitals, juvenile justice, private practice, and academia. Early consideration of degree tracks and training components aligned with career goals can maximize an individual's preparedness for acquiring competitive internship and job positions. Thus, graduate programs' coursework rigor (as mandated by accreditation and credentialing standards), opportunities for diverse clinical training, and faculty mentorship commitments are pivotal considerations. This chapter has offered guidance on each of these key factors. To support future planning, a Graduate Program Worksheet is provided.

GRADUATE PROGRAM WORKSHEET

Career Goal:							
	Action Plan	Specialization Coursework	Specialized Practica	Teaching, Research Goals	Publications, Presentations	Mentorship Needs	Licensure or Credential
Non-doctoral Degree and Doctoral Degree	Year 1						
	Year 2						
	Year 3						
Doctoral Degree Only	Year 4						
	Year 5						
	Year 6						

Although many of the essential elements of preparing for a career in school psychology will be supported by the existing training program infrastructure, graduate students may also utilize some strategies to enhance their education and networking options. These strategies include seeking specialized coursework and applied training experiences, participating in local and national interest groups, and becoming involved in state and national school psychology associations. Additionally, fostering strong mentoring relationships with faculty who are active in advocacy efforts, educational practice reform, and research addressing the needs of specific populations can provide valuable connections for pursuing those areas of interest. Ultimately, a career in school psychology offers significant opportunity for implementing principles of social justice and serving a wide range of youth and families.

DISCUSSION QUESTIONS

1. Compare and contrast the school psychology practitioner and academic faculty roles.
2. What are some factors to consider in seeking a mentor or supervisor? Which factors are most important to you?

3. How might you go about researching the populations and communities surrounding your university? Which individuals or resources might you consult?
4. Which types of employment settings and professional roles interest you most? What steps will you take to realize these goals?
5. How might you customize your professional preparation to emphasize a social justice perspective?

REFERENCES

American Psychiatric Association. (2013). *Diagnostic and statistical manual of mental disorders* (5th ed.). Arlington, VA: American Psychiatric Publishing.

Bennett, S. (2014). *The elements of résumé style: Essential rules for writing résumés and cover letters that work* (2nd ed.). New York, NY: American Management Association.

Castillo, J. M., Curtis, M. J., & Tan, S. Y. (2014). Personnel needs in school psychology: A 10-year follow-up study of predicted personnel shortages. *Psychology in the Schools, 51*, 832–849. doi:10.1002/pits.21786

Clopton, K. L., & Haselhuhn, C. W. (2009). School psychology trainer shortage in the USA: Current status and projections for the future. *School Psychology International, 30*, 24–42.

Grapin, S. L., Kranzler, J. H., & Daley, M. L. (2013). Scholarly productivity and impact of school psychology faculty in APA-accredited programs. *Psychology in the Schools, 50*, 87–101. doi:10.1002/pits.2165

Guiney, M. (2010). The state of NASP early career members. *Communiqué, 38*(7).

Harris, B., Shriberg, D., Ogg, J., Newton, J., & Sullivan, A. L. (2012, February). *Straight talk: Perspectives from early career trainers.* Symposium presented at the annual convention of the National Association of School Psychologists, Philadelphia, PA.

Harris, B., & Sullivan, A. L. (2012). Faculty roles: A primer for students and professional interested in careers in academia. *Communique, 41*(2).

Harvey, V. S., & Struzziero, J. A. (Eds.). (2008). *Professional development and supervision of school psychologists: From intern to expert.* Thousand Oaks, CA: Corwin Press.

Jackson, A. L., Geckeis, C. K., & NetLibrary, I. (2003). *How to prepare your curriculum vitae* (rev. ed.). Chicago, IL: VGM Career Books.

Joyce, D., & Grapin, S. (2012). School psychologists' role in facilitating successful post-secondary transitions for students with disabilities. *Communique, 41*(3), 1–22.

Joyce-Beaulieu, D., & Grapin, S. (2014). Support beyond high school for those with mental illness. *Kappan, 96*, 29–33.

Joyce-Beaulieu, D., & Rossen, E. (2016). *The school psychology practicum and internship handbook.* New York, NY: Springer Publishing.

Joyce-Beaulieu, D., & Sulkowski, M. (2015). *Cognitive behavioral therapy in K–12 school settings: A practitioner's toolkit.* New York, NY: Springer Publishing.

Kessler, R. C., Berglund, P., Demler, O., Jin, R., Merikangas, K. R., & Walters, E. E. (2005). Lifetime prevalence and age-of-onset distributions of *DSM-IV* disorders in the national comorbidity survey replication. *Archives of General Psychiatry, 62*, 593–602. doi:10.1001/archpsyc.62.6.593

Little, S. G., & Akin-Little, K. A. (2004). Academic school psychologists: Addressing the shortage. *Psychology in the Schools, 41*, 451–459.

Martínez, R. S., Floyd, R. G., & Erichsen, L. W. (2011). Strategies and attributes of highly productive scholars and contributors to the school psychology literature: Recommendations for increasing scholarly productivity. *Journal of School Psychology, 49*, 691–720. doi:10.1016/j.jsp.2011.10.003

Merrell, K. W., Ervin, R. A., & Gimpel-Peacock, G. (2012). *School psychology for the 21st century: Foundations and practices* (2nd ed.). New York, NY: Guilford Press.

National Association of School Psychologists. (n.d.). A career in school psychology: Frequently asked questions. Retrieved from https://www.nasponline.org/about-school-psychology/becoming-a-school-psychologist/a-career-in-school-psychology-frequently-asked-questions#where

National Association of School Psychologists. (2011). *Supervision in school psychology* [Position statement]. Bethesda, MD: Author.

Sulkowski, M., & Joyce, D. (2012). School psychology goes to college: The emerging role of school psychology in college communities. *Psychology in the Schools, 49,* 809–815. doi:10.1002/pits.21634

Walcott, C. M., Charvat, J., McNamara, K. M., & Hyson, D. M. (2016). School psychology at a glance: 2015 member survey results [PowerPoint slides]. Retrieved from https://www.nasponline.org/.../Membership%20Survey%202015%20Handout.pdf

Index

Gesell, Arnold, 26
graduate preparation
    accreditation, 50
    content and structure
        APA Standards for Health Service
            Psychology, 47–49
        ISPA Training Standards, 49
        NASP Graduate Preparation Standards,
            47
    doctoral degrees, 46–47
    non-doctoral degrees, 45–46
graduate program and faculty shortages, 218–219
Graduate Program Worksheet, 247
graduate student enrollment shortages, 218
group factors, 169

Hildreth, Gertrude, 26
hybrid years history, school psychology
    child study bureau, 25–26
    child study movement, 23–24
    civil rights movement impact, 28–29
    compulsory schooling, 23
    growth of training, 26–27
    intelligence-testing movement, 24–25
    labor force and education, 22–23
    NASP formation, 29–30
    overview of, 22
    professional organizations, 27
    psychology, Europe and United States, 22
    state associations, 29–30
    Thayer Conference, 29
    World War II impact, 27–28

ID. *See* intellectual disability
IDEA. *See* Individuals with Disabilities
        Education Act
IDEIA. *See* Individuals with Disabilities
        Education Improvement Act
IEPs. *See* Individualized Education Programs
Illinois Society for Child Study, 25
implementation, 125
implementation drivers, 203
implementers, 126
indirect observation, 106
Individualized Education Programs (IEPs), 13,
        31, 84
Individuals with Disabilities Education Act
        (IDEA), 36
Individuals with Disabilities Education
        Improvement Act (IDEIA), 36, 83–84,
        172–173
informants, 107
initial implementation stage, 201
innovation, 125
innovation stage, 201
instructional intensity, 142

intellectual disability (ID), 173
intellectual giftedness, 173–174
intelligence
    definition of, 168
    distribution of, 171–172
    interpretation of tests, 172
    measurement of, 169–171
    social justice and, 175
    structure of, 169
intelligence testing
    intellectual disability, 173
    intellectual giftedness, 173–174
    in schools, 172–175
    specific learning disability, 174–175
intelligence-testing movement, 24–25
internal consistency, 100
internship, 53, 237
intersectionality, 62–63
intervention, 115
intervention fidelity, 128, 206
intervention implementation
    components and stages, 125–126
    evaluating implementation outcomes,
        128–129
    maximizing contextual fit, 127
    training and technical assistance, 127–128
interviews, 108
intraindividual analyses, 172
introspection, 22
ipsative analyses, 172
IQ–achievement discrepancy, 174
ISPA Code of Ethics, 83
ISPA Training Standards, 49

James, William, 22

law, definition of, 78
least restrictive environment (LRE), 84
legal and ethical decision making model,
        87–88
legal, ethical, and professional practice, 10
legal violations, 90–91
Life Skills Training program, 126
local norms, 138
LRE. *See* least restrictive environment

Marzolf, Stanley, 29
math CBM, 135–136
McIntosh, Peggy, 70–71
medical model, 35
mental health consultation (MHC), 183–184
mentors
    academic careers, 241–242
    field-based practitioner careers, 237–239
meta-analysis, 190
MHC. *See* mental health consultation

riskiness, 127
RtI. *See* response to intervention

SBRJ. *See* school-based restorative justice
school-based mental health services providers, 87
school-based restorative justice (SBRJ), 68–69
school counseling, 13–14
school psychologists
  clinical psychologists vs., 14
  employment contexts, 11–12
  professional activities, 11–13
  role of, 223–225
school psychology
  APA definition, 4–5
  child clinical psychology vs., 14
  NASP definition, 4–5
  school counseling vs., 13–14
  social justice, 16–18
school psychology programs (SPPs), 49
scientist-practitioner model, 29
screening, 101–102
secondary implementers, 126
SEL. *See* social emotional learning
self-knowledge, 70–71
semistructured interviews, 108
service delivery, NASP Practice Model
  consultation and collaboration, 7
  data-based decision making and
    accountability, 6
  diversity in development and learning, 9–10
  legal, ethical, and professional practice, 10
  research and program evaluation, 10
shared vision, 199–200
single-blind peer review, 242
SLD. *See* specific learning disability
social, emotional, and behavioral (SEB) skills
  definition of, 150–151
  Tier 1 system
    assessment, 154–155
    class-wide behavioral interventions,
      153–154
    intervention, 151
    positive behavioral interventions and
      supports, 151–152
    social emotional learning, 152–153
  Tier 2 system
    assessment, 156–157
    direct behavior rating, 157–158
    intervention, 155–156
    permanent products, 158
    rating scales, 157
    systematic direct observation, 157
  Tier 3 system
    behavior intervention plans, 160–162
    functional behavior assessment, 158–160

other forms of diagnostic assessment, 160
  therapeutic interventions, 162
social emotional learning (SEL), 152–153
social intelligence, 168
social justice
  advocacy, 16–17
  aspirational goals of, 17
  definition of, 14–15
  intelligence and, 175
  multiculturalism and, 15–16
  rationale for, 16–18
  school psychology, 16–18
social justice connections
  advocacy consultation, 185–186
  assessment practices, 110
  cultural adaptation, 125
  legal and ethical decision making, 88–90
  minority racial/ethnic groups and other
    marginalized groups, 175–176
  MTSS, 143–144
  multicultural scholarship, 34
  preservice school psychologists, 244
  program evaluation, 205
  protective factors, mental health problems,
    162–163
  racial disparities, 68–69
  school psychology programs, 49
social skills, 150
social system, 126
sociocultural consciousness, 109
specialist-level degree, 219
specialized coursework
  academic careers, 241
  field-based practitioner careers, 236
specialized field placements
  academic careers, 241
  field-based practitioner careers, 237
specialized instructional support personnel, 87
specialty, 4
specific learning disability (SLD)
  IQ–achievement discrepancy, 174
  pattern of strengths and weaknesses
    approach, 175
  response to intervention, 174–175
spelling CBM, 136
SPPs. *See* school psychology programs
Spring Hill Symposium, 32–33
stakeholders, 126
state level practice credentials
  alternative/temporary credentialing, 55
  credentialing for practice in schools
    eligibility and education, 52–53
    exams, 53–54
    setting and scope of services, 54
    supervised field experiences, 53
    title, 54